THOMSON

COURSE TECHNOLOGY

Professional ■ Technical ■ Reference

Includes coverage of:
Word ■ Excel ■ Outlook ■ PowerPoint ■ Publisher

PICTURE YOURSELF
Learning
Microsoft® Office 2007

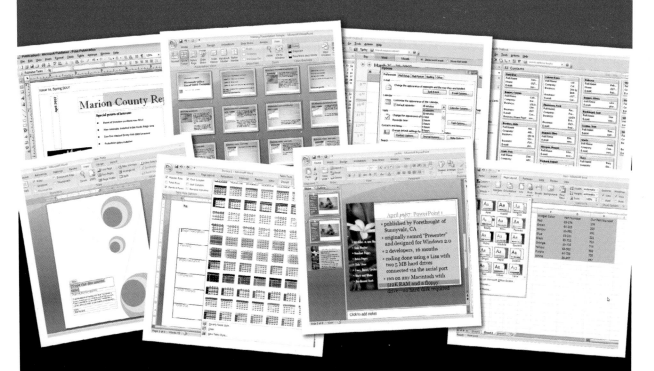

Step-by-Step Instruction for Creating Word Documents,
Excel® Spreadsheets, PowerPoint® Presentations, and More

Diane Koers

ISBN-10: 1-59863-378-3
ISBN-13: 978-1-59863-378-8
Library of Congress Catalog Card Number: 2006940092
Printed in the United States of America
07 08 09 10 11 BU 10 9 8 7 6 5 4 3 2 1

Thomson Course Technology PTR,
a division of Thomson Learning Inc.
25 Thomson Place
Boston, MA 02210
http://www.courseptr.com

THOMSON

COURSE TECHNOLOGY

Professional ■ Technical ■ Reference

Publisher and General Manager, Thomson Course Technology PTR:
Stacy L. Hiquet

Associate Director of Marketing:
Sarah O'Donnell

Manager of Editorial Services:
Heather Talbot

Marketing Manager:
Heather Hurley

Acquisitions Editor:
Megan Belanger

Marketing Assistant:
Adena Flitt

Project Editor & Copy Editor:
Dan Foster, Scribe Tribe

Technical Reviewer:
Lisa Bucki

PTR Editorial Services Coordinator:
Erin Johnson

Interior Layout:
Shawn Morningstar

Cover Designer:
Mike Tanamachi

Indexer:
Sharon Shock

Proofreader:
Steve Honeywell

To Mom

For just being the inspiration you are to me.
I'm sorry I've ignored you so much during this process.

Thanks for your patience. I love you!

Acknowledgments

SO MANY HARD-WORKING PEOPLE worked on this book, I hardly know where to begin. Many people worked behind the scenes, each as valuable as the next. First, I'd like to thank Megan Belanger for believing in me enough to let me write this book. I wish her all that life has to offer with her brand new baby! To Dan Foster, whose great patience and wonderful grammatical skills kept me going through the process. To Lisa Bucki, who used her incredible knowledge of Microsoft Office to keep me on track. To Shawn Morningstar, for exercising all her patience and layout talents in making this a beautiful book. From the proofreader, Steve Honeywell, the indexer, Sharon Shock, to Heather Talbot, Stacy Hiquet, and all the others working madly behind the scenes to get this book to market. To all of you, thank you from the bottom of my heart.

And finally, a huge note of appreciation goes to my husband of 38 years. Vern, thank you for your patience and understanding of the *many* late-night hours, for fending for yourself or both of us at supper time, and for keeping me encouraged and supplied with Diet Coke and working chocolate. I love you.

About the Author

DIANE KOERS owns and operates All Business Service, a software training and consulting business formed in 1988 that services the central Indiana area. Her area of expertise has long been in the word-processing, spreadsheet, and graphics areas of computing as well as providing training and support for Peachtree Accounting Software.

Diane's authoring experience includes over 35 books on topics such as PC Security, Microsoft Windows, Microsoft Office, Microsoft Works, WordPerfect, Paint Shop Pro, Photoshop Elements, Lotus SmartSuite, Quicken, Microsoft Money, and Peachtree Accounting, many of which have been translated into other languages such as French, Dutch, Bulgarian, Spanish, and Greek. She has also developed and written numerous training manuals for her clients.

Diane and her husband enjoy spending their free time camping, traveling, and playing with their four grandsons and their Yorkshire Terrier, Little Joe.

Table of Contents

Introduction

Welcome to the world of Microsoft Office 2007.

This new *Picture Yourself* guide from Course Technology will help you master the many and varied features of one of Microsoft's most popular products—Microsoft Office 2007. Microsoft Office is a powerful and popular suite of programs that supports many aspects of your everyday work style. This book provides information and advice to help you write a letter, create a spreadsheet, produce a professional-looking presentation, and manage your schedule and electronic mail. In addition, you'll learn how to create your own professional newsletters and other publications as well as create your own Web page.

Each of the individual programs interacts with the other programs in the suite. For example, you might need to prepare a business report in Word that contains graphs and charts based on data you enter in an Excel spreadsheet. Perhaps later, after you have delivered your report (possibly using Outlook's e-mail), you might need to prepare and schedule a PowerPoint presentation.

With this book you'll learn how to create Office documents, although what you create is totally up to you! Your imagination is the only limit to what you can do with Office documents after that. This book, however, cannot begin to teach you everything you can do with Microsoft Office, nor will it show you all the different ways to accomplish a task. What I have tried to do is give you a fast, fun, and easy way to get started with this exciting suite of programs.

Book Structure

This book includes 24 chapters divided into six parts. In Part I, I show you how to use basic Office commands—features that are common among most Office applications. Although it's not the most exciting part of the book, it's certainly the most practical. Look out, then—the fun begins! In Parts II through VI, you learn the basics of five popular Office applications: Word, Excel, PowerPoint, Publisher, and Outlook.

Who Should Read This Book?

I make a couple of assumptions about you for this book. First, I assume that you have worked with your computer enough to handle your mouse and be familiar with some terms such as save, open, and close. Second, most importantly and most obviously, since you're reading this right now, I assume that you want to know more. I will try to fill you with knowledge.

Whether you are computer challenged or have used Microsoft products before, you can quickly tap into the user-friendly integrated design and feature-rich environment of Microsoft Office 2007.

The Course Technology *Picture Yourself* guides use a visual approach with illustrations of what you will see on your screen linked with instructions for the next mouse movements or keyboard operations to complete your task. Computer terms and phrases are clearly explained in non-technical language, and expert tips and shortcuts help you produce professional-quality documents.

This book can be used as a learning tool or as a task reference. The easy-to-follow, highly graphical nature of this book makes it the perfect learning tool. No prerequisites are required from you, except that you know how to turn on your computer and how to use your mouse.

In addition, anyone using a software application always needs an occasional reminder about the steps required to perform a particular task. By using this *Picture Yourself Learning Microsoft Office 2007* guide, any level of user can look up task instructions quickly without having to plow through pages of descriptions.

Added Advice to Make You a Pro

You will notice that this book uses a lot of steps and keeps explanations to reasonable lengths to help you learn faster. Included in the book are a few elements that provide some additional comments to help you master the program, without encumbering your progress through the steps:

▶ **Tips** offer shortcuts for performing an action, or a hint about a feature that might make your work in Word quicker and easier.

▶ **Notes** give you a bit of background or additional information about a feature, or advice about how to use the feature in your day-to-day activities.

Read and enjoy this book. It certainly is the fastest and easiest way to learn Microsoft Office 2007. If you have any comments about this book, please feel free to contact me at diane@thepeachtreelady.com.

—Diane

Part I
Getting Started

You are about to embark on a journey into the world of Microsoft Office 2007. Office is a collection of multiple products and, depending on the flavor you purchased, you probably have Word, Excel, PowerPoint, Outlook, and possibly Publisher. Each application has its own purpose. You typically use Word for letters, Excel for mathematical calculations, PowerPoint for presentations, Outlook for appointments and e-mail, and Publisher for newsletters and Web pages. Each program is unique, yet all the programs have common features. This section takes you through some of the common functions used with all the different programs.

Discovering Office Common

Features

PICTURE YOURSELF SITTING DOWN at your new computer, ready to begin using it. You've already mastered the game of Solitaire, so now you're going to explore Microsoft Office. Microsoft Office isn't really a single program; rather, it's a collection of several applications. Some of the Microsoft Office 2007 applications include:

▶ **Word, which you use to write letters, faxes, and other documents.**

▶ **Excel, which you use to view and manage numbers and data.**

▶ **PowerPoint, which you use to create presentations and slide shows.**

▶ **Publisher, which you use to create publications, newsletters, brochures, and Web pages.**

▶ **Outlook, which serves as an e-mail program as well as a personal information manager.**

The specific applications included with your version of Office vary with the different Microsoft Office 2007 packages.

Opening Office Programs

I N MOST WINDOWS PROGRAMS, you see menus and toolbars from which you select your options. If you've used previous versions of Microsoft Office, you'll find some of the Office 2007 application screens very different from previous versions. In Word, Excel, and PowerPoint, Office provides a new interface that provides you with the right tools at the right time. Instead of the traditional look, Office applications now provide tabs with icon and button-laden ribbons containing your favorite features. Galleries and themes are also new additions, helping you maintain consistency and style in your documents' appearance. The Microsoft Publisher and the main Microsoft Outlook screens contain the traditional Windows menu and toolbars. As you perform different functions in Outlook, such as creating a new e-mail, you can also see the new interface.

Choose Start>All Programs>Microsoft Office, which displays a list of Office applications. Click the application you want to open. If you select Word, Excel, or PowerPoint, a blank document, workbook, or presentation appears on your screen ready for you to begin entering your data. You'll start working with Word in Chapter 2, Excel in Chapter 8, and PowerPoint in Chapter 14. Figure 1-1 illustrates the opening screens for Word, Excel, and PowerPoint.

> To place an Office application icon on your Windows desktop, right-click the application name under the Start>All Programs>Microsoft Office menu and choose Send To>Desktop (create shortcut).

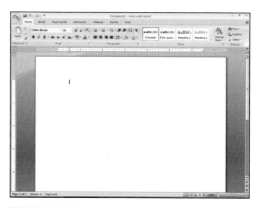

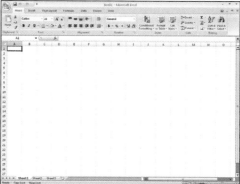

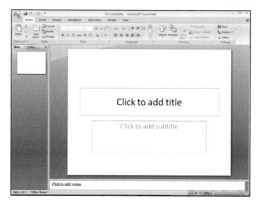

Figure 1-1
Ready to begin working in your Office application.

If you open Publisher, a list of templates appears (see Chapter 18), and the first time you open Outlook (Chapter 22), a startup wizard appears prompting you to configure Outlook and set up your e-mail accounts.

Whenever you finish working with a specific application, you exit the program to release the program from your computer's memory. Choose Office Button >Exit [application name] or click the Close button in the upper right corner of the application window. You may be prompted to save your file. Click Yes or No if prompted to save your file.

> Optionally, choose Office Button>Close. The current file closes, but the current program remains open.

Working with Office Elements

Designed to adjust to the way you work, instead of the traditional Windows menu bar and standard toolbars, the Word, Excel, and PowerPoint applications use a Ribbon. Take a look at Figure 1-2, and let's take a stroll through an Excel window and review some of the Office elements.

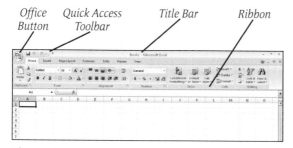

Office Button   *Quick Access Toolbar*   *Title Bar*   *Ribbon*

Figure 1-2
The Office Ribbon is designed to provide the right tool at the right time.

▶ **Title Bar:** Across the top you see a title bar that shows the program title and the document title. If you are working with a document created in an earlier version of Office, you may see the words "Compatibility Mode" displayed. You'll learn about Compatibility Mode later in this chapter.

▶ **Office Button:** Pause your mouse over the icon on the top left screen corner. Microsoft calls this icon the Office Button. As you stop your mouse over it, a description of the Office Button functions appears. The Office Button is where you access many common file functions such as Open, Save, and Print.

> When you click the Office Button, you see a list of options. Click the Office Button again to close the option list if you don't want to make a selection at this time.

▶ **Quick Access Toolbar:** The Office Quick Access Toolbar, provides fast and easy access to basic file functions. Pause your mouse over any of the four icons next to the Office Button. By default, the Office Quick Access Toolbar functions include Save, Undo, Redo, and QuickPrint.

▶ **Ribbon:** If you hover your mouse over the Ribbon area containing tabs, which are task orientated screens, a description of the feature appears in an Enhanced ScreenTip. The tabs are also broken down into subsections called groups, which break the tasks into smaller areas. Figure 1-3 shows the Excel Insert tab which includes the Tables, Illustrations, Charts, Links, and Text groups. As you click a different tab, the Ribbon changes to reflect options pertaining to the selected tab.

Tabs   *Groups*

Figure 1-3

Related items appear in groups.

▶ **Dialog Box Launcher:** Many options
include an icon at the bottom right edge
of the group option. Office calls this the
Dialog Box Launcher, and clicking it opens
a related dialog box. In Figure 1-4, the
Excel Page Setup dialog box opens.

Dialog Box Launcher

Figure 1-4

*See additional options through
a traditional dialog box.*

Click the Cancel button to close a dialog
box without making any changes.

▶ **Galleries:** Some Ribbon buttons display
a down arrow, which means there are
more choices available. In Figure 1-5,
you see an arrow on the Excel Format as
Table button. Click the arrow to display
a gallery of table styles. (Click the arrow
again to close the gallery.)

Gallery

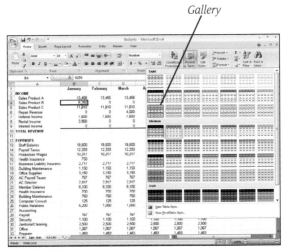

Figure 1-5

Click the arrow to expand the gallery.

▶ **Status Bar:** Along the bottom of the
Office application window you see a status bar that tells you if your keyboard's
Num Lock or Caps Lock is on, along with
a variety of other options. You can customize the display in the status bar by
right-clicking anywhere on the status
bar. The application displays a list of
options in the Customize Status Bar
menu similar to the one seen in Figure
1-6. Click any option without a checkmark next to it to activate the feature,
or click any option with a checkmark to
deactivate the feature.

Status bar

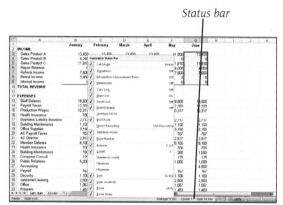

Figure 1-6
Display helpful information on the status bar.

Selecting Commands with the Keyboard

Sometimes you don't want to take your hands off the keyboard to make a choice from the Ribbon. Fortunately, Office provides easy ways to select commands using the keyboard instead of the mouse. Follow these steps to make a keyboard command selection:

1. If appropriate for the command you intend to use, place the insertion point in the proper word or paragraph.

2. Press Alt on the keyboard. Shortcut letters and numbers appear on the Ribbon. The letters control Ribbon commands, and the numbers control Quick Access Toolbar commands. See Figure 1-7.

Press F6 to change the focus of the program, switching between the document, the status bar, and the Ribbon.

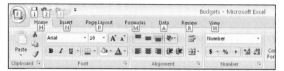

Figure 1-7
Make command selections using the keyboard.

3. Press a letter to select a tab on the Ribbon; for this example, press P. The application displays the appropriate tab and letters for each command on that tab.

4. Press a letter or letters to select a command. The application displays options for the command you selected.

Press the Escape key to revert the keyboard controls back one step.

5. Press a letter or use the arrow keys on the keyboard to select an option. If you use the arrow keys, press the Enter key after making a selection. The application performs the command you selected, applying the option you chose.

Working with Files

WHENEVER YOU WORK WITH an Office application, the application is creating a file. In Word, you create a document file; in Excel, a workbook file; and in PowerPoint, a presentation file. You can create the file and just throw it away when you're finished or you can save it on a disk drive for future reference.

Saving a File

The first time you save your file, the application prompts you for a name and a folder in which to save it. Choose Office Button>Save or click the Save button on the Quick Access Toolbar. The Save As dialog box appears, as shown in Figure 1-8. If you are using Publisher, choose File>Save.

> Optionally, press Ctrl+S to save your file.

Favorite links   *Save in folder*

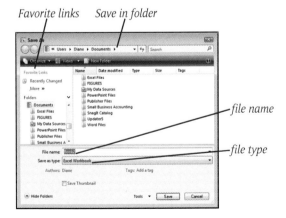

file name

file type

Figure 1-8
Saving a file for future reference.

From the Save As dialog box, you enter the following information:

▶ **Location: By default, Office applications save your files in your Documents folder. If you want to save your file in a different folder, use the Favorite Links pane to navigate to the folder or disk drive where you want to save the file.**

▶ **Name: In the File Name text box, type a descriptive name for the file. File names can contain any characters except an asterisk, slash, backslash, or question mark.**

▶ **Type: Each application has a specific file type it uses as a default. Word 2007 documents use a .docx file type, while Excel workbooks use the .xlsx file type. Most of the time you'll want to use the default file type, but if not, click the Save As Type down arrow and select a different file type. If someone who doesn't have Office 2007 will be opening your file, you might consider saving your file in a format that more closely matches their version, such as Word 97–2003. Older Word versions use a .doc file extension, and older Excel workbooks use the .xls file extension.**

Click the Save button. Excel saves the workbook in the location and with the name you specified. After assigning the file a name and a location, each time you click the Save button, the saved file is updated with any changes.

Depending on the file type you chose, Office may prompt you for additional information. In Figure 1-9, for example, you see a dialog box warning you of your workbook features used in Excel 2007 that aren't available when saving a file in an Excel XP or 2003 format.

Figure 1-9
Some Office 2007 features are not available in earlier Office versions.

Perhaps you want to make some changes to your file but you're not sure if you will like the changes. Or, maybe you wrote a proposal to a company and you need a similar one for a different company. One way to work around the changes is to save the file with a different name or in a different location. Office keeps the original version in the original location and keeps the modified version in the location you specified.

Don't wait until a project is finished to save it. A good rule of thumb is to save your work at least every 10 minutes.

To save a revised file without overwriting the original file, choose Office Button>Save As, which displays the Save As dialog box. From the Save As dialog box you can enter a new file name, select a different folder, or choose a different file type.

No two files can have the exact same name and file type in the exact same folder. You can place them in different folders, save them as different file types, or vary the name by at least one character.

Preserving a File in a PDF or XPS Format

Another way to save a file is with a fixed-layout format. Fixed-layout formats are electronic publishing formats that allow others to view a file, but not easily copy or change the data. Two popular fixed-layout formats include Adobe PDF or Microsoft XPS.

Before you can save an Office file in a PDF or XPS format, you must first install a free Office add-in utility to support the feature. You need only install the add-in once. Click the Office Button, and then pause your mouse over the Save As command to see saving options on the right side (Figure 1-10). Click Find Add-Ins for other file formats, which launches the Microsoft Download Center.

The PDF format requires the free Adobe Reader available from www.adobe.com. The Microsoft XPS format uses an Internet Explorer window to display your file.

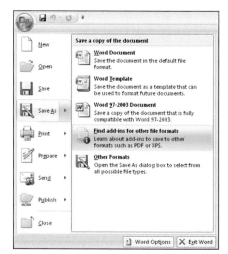

Figure 1-10
You must first install the Office PDF or XPF add in to create read-only files.

Click Continue and follow the on-screen instructions to download and run the Microsoft Save As PDF or XPS Add-In for 2007 Microsoft Office programs. See Figure 1-11.

Figure 1-11
Follow the onscreen instructions.

You must have Internet access to install the add-in.

Once you install the add-in you can save any Office document as a PDF or XPS file. Follow these steps:

1. Choose the Office Button or, in Publisher, click the File menu.

2. Hover your mouse over the Save As command, and then select PDF or XPS. (In Publisher, choose Publish as PDF or XPS). The Publish as PDF or XPS dialog box appears. See Figure 1-12.

Figure 1-12
Publish your file in a PDF or XPS format.

3. Select the folder where you want to save the file from the Save In drop-down list.

4. In the File Name text box, type a descriptive name for the file.

5. From the Save As Type drop-down list, choose either XPS Document or PDF.

If you don't want to view the PDF or XPS document after saving it, remove the check from Open File After Publishing.

6. Click Publish. Office saves the file and you see the file displayed in Adobe Reader or Internet Explorer.

Creating a New File

As mentioned earlier in this chapter, when you open most of the Office applications, a blank document appears. You can also generate a new document at any time by either choosing Office Button>New or, in Publisher and Outlook, choosing File>New. The application then displays the New dialog box prompting you for more information. Figure 1-13 illustrates the New Presentation dialog box seen when you choose Office Button>New in PowerPoint. By default, Office names each new file by the next numerical increment, such as Presentation2 or Workbook3.

Figure 1-13
Create any number of new files.

Optionally, press Ctrl+N to create a new file without opening the dialog box.

Opening an Existing File

When you've worked on and saved a file previously, you can reopen it to review or modify the file. There are several ways to open an existing file.

1. Choose Office Button>Open (or File>Open from Publisher or Outlook). An Open dialog box similar to the one seen in Figure 1-14 appears.

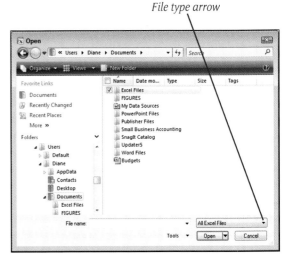

File type arrow

Figure 1-14
Open a previously saved file.

Optionally, press Ctrl+O to display the Open dialog box.

Office applications display recently used files on the right side of the Office menu. Click any listed file name to quickly open the selected file.

2. If needed, select the appropriate folder from the Look In drop-down list.

3. Select the file you want to open.

Click the file type arrow to display files saved in other formats.

4. Click the Open button. The document appears, ready for you to edit.

If the file you open was created in a previous version of Office, the words Compatibility Mode appear on the title bar, next to the document name (see Figure 1-15).

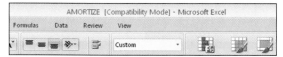

Figure 1-15
Some Office 2007 functions are not available when working in Compatibility Mode.

Renaming a File

When you first save your file, you're prompted to name it. But perhaps you didn't give it a name intuitive enough to know what the file represents. If you use the Office Button>Save As command and save your file with a different name, you have both the original file and the new file. If you just want to rename the existing file, you can use the Open or Save As dialog boxes. Follow these steps:

1. With the Office application open, but not the file you want to rename, choose Office Button>Open. The Open dialog box appears.

Optionally, choose Office Button>Save As and proceed using the Save As dialog box.

2. Locate and click once on the file you want to rename. Do not double-click the file as double-clicking the file will open it.

3. Choose Organize>Rename (see Figure 1-16). The original file name becomes highlighted.

4. Type the new file name and press Enter when you are finished typing. Excel renames the file.

5. Click the Cancel button, or press the Escape key, to close the Open (or Save As) dialog box.

Organize

Figure 1-16
Choose a new file name.

Deleting a File

Similar to renaming files, you can also use the Open or Save As dialog boxes to delete unwanted files. With the application open, choose Office Button>Open or Office Button>Save As. Either the Open or Save As dialog box appears. Locate the file you want to delete and choose Organize>Delete. A confirmation dialog box appears like you see in Figure 1-17. Choose Yes to delete the file, and then click the Cancel button (or press the Escape key) to close the dialog box

Figure 1-17
Delete unwanted files.

Previewing with Live Preview

Most Office 2007 applications include a new feature called Live Preview where you can see how formatting choices look in your document before you actually apply them to the document. By pointing to formatting options such as fonts or styles, you can see the effect on your document. If you want a different look, you simply move your mouse to a different option to view its effect.

Additionally, you can use Live Preview to view tables, charts, shapes, and graphics. However, Live Preview works only with Word, Excel, PowerPoint, and Outlook applications; it doesn't work in Publisher.

Take a look at Figure 1-18, where you see the effect of selecting a different font immediately display on the Word document heading. If you decide you like the effect, just click the mouse on the font to actually apply it to the text.

In Figure 1-19, choosing a different theme for a PowerPoint presentation allows you to see its effect on the current slide. If you don't want the new effect, just move your mouse to a different effect, or move the mouse off the Ribbon to make no changes.

Figure 1-18
Preview how a font changes affect your document.

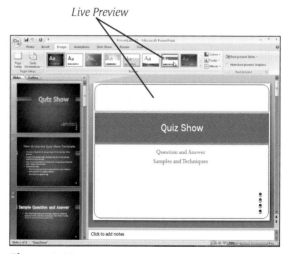

Figure 1-19
View style changes before actually applying a change.

Part II
Word

There are a number of essential things we need. Air and water certainly fit the bill, and many of us consider chocolate and true love right at the top. If you are using a computer, a good word-processing program is essential—and you have it. Microsoft Word is the most popular word-processing program in the world. It's abundance of features and ease of use leaves it unmatched. Whether you're making a grocery list or writing the great American novel, Word is the program for you. This section explains the fundamentals of working with Word and, even if you have worked with other word-processing programs, I am sure you will find Word's ease of use enriching

The Gettysburg Address

Gettysburg, Pennsylvania

November 19, 1863

Four score and seven years ago our fathers brought forth on this continent, a new nation, conceived in Liberty, and dedicated to the proposition that all men are created equal.

Now we are engaged in a great civil war, testing whether that nation, or any nation so conceived and so dedicated, can long endure. We are met on a great battle-field of that war. We have come to dedicate a portion of that field, as a final resting place for those who here gave their lives that that nation might live. It is altogether fitting and proper that we should do this.

But, in a larger sense, we can not dedicate -- we can not consecrate -- we can not hallow -- this ground. The brave men, living and dead, who struggled here, have consecrated it, far above our poor power to add or detract. The world will little note, nor long remember what we say here, but it can never forget what they did here. It is for us the living, rather, to be dedicated here to the unfinished work which they who fought here have thus far so nobly advanced. It is rather for us to be here dedicated to the great task remaining before us -- that from these honored dead we take increased devotion to that cause for which they gave the last full measure of devotion -- that we here highly resolve that these dead shall not have died in vain -- that this nation, under God, shall have a new birth of freedom -- and that government of the people, by the people, for the people, shall not perish from the earth.

2

Getting Started with
Word

PICTURE YOURSELF AS A SMALL CHILD looking through a glass door. The world looks huge when viewed through the perspective of a toddler, but generally children aren't afraid to explore the world around them. That's how they learn. In this chapter, you begin exploring the world of Microsoft Word.

Microsoft Word is a powerful word processing program that takes your documents far beyond what you can produce with a typewriter. Whether you want to write a simple letter to a friend, produce a newsletter for a professional organization, or even write a complicated, multiple-page report containing graphics and tables with numerical data, you can create it in Word.

If this is your first opportunity to use Microsoft Word, you may be a little overwhelmed by all the buttons and items on the screen. Just remember that although Word is a powerful program, it's also very easy to use, which is why most businesses have adopted it as a company standard. Don't worry. You'll be creating your first document after just a couple of mouse clicks.

Exploring the Word Window

A S MENTIONED IN CHAPTER 1, many items you see when you open the Word window are common to several other Office applications such as the Ribbon, tabs, groups, and status bar. The following list illustrates a few elements specific to Word (see Figure 2-1).

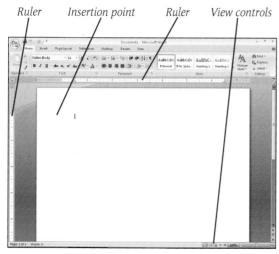

Figure 2-1
Word screen elements.

▶ **Mouse pointer:** The shape of the mouse pointer will change as you move it to different areas on the screen

▶ **Ruler:** Use the rulers to measure the document settings within the page margins. (See Chapter 4 for information on setting margins.)

By default, Word does not display the rulers. Show the rulers by choosing View>Show/Hide>Ruler.

▶ **Document screen:** The white area of the screen is where your typed text appears.

▶ **Insertion point:** The blinking vertical line in the document screen indicates where text will appear when you begin typing.

▶ **View controls:** Buttons on the status bar show you your document from various perspectives. (See Chapter 4 for more about changing views.)

Moving Around the Screen

A S YOU TYPE A FEW LINES OF TEXT, you'll notice that you don't need to press the Enter key at the end of each line. The program automatically moves down (or wraps) to the next line for you. Word calls this feature *word wrap*. You need only to press the Enter key to start a new paragraph.

To make changes to your document, you'll need to move the insertion point. Take a look at several methods Word provides for moving around the screen.

Using Click and Type

You can position the insertion point anywhere on the document using the Click and Type feature. Double-click your mouse pointer where you want to type. Word determines and sets any necessary paragraph formatting based on where you double-click.

The Click and Type feature works only if you are using Print Layout or the Web Layout view.

Before double-clicking the mouse, pay close attention to the appearance of the mouse pointer. If there are lines to the right of the I-beam pointer, the text you type will flow to the right of the insertion point. If the lines are to the left, the text will flow to the left of the insertion point, and if the lines are below the I-beam, the text will be centered at the insertion point (see Figure 2-2).

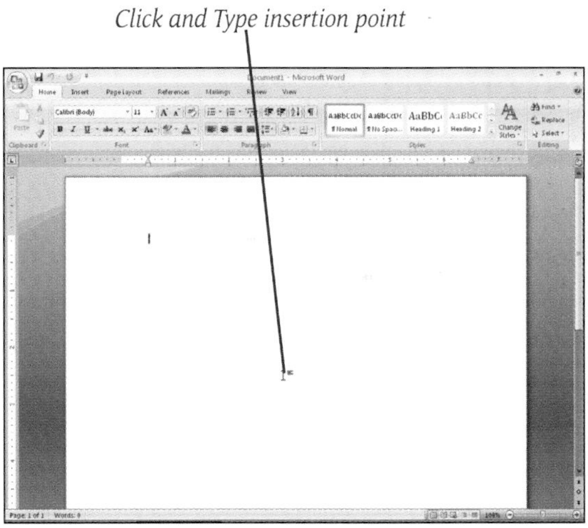

Click and Type insertion point

Figure 2-2
Using Click and Type.

Using the Scroll Bars

The Word document screen includes two scroll bars; a vertical scroll bar and a horizontal scroll bar; however, depending on the current view and the document zoom amount, you may not see the horizontal scroll bar. Figure 2-3 illustrates a document with both scroll bars visible.

Horizontal scroll bar   *Scroll box*   *Vertical scroll bar*

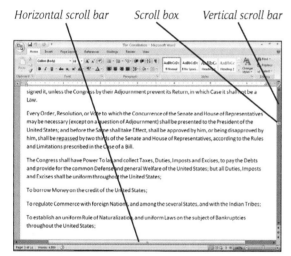

Figure 2-3
Word document scroll bars.

Click the arrow at either end of the scroll bar to move the document up or down in the window, or click the arrow at either end of the horizontal scroll bar to move the document left or right. Displaying text by using the scroll bars does not move the insertion point. You still need to click the mouse wherever you want to locate the insertion point.

> Optionally, drag the scroll box up or down to quickly move through a document.

Using the Keyboard

As you've seen, you can work on any part of the document that appears on your screen simply by clicking the mouse pointer where you want to work. You can also move around in a Word document by pressing the Up, Down, Right, or Left arrow keys on the keyboard. Each press of the key moves the insertion point one character or one line at a time.

There are also a number of shortcut keys designed to speed up the process of moving around in a Word document. Table 2-1 illustrates these shortcut keys.

Using the Go To Command

If you have a lengthy document, use the Go To command to jump to a specific location in the document. Follow these steps:

1. Choose Home>Editing and click the Find button drop-down arrow.

2. Choose Go To. The Find and Replace dialog box appears with the Go To tab in front (see Figure 2-4).

Figure 2-4
Quickly locate specific pages in your document.

Table 2-1

To Move	Do This
A word at a time	Press Ctrl+Right arrow or Ctrl+Left arrow
A paragraph at a time	Press Ctrl+Up arrow or Ctrl+Down arrow
A full screen up at a time	Press PageUp
A full screen down at a time	Press PageDown
To the beginning of a line	Press Home
To the end of a line	Press End
To the top of the document	Press Ctrl+Home
To the bottom of the document	Press Ctrl+End
To a specified page number	Press Ctrl+G, and then enter the page number

Two optional methods for displaying the Go To option are to press the F5 key or press Ctrl+G.

3. Type the page number you'd like to display and then click Go To or press the Enter key. Word displays the specified page with the insertion point located at the beginning of the specified page.

Editing Text

UNLESS YOU'RE A PERFECT TYPIST, you'll probably make a few mistakes in your document. Or, maybe you'll change your mind about some of the text in the document. In a word-processing program such as Word, corrections and changes are easy to make, and in some instances typing errors are even automatically corrected for you.

If the existing text doesn't move over, but disappears, you may have accidentally pressed the Insert key, which takes you out of Insert mode and into Overtype mode. Press the Insert key to return to Insert mode.

Adding New Text

When you want to add new text in the document, place the insertion point where you want to locate the new text and begin typing. As you type, Word inserts the characters and pushes the existing characters to the right or to the next line if necessary. Notice in the bottom example of Figure 2-5 how the added words "and seven" are inserted after the phrase "Four score," which makes some of the words in the top line drop down to the second line.

Deleting Existing Text

You can delete unwanted text one character, word, or paragraph at a time. Two common keys used to delete text are the Backspace and Delete keys. Pressing the Backspace key deletes one character at a time to the left of the insertion point, while pressing the Delete key deletes one character at a time to the right of the insertion point. In Figure 2-6, the word "continent" was deleted by pressing the Delete key repeatedly until the word disappeared.

Figure 2-6
Deleting unwanted characters.

Figure 2-5
Insert additional text wherever you want.

On most keyboards, the Backspace key shows a left-pointing arrow, which makes it an easy way to remember which direction the Backspace key deletes.

Optionally, make a selection in your document and press either the Backspace or Delete key to delete the selection. See the next section for more on selecting text.

Selecting Text

Before you can move, copy, delete, or change the formatting or placement of existing text, you must first select the text you want to edit. When text is selected, or *highlighted*, it appears on your screen as light type with a dark background—the reverse of unselected text. Word allows you to select sequential or nonsequential text for editing. The following list shows different selection techniques.

▶ **To select a single word, double-click the word.**

▶ **To select a sentence, hold down the Ctrl key and click anywhere in the sentence (see Figure 2-7).**

▶ **To select an entire paragraph, triple-click anywhere in the paragraph (see Figure 2-8).**

▶ **To select an entire document, hold down the Ctrl key and press the letter A.**

▶ **To select a single line of text, click once in the left margin with the mouse arrow pointing to the line you want selected.**

Selected sentence   *Selected word*

Figure 2-7
Selecting text to make additional changes.

Figure 2-8
Select an entire paragraph or the entire document.

Another way to select the entire document is choose Home>Editing>Select>Select All

▶ **To select a sequential text area, click at the beginning of the text you want selected, and then hold down the Shift key and click at the end of the text you want selected. Optionally, click and drag the mouse over the text you want to select.**

▶ **To select nonsequential text areas, select the first area you want selected, then hold down the Ctrl key and use the preceding techniques for each additional text area you want included (see Figure 2-9).**

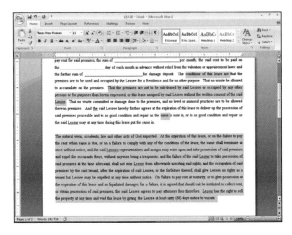

Figure 2-9
Selecting nonsequential areas in which to make changes.

To deselect text, click once anywhere in the document.

Discovering AutoCorrect

Word includes a fabulous feature that makes us look like better typists than we really are! The feature is called AutoCorrect, and, in many cases, if you mistype a word or forget to capitalize a sentence, Word automatically corrects it. Or, if you type something like (c), Word automatically understands that what you really want is a copyright symbol, and it changes the (c) to ©.

To take full advantage of the automatic correction feature, you have to understand how it works and how to customize it to better fit your needs. Follow these steps to review the AutoCorrect options:

1. Choose Office Button>Word Options, which displays the Word Options dialog box seen in Figure 2-10.

2. On the left side, choose Proofing.

Figure 2-10
Setting Word options.

3. Click AutoCorrect Options. The AutoCorrect Options dialog box opens (see Figure 2-11). On the AutoCorrect tab, you see the options Word automatically corrects for you.

Scroll down the list to see hundreds of predefined AutoCorrect words and symbols.

Figure 2-11
Create your own AutoCorrect items.

4. If you want to add your own common misspellings to the list, type your common mistake in the Replace text box and then type the correction in the With box. Click the Add button to add the correction to the list.

If you frequently use a lot of complex words such as chemical names or medical terms, enter an abbreviation for the term in the Replace box and put the complete term in the With box. After adding the term, when you need to add the term in your document, you need only type the abbreviation followed by a space, a period, or other character. For example, enter hctz to have Word replace it with Hydrochlorothiazide.

5. Click OK twice to close both the AutoCorrect and the Word Options dialog boxes.

Changing Text Case

As you just discovered, Word automatically corrects many text case errors. For example, if you type "SPringtime", Word automatically changes it to "Springtime." If, however, you type the entire word in uppercase ("SPRINGTIME"), you can quickly change it to "Springtime" or "springtime." You can apply a text case change to a word, a phrase, or any amount of selected text. Just follow these steps:

1. Select the text you want to change. The text becomes highlighted.

2. Click Home>Font>Change Case. A drop-down list of options appears as shown in Figure 2-12.

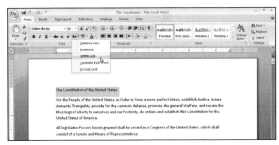

Figure 2-12
Quickly switch from lower to uppercase lettering.

3. Select an option from the drop-down list.

Optionally, make a text selection and press Shift+F3. Each time you press Shift+F3, a different case option applies.

Moving and Copying Text

WORD PROVIDES A NUMBER OF different methods with which you can copy and move text. Moving or copying text usually involves the Windows *Clipboard,* which temporarily holds text you place on it. You use the Clipboard feature to move or copy text from one place to another, thereby avoiding the need to retype it.

Moving Text

When you want to remove text from one place and put it into another location, you cut and paste the text. With cut and paste, Word deletes the selected text, holds it, and then places it into a new location. Just follow these steps:

1. Select to highlight the text you want to move.

2. Choose Home>Clipboard>Cut. The text disappears from the document, but Word stores it on the Windows Clipboard.

   Optionally, press Ctrl+X or right-click and choose Cut to cut selected text to the Clipboard.

3. Click the mouse where you want to place the text. The blinking insertion point appears at the new location.

4. Choose Home>Clipboard>Paste, or press Ctrl+V. Word places the text at the new location. In Figure 2-13, the highlighted paragraph was originally the first paragraph, but through cutting and pasting, it is now the fourth paragraph.

Paste   Cut   Copy

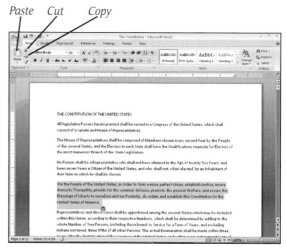

Figure 2-13
Save typing and editing time with Cut and Paste.

If you want to paste the text without the formatting, instead of clicking the Paste button directly, click the arrow beneath the Paste button and choose Paste Special. From the Paste Special dialog box (Figure 2-14), choose Unformatted text.

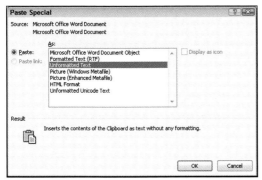

Figure 2-14
Paste without any formatting included.

Copying Text

The Copy and Paste features leave the selected text at its existing location and duplicate it into a new location. Working similarly to the Cut and Paste functions, Copy and Paste use the Windows Clipboard to temporarily store the text. Use the following steps to copy text to a new location:

1. Select to highlight the text you want to duplicate.

2. Choose Home>Clipboard>Copy or right-click and choose Copy. The text remains in the document, but Word also stores it on the Windows Clipboard.

Optionally, press Ctrl+C to copy selected text to the Clipboard.

3. Click the mouse where you want to place the text. The blinking insertion point appears at the new location.

4. Choose Home>Clipboard>Paste, or press Ctrl+V. Word places the text at the new location (see Figure 2-15). Notice that the second paragraph is repeated as the fourth paragraph.

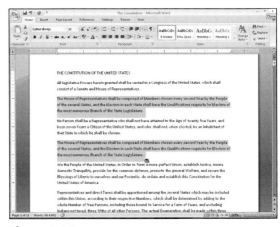

Figure 2-15
Duplicate text without retyping.

In some situations, when you paste or move text, you may see a small icon, called a Paste Options button, appear to the right of the pasted or moved text. See the section "Understanding Paste Options" later in this chapter.

Using Drag and Drop

Another, sometimes faster, method to move text from one location to another is to use the drag and drop editing function. The drag and drop feature works best for moving a relatively small amount of text a short distance. The following steps show you how to use drag and drop.

1. Select the text you want to move.

2. Position the mouse pointer on top of the highlighted text. The mouse arrow should point to the left.

3. Hold down the mouse button and drag the mouse pointer to the desired location. As you drag, a small box appears at the bottom of the mouse arrow and a gray line indicates the text position (see Figure 2-16).

New position for text

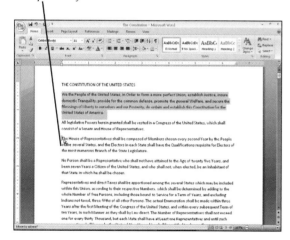

Figure 2-16
Select and drag text to a new location.

4. Release the mouse button to finish the text move.

To copy text instead of moving it, hold down the Ctrl key before dragging the selected text. Then release the mouse button before releasing the Ctrl key.

If you want to move text from one document to another, open both documents and display them side-by-side by choosing View>Window>Arrange All. Then highlight and drag the desired text from one document window to another (see Figure 2-17). Hold down the Ctrl key if you want to copy the text to the second document.

Figure 2-17
Move or copy text easily between documents.

Understanding Paste Options

By default, when you paste text, Word includes any formatting contained in the original text along with the text. For example, if the original text is underlined, the pasted text is underlined as well.

If the pasted text is a different font, size, or style than the text near where you pasted, you'll see the Paste Options button, which provides the option to paste text with or without formatting. (You'll learn more about formatting in Chapter 3, "Making a Document Look Good.")

Click the arrow next to the Paste Options button, as seen in Figure 2-18, and choose from the list of options:

▶ **Keep Source Formatting**: Leaves the pasted text formatted the same as the original text.

▶ **Match Destination Formatting**: Modifies the pasted text so it's formatted to match the closest existing text.

▶ **Keep Text Only**: Modifies the pasted text with the default document font.

Figure 2-18
Select paste options.

Using Undo and Repeat

I F YOU MAKE A CHANGE and then decide you really don't want to make that change after all, use Word's Undo function. You can use Undo to restore text that you deleted, to delete text you just typed, or to reverse a recently taken action. Word keeps track of several steps you've recently taken, so you can also undo your actions back several steps if you prefer.

Be aware that once you save your document, you cannot use Undo to "unsave" it. Also, if you close the document, when you reopen it, you cannot undo changes made in your previous editing session.

Undo   Undo multiple   Repeat
        steps

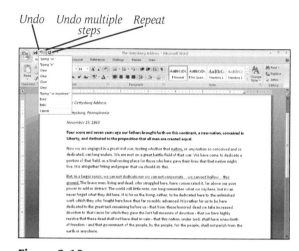

Figure 2-19
If you make a mistake, Undo it!

▶ To reverse the last action you took, click the Undo button on the Quick Access Toolbar.

▶ To repeat a previous action, click the Repeat button on the Quick Access Toolbar. If you just used the Undo button, the repeat button allows you to undo the previous Undo action.

▶ To undo multiple actions at once, click the arrow next to the Undo button and choose how far back you want to reverse your actions (see Figure 2-19).

Displaying Non-Printing Symbols

TO ASSIST YOU IN EDITING a document, Word can display hidden symbols it uses to indicate spaces, tabs, and hard returns, which are those created when you press the Enter key. These symbols do not print, but you can display them on your screen. Follow these steps:

Choose Home>Paragraph>Show/Hide. As shown in Figure 2-20, you see the paragraph symbol where a paragraph ends and you see dots that represent spaces and arrows that represent tabs.

To turn off the display of hidden characters, click the Show/Hide button again.

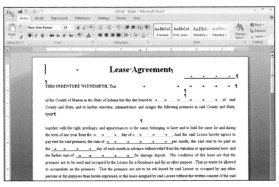

Figure 2-20
Viewing non-printing Word symbols.

RÉSUMÉ

John Q. Public
123 East Main Street, Some City, US 99999
(555)-123-4567
Johnq@myname.com

PROFILE

Skilled research engineer with doctorate in materials engineering. Strong background in manufacturing-process development and in product-improvement programs. Experienced in managing projects from conception to completion.

EDUCATION

Doctorate of Philosophy   2004
Oak Tree University
Dissertation topic: Alloy modifications to Deotel 61 to reduce additions of strategic elements while retaining the original material properties

Master of Science   2002
Elm College
Thesis topic: Optimizing the structure and properties of advanced cast irons to improve thermal fatigue resistance

Bachelor of Science   2000
Maple University

EXPERIENCE

Research Engineer   June 2002-present
Trey Research, Stamford, CT
Manage projects for several externally sponsored and company-funded manufacturing development programs.

- Handle the entire spectrum of the traditional material-removal processes, non-conventional techniques, tool design, process design, and expert systems.

- Manage projects from conception through development planning, budgeting, and scheduling; supervise technicians; present program highlights at executive conferences and trade shows.

- Revised research process to better coordinate with product marketing, resulting in more successful marketing programs and increased sales.

Professor's Assistant   Sept. 2001-May 2002
Oak Tree University
Assisted and instructed undergraduate students in classroom and laboratory settings.

- Created all materials for lectures and for semester and final exams.

- Helped revise curriculum and graduation requirements for students in materials engineering to better prepare them for the job market.

3

Making a Word Document
Look Good

PICTURE YOURSELF GOING FOR an important job interview. You need to make a good impression, so you want to look your best. So you make sure your clothes are clean and coordinated, your hair is combed and your shoes are shined. You put on your best smile and go forward into the interview.

When you create a Word document, especially one that others review, you want it to look the best. Besides making sure you've dotted all the i's and crossed all the t's, the document should have a clean, consistent, well defined appearance. Word's formatting features are what you use to modify your document's appearance.

Selecting Text Attributes

WHEN YOU SPEAK, the tone of your voice conveys how you feel. You can convey your enthusiasm (or lack of it), be friendly, or be sarcastic. In a similar way, *fonts,* which are families of design styles for the numbers, letters, and symbols that make up text, can provide additional information to the reader. Fonts can, for example, make your document appear mature and businesslike or young and casual.

Choosing a suitable font size can make a document easier to read. Other text attributes you might use to set the document tone include style settings such as bold, underline, italics, or even color.

For many text attributes, Word now offers a chance to "try before you buy" with its Live Preview feature. By pointing to various formatting choices you can see the effect the option has on your document before you actually choose the format choice. If you like it, you can simply click your mouse to choose the option. For example, if you pause your mouse over a font choice, the text appears dese-lected (it isn't) and displays with the font you are pointing to. Live Preview works with most font and paragraph formatting choices as well as styles and picture formatting changes.

> If you don't like the Live Preview option, you can turn it off. Choose Office Button>Word Options. Click Popular and remove the check mark from Enable Live Preview.

Choosing a Font

In addition to the many fonts you already have on your machine, Word comes with additional fonts. The default font used with Word 2007 is called Calibri. Fonts generally fall into two different categories: serif and sans serif. Serif fonts usually have details on the ends of some of the strokes that make up letters and symbols. A font that has serifs is called a serif font and a font without serifs is called sans-serif, from the French word *sans,* meaning "without."

Changing fonts is a very simple process. Select the text you want to modify and choose Home>Font> and from the Font drop-down list select the font you want to use (see Figure 3-1).

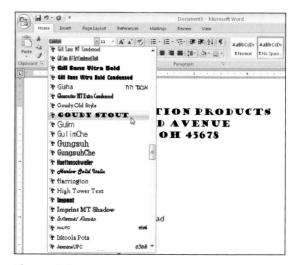

Figure 3-1
Choose a font from the list.

If you know the font name you want, you can quickly jump to that font by typing the first few characters of the font name. For example, if you want a Tahoma font, from the font list, type Ta, or for Arial, type Ari.

Selecting a Font Size

You can use any size for any font. Font sizes are measured in *points*, where a point is approximately 1/72 of an inch tall. Therefore, a 72-point font is approximately 1 inch tall.

Select the text you want to format and then choose Home>Font. Click the Font Size drop-down list arrow. You see a drop-down list of available sizes similar to those seen in Figure 3-2. Choose the size you want from the drop-down list, or type your own measurement in the Font Size box. And while you can enter a value between 1 and 1638, don't expect to be able to read a 1-point font, and a character as large as 1638 points won't even begin to fit on a standard page!

Optionally, you can click the Grow Font or Shrink Font button to increase or decrease your font size. Figure 3-2 illustrates a document with a title font size of 16 points.

The keyboard shortcut for Grow Font is Ctrl+> and for Shrink Font it's Ctrl+<.

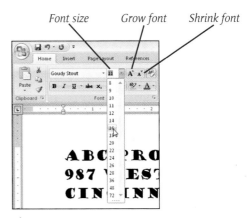

Figure 3-2
Changing font sizes.

Applying Formatting Attributes

Applying formatting attributes such as **bold**, *italic*, or <u>underline</u> calls attention to particular parts of your text. Additionally, you can assign a superscript or subscript notation to any text that makes it appear above or below the standard text, such as a copyright or trademark symbol. You can easily access these choices and others with the Home tab of the Ribbon.

To insert a copyright, trademark, registered trademark, or any of hundreds of different symbols, choose Insert>Symbols>Symbol and make a selection from the Symbol gallery. Clicking More Symbols displays the Symbol dialog box as seen in Figure 3-3.

Symbol gallery

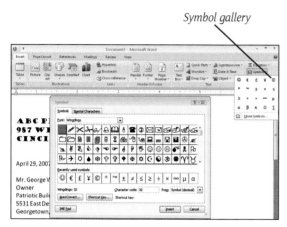

Figure 3-3
Inserting special symbols and language characters.

Select the text you want modified and from the Home tab, the Font group as shown in Figure 3-4, choose the attribute you want to apply.

Bold   Italic   Underline   Strikethrough   Subscript

Superscript

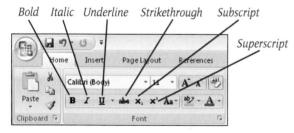

Figure 3-4
Applying special text attributes.

Some formatting shortcuts include Ctrl+B for bold, Ctrl+I for italic, and Ctrl+U for single underline.

If you want your text underlined, you can click the down arrow next to the Underline button and select an underline style and color from the drop-down list shown in Figure 3-5.

Figure 3-5
Choosing an underline style.

Choosing More Underlines displays the Font dialog box where you can select even more underline styles.

Adding Color

Another way to add impact to your document is by adding color to your text. Color becomes very effective when printing to a color printer or viewing your document on screen. Follow these steps to apply color to your text:

1. Select the text you want formatted.

2. Choose Home>Font>Font Color, or if you want to select a specific color, click the down arrow next to Font Color and make a choice from the resulting gallery as shown in Figure 3-6.

Figure 3-6
Add WOW to a document with color.

> Notice how the gallery colors are grouped together in themes. Office document themes, available in Word, Excel, and PowerPoint, contain colors, fonts, and other formatting options, all designed to give your documents a polished, professional appearance.

the down arrow next to Text Highlight Color and make a choice from the resulting gallery. Word deselects the text and applies the highlighting. Figure 3-7 shows text with pink highlighting.

Figure 3-7
Call attention to special areas with highlighting.

> To remove highlighting, choose No Color from the available color selections.

Highlighting Text

You can highlight text in your document in the same manner you highlight text with a marker in a book. You can even choose the color of highlighter you want to use. While on a monitor or with a color printer, you see the highlight color, on a black and white printer, highlighting prints as gray shading over the text. Highlighting calls attention to specific areas of your document.

Select the text you want to format with highlighting and then choose Home>Font>Text Highlight Color, or if you want to select a specific color, click

Using the Mini Toolbar

Word (along with Excel and PowerPoint) contains a semitransparent Mini Toolbar designed to provide quick access to many text and paragraph formatting features so you don't have to move your mouse so far to select the commands from the Ribbon.

The Mini Toolbar appears whenever you select some text. As your mouse points to the selected text, the transparent toolbar appears. As you move your mouse pointer so it rests on top of the toolbar, the Mini Toolbar appears in full opacity (see Figure 3-8).

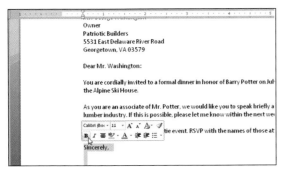

Figure 3-8
Save mouse movement by using the Mini Toolbar.

Available choices on the Mini Toolbar include:

▶ **Font**

▶ **Font Size**

▶ **Grow Text**

▶ **Shrink Text**

▶ **Quick Style**

▶ **Format Painter**

▶ **Bold**

▶ **Italic**

▶ **Center**

▶ **Text Highlight Color**

▶ **Font Color**

▶ **Decrease Indent**

▶ **Increase Indent**

▶ **Bullets**

If you find the Mini Toolbar distracting, you can turn it off. Choose Office Button>Word Options. Click Popular and remove the check mark from Show Mini Toolbar on Selection.

Using the Font Dialog Box

Another way to apply formatting to your selected text is through the Font dialog box, where you can make all your font choices via a single box. Also, you'll find that the Font dialog box offers additional attribute options not available on the Ribbon. Use the following steps to work with the Font dialog box:

1. Select the text you want formatted.

2. From the Home tab, click the Fonts group Dialog Box Launcher or press Ctrl+Shift+F. You see the Font dialog box displayed in Figure 3-9.

Dialog Box Launcher

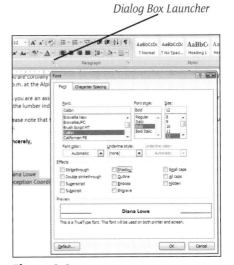

Figure 3-9
The Font dialog box.

3. Make any desired text attribute changes. The preview box at the bottom of the dialog box illustrates your choices. Live Preview isn't available from the Font dialog box.

4. Click the OK button.

Removing Formatting

If you decide you really liked the original formatting in your document, you can easily return it to the default document settings. After selecting the text from which you want to remove formatting, choose Home>Font>Clear Formatting. All text and paragraph formatting choices return to the default setting with the exception of highlighting. Any applied highlighting remains on the selected text. Figure 3-10 illustrates a document showing all the formatting removed from the second paragraph.

Clear Formatting

Figure 3-10
Easily remove unwanted formatting.

Changing the Default Font

As mentioned earlier in this chapter, Word 2007 uses 11-point Calibri as the default font. If your company has a different font as its company standard or you just prefer a different font for most documents, you can change the default font for any new Word documents. Changing the default font does not affect any existing documents.

You can set the default font from any blank document, or any currently open document. Just follow these steps:

1. From the Home tab, click the Fonts group Dialog Box Launcher or press Ctrl+Shift+F.

2. Select the font and size you want as your default.

3. Click the Default button. A confirmation message like the one seen in Figure 3-11 appears.

Figure 3-11
Confirm the Default font change.

4. Click Yes.

Formatting Paragraphs

WORD INCLUDES MANY FEATURES designed to assist you in placing text on the page just the way you want it. You can align text left-to-right using tabs or alignment options, or you can adjust your text vertically using line spacing options. Take a look at some of the available paragraph formatting choices:

Aligning Text

Alignment arranges the text to line up at one or both margins, or centers it between the margins. Alignment applies to entire paragraphs. In other words, you can't center align part of a paragraph and left align another part of the same paragraph.

You can align text to the left, right, or center, or you can *justify* your text, which means that the text becomes evenly spaced across the page from the left margin to the right margin. Apply alignment options by selecting the text you want to align, then choosing Home>Paragraph and clicking one of the following alignment buttons:

> ▶ **Align Text Left:** The text aligns evenly at the left margin. This is the default choice.
>
> ▶ **Center:** The text centers evenly between the left and right margins.
>
> ▶ **Align Text Right:** The text aligns along the right document margin.
>
> ▶ **Justify:** The text fills with micro spaces so it aligns evenly on both the left and right margins.

Figure 3-12 illustrates a document with text matching each alignment option.

Figure 3-12
Changing alignment of selected text.

Adding Paragraph Borders

Word includes borders that you can apply to any size block of text, which draw the reader's eye to specific areas for a "quick read." Use a border to place a frame around a word, phrase, paragraph, or group of paragraphs to frame the text and call specific attention to the areas. A border can encase the entire area or be any combination of lines around the text, such as above and/or below the text. Select the text you want bordered and choose Home>Paragraph. Click the drop-down arrow next to the Borders button, which displays a list of options like the one you see in Figure 3-13. Choose the border option you want.

Figure 3-13
Adding borders around text.

Word automatically adds a thin single-line border if you type three dashes in a row and then press the Enter key. Typing three underscore characters in a row and pressing Enter automatically creates a thicker border line.

Shading Text

Shading helps you distinguish headlines and important passages such as sidebars by creating a *screen*, which is typically light gray shading against the standard black text. Screens can add contrast to and enhance the readability of your document. Shading especially looks good when used in combination with a border.

A great way to add enhancement is to use a black or dark gray shading with white text.

Select the text you want shaded and choose Home>Paragraph, and then click the Borders drop-down arrow. From the list, select Borders and Shading, which displays the Borders and Shading dialog box. Click the Shading tab (see Figure 3-14).

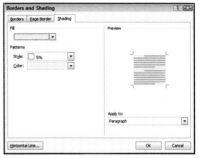

Figure 3-14
Adding shading to text.

The Shading tab provides several different shading options:

▶ **Click the Fill drop-down arrow to select a fill color. Choices are available in themes or standard colors.**

▶ **Click the Style drop-down list to select a pattern. Choices range from a light 5% shade to patterns such as diagonal stripes or polka dots.**

Use caution with patterns. Using a busy pattern can make your text very difficult to read.

▶ **Click the Color drop-down list to select a color for the pattern.**

The Borders and Shading dialog box also provides border setting options for the selected paragraphs or the current page.

Indenting Text

Typically, text runs between the left and right margins, but you may want to indent particular paragraphs. Surprise! Word contains a tool for indenting. Select the text you want to indent and then choose Home>Paragraph>Increase Indent. Each click of the Increase Indent button indents the text one-half inch from the left margin. Click the Decrease Indent button to move the text back one-half inch.

If you want to indent the right margin or you want to manually set how much indentation Word applies, you can use the Format Paragraph dialog box. Click the Paragraph Dialog Box Launcher, which displays the Paragraph dialog box seen in Figure 3-15.

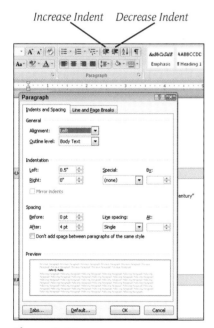

Figure 3-15
Set text apart by using indentation.

Click the spinner arrows for the Left or the Right text boxes to specify the number of inches to indent the left and right edge of the paragraph. The Preview box at the bottom shows the effects of your settings. Optionally, click the Special drop-down list and select an indenting option:

- ▶ **First line: This option indents only the first line of the paragraph and leaves the rest of the paragraph even with the left margin.**

- ▶ **Hanging: This option indents all lines *except* the first line of the paragraph.**

Click OK after you finish making selections. Word applies the paragraph indentation settings you selected.

Another way to control indention is by dragging the indentation icons on the ruler:

- ▶ **Left Indent**

- ▶ **Hanging Indent**

- ▶ **First Line Indent**

- ▶ **Right Indent**

Working with Tabs

By default, each time you press the Tab key, Word moves the insertion point a half inch to the right. However, you can set tab stops at desired points along the ruler so that when you press the Tab key, the insertion point moves to that point automatically, instead of stopping every half inch. The following steps show you how to set your own tab settings:

Do not try to line up text by pressing the space bar. Even if the text looks evenly aligned on the screen, it won't be lined up when printed. Use tabs instead.

1. Click the mouse pointer at the location you want to create a tabbed paragraph.

If you want to set tabs for multiple previously typed paragraphs, select the paragraphs before proceeding to Step 2.

2. Make sure the ruler display is turned on. If you don't see your rulers, choose View>Show/Hide>Ruler.

3. Click the Tab button located at the left end of the horizontal ruler as often as needed until you see your desired tab alignment icon (see Figure 3-16). Some tab choices include:

Tab button

Figure 3-16
Setting manual tabs.

▶ **Left:** The Tab button defaults to the left tab symbol, which looks like an "L." When using a left tab, text appears with the left edge of the text at the tab.

▶ **Center:** When you select a center tab symbol, the Tab button looks like an upside-down "T." When using a centered tab, text centers at the tab stop.

▶ **Right:** When you select the right tab symbol, the tab button looks like a backward "L." When using a right tab, text appears with the right edge of the text at the tab stop.

▶ **Decimal:** If you display the decimal tab, the Tab button appears as an upside-down "T" with a dot on the right. When writing out dollar and cent amounts, for example, decimal points align to the tab.

▶ **Bar:** Bar tabs are very different from the previous four tabs. Text doesn't position around bar tabs. Instead, Word inserts a vertical bar at the top position and runs through the depth of the paragraph.

4. Click on the horizontal ruler to set the tab for the current paragraph or the currently selected paragraphs. Depending on the tab type you selected, a left, right, center, decimal, or bar tab symbol appears where you clicked the ruler.

5. Click in the paragraph and press the Tab key. Notice how the insertion point moves to the tab setting you created.

6. Type some text. The text you type appears on the page. In Figure 3-17, you see examples of center and right align tabs as you might use them in a document. (To make the tabs easier to see, I've also displayed the hidden characters.)

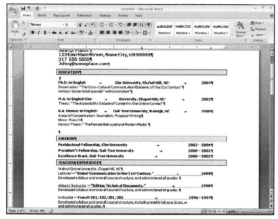

Figure 3-17
Line up text with tabs—not spaces.

Pressing Enter continues the tab settings to the next paragraph.

Moving a Tab

If you're not happy with the position of your tab stop, you can easily move it. Select to highlight the paragraphs that have a tab you want moved, and then drag the tab to a new location on the ruler bar. As you drag the tab, a vertical, dotted line like the one shown in Figure 3-18 illustrates the new tab position. When you release the mouse button, the text moves to the new tab position.

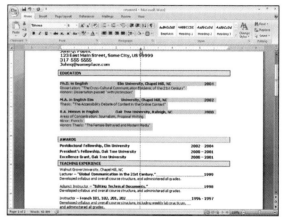

Figure 3-18
Easily move manual tabs to a different area.

Deleting a Tab

Like moving a tab, the ruler makes deleting a tab a very simple process. Select the paragraphs that have a tab you want to delete and then drag the current tab setting off the ruler, into the body of the document. A vertical dotted line appears. When you release the mouse button, the tab disappears from the ruler and text realigns according to your new tab settings. If there is no previous manual tab stop, the default tab settings take effect.

Using the Tabs Dialog Box

If you want your tab stops at more precise positions than you get by clicking the ruler, or if you want a dot leader before the tab, use the Tabs dialog box. Select the text where you want to set the tab. From the Home tab, click the Paragraph Dialog Box Launcher.

> Optionally, double-click any manual tab stop on the ruler.

Click the Tabs button, which displays the Tabs dialog box shown in Figure 3-19.

Figure 3-19
The Tabs dialog box.

In the Tab stop position text box, type the location you want for the new tab and choose an Alignment and optional Leader style for the tab. Click the Set button. Repeat this action for each tab you want set. Click OK to close the Tabs dialog box.

> Optionally, use the Tabs dialog box to change the default tab stop setting from 0.5" to any desired amount.

Changing Line Spacing

Line spacing is the amount of vertical space between each line of text. You might want to change line spacing when you want to make a document such as a contract easier to read or to make room for changes when writing a document draft. Like text alignment, line spacing applies to complete paragraphs. Use the following steps to change line spacing:

> Word 2007 uses a default line spacing of 1.15. Previous versions of Microsoft Word used single spacing (1.0) as the default setting.

1. Select the text you want to change.

2. Choose Home>Paragraph>Line Spacing. A list of options appears (see Figure 3-20).

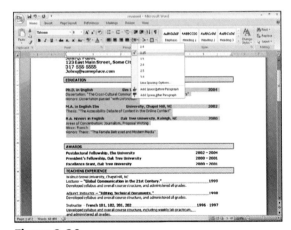

Figure 3-20
Choosing a line spacing option.

3. Select a line spacing option. Word applies the spacing you select to the highlighted text.

Shortcut keys for setting line spacing are: Ctrl+1 for single spacing, Ctrl+2 for double spacing, and Ctrl+5 for 1.5 line spacing.

Changing Spacing Between Paragraphs

Paragraph spacing is the amount of vertical space between each paragraph of text. Remember that whenever you press the Enter key, you start a new paragraph. In previous versions of Word, the default was no spacing between paragraphs, so, traditionally, you would press the Enter key a second time to leave space between two paragraphs. Word 2007 uses a different default setting. The default setting allows for 10 points of blank space at the bottom of every paragraph, thereby eliminating the need to press the extra Enter key.

However, you have complete control over how much spacing, if any, you want between two paragraphs. Similar to indentation, paragraph spacing is controlled through the Paragraph dialog box. From the Home tab, click the Paragraph Dialog Box Launcher, which displays the Paragraph dialog box (see Figure 3-21).

Figure 3-21
Manually setting the desired amount of spacing between paragraphs.

The Spacing section is where you determine the amount of space you want before or after each paragraph. Settings are measured in points and range from -1 to 1584.

Copying Formatting

I F YOU SPEND SEVERAL MINUTES setting up just the right text and paragraph formatting, and you know you'll need the same formatting several more times in your document, you don't want to have to remember all your settings and repeat them over and over again. Instead, you can copy formatting from one area to others by using the Format Painter tool. Follow these easy steps to copy formatting:

1. Select some of the text containing the formatting you want to use elsewhere. Your selection could include just a few characters or an entire paragraph.

2. Choose Home>Clipboard>Format Painter. Your mouse pointer changes to the shape of a paintbrush.

3. Press and hold the mouse button and drag over the text you want formatted.

4. Release the mouse button. Notice, as shown in Figure 3-22, how the third paragraph takes on the formatting attributes of the first paragraph.

Format Painter

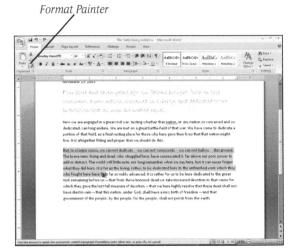

Figure 3-22
Save formatting time by using the Format Painter tool.

To keep the Format Painter function active for repeated use, double-click the Format Painter button. When you finish using the Format Painter function, click the Format Painter button again, which turns it off.

Working with Lists

YOU CAN USE BULLETS OR NUMBERS to call attention to lists in your documents. Traditionally, you use bullets when the list items do not follow any particular order (such as a list of options), and you use numbers when you want the items to follow each other in numerical order (such as the steps in this book). Select the text for which you want to add bullets or numbers. Then, choose Home>Paragraph and click either the Bullets button or the Numbering button. Both items have a drop-down arrow from which you can select a bullet or number style (see Figure 3-23). You can preview the options with Live Preview by pausing your mouse over any option before selecting.

If you choose bullets and then decide you want numbering, or vice-versa, select the text, and then choose the other option. If you decide you don't want a bulleted or numbered list, select the text and click the bullet or number button again, which removes the selected option.

If you have not already typed your list, Word monitors your keystrokes and, depending on what you type, automatically converts a list to a bulleted or numbered list. If you type a 1 followed by a period and then either a space or tab, Word automatically converts the item to a numbered list. If you type an asterisk * followed by a space or a tab, Word automatically changes the asterisk into a bullet. When you finish typing and press the Enter key, Word creates the next numbered item, or adds another bullet.

Bullets   Numbering

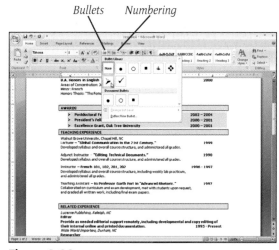

Figure 3-23

Grab readers' attention by using bullets or numbering.

Other features Word monitors and automatically changes include changing fractions to fractional characters like 1/2 to ½ or applying ordinals such as changing 1st to 1st.

When Word formats the entry as a list, you see an AutoCorrect Options button next to the bullet or number (see Figure 3-24). If you don't want Word to change the list formatting, click the AutoCorrect Options button and choose Undo Automatic Numbering or Undo Automatic Bullets.

To permanently turn off the automatic numbering or bullet formatting, choose Office Button>Word Options. In the Proofing section, click AutoCorrect Options. Click the AutoFormat As You Type tab and turn off Automatic Bulleted Lists and Automatic Numbering.

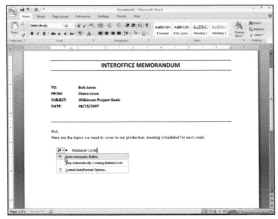

Figure 3-24
Word's AutoFormat As You Type feature.

Using Quick Styles

THIS ENTIRE CHAPTER IS ABOUT
making your document look good by using
Word's many formatting tools. However,
there is a faster way to quickly apply formatting.
Styles are predefined sets of formatting that can
include font, paragraph, list, border, and shading
information. Using styles also helps maintain consistency in your document. Use the following steps
to work with Quick Styles:

1. Select the text to which you want to apply
   formatting.

2. Choose Home and click the More button
   next to the Styles scroll bar. A gallery of style
   options as you see in Figure 3-25 appears.

Figure 3-25
Choose from Word's predefined styles.

3. As you position your mouse over the styles,
   Live Preview shows you the effect on your
   selected text. Select the option that best suits
   your text.

Optionally, choose Home>Styles>Change
Styles>Style Set and view additional style
options (see Figure 3-26).

Figure 3-26
More Word predefined style formats.

4

Managing Word

Pages

PICTURE YOURSELF TAKING YOUR FAMILY to an amusement park. The older children want to go this way, and the younger children want to go another way. Grandpa just wants to sit, rest, and watch. How will you manage everything?

Balancing a document's *white space*—the amount of blank space on a page—is an important aspect of designing professional-looking pages. You can increase or decrease white space by adjusting margins and the amount of text you place on a page. Additionally, Word provides the ability to work with multiple documents at the same time, as well as methods for quickly comparing information between two documents. When multiple windows are active, you'll need a way to manage them all. That's what this chapter is about...managing Word pages.

Creating Page Breaks

WORD AUTOMATICALLY INSERTS a page break when text fills the page. This page break sometimes doesn't fall where you want it to. You can override Word's automatic page break by creating your own page break. You can make a page break at a shorter position than Word chooses, but you cannot make a page longer.

A manual page break is sometimes called a hard page break because, unlike the page breaks that Word inserts, a manual page break doesn't move if you delete text above it, adjust the margins, or otherwise change the amount of text on the page. Insert a manual page break by positioning the insertion point where you want the new page to begin and choosing one of the following methods:

- ▶ **Choose Insert>Pages>Page Break**
- ▶ **Choose Page Layout>Page Setup> Breaks>Page**
- ▶ **Press Ctrl+Enter**

If you are in the default Print Layout view, you see the text below the insertion point move down to the next page of the document, such as you see in Figure 4-1. However, if you have the Show/Hide characters active, you see the words "Page Break," along with a dotted line, where the new page begins. (Document views are discussed later in this chapter.)

Word's automatic page breaks cannot be deleted, but the hard page breaks that you have inserted manually can be deleted at any time. Simply click the mouse pointer at the beginning of the text after the page break indication and then press the Backspace key. Word deletes the manual page break and the document text readjusts to fit on the pages correctly.

Figure 4-1
Manually starting a new page.

Using Section Breaks

When you need to apply different page formatting options to only a portion of the document, you need to break the document into *sections*. For example, when page 1 requires different margin settings from the rest of the document, you must break page 1 into its own section. If only pages 16–18 need to be printed in landscape orientation, you can break pages 16, 17, and 18 into a section.

Most section breaks involve entire pages; however, if you need different columns, they don't necessarily have to be on different pages. Word allows for three different types of section breaks:

- ▶ **Next page:** Inserts a section break and starts the new section on the next page.
- ▶ **Continuous:** Inserts a section break and starts the new section on the same page.

▶ **Odd page**: Inserts a section break and starts the new section on the next odd-numbered page.

▶ **Even page**: Inserts a section break and starts the new section on the next even-numbered page.

Section formatting options include the following, many of which are covered in this chapter:

▶ **Margins**: The amount of space between the text and the paper edge

▶ **Paper size**: The paper size you intend to use when printing

▶ **Paper orientation**: The direction the text prints on the paper edge

▶ **Paper source**: When printing, which paper tray the printer should pull paper from.

▶ **Page borders**: Bordered lines that appear around the entire document page

▶ **Vertical alignment**: The placement of text between the top and bottom margins

▶ **Headers and footers**: Text that appears at the top or bottom of every document page

▶ **Columns**: How text in newsletter-style columns flows from one column to the next on the same page.

▶ **Page numbering**: Sequential numbering for each document page

▶ **Line numbering**: How Word automatically counts the lines in a document and displays the appropriate number beside each line of text.

▶ **Footnotes and endnotes**: A note of text placed at the bottom of a page or at the end of the document typically citing a reference used in the document.

To insert a section break, position the mouse where you want the new section to begin and choose Page Layout>Page Setup>Breaks and select the desired section break type from the drop-down list as shown in Figure 4-2. A section break controls the formatting of the text that precedes it.

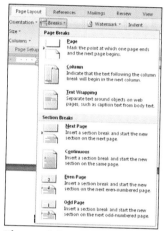

Figure 4-2
Types of page and section breaks.

Depending on the type of section break you choose, from the default Print Layout view, you see the text below the insertion point remain at the same location or move down to the next page of the document. However, if you are in Draft view or you have the Show/Hide characters active, you see the words "Section Break" and the type of section break in action, along with a dotted line, where the previous section ends (see Figure 4-3).

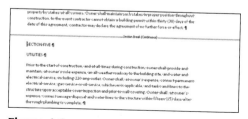

Figure 4-3
Section break indication.

Managing Page Layouts

S OMETIMES WORKING WITH A LONG
document can feel a bit overwhelming.
Fortunately, Word contains many features
designed to assist you, such as those which allow
you to set the page size and layout, mixing and
matching them as needed.

Setting Margins

Margins are the space between the edges of the
paper and where the text actually begins to appear.
Word allows you to set margins for any of the four
sides of the document and also allows you to mix
and match margins for different pages. Word sets
the default margins as 1" on each of the top, bottom, left, and right sides.

You can set the document margins before you
begin entering text into a document, after you've
completed the entire document, or at any time in
between.

Choose Page Layout>Page Setup>Margins and
select from the choices you see in Figure 4-4, or
click Custom Margins, which displays the Page
Setup dialog box where you can set your own
choices. By default, Word applies the new settings
to the entire document.

If you want to change margins for only part of the
document, select the portion you want to change.
From Page Layout>Page Setup>Margins, choose
Custom Margins. Set the margins you want and,
from the Apply to drop-down list, choose Selected
Text (see Figure 4-5). Word creates section breaks
and applies the new margin settings.

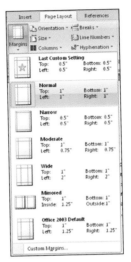

Figure 4-4
Choosing from standard margin options.

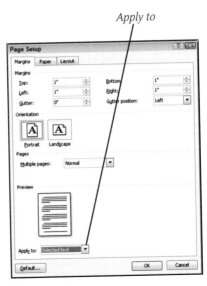

Figure 4-5
Applying margin settings to only part of a document.

Changing Document Orientation

Webster's dictionary describes orientation as a position in relation to a specific place or object. In word processing, orientation refers to how the text is positioned to the top of a page. Two orientations exist: Portrait, the default orientation, prints the text beginning along the short edge of the paper, and Landscape orientation prints along the long edge of the page.

Choose Page Layout>Page Setup>Orientation and choose Portrait or Landscape as seen in Figure 4-6.

Figure 4-6
Choosing a document orientation.

Similar to margin settings, if you want to change the orientation for only part of the document, select the portion you want to change and, from the Page Setup dialog box, choose your orientation and from the Apply to section, choose Selected Text. Word creates section breaks and applies the new settings to the selected section.

Setting the Paper Size

Word assumes you want your document printed on standard paper 8.5 inches wide by 11 inches long, but you may want some or your document printed on a different paper size. Although Word can work with many different sizes of paper, often the available selections depend on the printer you have. In many situations, you can even create your own custom paper size.

Word provides a number of different ways to manage document paper sizes.

▶ **To change the paper size for the entire document, choose Page Layout>Page Setup>Size and select a size from the resulting drop-down box (see Figure 4-7).**

Figure 4-7
Selecting the desired paper size.

▶ **To change the paper size from a certain location through the rest of the document, position the insertion point where you want the new paper size to take effect, and then choose Page Layout>Page Setup>Size and select More Paper Sizes. From the Paper tab of the Page Setup dialog box, select the paper size you want and then, in the Apply to drop-down list, choose "This point forward."**

▶ **To change the paper size for a particular section, create the section breaks where needed and click anywhere inside the section you want to change, or select the text area. Choose Page Layout>Page Setup>Size and select More Paper Sizes. From the Paper tab of the Page Setup dialog box, select the paper size you want and then, from the Apply to drop-down list, choose "This section" or "Selected sections."**

Viewing a Document

WORD PROVIDES SEVERAL different view perspectives to use when displaying a document, each having its own purpose. For each of the following views, except Print Preview, choose View>Document Views and choose an option.

Word also displays icons along the status bar that allow you to choose most of the view options.

▶ **Print Layout:** The default view, Print Layout, allows you to see how text, graphics, and other elements will be positioned on the printed page. This view is especially helpful if you are working with text columns. In Print Layout view, you'll see the document's top and bottom margins, as well as the headers and footers. The top and bottom margins appear, and page breaks between pages are indicated by a darker area.

▶ **Full Screen Reading:** Using the Full Screen Reading view hides most of the Ribbon and other screen elements and displays your document two pages at a time, usually in a larger font size, scaling the contents of your document to pages that fit comfortably on your screen, making it easy to read. When in Full Screen Reading view, the page breaks are not necessarily the same page breaks as in the printed document.

You can adjust the reading font size without actually affecting the document itself. (Choose View Options>Increase Text Size). See Figure 4-8 for an example of a document in Full Screen Reading view.

View Options

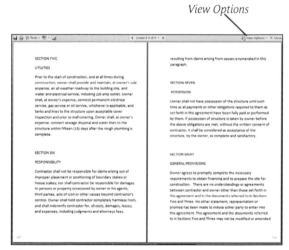

Figure 4-8
Full Screen Reading view.

Use the View Options button to change Full Screen Reading view options. Click the Close button to return to the previously used view.

▶ **Web Layout:** When in Web Layout view you see how the document looks as viewed in a Web browser.

▶ **Outline**: Outline view displays your text in an outline format that includes the outlining tab from which you can display levels as well as promote and demote headings. (See Chapter 6, "Discovering Word Tools" for information on outlines.)

▶ **Draft**: Draft view is a text-only view used for typing, editing, and formatting text. It simplifies the layout of the page so that you can type and edit quickly. Page breaks are indicated by a dotted line, and headers, footers, page margins, backgrounds, and some other objects do not appear in Draft view.

▶ **Print Preview**: This view allows you to see the document as it will appear when printed. For Print Preview, choose Office, pause the mouse over the Print command, and then choose Print Preview. (See Chapter 6, "Discovering Word Tools".)

Using the Zoom Feature

Word's ability to zoom in on a document allows you to examine your document more closely or in greater detail through a close-up view of your text. You can also zoom out to see more of the page at a reduced size. Zoom settings do not affect the arrangement of text when you print the document. Choose View>Zoom, and you see that Word provides a number of different ways that you can zoom in or out of your document:

> Using the Zoom feature does not alter the size at which the document will print.

▶ Click the Zoom button to display the Zoom dialog box (see Figure 4-9) where you can choose the zoom percentage you want.

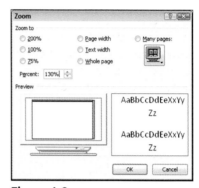

Figure 4-9
Choosing a Zoom percentage.

▶ Choose One Page to view the entire page (see Figure 4-10).

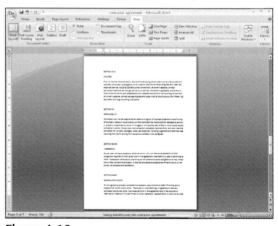

Figure 4-10
Viewing a single page.

► **Choose Two Pages to view two pages side by side. Use the scroll bar to scroll down through the document two pages at a time.**

► **Choose Page Width to view the page by page width.**

Setting the Zoom to Page Width can be very helpful if your document page orientation is set to landscape.

► **Choose 100% to return to the normal zoom rate of 100%**

► **Drag the zoom slider located on the status bar to zoom in and out as desired (see Figure 4-11). The current zoom rate appears next to the zoom slider.**

Figure 4-11
The zoom slider controls.

If your mouse has a scroll button on top, you can use it to zoom in and out. Hold down the Ctrl key and move the scroll button forward to zoom in or backward to zoom out.

Working with Split Windows

If you want to see two parts of a document, but you can't get them on the screen at the same time, you can split a window. Doing so enables you to view part of the document in the upper window while you view another part of the document in the lower window.

When you split a window each window panel contains its own scroll bar. Choose View>Window>Split. A horizontal line with a double headed arrow appears at the mouse pointer. Click the mouse where you want the window divided, which then locks in the split. The window divides into two sections with each section having its own scroll bar and rulers. Take a look at Figure 4-12 where you see page 1 in the top section and page 7 in the bottom section.

Figure 4-12
Viewing two different document areas.

To resize the windows, position the mouse at the top of the bottom window until it becomes a double-headed arrow and then drag the line until the windows are the desired size.

When you want to remove the window split, choose View>Window>Remove Split. Your document reappears in a single window.

Comparing Documents Side by Side

Occasionally, you may want to view two documents side by side, perhaps to compare one version to another. Word provides the ability to view any two open windows next to each other.

Choose View>Window>View Side by Side. If you have more than two Word documents open, Word first requests which window you want to compare to the top current window (see Figure 4-13). If you have only two open Word documents, you do not see this Compare Side by Side dialog box.

Figure 4-13
Viewing two different documents.

To edit a document, click anywhere in the document window.

By default, the two windows are synchronized so that as you scroll through one window, the other one scrolls with it. If you want to scroll through the windows independently, you need to turn off Synchronous Scrolling. From either window, choose View>Window>Synchronous Scrolling (see Figure 4-14).

To return to a single document window, deactivate the feature by choosing View>Window>View Side by Side.

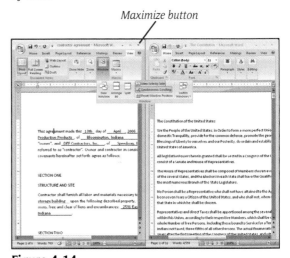

Maximize button

Figure 4-14
Managing Synchronous Scrolling.

Using the Document Map

If your document is quite lengthy, it can be difficult and time consuming to navigate through the document. However, if your document contains heading styles, you can use the Document Map feature to ease navigation. The Document Map also allows you to examine the document flow for completeness and ensure that formatting is consistent. Think of a Document Map as a simple Table of Contents. Choose View>Show/Hide>Document Map. The Document Map pane, like the one seen in Figure 4-15, appears on the left side of the screen.

If the document does not contain any heading styles, the Document Map will be blank.

Each item in the Document Map panel represents a heading in your document; you can click any item to move the insertion point to that place in the document. You can click the plus sign to expand a heading or click the minus sign to hide subheadings.

To hide the Document Map, choose View> Show/Hide>Document Map, which removes the checkmark in Document Map and closes the Document Map pane.

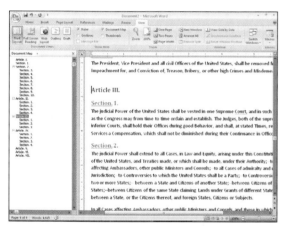

Figure 4-15

Working with a Document Map.

Adding Headers and Footers

EADERS AND FOOTERS ARE FEATURES used for placing information at the top or bottom of every page of a document. As you'd expect, a header prints at the top of every page, and a footer prints at the bottom. You can place any information in headers and footers, such as a company logo, the document title, page numbering, and so forth.

Using Header and Footer Styles

In keeping with the themed concept of Office 2007, the predefined headers and footers contain elements designed to make your document more visually appealing. Choose Insert>Header & Footer>Headers (or Footers) which displays a gallery of 24 unique header (or footer) styles, as seen in Figure 4-16.

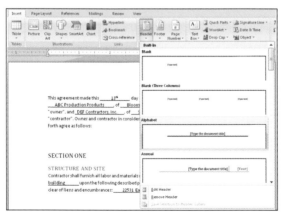

Figure 4-16
Creating a header or footer.

Select the style you want. The document header area becomes visible and Word displays an additional tab on the ribbon. You can now use the Header & Footer Tools>Design tab for creating your personalized header or footer.

In the header example shown in Figure 4-17, Word inserts a placeholder for the document title. Click the placeholder and enter the desired text. Also in the same figure, you see a placeholder that says Pick the Date. If you click the down arrow, Word displays a calendar from which you can select the date you want in the header. Optionally, you can just type a date in the date field. The actual choices you see depend on which header or footer style you select.

Placeholder   *Design tab*

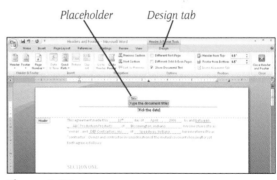

Figure 4-17
Working with text placeholders.

If you don't want the predefined placeholder, click the small tab above the placeholder and press the Delete key.

Now take a brief look at some of the tool groups on the Header & Footer Tools>Design tab, as seen in Figure 4-18.

Figure 4-18
The Header & Footer Tools Design tab.

▶ **Header & Footer:** Use this group to change the header or footer style or to insert the page number in the header or footer.

▶ **Insert:** From this group you can insert the current date or time, a picture, or a piece of clip art. You can also select from Quick Parts and choose one of the document properties shown in Figure 4-19.

Figure 4-19
Adding document Quick Parts.

▶ **Navigation:** Use the tools in this group to move between the document headers and footers.

▶ **Options:** The Options group allows you to choose whether the first page of your document should have a different header or footer from the rest of the document. You can also choose different headers for the odd or even numbered pages.

▶ **Position:** This group contains settings for exact header and footer placement in relation to the top or bottom of the document paper edges.

▶ **Close:** Use this button to close the header or footer and return to the document body. You can also double-click anywhere in the document body to close the header or footer.

Every page of the document displays the header and/or footer you created (see Figure 4-20). Remember, however, that documents displayed in Outline or Draft view do not show headers or footers.

> **For further editing, double-click the header or footer area.**

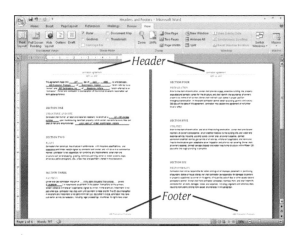

Figure 4-20
Viewing a document header and footer.

SPECIAL REQUESTS

- **We love our children** playing in their front yards and with friends on the street but please remember to put toys away when not in use and to keep sidewalks clear of toys.
- **Thank you to all those** residents who rescheduled weekend landscaping to weekdays. Your neighbors appreciate it.
- **A friendly reminder to** dog owners to keep their dogs leashed when on the streets. We have had reports of some dogs joining their neighbors at the dinner table!

SAFETY ALERTS

Please check your supporting structures (balcony posts etc) for wood rot. You may report it to Chris Doe, New Home Warranty, Trophy Homes.

You may have seen one of many media releases

regarding manufacturing defects in attic furnaces that pose potential fire

threat. Homeowners with attic or under-floor furnaces installed between 1984 and 1999 should verify the Brand name and model number of furnaces in their home to determine if they are defective. Any air conditioning contractor or maintenance personnel can make this determination.

VOTING OPINION POLLS

Thank you to the approximately 100 residents who responded to the opinion polls mailed by Keystone Pacific during the months of November and December. Here are the actual results:

OPINION SURVEY	YES	NO
I would like the Association to proceed with the Guardhouse	48	46
I would like the Association to proceed with changing the legal documents regarding the approval percentage	50	45

These numbers indicate insufficient support to justify the Board pursuing either option in the immediate future. The Board voted that it would not be prudent to expend association funds on feasibility studies and legal fees when there is no guarantee that either measure would pass when put to the membership for a formal vote. Both issues were tabled for six months.

DID YOU KNOW …?

It costs the Snoozie Homeowners Association $774 per month to keep our gutters and streets free of debris and algae. The street sweeper comes twice a month on the first and third Wednesday. It is unfortunate that the street sweeper is unable to effectively do its job because cars parked on the street continue to obstruct its work. All homeowners are requested to ensure that their own cars as well as cars belonging to visitors (including domestic help) are parked in driveways and off the street on the days the street sweeper is scheduled.

Warning notices will be issued to cars in violation for the next couple of street sweepings, however if this problem

1

5

Working with Columns and *Tables*

PICTURE YOURSELF CRAWLING OUT of your warm bed after a good night's sleep. A luxurious aroma wafts through the house and you anticipate your first cup of hot coffee. You sit at the table and begin reading the morning paper, scanning the headlines and reading some articles in their entirety. You look at the financial section to check your stocks and you review the weather forecast for the next few days.

When you read a newspaper or magazine article, you read in columns. When you look at the financial page or the weather forecast, you're usually looking at a table, which is a grid consisting of rows and columns. That's what this chapter is all about...creating the type of document designed for reading large amounts of information quickly and easily.

Using Columns

NEWSPAPERS AND MAGAZINES are just a few of the documents that use columns to break up stories, with the text flowing from the bottom of one column to the top of the next. Of course, columns can be used for many other items, such as creating attractive newsletters, forms, or marketing materials.

Word applies columns to the entire document unless you first select the portion you want changed into columns, or you create section breaks and apply the column settings to the current section.

Choose Page Layout>Page Setup>Columns. As shown in Figure 5-1, you see a drop-down list of preset column options. Take a look at what each choice represents:

Figure 5-1
Choosing column settings.

▶ **One:** Use this choice to transform the document (or section) from multiple columns back to a single column.

▶ **Two:** Select this to divide the page into two equally spaced columns.

▶ **Three:** If you want three equally spaced columns on the page, choose this option.

▶ **Left:** The Left option divides the page into two columns, but the left column is smaller than the right (see Figure 5-2).

Figure 5-2
The left column is smaller than the right.

▶ **Right:** The Right option divides the page into two columns, but the left column is larger than the left.

▶ **More Columns:** This option displays the Columns dialog box where you can customize your column settings.

For better column setting controls, choose the More Columns option. The Columns dialog box, as shown in Figure 5-3, provides a plethora of column options.

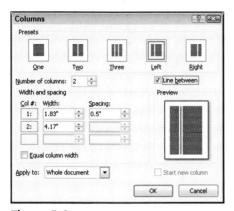

Figure 5-3
The Columns dialog box.

Remember that if you want to make column changes to only a portion of the document, you must select that portion, or click in the section before choosing options from the Columns dialog box.

▶ **Choose from any of the five preset column options.**

▶ **Manually set the number of columns, ranging from 1 column to 45 columns, by clicking the up/down arrows.**

▶ **Check the "Line between" check box to add a solid line between the columns. Vertical lines between columns can make it easier to separate the columns when reading the text.**

▶ **Select a column and manually set the column width and the spacing between two columns. The white space between the columns is called the *gutter*. Each column can have its own width and gutter.**

▶ **Choose the "Equal column width" box if you want all columns equally spaced.**

By default, text will flow down one column, then over to the next column. If you want the column to break at a particular point, you can insert a manual column break. Column breaks are similar to page breaks in that you cannot create a manual column break to make the column longer than the page margins, but you can make a column shorter. To create a manual column break, choose Page Layout>Page Setup>Breaks>Column

Figure 5-4 illustrates a newsletter created in Word using columns, sections breaks and column breaks, page borders, shading, and a few graphics.

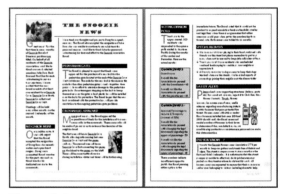

Figure 5-4
A finished newsletter.

To create the large first letter, called a *drop cap*, select the first letter and choose Insert>Text>Drop Cap>Dropped.

Working with Tables

T ABLES ARE GREAT FOR ORGANIZING information. A table is a grid of columns and rows, and the intersection of a column and row is called a *cell*. When you need to compare data or follow information across several columns, it's easier if the information is displayed in a table. You can use tables to place pieces of data side-by-side in a document—for example, in the various sections of an invoice or address list.

If you have used Microsoft Excel or another spreadsheet program, you will find working with tables in Word very similar. In fact, on a very small scale, Word tables are small spreadsheets.

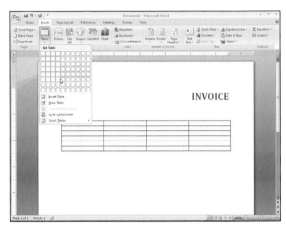

Figure 5-5
The table grid.

Creating a Simple Table

When you create a table, all you need to do is estimate the number of rows and columns you need. Notice I said *estimate*. You'll find it easy to add or delete rows or columns after you create the table. Use the following steps to create a table:

1. Position the insertion point where you would like the table to begin.

2. Choose Insert>Tables>Table, which displays a table grid like the one you see in Figure 5-5.

3. Drag the mouse across the squares that represent the number of rows and columns you want in your table. Word's Live Preview feature draws a sample of the table in your document.

> If you don't want to drag across the table grid to set the table size, choose Insert Table. The Insert Table dialog box appears, in which you can type how many rows and columns you want in your table.

4. Click the square that represents the lower right corner of your table. Word places the table into your document.

Notice in Figure 5-6 that the blinking insertion point is in the first table cell and that the Ribbon now contains two Table Tools tabs: Design and Layout.

A table cell is a box that appears at the intersection of a row and column. Although the names don't display, each column takes an alphabetic letter, A, B, C, and so forth. Each row is indicated by number. A cell, then, is referred to by both the column and row, such as A2 or B5. This is especially important if you create a formula in your table. (See "Creating Table Formulas" later in this chapter.)

Figure 5-7
Table cells expand to accommodate entered text.

Converting Tables

Another method you can use to insert a Word table is by using existing text. If you already have a list where each column is separated by a tab, a comma, or other consistent character, you can easily convert that list to a table so you won't have to create the table and retype all the text. Conversely, if you put text into a table and then decide you would prefer it in tabular columns, you can convert the table into a list.

In order for the conversion feature to work correctly, you must be consistent with the character you use to separate the items.

To convert a text list into a Word table, select the list and choose Insert>Tables>Table>Convert Text to Table. The Convert Text to Table dialog box shown in Figure 5-8 appears.

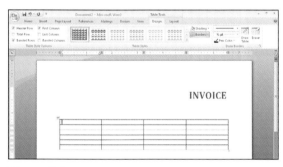

Figure 5-6
Creating a table.

Entering Text

Once you have your table in the document, you can start adding text to it. Click in the cell where you want to enter information and begin typing. If needed, Word automatically wraps the text and expands the row height to accommodate the text, as seen in Figure 5-7. You can press the Tab key to move to the next cell or press Shift+Tab to move to the previous cell. You can also use the up and down arrow keys to move up or down a row at a time.

Other separation character

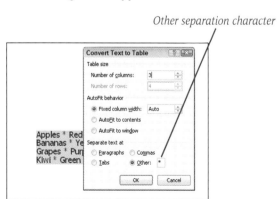

Figure 5-8
Converting an existing list into a Word table.

Based on the data you selected, Word guesses the number of columns you want. If you did not separate your columns with commas or tabs, in the "Separate text at" section, choose Other and type the character you used, such as an asterisk or dash. Click OK and Word converts the list into a table.

If your text is already in a table, but you would prefer it in a tabular list, click anywhere in the table and choose Table Tools Layout>Data>Convert to Text. You see the Convert Table to Text dialog box seen in Figure 5-9. Choose the printing or non-printing character you want the text separated with and then click OK. The table disappears and the text remains.

Figure 5-9
Converting a table back to standard text.

Creating a Quick Table

A third method for creating a table is using one of Word's Quick Tables. Quick Tables are nine predefined tables that include sample data and formatting. If you find a Quick Table close to what you actually need, you can save time by choosing the Quick Table and then changing the elements you want changed. Choose Insert>Tables>Table>Quick Tables and choose from one of the preformatted templates like you see in Figure 5-10.

Figure 5-10
Choosing a Quick Table style.

If you create and format a table style you like and frequently use, select the table and choose Insert>Tables>Table>Quick Tables> Save Selection to Quick Tables Gallery. The next time you need that table you can select it from the Quick Tables gallery.

Okay...one more, rather fun way to create a Word table is by simply typing out a string of plus signs (+) and minus signs (-). Word uses its AutoCorrect feature to interpret your typing and convert it to a table. Type a plus sign and then type a series of minus signs until you have the first column width you want for your table. Type another plus sign, followed by more minus signs. Repeat these steps, placing a plus sign at the end of the series of minus signs (see Figure 5-11). When you press Enter, Word automatically converts it to a table.

Typing this...   *Results in this*

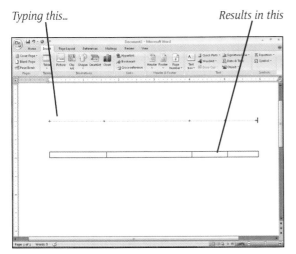

Figure 5-11
Manually typing table boundaries.

No matter which method you used to create your table, you enter the data as well as format or modify the table in the following ways.

Changing Table Size

OK, now you have your table created, but it doesn't contain the right number of rows or columns. You can easily change the table size by adding or deleting rows or columns from your table. Table 5-1 illustrates some of the different ways you can change the table size:

Figure 5-12
Deleting unwanted table areas.

Table 5-1 Changing Table Size

To	Do This
Add rows to the table end	Click in the last table cell and press the Tab key or click in the last row and choose Table Tools Layout>Rows & Columns>Insert Below.
Add rows in the table middle	Click in a cell and choose Table Tools Layout>Rows & Columns>Insert Below (or Insert Above).
Add columns	Click in a cell and choose Table Tools Layout>Rows & Columns>Insert Left (or Insert Right).
Delete a column	Click in the column you want to delete and choose Table Tools Layout> Rows & Columns>Delete>Delete Columns.
Delete a row	Click in the row you want to delete and choose Table Tools Layout> Rows & Columns>Delete>Delete Rows.
Delete an entire table	Click anywhere in the table and choose Table Tools Layout>Rows & Columns>Delete>Delete Table (see Figure 5-12).

Adjusting Column Width and Row Height

When you begin typing in a cell, you see that as you type, the text wraps to the next line in the same cell. You may find that you don't want the data to wrap around, but the column is not wide enough to hold your data. You can easily change the width of columns or the height of rows. You can manage the task with the mouse or you can choose options in the ribbon. First, look at the methods you can use to change column width:

▶ Position the mouse over the edge of any cell in the column you want to adjust. Notice the mouse pointer changes to a bar with both left and right pointing arrows. Drag the edge of the cell until the column is the width you want (see Figure 5-13).

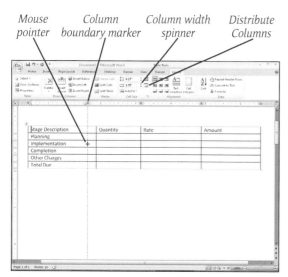

Figure 5-13
Drag to resize a column.

▶ Drag the column boundary marker on the ruler.

▶ Click in any cell of the column you want to adjust and choose Table Tools Layout>Cell Size>Table Column Width. Use the up/down arrows to set the desired column width.

▶ To force the column width so it's wide enough to fit the widest entry in the column, position the mouse pointer over the left edge of any cell in the column. When the mouse pointer changes to a bar with the left and right pointing arrows, double-click the mouse. Word automatically expands the column to fit the widest entry.

▶ To force all columns to the same width, choose Table Tools Layout>Cell Size> Distribute Columns

▶ To adjust the width of *all* of the table columns to fit their widest entry, choose Table Tools Layout>Cell Size>AutoFit> AutoFit Contents.

The methods for modifying row height are very similar to those you use to change column width:

▶ Position the mouse over the bottom edge of any cell in the column you want to adjust. Notice the mouse pointer changes to a bar with both up and down arrows. Drag the bottom edge of the cell until the row is the height you want.

▶ Click in any cell of the row you want to adjust and choose Table Tools Layout> Cell Size>Table Row Height. Use the up/down arrows to set the desired row height.

▶ To adjust the height so it's tall enough to fit the tallest data entry, position the mouse pointer over the bottom edge of any cell in the row and double-click the mouse.

▶ To force each row to the same height, choose Table Tools Layout>Cell Size>Distribute Rows.

Changing Table Dimensions

If you find that your table dimensions don't quite provide the look you want, besides changing column widths and row heights, you can easily change the table size. Just follow these steps:

1. Pause your mouse anywhere over the table until you see a sizing handle appear in the lower right table corner. (You must be in Print Layout view or Web Layout view to use this feature.)

2. Position the mouse pointer over the handle until the pointer changes to a diagonal double headed arrow. (See Figure 5-14).

Stage Description	Quantity	Rate	Amount
Planning			
Implementation			
Completion			
Other Charges			
Total Due			

Figure 5-14
Resizing a table.

3. Drag the sizing handle, which resizes the table. As you drag the handle you see a dashed line that represents the new table size.

4. Release the mouse button to resize the table.

Moving a Table

The first step when creating a new table was to position the insertion point where you want the table. If you didn't have your insertion point in the right location, or you just decide you want to move the table, you can easily drag it to a different document area.

From Print Layout view or Web Layout view, as you move your mouse over the table, notice the upper left table corner has a small box with a four-headed arrow in it. This is the Table Move handle. Position your mouse pointer over the Table Move handle until the mouse pointer also changes to a four-headed arrow, and then drag the table to a new location. As you move the table, you see a dashed line which represents the new table position. See Figure 5-15 for an example.

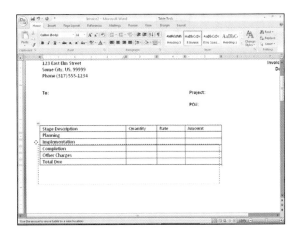

Figure 5-15
Moving a table.

If you want to copy the table instead of moving it, hold down the Ctrl key as you drag the table.

Selecting Table Areas

Often you want to make changes to an entire column or an entire row. Or perhaps you want to apply a certain formatting option to the entire table. While you could make any desired changes one cell at a time, Word includes several methods you can use to select portions of the table so you can quickly apply any changes to the entire selection. The following list shows you several ways to select table cells:

▶ **To select sequential cells, click in the first cell, then hold down the Shift key and select the last cell you want. Optionally, drag the mouse over a group of cells to select a sequential area. All cells in the selected area are highlighted.**

To select non-sequential cells, hold down the Ctrl key and click each additional cell you want to select. Figure 5-16 shows non-sequential cells selected and highlighted in blue.

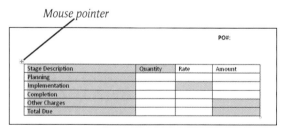

Mouse pointer

Figure 5-16
Selecting cells.

▶ **To select a single entire column, position the mouse pointer at the top of a column until the mouse turns into a down-pointing arrow, and then click. You can see the mouse pointer illustrated in Figure 5-16.**

▶ **To select multiple columns, make sure the mouse pointer is the down-pointing arrow, and then drag across multiple columns.**

▶ **To select a single entire row, position the mouse pointer at the left of the row column until the mouse pointer turns into a white, right-pointing arrow, and then click.**

▶ **To select multiple rows, make sure the mouse is the right-pointing white arrow and then drag across multiple rows.**

When making non-sequential cell selections, you can include entire rows and entire columns along with individual cells or groups of cells.

▶ **To select the entire table, click the small box in the upper left table corner.**

▶ **To clear any selection, click any nonselected cell or click outside of the table.**

Formatting Cell Contents

If you want to change the appearance (formatting) of the table cells, select the cells you want to modify and apply any of the standard formatting choices such as fonts, shading, and borders that you discovered in Chapter 3. However, Word also supplies a quick and easy way to format your table. By selecting from Word's large gallery of table styles you can apply attractive formatting with a click of the mouse. You can make any additional adjustments to better meet your needs.

Take a look at the Design tab, shown in Figure 5-17. With the insertion point anywhere in your table, the Design tab displays a number of different pre-defined themed formats. As you pause your mouse over any design option, Live Preview allows you to see the formatting as it would look in your actual document. When you find the style you want, click the mouse to actually accept the style.

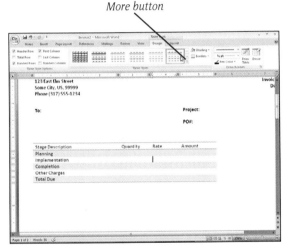

Figure 5-17
Use the Design tab to apply table styles.

Click the More button to display many more choices, such as seen in Figure 5-18.

You can also easily adjust table formatting options by experimenting with the choices in the Table Style Options group.

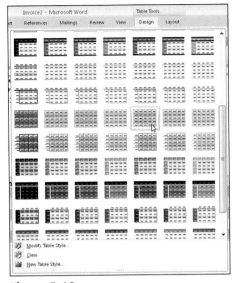

Figure 5-18
Choose from any of the many themed table styles.

Merging and Splitting Table Cells

By default, Word creates tables with each cell in a column the same width as the cell below it. Sometimes, however, especially if you are creating a form with your table, you may find some cells too small. Fortunately, you can combine adjacent cells to become larger cells. This is especially useful if you want to create a table header row such as the one seen in Figure 5-19.

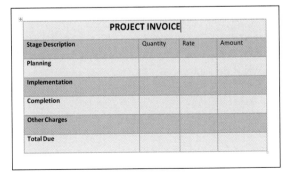

Figure 5-19
Merging multiple cells into one larger cell.

Drag across the two or more cells you want to merge and then choose Table Tools Layout>Merge> Merge Cells. The highlighted cells combine into one larger cell.

If you want to split a cell into smaller cells, you need to tell Word into how many columns and rows you want the cell. Click anywhere in the cell you want to split and choose Table Tools Layout>Merge>Split Cells. The Split Cells dialog box appears. Choose how many columns and rows you want and then click the OK button. The cell splits apart as seen in Figure 5-20.

Split Cells

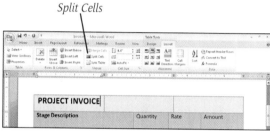

Figure 5-20
Dividing a cell into multiple cells.

Creating Table Formulas

If you have a complex table with lots of calculations, consider using Excel to perform the calculations and then insert the spreadsheet into Word. The next section shows you how to accomplish that. But if you want a simple calculation such as adding a column of values, go ahead and let Word do the work for you.

There are two rules you must follow when creating Word calculations. One is that the entire calculation must be enclosed in a Word field. Word fields, which you'll see how to create shortly, are displayed with opening and closing curly brackets, { and }. The second rule is that all calculations must begin with an equal sign (=).

You create Word arithmetic formulas using operators to perform the calculation you want. Table 5-2 shows the mathematic operators used in Word tables along with an example of each.

Table 5-2 Mathematical Operators Used in Word

Name	Operator	Example	Result
Addition	+	{=6+3}	9
Subtraction	-	{=6-3}	3
Multiplication	*	{=6*3}	18
Division	/	{=6/3}	2
Percentage	%	{=6%}	.06
Exponentiation	^	{=6^3}	216

When creating a calculation, the power comes in to play in that you typically don't use the actual values; instead, you create a reference to them. Suppose cell B2 has a value of 6 and cell B3 has a value of 3. Now, suppose you want, in cell B4, to multiply those two values. In cell B4, you won't enter =6*3; instead, you'll enter =B2*B3. The advantage is that if you later change the value in cell B2 from 6 to 8, you won't have to retype the calculation—you'll simply tell Word to recalculate it. Look at how this is all accomplished:

1. First you must realize that calculations in Word tables are generated from formula fields. Click the cell in which you want a formula field and choose Table Tools Layout>Data> Formula. You see the Formula dialog box shown in Figure 5-21.

Figure 5-21
The Formula dialog box.

2. Highlight the existing text in the Formula text box and type an equal sign (=).

3. Type the rest of your formula such as you see in Figure 5-22. In this example, I am multi-plying the Quantity times the Rate, which will give the Amount.

Figure 5-22
Creating a calculation.

4. Optionally, choose an option from the Number Format drop-down list. This option determines the appearance of your answer such as whether to include a dollar sign, a percent symbol, or two decimal points.

5. Click OK. Word calculates the formula and displays the results.

If you want to see the actual formula instead of the result, right-click over the answer and choose Toggle Field Codes. To view the answer again, repeat the action.

If you later make a change to any of the table cells referenced in the formula, Word doesn't automati-cally update the formula answer. Right-click over the current answer and choose Update Field.

Word contains a number of predefined calculations, called *functions*, that you can plug into your formula fields. For example, if you simply want to add adjacent cells, use the Sum function, such as =SUM(ABOVE) or =SUM(LEFT). The ABOVE reference tells Word to add all the non-blank cells directly above the answer cell. The LEFT reference tells Word to all add the non-blank cells directly to the left of the answer cell. To use a function choose Table Tools Layout>Data>Formula. You can either accept the suggestion provided by Word, or click the Paste function drop-down list and choose a different function (see Figure 5-23).

> **Word cannot total the entire column or row if your column or row contains blank cells or cells with text instead of values.**

Take a look at the finished document as seen in Figure 5-24. The formatting tools along with the table tools enabled the creation of a nice looking invoice.

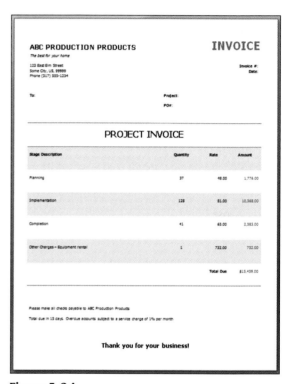

Figure 5-24
The final invoice created in Word.

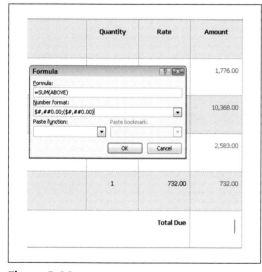

Figure 5-23
Using calculation functions.

Adding an Excel Table to a Word Document

IN THIS CHAPTER YOU'VE SEEN SOME of the power behind a Word table. As mentioned at the chapter beginning, a Word table is basically a small spreadsheet. You'll discover later in this book how to work with Excel worksheets, but you should also know that once you create an Excel worksheet, you can insert it into a Word document. Just follow these steps:

1. Position the insertion point where you want the Excel worksheet placed.

2. Choose Insert>Text>Object>Object. You see the Object dialog box.

3. Click the Create from File tab.

4. Click the Browse button. A Browse window opens.

5. Locate and double-click the file you want to insert. The Object dialog box reappears with the file name you selected (see Figure 5-25).

6. Click OK. The Excel worksheet along with any formulas and formatting appears in your document. See the example in Figure 5-26.

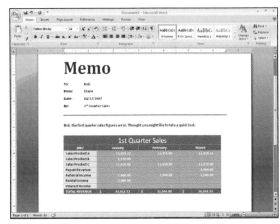

Figure 5-26
An Excel worksheet in a Word document.

Word considers the table an object in the document. To make any changes, double-click the inserted Excel worksheet where you will see the Excel worksheet Ribbon and options. Click outside the table to return to Word. Changes you make in the Word table do not affect the saved Excel worksheet.

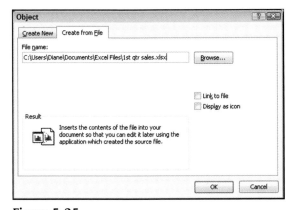

Figure 5-25
Select the Excel file you want to include.

6

Using Word for Mail

Merge

PICTURE YOURSELF OPENING THE MAIL. On the front of the envelope it says in big bold letters that "You have won TEN MILLION DOLLARS." Then, of course, in teeny tiny print it says "*if* you are the lucky winner." It has your name printed in big letters right there on the certificate! The funny thing is that each of your neighbors got exactly the same letter with their name on the envelope and certificate. Probably millions of copies of exactly the same letter arrived in mailboxes all around the country.

Although our society has become a little more paperless than just a few years ago, realistically we still use snail mail for lots of things. We still rely on the postal service for delivery of our bills, catalogs, Christmas cards, and lots of other types of correspondence. And let's not forget the hard working trash collectors. They might be out of work if it weren't for all the junk mail we all receive!

This chapter is all about mail. Creating envelopes, labels, and mass mailings are all easy tasks when you use Word.

Generating a Single Envelope

BECAUSE OF THE AUTOMATION USED by the post office when sorting mail, it's important to make sure the address is clear and concise. Hand addressed envelopes can easily be misread by both man and machine and, frankly, they often look very unprofessional.

By using Word to address your envelopes, you can create neat, accurate addresses for both the mailing address and the return address. You can even add a bar code that can often speed up delivery time or a graphic image to make your envelope personalized.

Creating the Envelope

When you generate an envelope, Word displays an Envelopes and Labels dialog box. Obviously, for the envelope, you'll need a delivery address. First take a look at several methods Word uses to obtain a delivery address:

▶ **If you have a letter or other document already on your screen, you can let Word automatically find the recipient address and fill it directly into the Delivery address box. By far, this is the fastest and easiest method! See Figure 6-1 for a sample letter that contains a recipient address.**

▶ **You can type the address directly into the Delivery address box in the Envelopes and Labels dialog box.**

▶ **From the Envelopes and Labels dialog box, you can choose an address from your Outlook contact list. (See Chapter 23 for information about the Outlook contact list.)**

▶ **You can copy the address from another source and then paste it into the Delivery address box. Use the Ctrl+V keyboard shortcut to paste the address.**

Figure 6-1
Word can pick up the mailing address from the current document.

Choose Mailings>Create>Envelopes. The Envelopes and Labels dialog box seen in Figure 6-2 appears. If your document contained the mailing address, the address already appears in the Delivery address area. If you don't see the delivery address in the dialog box, you need to enter the address using one of the previously listed methods.

Insert Address

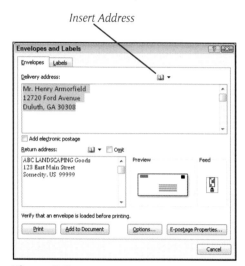

Figure 6-2
Envelope settings.

Following are the other choices on the Envelopes tab:

▶ **If you subscribe to an electronic postage service such as Stamps.com, check the "Add electronic postage" check box. You also should then click the E-postage Properties button to set any desired options for your e-postage subscription.**

▶ **Enter your return address in the Return address dialog box, or click the Address book button above it to extract your address from your Outlook contact list. When you exit the Envelopes and Labels dialog box, Word asks whether you want to save the return address as the default return address. If you choose yes, the next time you open the Envelopes and Labels dialog box, your address will already be listed in the Return address section. You can change the default return address at any time.**

▶ **Click the Omit check box if you don't want Word to add a return address to the envelope.**

▶ Click the Options button to display the Envelopes Options dialog box. From this dialog box you select the envelope size as well as a default font you want for the addresses.

▶ The Printing Options tab displays options for feeding envelopes, but I recommend you leave it at Automatically Select since Windows already knows how your current printer accepts envelope feeds.

> **Each printer model handles envelopes a little differently than the next one. Review your printer manual for envelope feed information.**

Once you select the envelopes options, you now can either create or print the envelope. If you click the Print button, Word sends the printing information directly to your default printer. Make sure you have the printer on and the envelope inserted into the appropriate location. If you click the Add to Document button, Word adds a new page to the top of the document and displays the envelope (see Figure 6-3).

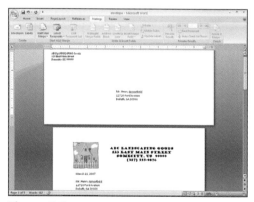

Figure 6-3
Adding an envelope to your document.

If you add the envelope to the document, using the Word tools you already know, you can edit the envelope addresses, change fonts, or even add a graphic to the envelopes. If you want to change the envelope options, click anywhere inside the envelope area and choose Mailings>Create> Envelopes again, which redisplays the Envelopes and Labels dialog box. Make any desired changes and then click Change Document.

Adding a US Bar Code

The computerized sorting equipment used by the United States Post Office relies on delivery point bar codes, which are also known as POSTNET bar codes. You can easily add a bar code to your envelope. Follow these steps:

> If you are processing a bulk mailing, you can save money by presorting the envelopes and including the POSTNET bar codes. Contact your post office for more information on bulk mail postal rates and requirements.

1. Add the envelope to your document. (See the previous section.)

2. Click the insertion point where you want the POSTNET bar code located, which is typically directly above or directly under the delivery address.

3. Choose Insert>Text>Quick Parts>Field. The Field dialog box appears.

4. In the Field names list, click once on BarCode. Bar code options appear on the right side of the dialog box as shown in Figure 6-4.

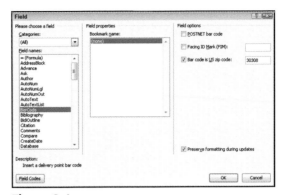

Figure 6-4
Generating a bar code.

5. In the Field options section, click the "Bar code is US zip code" option.

6. Next to the "Bar code is US zip code" option, type the recipient zip code and then click the OK button.

As you see in Figure 6-5, Word inserts the bar code at the insertion point.

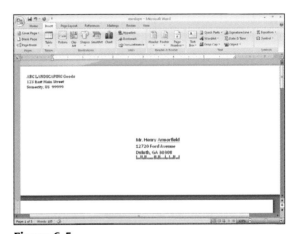

Figure 6-5
A POSTNET bar code.

Creating Labels

YOU CAN PURCHASE SHEETS OF LABELS that feed easily into both inkjet and laser printers, making mailing labels easy to produce using Word's label function. Labels are especially useful if you have large quantities of letters to mail, and, of course, some envelopes are simply too big or bulky to fit into your printer. You can also use labels to create hundreds of different items such as name tags, product information, file folder labels, or return address labels.

Like an envelope, if you want Word to pick up the address automatically, create it in the form of a letter or document before you begin label creation. Otherwise, start with a blank document, and then follow these steps:

1. Choose Mailings>Create>Labels. The Envelopes and Labels dialog box appears with the Labels tab on top.

2. Click the Options button. The Label Options dialog box seen in Figure 6-6 appears.

3. Click the Tray drop-down list and select the printer tray you plan on using for labels.

4. Click the Label vendor's drop-down list and select the manufacturer of the labels you plan on using.

5. Click the label Product number you want to use. A description of the selected label appears on the right side.

6. Click the OK button. You return to the Envelopes and Labels dialog box.

7. Choose "Full page of the same label." Select this option even if you want to enter different information on each label.

8. If you want a full page of the same label, enter or edit the label information in the Address section or click the Insert Address icon to choose from an Outlook contact (see Figure 6-7).

If you want to type individual information on each label, leave the Address box blank.

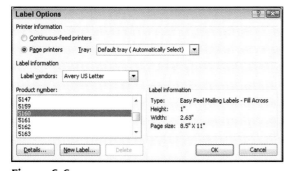

Figure 6-6
Choosing a label size.

Figure 6-7
Enter address label information.

Figure 6-8
A full page of labels.

9. Click New Document. A screen full of labels or a label grid appears on your screen.

> Word uses tables when creating labels. If you don't see the gridlines indicating labels, click Table Tools Layout>Table>View Gridlines.

> If you find that your labels are printing too close to the left edge of the label, press Ctrl+A to select all of the labels, and then drag the left indent mark a little to the right on the ruler.

10. You can now optionally edit the individual labels and print them whenever you're ready (see Figure 6-8).

Using Mail Merge

WHEN YOU PLAN ON SENDING A GROUP of recipients the same basic letter, that letter is called a *form letter.* A form letter results from merging together a standard generic letter and personalized information. To create form letters in Word, use the Mail Merge function.

You need two things to create a personalized mailing with a mail merge: a letter, which is called the main document and contains the information that doesn't change, and codes, called merge fields, that act as placeholders for the variable information. This variable information is usually a list of names and addresses, called the data source, and contains the information that changes for each letter. When you merge the two, the result is an individualized form letter, called the merge document.

Creating the Main Document

For the main document, you can use a letter that you've previously created or you can create a letter from scratch. Type your letter without filling in any of the information that will vary from recipient to recipient such as addresses, meeting dates, and such.

The following steps show you how to begin the mail merge process:

1. Open or type the letter you want as the main document.

2. Choose Mailings>Start Mail Merge>Start Mail Merge>Letters. If you were not already in Print Layout view, Word switches to Print Layout view (see Figure 6-9).

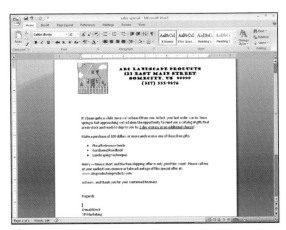

Figure 6-9
A mail merge main document.

Specifying Data for Your Mail Merge

Once you create your main document, you need to link the document to a file that contains your data. The data source could be in the form of a comma-separated value Word document or it could be in an Excel worksheet or an Access database. See Figure 6-10 for an example of each document type—Word, Excel, and Access.

Two terms commonly used with merge data files are fields and records. A *field* is an individual piece of information about someone or something such as a zip code, first name, or product description. A *record* is the complete picture of information with all the fields put together.

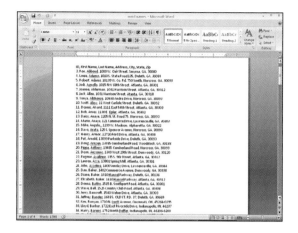

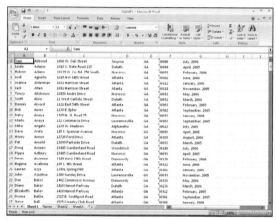

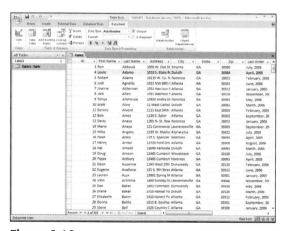

Figure 6-10

Possible data sources.

Selecting a Data Source

You can select from a preexisting list as your data source or you can create a new one using Word. If you want to choose from an existing file, choose Mailings>Start Mail Merge>Select Recipients>Use Existing List (see Figure 6-11). The Select Data Source dialog box opens. Locate your data file and choose Open.

Figure 6-11

Selecting an existing data source.

If you have not already created a data source, you can create one with Word. Following are the steps for creating a data source in Word:

1. Choose Mailings>Start Mail Merge>Select Recipients>Type New List. The New Address List dialog box appears. Word tries to anticipate your needs by providing the most commonly used data fields. You'll soon see how you can add extra fields.

2. Enter the data for the first recipient. You do not need to enter data into every field as you see in Figure 6-12.

Figure 6-12

Adding records.

Use the Tab key to move from one field to the next, or press Shift+Tab to return to a previous field.

3. Click the New Entry button, which creates a blank line for the next recipient. Optionally, as you press Tab after the last field, Word automatically adds a line for the next recipient.

4. Repeat steps 2 and 3 for each additional recipient.

Although Word includes commonly used data fields, you may need to add your own fields or remove the predefined fields you don't want. Click the Customize Columns button in the New Address List dialog box. The Customize Address List dialog box appears, like the one seen in Figure 6-13. Make any desired changes and then click OK. Here are the options available in the Customize Address List dialog box:

Figure 6-13
Customizing data fields.

▶ **Add:** To add additional fields, click the Add button. As seen in Figure 6-14, Word prompts you for a name for the new field. Type the name and click OK.

Figure 6-14
Adding an additional data field.

▶ **Delete:** To delete an unwanted field, click a field name and then click the Delete button. A confirmation message appears. Click Yes to confirm the deletion.

▶ **Rename:** To rename a field, click the field name and then click the Rename button. Enter the new name in the resulting dialog box and click OK.

▶ **Move up:** To move a field further up in the list, click the field name and click the Move Up button until the field is located where you want it.

▶ **Move down:** To move a field further down in the list, click the field name and click the Move Down button until the field is located where you want it.

When you have all your entries in the New Address List, click the OK button.

If you want to delete a record, click anywhere in the record and click the Delete Entry button. Click Yes to the resulting confirmation message.

Word prompts you to save your address list. By default, Word attempts to save the file in the Documents>My Data Sources folder. Select a different folder if desired. Enter a file name and then click Save.

Word saves the data file as an MDB file, which is an Access database file.

Selecting Recipients

You may have a number of names in your data file, but perhaps you don't want to send the merged letter to everyone in the file. By default, Word assumes you want everyone in the data file, but you can pick and choose which recipients you want to use. Just follow these steps:

1. Choose Mailings>Start Mail Merge>Edit Recipient List. You see a Mail Merge Recipients list similar to the one displayed in Figure 6-15.

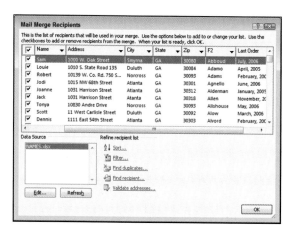

Figure 6-15
Deselect any recipient you don't want to include.

Click any column heading to sort the records by the selected column.

2. Click the check box to the left of the name for any recipient to whom you don't want to send the form letter. The check mark will be removed.

To edit recipient information, click the data source name, then click the Edit button. The Edit Data Source dialog box appears, from which you can make any desired changes.

3. After determining that the desired recipients are checked, click the OK button.

Inserting Merge Fields

Now that you've created the main document and have selected a data source, the next step is to enter the merge fields (also called merge codes) into the main document, thereby instructing Word exactly where you want those data fields placed.

You have the option of placing a group of fields together or choosing the individual fields you want to enter. The field groups come in the two different forms. The first group is for an Address Block which consists of the following fields: Title, First Name, Last Name, Company Name, Address Line 1, Address Line 2, City, State, and ZIP Code. The second group is for the Greeting Line, which includes a greeting such as "Dear" or "To," followed by the First Name and Last Name, and then a punctuation choice such as a comma.

Adding an Address Block

Begin by adding an Address Block. In the main document, click the insertion point where you want the recipient name and address. Choose Mailings>Write & Insert Fields>Address Block. The Insert Address Block dialog box appears, as seen in Figure 6-16.

Match Fields

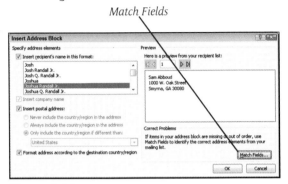

Figure 6-16
Setting options for an address block.

Since Word recognizes the individual fields—including name, address, city, state, and ZIP—as part of the address block, using the address block saves you the steps of inserting each of those fields individually. You can, however, choose the style of address block you prefer. Click on the various address formats and review in the preview panel how your data looks with each format.

> If the fields in your address block don't match your data, you can manually pair them together. For example, if you expect to see someone's first name, but instead you see their country, click the Match Fields button to identify and match the fields.

Click OK when you've decided on the format you want. Word returns to the main document and inserts a field <<AddressBlock>> at the insertion point. This is a hidden code to Microsoft Word. Don't try to type <<AddressBlock>>.

Selecting a Greeting Line

Most form letters also include a personalized greeting. Use the Greeting Line field box to assist you. Begin by positioning the insertion point where you want the greeting line, usually two lines under the Address Block. Choose Mailings>Write & Insert Fields>Greeting Line. The Insert Greeting Line dialog box appears (see Figure 6-17).

Figure 6-17
Choosing a greeting line format.

Select a greeting from the first drop-down list. Choices include "Dear," "To," or nothing at all. From the second drop-down list, select the name format you like best and then from the third drop-down list, choose a punctuation mark of comma or a colon, or choose no punctuation.

In the event that one or more of your recipients doesn't have data in the first and last name fields, the Greeting line for invalid recipient names drop-down list provides a couple of alternatives. Select the one you prefer for your document.

Click the OK button, which returns you to the Word main document where you now see the <<Greeting Line>> field code.

Adding Individual Fields

If the field information you want to insert into your document doesn't fall into the Address Block or Greeting Line groups, you can manually insert fields into desired document areas. Just click the mouse pointer where you want the field to appear. Choose Mailings>Write & Insert Fields>Insert Merge Field and select the field you want in the letter.

> **It's not necessary to use all fields in a form letter, and you can use fields multiple times in the same document.**

Figure 6-18 illustrates a sample form letter with an Address Block, Greeting Line, and an individual data field entered into the letter.

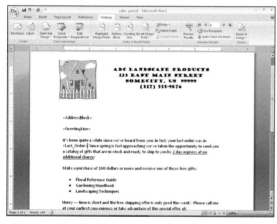

Figure 6-18
A sample form letter.

Finishing the Merge

Before you actually print all the records, you should preview them. Choose Mailings>Preview Results>Preview Results. You see your letter with data filled in from one of the records (see Figure 6-19). In the Preview mode, you can manually make any formatting or text changes, and the changes will appear for all recipients.

Use the Preview Results scroll buttons to browse between the previous and next records, or the first and last records.

Preview Results scroll buttons

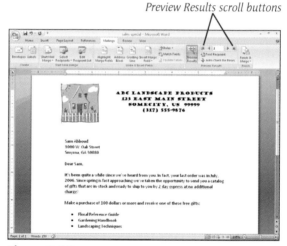

Figure 6-19
Previewing the merged letter.

When you are satisfied with the results, you're ready to finish the merge. Choose Mailings>Finish>Finish & Merge. A menu of options appears where you can edit the individual documents, print the documents, or send the documents via e-mail.

▶ **Edit the individual documents:** Choose this option if you want to personalize your letters. This option creates a new Word document where each letter is on its own page and any changes you make affect the individual current record only—not the other recipients. You have the option to merge all records, the current record, or a range of record numbers (see Figure 6-20).

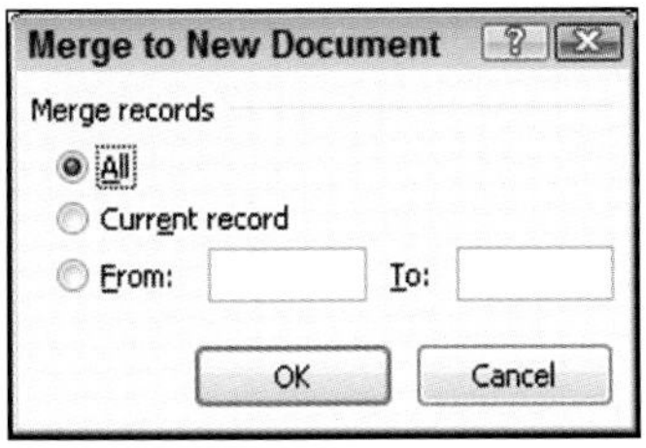

Figure 6-20
Merging records to a new Word document.

▶ **Print documents:** Choose this option if you don't need to make any individual changes and just want to print the merged documents. When you choose this option you can choose to merge all records, the current record, or a range of record numbers.

▶ **Send E-mail messages:** This option sends the document to the recipient via e-mail. The e-mail option only works if the individual record data includes e-mail addresses. When you choose this option, like the others, you can merge all records, the current record, or a range of record numbers. Additionally, as seen in Figure 6-21, you determine which field in your data source contains the e-mail address as well as enter a subject line. Also, you determine if you want the letter sent as an attachment to the e-mail, in HTML format, in the e-mail, or in just a plain text with no formatting in the e-mail.

Don't leave the subject line blank. Many e-mail filters will not display an e-mail without a subject.

Figure 6-21
Sending the merged letters via e-mail.

7

Discovering Word
Tools

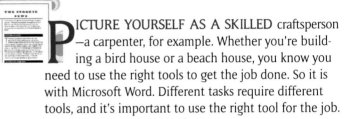

PICTURE YOURSELF AS A SKILLED craftsperson —a carpenter, for example. Whether you're building a bird house or a beach house, you know you need to use the right tools to get the job done. So it is with Microsoft Word. Different tasks require different tools, and it's important to use the right tool for the job.

Up to this point, you've used quite a few of the basic Word features. This chapter is sort of a hodgepodge of some additional tools provided with Word that can make your word-processing tasks easier and faster, and help improve the quality of your writing. Besides looking at tools for speed and quality, we'll also review features you might use to finish up a project such as printing or e-mailing a document. We'll also take a look at document security and how you can better protect your work.

As you work with Word, you may find you use some of the tools a lot and other tools very seldomly, but as you proceed with your Word documents, at some time I'm sure you'll find yourself looking at your screen and thinking, "Aha! I can use the [xyz] feature to accomplish this."

Employing Tools for Quality

WHETHER YOU ARE WRITING THE great American novel, a standard business letter, or a résumé, spelling or grammatical errors can ruin the impression you're trying to create. Not only does Word have spelling and grammar checkers to correct document errors, it also has a thesaurus to help you find just the right word to convey your ideas.

If Word interprets a word as a misspelling, but it is a word you use frequently, such as a name or business term, you can add it to your dictionary so Word won't see it as a misspelling.

Correcting Errors

Word has built-in dictionaries and grammatical rule sets that it uses to check your document. Word can identify possible problems as you type, and it also can run a special spelling and grammar check that provides you with more information about the problems and tools for fixing them. These features aren't infallible; if you type "To *air* is human" instead of "To *err* is human," Word probably won't be able to tell you that you're wrong. However, combined with a good proofreading, these tools are very helpful.

Add to Dictionary

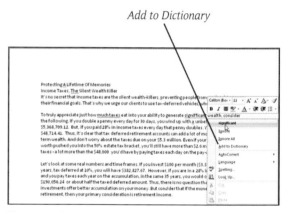

Figure 7-1
Fixing errors as you type.

Checking Spelling and Grammar as You Go

As you type your document, Word operates the spell checker tool in the background and identifies problems. Word tags potential spelling errors with a red wavy line under them. Right-click on an unrecognized word and you see a shortcut menu appear with possible suggestions for correction (see the example in Figure 7-1). Click on the correct spelling and the misspelled or unrecognized word is replaced with your selection. Occasionally Word cannot provide a suggestion. In those cases, you need to correct the error yourself.

As with spelling errors, Word identifies potential grammatical errors by placing a green wavy line under the questionable text. Right-click on the questionable word or phrase to display a shortcut menu with suggested grammatical corrections. Click the appropriate option and Word replaces the incorrect word or phrase with your selection. Sometimes, however, Word cannot provide a suggestion; in those cases, you need to correct the error yourself.

Do *not* rely on Word's spell check and grammar features to catch all your errors. The tools are very helpful, but they are far from perfect and can miss many items. They can also flag items as errors that really are okay and can suggest wrong ways to fix both real problems and false errors. You alone are the one who knows what you want your document to say. Proofread it yourself!

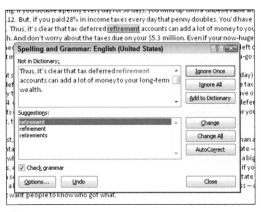

Figure 7-2
Using the Spelling and Grammar check to improve your document

Running a Spelling and Grammar Check

If you don't want to correct items as you type, Word can run a spelling and grammar check at the same time. Running the spell and grammar check also provides additional options for dealing with incorrect items. Use the following steps:

1. Position the insertion point at the beginning of the document to check the entire document. If you only want to check a portion of the text, select the text first.

2. Choose Review>Proofing>Spelling and Grammar. If there are no errors in the document, a message box appears advising you that the checks are complete; otherwise, Word displays the Spelling and Grammar dialog box seen in Figure 7-2, referencing the first error, whether spelling or grammar.

Optionally, press F7 to launch the Spelling and Grammar check.

3. If the error is a spelling error, do one of the following:

   ▶ **Change:** Choose a word from the Suggestion list and then click Change, which changes just this incident of the spelling mistake.

   ▶ **Change All:** After selecting a replacement from the Suggestion list, choose Change All if you think you could have made the same mistake more than once.

   ▶ **Ignore Once:** Click this if you don't want to correct this instance of the spelling.

   ▶ **Ignore All:** Click this if you don't want to correct any instances of the spelling.

   ▶ **Add to Dictionary:** Choose this to add the word to the dictionary so that in the future Word won't flag it as an error.

   ▶ **AutoCorrect:** After making a selection from the Suggestion list, click this option to add the unknown word and the correction as an AutoCorrect entry. If you make the same misspelling in a future document, Word automatically changes it to the correction.

4. If the error is a grammatical error, such as you see in Figure 7-3, take one of these actions:

> If you don't want Word to check grammar, remove the check mark from the Check Grammar option.

Check Grammar

Figure 7-3
Catching grammatical mishaps.

▶ **Ignore Once:** Click this option if you don't want to change this instance of the grammatical problem.

▶ **Ignore Rule:** Click this option to ignore all instances of the same grammatical problem type.

▶ **Next Sentence:** Click this option to skip the error and continue the check. All instances of the same error are ignored.

▶ **Change:** Choose an option from the Suggestion list and then click Change, which changes just this incident of the grammatical mistake.

▶ **Explain:** Click this option to launch an article that explains the error and offers suggestions for avoiding the error.

5. When all potential mistakes are identified, Word notifies you that the spelling and grammar check is complete. Click the OK button.

Changing Spelling Options

Word provides quite a few options for both the spelling and grammar correction features. For example, if you don't want Word to check your spelling or your grammar as you type, you can turn off the feature. Choose Office Button>Word Options or, from the Spelling and Grammar box, click the Options button.

From the Proofing section, as seen in Figure 7-4, you can set or turn off any desired proofing options. Some of the options apply to all Office 2007 applications and some apply only to Microsoft Word. There are even a few options that apply only to the current document.

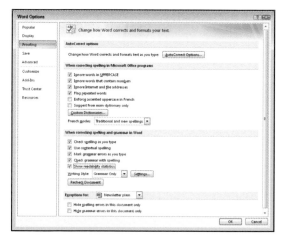

Figure 7-4
Setting proofing options.

Click the "Show readability statistics" check box, and after running a Spelling and Grammar check, Word displays statistics such as the number of words, characters, paragraphs, and sentences, as well as average words per sentences or the readability grade level. See Figure 7-5 for an example.

Readability Statistics

Counts	
Words	979
Characters	4701
Paragraphs	22
Sentences	55

Averages	
Sentences per Paragraph	3.9
Words per Sentence	16.6
Characters per Word	4.5

Readability	
Passive Sentences	1%
Flesch Reading Ease	54.3
Flesch-Kincaid Grade Level	9.4

OK

Figure 7-5
Viewing document statistics.

Finding Elusive Words with the Thesaurus

A key to good writing is using words that add interest and flair. However, remember that you need words appropriate for your audience. If you are addressing a group of grade school children, you'll use simpler words than if you are writing your college thesis. If you need a little help finding just the right word, try using Word's thesaurus.

Click anywhere in the word you want replaced and then choose Review>Proofing>Thesaurus. Optionally, press Shift+F7 to launch the thesaurus. A Research pane similar to the one seen in Figure 7-6 appears on the right side of the screen and displays various meanings of the current word and possible replacements. If you don't see the exact word you want, click a similar word, which displays its synonyms. Click the Back button to return to the previous word. When you locate the word that best fits your document, click the arrow next to it and choose Insert. Word replaces the current word with your selection.

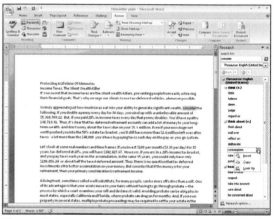

Figure 7-6
Locating synonyms with the thesaurus.

Click the Research close box to close the Research pane.

Using Find and Replace

Word's Find and Replace features are real time savers. For example, you can quickly find out if you covered a particular topic in a lengthy report, or you can changes names, dates, and prices throughout documents with just a few keystrokes.

Using Find

Word's Find command is useful when you want to seek out text that you may have trouble visually locating in a document. The Find command doesn't change any text; it simply locates and highlights the specified text for you. Follow these steps:

1. Choose Home>Editing>Find, or press Ctrl+F. The Find and Replace dialog box appears with the Find tab on top.

2. In the "Find what" text box, type the word or phrase that you want to search for.

3. Click Find Next. Word takes you to the first occurrence of the word or phrase you're looking for (see Figure 7-7).

Figure 7-7
Finding document text.

The Find command begins its search at the location of the insertion point.

4. If you want to continue the search, click Find Next, which takes you to the next occurrence of the text. If you want to discontinue the search, click the Cancel button.

Unless you specify whole words (see the next section), Word locates any instance containing the letters you specify. For example, if you enter *read* in the Find box, Word also locates words like *bread* or *reading*.

5. When all occurrences of the search text are located, Word displays a message box. Click OK to close the message box and then click Cancel to close the Find and Replace dialog box.

Extending Search Options

If you need to be a little more specific about what you're searching for, Word provides a number of extended options to assist you.

Open the Find and Replace box by choosing Home>Editing>Find, or press Ctrl+F. In the "Find what" text box, type the word or phrase for which you want to search. Expand the Find and Replace dialog box to the one you see in Figure 7-8 by clicking the More button and then selecting the options you want.

Figure 7-8
Specifying search options.

Take a brief look at each extended option:

▶ **Search**: Select which direction in the document you want to search. Choices are Up, Down, or All.

▶ **Match case**: Check this to locate instances that match the upper and lower case letters as you entered in the Find box. For example, if you typed *Go*, Word will not locate *go* or *GO*.

▶ **Find whole words only**: Check this to locate instances of the entire words only. For example, if you enter *read* in the Find box, Word will ignore words like *bread* or *reading*.

▶ **Use wildcards**: Check this to use the wildcards ? or * in your search. The ? character matches any single character and the * character matches any number of characters. For example, if you enter *b?d* in the Find box, Word finds *bad, bed,* or *bidding,* but not *bread*. If you enter b*d, Word locates words like *bad, bed, abide, bidding, bread, bored,* and so forth.

Word also recognizes additional wildcard characters such as @ or <. See the Word help system for a complete description.

▶ **Sounds like**: Check this to locate instances that are phonetically the same as the text in the Find box. For example, if you entered *foul*, Word also locates *fowl*.

▶ **Find all word forms**: Check this to locate all grammatical forms of the search word. For example, if you enter *they*, Word also locates *their, theirs, them,* and *themselves.*

▶ **Match prefix**: Check this to locate words that only begin, not contain or end, with the search word. For example, if you enter *mini*, Word also locates *minimum* or *miniature,* but not *administration.*

▶ **Match suffix**: Check this to locate words that only end, not contain or begin, with the search word. For example, if you enter *ration*, Word also locates *demonstration* but not *rational.*

▶ **Ignore punctuation characters**: Check this to ignore punctuation marks such as '?-"!;:,. and /. For example, if you entered *1478*, Word also locates *1,478* and *14.78.*

▶ **Ignore white space characters**: Check this to ignore spaces and tabs. For example, if you enter *lonestar*, Word also locates *lone star.*

Finding Formatted Text

You can also locate text that contains a specified type of formatting. For example, you want to locate the word *apple* but only if you underlined the word. Follow these steps:

1. From the expanded Find and Replace dialog box, click the Format button. You see a list of formatting options as shown in Figure 7-9.

Figure 7-9
Specifying search options.

2. Click the formatting type you want to locate. Choices include Font, Paragraph, Tabs, Language, Frame, Style, and Highlight. A dialog box appropriate to your selection appears. In Figure 7-10 you see the Find Font dialog box.

3. Select the formatting you want to search for and then click OK.

Instead of choosing font options from a dialog box, you can press a formatting shortcut key such Ctrl+B for bold.

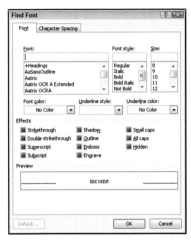

Figure 7-10
Searching for formatting.

4. In the "Find what" text box, enter the text you want to search for, or, if you want to find the formatting only, regardless of the text, leave the "Find what" box empty.

5. Specify any other search options and click Find Next to begin your search.

Click the No Formatting button to remove any formatting specifications.

Finding Special Characters

In Chapter 2, you discovered that Word hides many characters such as the dots used for spaces, or an arrow for tabs, or even the paragraph mark ¶ at the end of a paragraph. You can have Word search for a number of special characters.

From the expanded Find and Replace dialog box, click the Special button. You see a list of formatting options as shown in Figure 7-11. Choose the special character for which you want to search. Word places a code for the character in the Find What text box. Specify any other search options and click Find Next to begin your search.

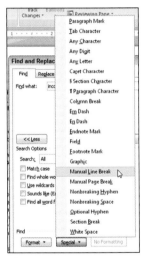

Figure 7-11
Searching for special characters.

Using Reading Highlight

Instead of jumping from one instance to the next of a search word or phrase, you can have Word highlight all occurrences of matching text. You can then review the document in its entirety, perhaps to see if you used a certain word too many times, or to view the phrase in different contexts.

After entering your search specifications, click Reading Highlight and choose Highlight All. In the Find and Replace dialog box, Word indicates how many items it highlighted. Figure 7-12 illustrates both the Find and Replace dialog box as well as a document in which Word highlighted all occurrences.

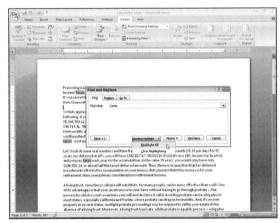

Figure 7-12
Highlighting all occurrences.

> **The reading highlighting does not print.**

To remove the highlighting, click Reading Highlight and choose Clear Highlighting.

Using Replace

If you want to locate some particular text and change it to something else, let Word do it for you with the Replace feature. The Replace feature is very similar to the Find function you just discovered. You can locate text and replace it with different text, or you can locate text and replace it with the same or different text, but perhaps with different formatting. Follow these simple steps:

1. Choose Home>Editing>Replace, or press the Ctrl+H keys. The Find and Replace dialog box appears with the Replace tab on top.

2. In the "Find what" text box, enter the text you want to search for.

3. Click in the "Replace with" text box and type a replacement word or phrase (see Figure 7-13).

Figure 7-13
Entering Find and Replace text.

To delete the "found" text, leave the "Replace with" text box empty. Word will replace the found text with nothing.

4. Specify any additional search or replace options such as matching case or a particular format.

5. Click Find Next. Word locates the first match.

6. Choose one of the following:

   ▶ **Click Replace if this is the text you want to change. Word replaces the text and locates the next occurrence.**

   ▶ **Click Replace All to replace all occurrences of the found text with the replacement text. Word displays a dialog box indicating how many occurrences it replaced.**

Use the Replace All button cautiously. Remember that Word takes you very literally. Make sure the Find and Replace options are exactly as you want them.

   ▶ **Click Find Next to skip making changes on this occurrence and locate the next match.**

7. Word notifies you when no more occurrences of the search text exist. Click OK to close the message box and click Cancel to close the Find and Replace dialog box.

Applying Tools for Speed

WORD INCLUDES A NUMBER of tools that help speed up the process of creating and editing documents—tools that can locate mistakes and correct them automatically, tools that do your typing for you, and tools that let you quickly make changes in your document.

Creating Bookmarks

Just like you use a bookmark to mark a certain place in a book, electronic bookmarks identify specified text locations for future reference. As an example, you might use a bookmark to help you quickly jump to certain topics in your document.

> **Bookmarks are useful for electronic reading only and do not affect a printed document.**

Place the insertion point where you want to create a bookmark and choose Insert>Links>Bookmark. The Bookmark dialog box seen in Figure 7-14 appears.

Figure 7-14
Creating a bookmark.

Type a name for the bookmark and click Add. Word saves the bookmark and closes the Bookmark dialog box.

> **Bookmark names cannot include spaces or special characters except the underscore character (_).**

Now instead of scrolling through the document to locate the text, you can go to it by using the Go To option, also found on the Find and Replace dialog box. Choose Home>Editing and then click the down arrow next to the Find option. Choose Go To. The Find and Replace dialog box appears with the Go To tab on top (ee Figure 7-15).

> Two alternative methods of displaying the Go To option are pressing F5 or pressing Ctrl+G.

Click Bookmark and then from the "Enter bookmark name" drop-down list, choose the bookmark you want. Click Go To and Word instantly jumps to the bookmark location.

Figure 7-15

Locating a bookmark.

If you want to see the bookmarks in your document, choose Office Button>Word Options. Click Advanced and scroll down to the "Show document content" section and check Show Bookmarks. Word indicates bookmarks in [brackets].

Specifying Hyperlinks

Hyperlinks, similar to bookmarks, take you to a specific location. However, not only can hyperlinks jump to a location in your document, they can also jump to another file on your computer, on your network, or to a Web page. Like bookmarks, hyperlinks are useful for electronic reading only and do not affect a printed document.

Word automatically creates some hyperlinks for you. For example, if you type a Web address or e-mail address, as soon as you press Enter or the spacebar, Word underlines the area and creates the link. The AutoFormat As You Type function is what controls the automatic link creation behavior. You will learn more about the AutoFormat As You type later in this chapter.

If you want to manually create a link, first select the text or graphic you want the reader to click to launch the hyperlink. Choose Insert>Links>Hyperlink, which display the Insert Hyperlink dialog box. The Insert Hyperlink dialog box offers several different options from which you can select:

▶ **If you want to link to a different file or to a Web site, choose Existing File or Web Page. For a different file, locate and select the file name so when the user clicks the link, the referenced file will open. However, if you want to link to a Web site, enter the Web address in the Address text box. When the user clicks the link, the Web browser will open to the referenced Web page. Figure 7-16 illustrates a link to a Web site.**

Figure 7-16

Creating a hyperlink to a Web site.

▶ **If you want to link to a different location in the current document, click the Place in This Document button, then specify which heading or bookmark you want to reference. When users click on this link they will be redirected to the specified location.**

▶ **If you wantto create a new document, when the hyperlink is clicked, choose Create New Document and then enter a name and folder for the new document.**

▶ **If you want to send an e-mail when the link is selected, click the E-mail Address button, then enter the recipients e-mail address and a subject. When the user clicks the link, the user's e-mail program starts. Figure 7-17 illustrates the e-mail link options.**

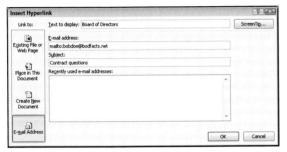

Figure 7-17
Creating an e-mail hyperlink.

Word displays hyperlinks in a different color text and with an underline. Press Ctrl and click any link to jump to the specified location. As you pause your mouse over the link, a tip appears with instructions for following the link and a notation to where the link will take you (see Figure 7-18).

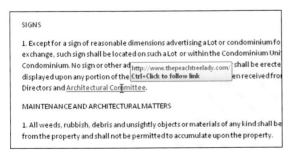

Figure 7-18
Hold down the Ctrl key and click the link.

Generating Text with Building Blocks

Are you tired of typing your address over and over when composing letters? Or, do you have a standard phrase that you need to frequently add to your documents? Word provides a couple of different methods you can use to quickly add the text into your document.

The first method is using Word's AutoCorrect function, which you discovered in Chapter 2. Not only can you add words and symbols, you can generate a text paragraph or even a graphic with your signature. The only problem is that the AutoCorrect function limits each entry to 255 characters.

Office 2007 is designed to be modular, so it now uses a function called Building Blocks that are divided into 14 different galleries. Think of building blocks as recycled material. You've already been introduced to some of the building blocks when you discovered some of the built-in options in Headers, Footers, Page Numbering, and Quick Tables. Take a brief look at the different building block galleries and what type of element each gallery holds:

▶ **AutoText: Holds small text entries or graphics that you want to use again, such as a standard contract clause or a mission statement.**

▶ **Bibliography: Holds text in the form of a reference list of works by author, subject, or other relevant information.**

▶ **Cover Pages: Holds preformatted cover pages such as those you might use for reports. Figure 7-19 illustrates one of the sample Cover Page building blocks.**

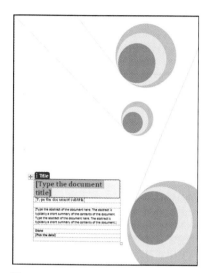

Figure 7-19
The Mod cover page.

▶ **Quick Parts**: Holds miscellaneous building blocks that don't fit any other gallery.

▶ **Equations**: Holds predefined equations.

▶ **Footers**: Holds a number of predefined footers that appear at the bottom of the page.

▶ **Headers**: Holds a number of predefined headers that appear at the top of the page.

▶ **Page Numbers**: There are four different page number galleries that hold predefined page numbers—some at the current location, some at the bottom or top of the page, and some in the margins.

▶ **Table of Contents**: Holds predefined tables of contents that are created based on heading styles in the document.

▶ **Tables**: Holds a series of predefined tables such as those in the Quick Tables.

▶ **Text Box**: Holds predefined text box layouts and formatting

▶ **Watermarks**: Holds several predefined watermarks such as Draft, Do Not Copy, or Confidential. Watermarks are in light gray shading and appear in the background of a document such as you see in Figure 7-20.

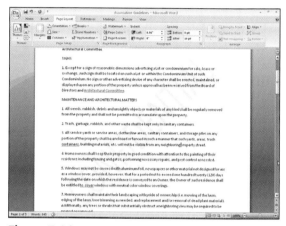

Figure 7-20
A watermark building block.

Inserting Building Blocks

Now that you see all the different types of building blocks, take a look at how to insert any of the existing blocks into your document. Just follow these steps:

1. Position the insertion point where you want to insert the building block.

2. Choose Insert>Text>Quick Parts>Building Blocks Organizer. The Building Blocks Organizer appears.

3. Click a building block to display a preview on the right side, such as you see in Figure 7-21.

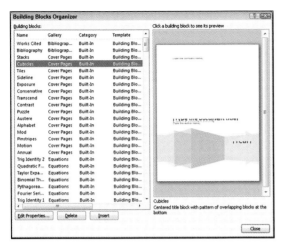

Figure 7-21
Click the Building Block Organizer to see a preview.

Click any building block column heading to sort the building blocks by that column.

4. Click the Insert button. Word inserts the building block into your document.

Some building blocks prompt you to insert text such as your company name or a document title. Click the placeholder and type the appropriate text.

Creating Custom Building Blocks

If none of the predefined building blocks suit your needs, you can create your own custom building block. Additionally, you can start with one of the existing building blocks and customize it to a better fit and then save it for future use. Just follow these simple steps:

1. Create the text and formatting for the new building block.

2. Select the area you want to save as a building block

3. Choose Insert>Text>Quick Parts>Save Selection to Quick Part Gallery. The Create New Building Block dialog box appears.

4. Fill in the appropriate information as seen in Figure 7-22.

Figure 7-22
Naming a custom building block.

▶ **Name:** By default, Word picks up the first few characters of the text you selected; however, you can give the building block a short, more descriptive name.

▶ **Gallery:** Select which of the Galleries you want. Most likely, you'll want to use the Quick Parts gallery.

▶ **Category:** You can further differentiate the items in a gallery by creating and assigning categories.

▶ **Description:** Enter a longer description to help you identify the building block and its purpose.

▶ **Save in:** Select whether to save the new item under the Building Block area, which makes it available no matter which template you use, or choose to save it only if you are using the Normal template. (Templates are discussed later in this chapter.)

▶ **Options:** Choices include whether to insert the building block at the current cursor position, start a new paragraph and then insert the building block, or to start a new page and then insert the building block.

5. Click OK. Now when you open the Building Blocks Organizer, you'll see your custom building block.

When you exit Word, you see the message box seen in Figure 7-23. Choose Yes to save the changes.

Figure 7-23
Saving building blocks for future use.

If you no longer want a custom building block, display the Building Blocks Organizer, select the building block you want to delete, and click the Delete button. Click Yes to the confirmation message that appears.

Adding Automatic Date Codes

When you create a document and you type in a date, the date is said to be static, meaning it doesn't change when the date changes. So if you type September 16, 2007, the document will always read September 16, 2007. If, however, you want the date or time to change with the calendar, you need to insert a dynamic date or time. Word handles these in the form of a field code. Just follow these steps:

1. Position the insertion point where you want the date.

2. Choose Insert>Text>Date and Time. The Date and Time dialog box appears (see Figure 7-24).

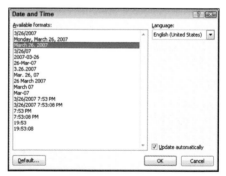

Figure 7-24
Adding an automatic date in the format you need.

3. Click the date format you want to use.

4. Click the "Update automatically" check box and then click OK.

If you only want the current static date and not a dynamic date, do not check the Update automatically option.

Word inserts the current date field into the document. As you pause your mouse over the date, the field becomes shaded and if you click the field, the field placeholder appears (see Figure 7-25). Fields update automatically each time you open the document, but if you want to update a field manually, click the Update button at the top of the field placeholder.

Figure 7-26
Inserting an existing file.

Locate and click the file you want and then choose Insert. The entire file appears in the current document.

Selecting a Template

Templates are another time-saving feature. Every Microsoft document is based on a template, which determines the basic structure for a document and contains settings such as styles, AutoText, fonts, macros, menus, page layout, and any special formatting. Templates appear as untitled documents with text, graphics, formatting, and other attributes applicable to that template. The advantage of a template is that you cannot easily permanently overwrite it. When you create a document based on a template, Word prompts you to save the document with its own name.

Most new documents are based on the default Normal template. However, you can create documents based on templates for memos, faxes, and lots of other types of documents. Word provides a variety of ready-to-use document templates. Just follow these steps to create a new document based on a template.

Figure 7-25
Word fields appear with shading.

Inserting Another File

If you have already created a file and need to insert it into the current document, you *could* open the document you want to insert, select the entire document, copy it, and then paste it into the new document.

Another method, however, is to position the insertion point where you want the file to begin and then choose Insert>Text>Object>Text from File. The Insert File dialog box seen in Figure 7-26 appears.

1. Choose Office Button>New. The New Document dialog box shown in Figure 7-27 appears.

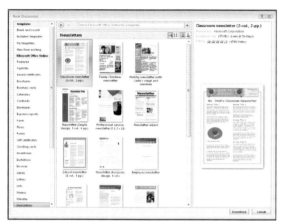

Figure 7-27
Choosing a template category.

2. From the left side, chose a category. If you don't have an Internet connection, choose Installed Templates or My Templates; if you have an Internet connection, Word can also display thumbnail representations from the hundreds of templates available from Microsoft Office Online.

You cannot access the Word templates by pressing Ctrl+N. The Ctrl+N keystroke automatically creates a new document based on the Normal template.

---

3. If you want one of the already installed templates, click the template and then click Create. If you select one of the templates from Office online, click the template and then click Download. Word then downloads the template and displays it on your screen.

In many templates, Word places prompt fields in the areas where you probably want to enter information (see Figure 7-28).

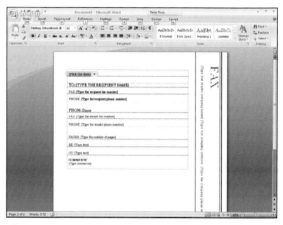

Figure 7-28
A template with prompt fields.

You only have to download a template once. The next time you want the template, you see it listed under the "Blank and recent" category or under My Templates, which displays the New dialog box shown in Figure 7-29.

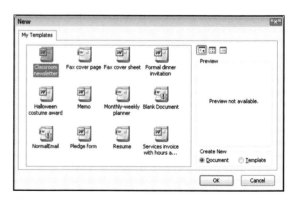

Figure 7-29
Downloaded and personally saved templates.

Creating Footnotes and Endnotes

OFTEN REPORTS PRESENT MATERIAL that requires notes set off from the regular text—for example, when you credit material from another source. You can use the Word Footnote or Endnote feature to add these explanatory or source notes to your document.

Generating a Footnote or Endnote

To give credit where credit is due, you can use the Word Footnote or Endnote feature. Word places footnotes at the bottom of the page where the note reference mark appears, and places endnotes at the end of the document.

When creating a footnote, Word automatically adds a number or character to mark the reference as well as a separating line. If you have both footnotes and endnotes in a document, Word numbers them independently.

Position the insertion point where you want the note reference mark to appear and choose References>Footnotes>Insert Footnote. The insertion point drops to the bottom of the screen where you can cite the actual reference (see Figure 7-30). As you create additional notes, Word numbers the references sequentially.

Footnote reference mark

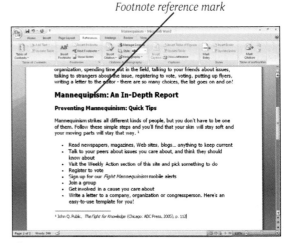

Figure 7-30
Creating footnotes.

If you want an endnote instead of a footnote, choose References>Footnotes>Insert Endnote. Word jumps to the end of the document where you can cite your reference.

If you position the mouse pointer over the note reference mark in the body of the document, the note text will appear in a box similar to a ToolTip.

Copying Notes

Sometimes you will refer to a source more than once in a document. Fortunately, as another time-saving measure, you don't have to retype the text for the footnote; you can copy and paste it into a new location. Word will renumber all the notes affected by the change. Follow these steps:

1. Select the note reference mark of the footnote or endnote that you plan to copy. The reference mark will be highlighted.

2. Choose Home>Clipboard>Copy. It won't look like anything happened, but Word is keeping track for you.

3. Position the insertion point at the location for the duplicated note.

4. Choose Home>Clipboard>Paste. The note reference mark of the copied footnote or endnote appears in the original and new location, and the footnote or endnote appears in the footnote or endnote text area with the correct numbering. In Figure 7-31, footnote number 2 was duplicated and now also appears as footnote number 4.

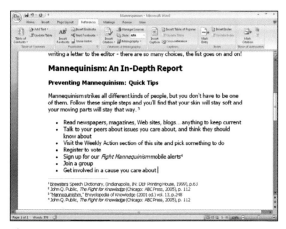

Figure 7-31
Duplicate footnotes without retyping them.

Moving Notes

You can move a footnote or endnote to a new location, and Word will renumber all of the notes affected by the move. Select the note reference mark of the note that you plan to move. If you want to move any surrounding document text along with the reference number, highlight it as well. Choose Home>Clipboard>Cut and then position the insertion point at the location for the duplicated note. Choose Home>Clipboard>Paste. The note reference mark of the copied footnote or endnote appears in the new location, and the footnote or endnote appears in the footnote or endnote text area with the correct numbering (see Figure 7-32).

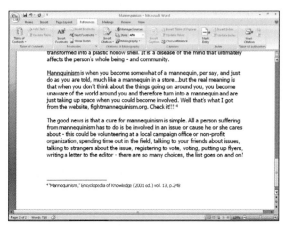

Figure 7-32
Using Cut and Paste allows you to easily move footnotes or endnotes.

Delete a footnote or endnote by highlighting and deleting the note reference mark, not by deleting the footnote or endnote. After pressing the Delete key, Word deletes the note reference mark and the footnote or endnote in the text area and then renumbers all the notes affected by the deletion.

Converting a Footnote to an Endnote

What happens if you create footnotes throughout your report and then decide that you should have used endnotes? Word can convert footnotes to endnotes and endnotes to footnotes, thereby saving you the headache of retyping each entry.

In the reference area at the bottom of the page or at the bottom of the document, locate and highlight the reference you want to change. Right-click the reference and choose Convert to Endnote or Convert to Footnote, depending on which reference you currently selected (see Figure 7-33).

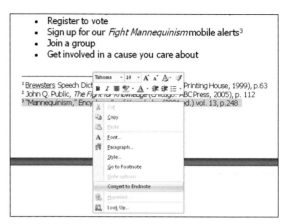

Figure 7-33
Converting a footnote to an endnote.

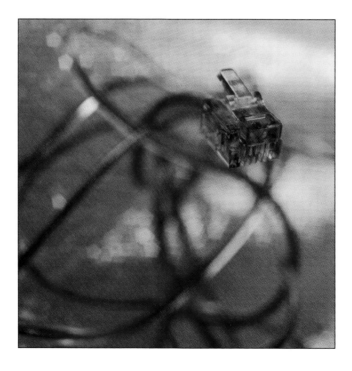

Working with Outlines

A GREAT ORGANIZATIONAL TOOL, Word outlines assist you by using headings and subtopics to categorize a task and its sub tasks. The easiest way to create an outline is by beginning in the Outline view. Choose View>Document Views>Outline or, optionally, just click the Outline view button located on the status bar.

While in Outline view, you see a new tab at the beginning of the Ribbon. The Outlining tab is designed to assist you in creating your outline (see Figure 7-34).

Promote   Current Level   Demote

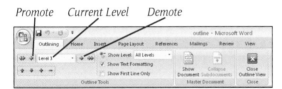

Figure 7-34
The Outlining Ribbon.

Generating Headings

Word considers the first line of text you type in an outline to be a Level 1 heading, the top-most level. Word uses styles to track outline headings and sub-headings, and a Level 1 heading is a style. You use the Tab key to demote your headings and the Shift+Tab keys to promote your headings.

Type the first line of your outline and then press the Enter key, which moves the insertion point to the next line. Type the second line of your outline. Notice that the text still appears as a Level 1 heading. When you want to create subheadings, use the Tab

key to indent the text. Word automatically assigns a Level 2 heading. Each time you press the Tab key, Word creates a lower level subheading. A Word outline can contain up to nine different heading levels.

When you need to return to a higher level, press the Shift+Tab keys. Figure 7-35 illustrates a sample document outline with several heading levels.

Move up   Move down   Demote to Body Text

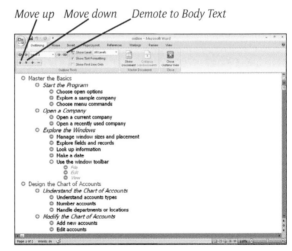

Figure 7-35
A sample outline.

If you want to add text to your outline that isn't really an outline heading, you create body text. Typically, body text elaborates more on the outline level heading directly above it. You create body text by using the Outline toolbar. Type the text you want as body text and click the Demote to Body Text button.

As you organize your thoughts and ideas in an outline, you might change your mind and want to cover a topic earlier than originally planned. You can move selected headings along with any associated subheadings and body text up or down to any location in your outline. Click the Heading icon of the section you want to move and either click the Move Up button or click the Move Down button. The selected section moves up or down one line with each click of the button.

Promoting or Demoting Headings

A Level 1 heading is the highest level in an outline and a Level 9 heading is the lowest. To change the heading level of existing text, place the insertion point anywhere in the line you want to promote and press the Tab key, or use the Shift + Tab key to demote or promote the text. Optionally, you can use the Outlining tab on the Ribbon to demote or promote your text.

Click anywhere in the line you want to change and click the promote or demote button, or you can click the Current Outline level drop-down list and choose from the resulting list seen in Figure 7-36.

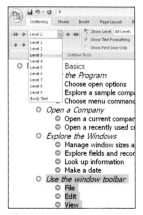

Figure 7-36
Choosing a new level.

The Outlining tab on the Ribbon also contains a button with double arrowheads pointing right. Click that button to quickly promote the current line to a Heading 1, the highest level.

Viewing the Outline

While in Outline view, you can expand or collapse the various levels to view only the portions you want to see. For example, you can view headings only to get an overview of the entire document, thereby helping you further organize your thoughts. Additionally, you can turn the formatting display on or off. Word includes several areas on the Outlining tab to assist you with viewing your outline.

▶ **On the outline body, double-click the Heading button, which looks like a circle with a plus sign in it. If the Heading button has a minus sign, there are no subheadings or body text under that heading; however, a plus sign indicates additional items. Word collapses the body text and subheadings of the first level below the currently selected heading, or, if the heading is already collapsed, Word expands the first heading level below the currently selected heading. Each double-click will collapse or expand additional headings.**

Optionally, double-click a Collapse and Expand icon to fully open the selected heading.

▶ From the Outlining tab, the Outlining Tools group, click the Show Level down arrow, which displays a drop-down list of heading options. Select a level and Word displays only the headings at the level you chose and those that are higher. For example, as shown in Figure 7-37, if you select Show Level 2, both Level 1 and Level 2 headings appear but not Level 3 or Level 4 headings.

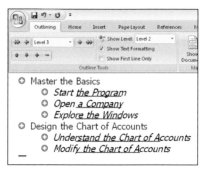

Figure 7-37
Displaying only the levels you want to view.

Click on Show All Levels to view the entire outline.

▶ Choose Outlining>Outline Tools>Show First Line Only. The outline display toggles between displaying all the body text or only the first line of each body text paragraph.

▶ Choose Outlining>Outline Tools>Show Text Formatting. The outline view toggles between displaying the outline with or without character formatting. Figure 7-38 illustrates the outline without text formatting.

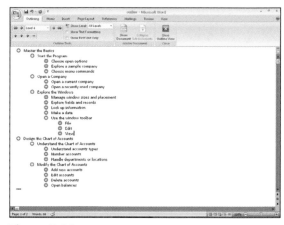

Figure 7-38
Viewing an unformatted outline.

Choose Outlining>Close>Close Outline View to close the outline and return to Print Layout view.

When you print an outline, Word prints the outline in its entirety as it displays in Print Layout view, without the indentation you see in Outline view.

Keeping Documents Secure

MANY DOCUMENTS CONTAIN DATA that is confidential in nature, such as business plans or personal diaries. In today's world of electronic snooping, it's up to you to protect your work against prying eyes. Even if you allow others to view your documents, you may want to prevent accidental or intentional changes. Fortunately, Word provides several security tools including password protection.

Inspecting for Personal Information

Many Word documents contain *metadata,* which is somewhat hidden information that others could see—data such as the names of people who have previously edited the document, file locations, and even e-mail addresses. You may not want others to have access to this information. Fortunately, you can eliminate the metadata by using the Document Inspector.

If you are collaborating with others using features such as comments or tracked changes, you may not want to remove the metadata until the collaboration is complete. Typically, you run the Document Inspector just prior to publication. You'll discover comments and tracked changes later in this chapter.

First save your file and then choose OfficeButton> Prepare>Inspect Document. You see the Document Inspector dialog box shown in Figure 7-39.

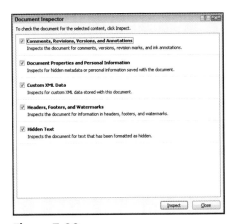

Figure 7-39
Inspecting your document for personal information.

Deselect any options you do not want to check and click the Inspect button. Word inspects the document for various types of potential personal information. When the inspection is complete, the Document Inspector reappears with information as seen in Figure 7-40.

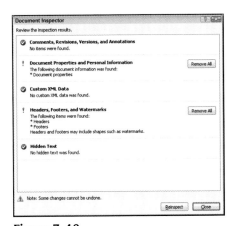

Figure 7-40
The Document Inspector reveals potential problem areas.

Click the Remove All button next to any option you want removed. Word removes the selected information and the Remove All button next to the option disappears. Repeat this for any additional items you want to remove. When finished, click the Close button and resave your file.

Restricting Formatting Changes

One method of protection you can apply is to protect the document against formatting changes. Then, before someone can change the document appearance, they must first enter a password. If you apply a file password (which you'll see how to do later in this chapter), with that password you or others can open or modify the document. If you can modify a document, you can modify any portion of it—text or formatting. Follow these steps to lock-in document formatting:

1. Choose Review>Protect>Protect Document. A Restrict Formatting and Editing pane opens on the left side of the screen as seen in Figure 7-41.

Settings

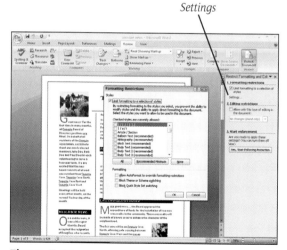

Figure 7-41
Stop unwanted formatting changes.

2. Click the "Limit formatting to a selection of styles" check box.

3. Click the Settings link. The Formatting Restrictions dialog box appears (also seen in Figure 7-41). By default, changes to any styles are allowed.

4. Click the None button. All choices are deselected; however, if you do want to allow formatting changes to a particular style, you can recheck that style name.

5. Click the OK button. If you get a message box saying "This document may contain formatting or styles that aren't allowed. Do you want to remove them?," click No.

6. Click Yes, Start Enforcing Protection. The Start Enforcing Protection dialog box appears.

7. Enter an optional password and then reenter the password to confirm it. The password you type appears as a series of black dots.

8. Click OK. Notice how any Ribbon option that affects formatting becomes unavailable.

If you want to make any formatting changes, you must first click the Stop Protection button. If you don't see the Restrict Formatting and Editing pane, choose Review>Protect>Protect Document. You must then enter the password to stop the protection and allow formatting changes.

Marking a Document as Final

To protect your document against accidental changes, Word includes a feature called Mark as Final. After choosing the option, the document cannot be changed unless you choose the Mark as Final option again, which then allows document changes.

Choose Office Button>Prepare>Mark as Final. A confirmation message appears. Click OK. Next, the confirmation message you see in Figure 7-42 appears. Click OK to that message also.

Figure 7-42
Disable editing by marking a document as final.

Marking a document as final disables every option in the Ribbon that could change the document in any way. An icon appears in the status bar indicating the document is marked as final and if you attempt to make any changes, the icon changes to a message stating the modification is not allowed.

This feature is easily bypassed. Suppose you need to change a date in the document or you forgot to list a particular item. You can "unmark" the document from being final by simply going back into Office Button>Prepare>Mark as Final.

Saving a File as Read-Only

If your goal is to prevent accidental changes either by you or others, one of the easiest methods is to save the file with a read-only recommendation. When a file is read-only, you can still make changes to the document, but the only way you can save those changes is to save the file to a different file name or folder.

1. Choose Office Button>Save As.

2. Optionally, select a different folder in which to save the file.

3. Enter a file name if you haven't already assigned a name.

4. Choose Tools>General Options (see Figure 7-43).

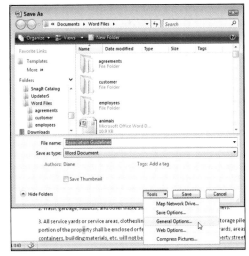

Figure 7-43
Choosing general file options.

5. From the General Options dialog box, click the Read-Only recommended check box

6. Click the OK button, which returns you to the Save As dialog box.

7. Click the Save button.

When you or another user attempts to open the file, the message shown in Figure 7-44 is displayed. Click Yes to open the File as a Read-Only file. If you choose No, Word again recommends you open the file as Read Only, but if you click No again, the file finally opens as a standard file where changes can be made.

Figure 7-44
The read-only recommendation box.

Assigning a File Password

Another method to protect your documents, and probably one of the safest methods, is to assign a password. When you assign a file password, the application uses a key to encrypt the document's contents. Word, Excel, and PowerPoint all allow you to assign passwords. There are two levels of password protection you can use. One forces anyone who attempts to even open the file to supply a password. Of course, if they cannot open the file, they cannot view it or modify it. The second level is where you could allow others (with or without password protection) to open the file and view it, but not allow them to edit the file in any way without first providing another password.

To create file passwords, choose Office Button>Save As. Select a folder for your file and enter a file name. Choose Tools>General Options. The General Options dialog box appears. Type a password in the Password to Open text box if you want users to enter a password before they can open and view the document. Word displays passwords with a black dot for each character, like those shown in Figure 7-45.

Figure 7-45
Assigning a file password.

Good passwords should be at least eight characters and should contain a mixture of numbers as well as upper and lower-case letters. Passwords are case sensitive. Don't, however, make your passwords so difficult you can't remember them. If you lose the password to your Word, Excel, or PowerPoint document, it cannot be recovered!

Optionally, you can leave the Password to Open box empty and enter a password in the Password to Modify text box. Using this option allows others to open the file, but they cannot make any changes without keying in the password. Click OK and a message box appears prompting you to reenter the passwords just in case you typed them incorrectly the first time. Reenter the passwords as prompted and click OK; then, click the Save button to save the password security.

If you want to use both a password to open and a password to modify, it's a good idea to use different passwords for each function.

When you or anyone opens the file, they are prompted to enter the password (see Figure 7-46).

Figure 7-46
Enter the required password to open the file.

To remove file passwords, from the General Options dialog box, delete the characters from the Password to Open or Password to Modify text box and resave the file.

Printing and Publishing

Y OU DID IT! You created a great document, and now it's time to use it. With the adoption of e-mail within most corporations and homes, many documents today might never be printed on paper—they may only ever exist in an electronic form; however, there may still be times when you need a paper copy. This section shows you how to distribute your document both electronically and on paper.

Using Print Preview

Before you print your document, you should preview it on the screen so you can sit back and look at how document layout settings such as the margins will look in the printed document. In Print Preview, although you can only view the document and cannot edit it, you can tell quite a bit about it from a different perspective. The following steps walk you through the Print Preview process:

1. Choose Office and pause your mouse over the Print option. A selection of choices appears.

2. Choose Print Preview. The Print Preview window opens so that an entire page is visible on the screen. Notice in Figure 7-47 how the mouse pointer becomes a magnifying glass with a plus sign on it.

Press the Page Down or the Page Up key on your keyboard to view other pages of the document.

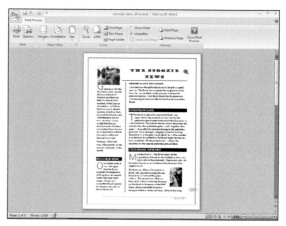

Figure 7-47
Previewing your document before printing it.

3. Click anywhere on the document body. The text zooms in and becomes larger on the screen. Click anywhere on the document body again to make the text zoom out.

Take a closer look at the Print Preview Ribbon tab seen in Figure 7-48. You see buttons that let you print the document, change the way the page is set up, control the zoom percentage or view, or hide items such as the ruler.

Figure 7-48
The Print Preview ribbon.

Press Escape or click the Close Print Preview button to return to the standard document screen.

Printing a Document

When your document is complete and you've reviewed it for any changes, you may want to make a hard copy of it to file away or to share with others. Choose Office Button>Print. The Print dialog box seen in Figure 7-49 illustrates the many printing options. Take a look at a few of them:

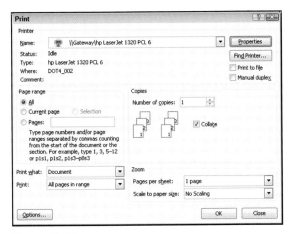

Figure 7-49
The Print dialog box.

▶ **Name:** If you are connected to more than one printer, you can select which printer you want to use from the Name drop-down list.

▶ **Page Range:** Determine which pages you want to print. If you highlight a document area before you display the Print dialog box, you can choose Selection to print only that area. If you want to print only selected pages, enter into the Pages text box the page numbers separated by a comma or a dash. For example to print only the first three document pages, enter 1, 2, 3 or 1-3.

▶ **Copies:** Select the number of copies you want to print and whether you want the pages printed in the order you created them (collated). (On a few printer models, the collate option is not available.)

▶ **Print:** Choose Odd Pages or Even Pages from this option if you only want to print the odd number pages or the even numbered pages.

▶ **Pages per sheet:** Choose this option to determine how many document pages you want to print on a single sheet of paper. The formatting and document page layouts do not change; Word simply reduces the size of each printed page to fit the number of pages that you select. This feature is helpful as an overview or handout document.

▶ **Scale to paper size:** While you can choose this option to select the paper size you want to use, it's really better to choose that from inside the document itself (Page Layout>Page Setup>Size).

Choose any desired options and then click the OK button to begin printing.

E-Mailing a Document

If you have e-mail access, you can send a document directly to another person. Word copies the content of the document as an attachment to an e-mail message. While many e-mail applications work fine with this feature, Office works best with Outlook and Outlook Express.

With the document open and ready to send, choose Office Button>Send>E-mail. Word launches your e-mail application with the file listed as an attachment. Type the recipient's e-mail address or click the To button to select from your Outlook Contact List (see Chapter 23, "Working with Outlook Contacts"). Word automatically adds the document name as the subject, but you can click the Subject text box and change the subject. Optionally, you can type a message in the message body (see Figure 7-50). Click the Send button when you are finished.

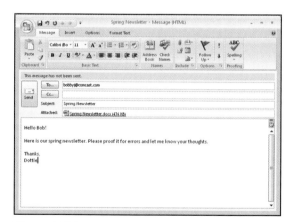

Figure 7-50
E-mailing a Word document as an attachment.

Publishing to a Blog

Rapidly gaining in popularity are Internet *blogs* (derived from *Web Log*). Blogs typically provide commentary or news on a particular subject, such as food, politics, or local news, and many function as more personal online diaries. A blog might even combine text, images, and links to other blogs, Web pages, and other media related to its topic. The entries are usually in reverse chronological order and depict a simple journal style. Millions upon millions of blogs are updated daily by their users.

If you have a blog account, Word 2007 now provides the ability to publish a document directly to your blog. If you don't have a blog account, Word 2007 offers several suggestions as to where you can sign up for one.

To post your document as a blog, choose Office Button>Publish>Blog. Word creates a new document with the document text. The Ribbon changes to include two tabs relative to blogs (see Figure 7-51).

You must register your blog address into Office before you can publish your blog post. Follow the onscreen prompts.

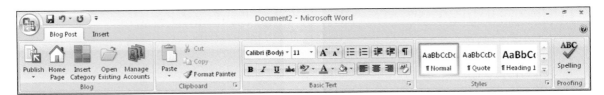

Figure 7-51
The Blog Post tab.

If you have not already formatted your document for your blog post, Word provides tools for items such as fonts, bullets and numbers, and alignment. Use these tools just as if you were using them in a standard Word document.

You can create categories for your blog—such as family news, jokes, discussions, and so forth. Click the Insert Category to choose one of the existing categories or type a new one.

When you are ready to publish to your blog, choose Blog Post>Blog>Publish>Publish. Word displays an informational message. Click Yes. A message appears at the top of the blog text confirming the post was published to the blog (see Figure 7-52).

When you log in to your blog, you see the document you published. Figure 7-53 shows an example.

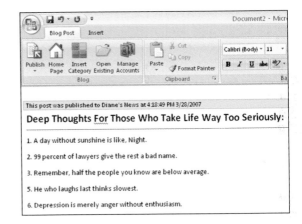

Figure 7-52
Confirming a blog posting.

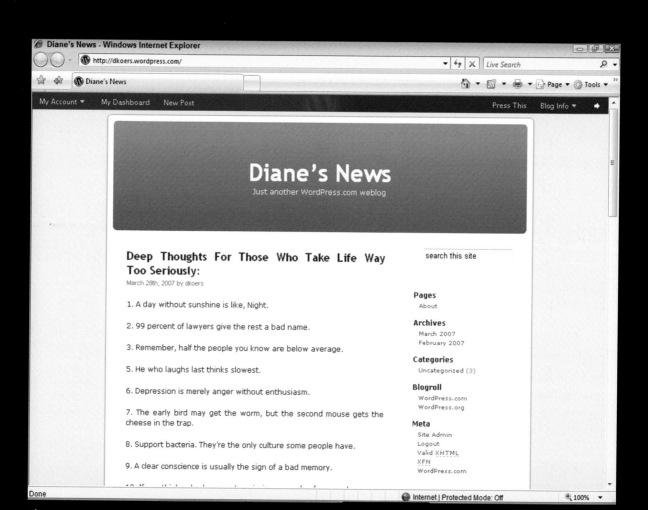

Figure 7-53
A finished blog entry.

Part III
Excel

When it comes to software for crunching numbers, there is nothing better than Microsoft Excel. You can use Excel for tasks such as balancing your checkbook, projecting company profits, tracking your CD collection, or tallying up recent trip expenses. Excel performs all the math for you quickly and accurately. This section explains the fundamentals of working with the Excel workbook and, even if you have worked with spreadsheets before, I'm sure you will pick up a few tips and tricks along the way.

8

Creating a Basic
Worksheet

© *imagepro – FOTOLIA*

PICTURE YOURSELF STARING OUT across the horizon. As you view the sun reflecting on the crystalline water, you are contemplating a decision you must make. You're probably making a mental list about the decision, listing the pros in one column and the cons in another column.

Welcome to Excel, the most powerful and popular spreadsheet program in the world. "What is a spreadsheet program?," you may ask. Well, it's a computer program that features a huge grid designed to display data in rows and columns. You use it to perform calculations, sort large amounts of data, and extract information that meets criteria you specify, all of which can help you make better decisions. Whether you need a list of names and addresses or a document to calculate next year's sales revenue based on prior years' performance, Excel is the application you want to use.

But every Excel task you tackle begins with a blank sheet. And that's where this chapter begins—with a blank sheet. This chapter begins with the basics of Excel.

Exploring the Excel Window

PREVIOUSLY, YOU MAY HAVE USED a
paper, pencil, and calculator to track information, whether to figure a simple calculation
or track a list of items in alphabetical order. Excel
handles those tasks and many more, including
complex calculations. At first glance, however, the
Excel opening screen can appear very intimidating
with all its buttons, options, rows, and columns.
Once you understand the purpose for those options,
you will feel much more comfortable with the
Excel screen.

Identifying Screen Elements

As mentioned in Chapter 1, many items that you
see when you open a new worksheet (also called a
spreadsheet) are standard to most Microsoft Office
programs. You see the Ribbon with its tabs and
groups, and you see the status bar at the bottom of
the window. However, the following list illustrates
a few elements that are specific to Excel (see
Figure 8-1).

- ▶ **Worksheet area:** A rectangular grid consisting of rows and columns. Columns
  are labels with letters across the top,
  and rows are indicated by numbers.

- ▶ **Cell:** The intersection of a row and a
  column, also known as a cell address.
  When referring to a cell address, Excel
  references the column letter first, then
  the row number. For example, Excel
  refers to a cell address as C13 not 13C.
  The current cell has a heavy border
  around it.

Name box   Current cell   Formula bar

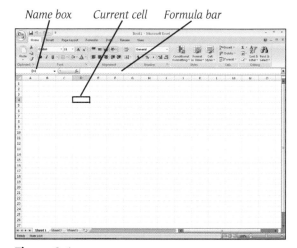

Figure 8-1
The Excel screen.

- ▶ **Edit line:** The edit line consists of three
  parts: the Name box, the Insert
  Function button, and the Formula bar

- ▶ **Selection indicator:** Shows the address
  or name of the currently selected cell.
  You can also use this area to create or
  use a range name. (See "Working with
  Ranges" later in this chapter).

- ▶ **Insert Function button:** Provides a means
  to insert Excel functions. (See Chapter 9,
  "Working with Formulas and Functions").

- ▶ **Formula bar:** Displays the contents of
  the currently selected cell.

- ▶ **Scroll bars:** The screen has both
  horizontal and vertical scroll bars.

- ▶ **Sheet tabs:** Each Excel file begins with
  3 worksheets.

Moving Around the Screen

Each worksheet has 16,384 columns, beginning at column A and extending to column XFD, and 1,048,576 rows. That's over seventeen *billion* cells in a single worksheet! Because of the size of an Excel worksheet, you need ways to move around quickly. You can use your mouse or keyboard to move around a worksheet.

Using the Mouse

Because there are over 17 billion possible cells in a single worksheet, you may find that using the mouse is an easy way to move around in the worksheet.

Click the mouse pointer on any cell to move the active cell location to that cell. You can use the scroll bars to see more of the worksheet. Both the horizontal and vertical scroll bars have arrows at each end to extend the worksheet scroll amount (see Figure 8-2).

Figure 8-2
The worksheet scrollbars.

Also, by default, Excel displays three worksheets, labeled Sheet1, Sheet2, and Sheet3. Clicking any worksheet tab makes that Sheet appear on top of the other worksheets. You'll learn more about working with multiple worksheets in Chapter 11, "Managing Large Amounts of Excel Data."

Using the Keyboard

As you have just discovered, you can use your mouse to move around an Excel worksheet; however, you may like using the keyboard better. Table 8-1 describes keyboard methods for moving around a worksheet.

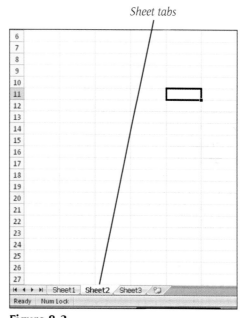

Figure 8-3
Viewing Sheet2.

Table 8-1 Excel Movement Keystrokes

Keystroke	Result
Arrow keys	Moves one cell at a time up—down, left, or right
Page Down	Moves one screen down
Page Up	Moves one screen up
Home	Moves to column A of the current row
Ctrl+Home	Moves to cell A1
Ctrl+End	Moves to the lower-right cell of the worksheet that contains formatting or data
Ctrl+Arrow key	Moves to the beginning or end of a row or column
Ctrl+Page Down	Moves to the next worksheet (see Figure 8-3)
Ctrl+Page Up	Moves to the previous worksheet
F5	Displays the Go To dialog box

Using the Go To Command

You have discovered that you can press the F5 key to display the Go To dialog box. You can use the Go To command to jump to a specific cell or area of the worksheet. The Ribbon command for executing the Go To command is Home>Editing> Find & Select>Go To. The Go To dialog box displays. In the Reference box, enter the address of the cell you want to make active and then click the OK button (see Figure 8-4.) The Go To box also displays any recently accessed cells and range names in the current workbook.

Figure 8-4
The Go To dialog box.

Cell addresses are not case sensitive.

A cell's location is designated by the column letter followed by the row number.

Entering Excel Data

HERE'S AN OLD ADAGE THAT SAYS "You have to crawl before you can walk." That saying applies to Excel worksheets as well. You need to learn the basics before you learn the more complex Excel features. This section shows you how to get basic data into your worksheet.

Worksheet data is made up of three components: labels, values, and formulas. This section discusses entering labels and values, and you'll learn about creating and entering formulas in Chapter 9, "Working with Formulas and Functions." When you are ready to enter data into a worksheet cell, you must first click on the cell in which you want the information.

Entering Labels

Labels are traditionally descriptive pieces of information, such as names, months, or other identifying information. Excel automatically recognizes information as a label if it contains alphabetic characters. Don't worry if the entire label does not appear to fit into a cell width. If needed, Excel automatically extends the data past the cell width, and you'll soon discover how you can manually widen a cell.

Excel aligns the data to the left side of the cell. If the descriptive information is too wide to fit in a cell, Excel extends that data past the cell width as long as the next cell is blank. If the next cell is not blank, Excel displays only enough text to fit the display width. Widening the column displays additional text.

Click the cell in which you want to place the label and type the text. Press the Enter key and Excel accepts the label and aligns the data along the left edge of the cell. After pressing Enter, the cell below the one in which you just entered data becomes the current cell. If you make a mistake and have not yet pressed the Enter key, press the Backspace key to delete characters and type a correction, or press the Escape key to cancel typing in the selected cell.

> Optionally, instead of pressing the Enter key, press the Tab key, which makes Excel move to the right instead of down. Or, you can press an arrow key instead of the Enter key, which moves the next selection in the direction of the arrow key.

Figure 8-5 illustrates a worksheet with several labels. Also notice that Excel displays the contents of the current cell in the formula bar.

Current cell contents

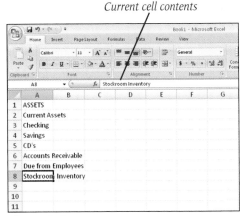

Figure 8-5

Labels appear aligned to the left side of the cell.

Entering Values

Values are the raw numbers that you track in a worksheet. When you enter a value, you don't need to enter commas or dollar signs. In Chapter 10, "Making the Worksheet Look Good," you'll learn how to let Excel do that for you.

Click on the cell in which you want to place the value and type them in. Press Enter to accept the value. Excel enters the value into the cell and aligns it along the right cell edge (see Figure 8-6).

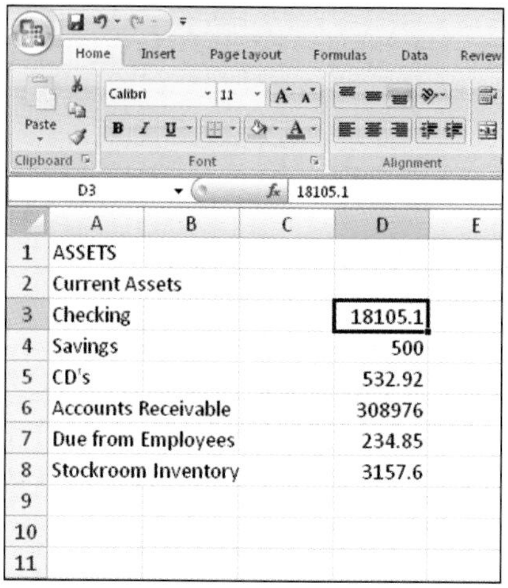

Figure 8-6

Entering values.

As you can see, Excel drops the leading and trailing zeros. For example, if you enter the value of 0123, Excel sees it as 123. If you enter 123.40, Excel displays it as 123.4. The trailing zero is not lost; it simply doesn't display.

To enter a value as a label, type an apostrophe (') character before the number. The apostrophe character tells Excel to treat the information as a label instead of a value.

If your value is too large to fit into the cell width, Excel may display a series of number signs (####), or it may round the value display. Don't worry about the appearance that displays in Excel. Remember that you'll discover how to change the display of your data in Chapter 10. Table 8-2 illustrates some of the ways that Excel, by default, displays numeric data.

Table 8-2 Excel Value Appearances

Keystroke	Result
1074	1074
0174	174
'0174	0174
39.95	39.95
39.50	39.5
39.501	39.501
4789547.365	4789547.37

Entering Dates

Although dates contain characters, and look like a label, Excel technically considers them values, because Excel can calculate the time between dates, which you will learn about in Chapter 9, "Working with Formulas and Functions." For example, day 1 is January 1st, 1900, day 2 is January 2nd, 1900, and so forth.

When you enter a date, by default Excel may not display it on the screen in the same way that you type it. You will discover how to format dates in different perspectives in Chapter 10, "Making the Worksheet Look Good." Figure 8-7 and Table 8-3 show how Excel automatically displays dates.

You type this...   *Excel displays this*

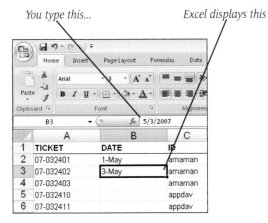

Figure 8-7
Entering dates into the worksheet.

Table 8-3 Entering Dates

You Type	Excel Displays
January 23, 2007	23-Jan-07
January 23	23-Jan
Jan 23	23-Jan
1/23	23-Jan
1-23	23-Jan
1-23-07	1/23/2007
1/23/07	1/23/2007

Depending on the Regional and International settings of your computer, your system may display differently, such as displaying only the last two digits of a year.

Extending a Series with AutoFill

Excel includes a great built-in, time-saving feature called AutoFill. If you provide Excel the beginning pattern, such as a month, day, or numbers, Excel can fill in the rest of the pattern for you. For example, if you type January, Excel fills in February, March, April, and so on. AutoFill works with days of the week, months of the year, or yearly quarters such as 2nd Qtr. You can enter the entire word or you can enter the abbreviated form such as Wed or Sep. The following steps show you how to use the AutoFill feature.

1. Type the first cell of data with data such as a day or month, such as Wednesday or September.

2. Press Enter, which accepts the data entry.

3. Select the cell in which you just entered the data.

4. Position the mouse pointer on the small black box at the lower-right corner of the data cell (fill handle). Your mouse pointer turns into a small black cross.

To AutoFill a series of numbers, enter two values in two adjacent cells, such as 1 and 2 or 5 and 10. Select both cells, and then use the AutoFill box to highlight cells. Excel continues the series as 3, 4, 5, or 5, 10, 15 and so forth.

5. Drag the small black box across the cells you want to fill. You can drag the cells up, down, left, or right.

6. Release the mouse. Excel fills in the selected cells with a continuation of your data. Figure 8-8 shows how Excel fills in the cells with a continuation of the months.

If you use AutoFill on a single value or a text word, Excel duplicates it. For example, if you use AutoFill on a cell with the word Apple, all filled cells contain Apple.

Fill Handle

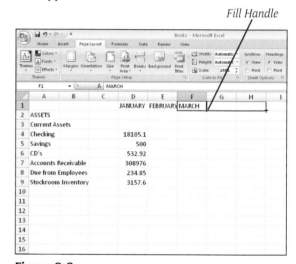

Figure 8-8
Using AutoFill for calendar months.

Learning Selection Techniques

TO MOVE, COPY, DELETE, OR CHANGE the formatting of data in a worksheet, you must first select the cells you want to modify. Selected cells appear darker on screen—just the reverse of unselected text, with the exception of the first cell. The first cell does not appear darker; it just has a dark border around it.

Make sure the mouse pointer is a white cross before attempting to select cells.

To select more than one cell perform one of the following actions:

▶ To select a single entire row, click the row number. As the mouse is on the row number it appears as a black arrow pointing right.

▶ To select multiple rows, drag across multiple row numbers, as seen in Figure 8-9.

▶ To select a single entire column, click a column heading. As the mouse is on the column heading, it appears as a black arrow pointing down.

▶ To select multiple columns, drag across multiple column headings.

▶ To select sequential cells, click the first cell, hold down the Shift key and select the last cell you want to select. Excel designates a sequential cell range with a colon dividing the beginning and end. For example, B1:C3 means cells B1, B2, B3,C1, C2 and C3 are included.

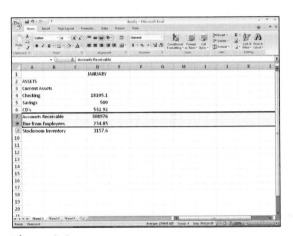

Figure 8-9
Selecting multiple rows.

Optionally, click and drag the mouse over a group of cells to select a sequential area.

▶ To select non-sequential cells, click the first cell, hold down the Ctrl key and click each additional cell you want to select. Figure 8-10 shows the non-sequential cells A3, A13, D1, and D4 through D12 selected. When making non-sequential cell selections, you can include entire rows and entire columns along with individual cells or groups of cells.

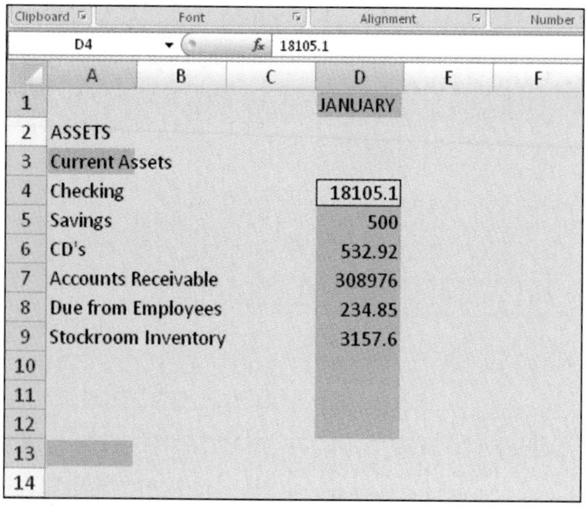

	A	B	C	D	E	F
1				JANUARY		
2	ASSETS					
3	Current Assets					
4	Checking			18105.1		
5	Savings			500		
6	CD's			532.92		
7	Accounts Receivable			308976		
8	Due from Employees			234.85		
9	Stockroom Inventory			3157.6		
10						
11						
12						
13						
14						

Figure 8-10

Selected non-sequential cells.

- ▶ **To select the entire worksheet, press Ctrl+A or click the small gray box located to the left of column A and above row 1.**

Click any non-selected cell to clear the selection.

If you are inputting data, you can save time by leaving your hands on the keyboard, so Excel also provides ways you can make many selections with your keyboard, instead of the mouse. Here are a few of the methods you can use:

- ▶ **Select a contiguous range by using an arrow key to move to the beginning of the range you want and then hold the Shift key while you arrow-key to the last cell of the range.**
- ▶ **Select an entire column by pressing Ctrl+Spacebar.**
- ▶ **Select multiple adjacent columns by first selecting a cell in each column and then pressing Ctrl+Spacebar.**
- ▶ **Select an entire row by pressing Shift+Spacebar.**
- ▶ **Select multiple adjacent rows by first selecting a cell in each row and then pressing Shift+Spacebar.**
- ▶ **Select all data filled cells adjacent to the current cell by pressing Ctrl+* (asterisk). (See Figure 8-11). The current cell does not have to be at the beginning of the range.**

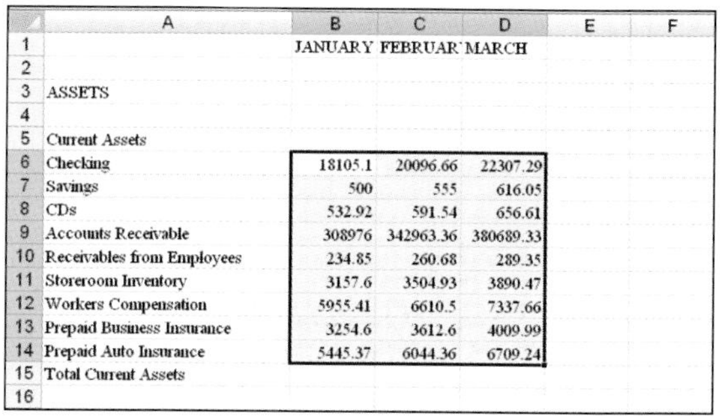

	A	B	C	D	E	F
1		JANUARY	FEBRUAR'	MARCH		
2						
3	ASSETS					
4						
5	Current Assets					
6	Checking	18105.1	20096.66	22307.29		
7	Savings	500	555	616.05		
8	CDs	532.92	591.54	656.61		
9	Accounts Receivable	308976	342963.36	380689.33		
10	Receivables from Employees	234.85	260.68	289.35		
11	Storeroom Inventory	3157.6	3504.93	3890.47		
12	Workers Compensation	5955.41	6610.5	7337.66		
13	Prepaid Business Insurance	3254.6	3612.6	4009.99		
14	Prepaid Auto Insurance	5445.37	6044.36	6709.24		
15	Total Current Assets					
16						

Figure 8-11

Selected sequential cells with data.

Editing a Worksheet

WHEN YOU CREATE A WORKSHEET, a lot of data entry is usually involved. Excel has features to assist you with some of the repetitive work, but unfortunately you'll probably still make mistakes. You may need to edit the entries you made in some cells, and you may want to make changes to the construction of your worksheet. Excel includes the ability to reorganize your worksheet without having to reenter any data.

Editing Cell Data

You can edit your data in a variety of ways. You might need to change the contents of a cell or delete its current content. If you enter data into a cell and later decide you do not want the information in the worksheet, you can delete the entire contents of a cell by pressing the Delete key or by choosing Home>Editing>Clear>Clear Contents.

There are several methods you can use to edit cell data. One simple method of changing cell content is to select the cell and type the new data. When you type the new data and press Enter, it replaces the current cell content. Optionally, you can use the Edit feature. You'll find the Edit feature very useful if your cell has a lot of information in it and you need only to change a few characters. In some situations, editing may be faster than retyping the entire cell contents. Follow these steps to edit the cell contents:

1. Double-click the cell you want to edit. The insertion point blinks within the cell and the status bar indicates you are in Edit mode (see Figure 8-12).

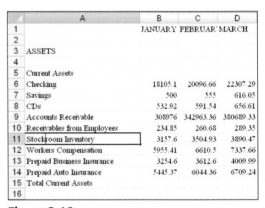

Figure 8-12
Edit cell contents without having to start over.

Optionally, press F2 to launch the Edit mode.

2. Press the arrow key until the insertion point is located where you need to make a change.

3. Type the changes, whether adding new characters or pressing Backspace or Delete to remove existing characters. As you type, the changes appear in the current cell.

4. Press the Enter key to accept the changes.

Using Undo and Redo

If you make a change and then determine you really didn't want to make that change, Excel provides an Undo feature. You can use Undo to restore text that you deleted, delete text you just typed, or reverse a recently taken action. An exception to the Undo function is that if you save your worksheet, you cannot "unsave" it. Also, if you close the worksheet, you cannot undo changes made in the previous editing session when you reopen the worksheet.

To undo any actions or correct any mistakes you make when entering data, perform one of the following options:

▶ **Choose Undo from the Quick Access Toolbar.**

▶ **Press Ctrl+Z.**

▶ **To undo several steps at once, click the arrow on the Undo button and select the step from which you want to begin the Undo action (see Figure 8-13).**

To repeat your last action, click the Redo button on the Quick Access Toolbar or press Ctrl+Y.

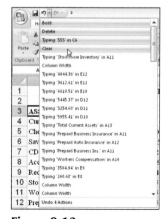

Figure 8-13
Select the steps you want to reverse.

Inserting Areas

Occasionally you need to insert a column, row, or a single cell in the middle of existing information. Inserting columns, rows, or cells moves existing data to make room for new rows or columns.

You can insert a column or row anywhere you need it by first selecting a cell where you want the new column or row located. Choose Home>Cells>Insert (arrow) and choose Insert Sheet Rows or Insert Sheet Columns. Figure 8-14 illustrates a newly inserted column F.

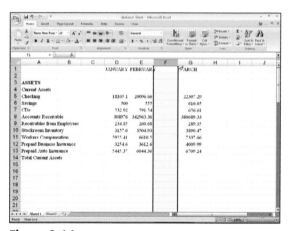

Figure 8-14
Inserting additional columns.

To insert multiple columns or rows, select headings or row numbers across multiple columns or rows.

If you insert a column, Excel moves information in the current column and all columns to the right of the current column to the right. If you insert a row, Excel moves information in the current cell and all cells below the current row down.

No matter how many rows or columns
you insert, Excel cannot exceed its
original worksheet size of 16,384
columns and 1,048,576 rows.

Figure 8-16
Inserting cells where needed.

Instead of inserting an entire column or an entire
row, you can also insert just a single cell or even a
group of cells. Excel then moves existing data
down or to the right, depending on an option you
specify. Begin by selecting the cells where you
want new cells. Then choose Home>Cells>Insert
(arrow) and choose Insert Cells. You see the Insert
dialog box seen in Figure 8-15.

Figure 8-15
Choose the direction you want existing cells to move.

Click the desired insert option and then click OK.
Excel shifts existing data according to your selection.
In Figure 8-16, a blank cell was inserted in cell E7.

To bypass the Insert dialog box and just
insert a cell, choose Home>Cells>Insert.

Deleting Areas

Like inserting areas, you can delete unwanted
columns, rows, or cells. Excel moves existing data
to take up the room made by the deletion. Use
caution when deleting entire rows or columns.
Excel deletes the entire row of sixteen thousand
plus columns or one million plus rows. Any data in
the selected row or column gets deleted as well. No
confirmation appears before Excel deletes the area.

When you delete columns, Excel pulls the remaining columns to the left; when you delete rows,
Excel pulls the remaining rows up. You can delete
multiple rows or multiple columns, whether
sequential or non-sequential; however, you cannot
delete both rows and columns at the same time.
Choose Home>Cells>Delete (arrow) and choose
Delete Sheet Rows or Delete Sheet Columns
(see Figure 8-17).

Figure 8-17

Deleting unnecessary columns or rows.

You can also delete a single cell by choosing Home>Cells>Delete or Home>Cells>Delete (arrow) and choosing Delete Cells. You may be prompted which direction to move the remaining cells.

Moving Data

If you're not happy with the placement of data, you don't have to delete it and retype it. Excel makes it easy for you to move it around. In fact, Excel provides several methods to move data. You can cut and paste it or you can use the drag and drop method.

Using Cut and Paste

Excel uses the Windows Clipboard, which allows you to collect text and other items from Excel or any Office document—even other programs—and then paste them into an Excel worksheet. If you want to move cells from one place to another, the clipboard is a great tool to assist you. The process involves selecting cells and either cutting (moving) or copying (duplicating) them to the clipboard, and then telling Excel where to paste (place) them.

1. Select the area of data you want to move.

2. Choose Home>Clipboard>Cut. A marquee (which looks like marching ants) surrounds the cells (see Figure 8-18).

To duplicate (instead of move) the selected cells to a new location, choose Home>Clipboard>Copy.

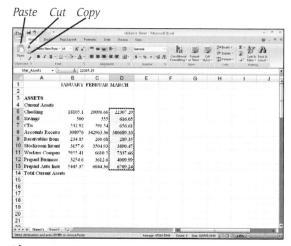

Paste   Cut   Copy

Figure 8-18

A marquee ("marching ants") forms around a cut or copied area.

3. Click the cell to which you want to move the selected area.

4. Choose Home>Clipboard>Paste. The selected cells are pasted into the new location.

Make sure the cells you paste into are empty. Pasting overwrites any existing data.

5. Paste the cells into another location or press Esc to cancel the marquee.

Optionally, press Ctrl+C to copy the selected cells and Ctrl+X to cut the selected cells, or Ctrl+V to paste the selected cells.

Dragging and Dropping Data

Drag and drop is another method often used to move data from one location to another. The drag and drop method works best when moving a few cells of data a short distance. Just follow these steps:

1. Select the cells you want to move.

2. Position the mouse pointer on the border edge of the highlighted cells. The mouse pointer must appear as a white arrow pointed to the left with four black arrowheads (see Figure 8-19).

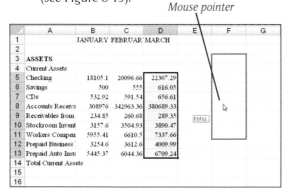

Mouse pointer

Figure 8-19

Pay attention to the mouse pointer before dragging cells.

3. Hold the mouse button down and drag the mouse to the desired location. A gray border appears around the cells you point to. Additionally, a tool tip appears confirming the cell location.

4. Release the mouse button to move the cell data to the new location.

To copy text with drag and drop, hold down the Ctrl key before dragging the selected cells. Release the mouse button before releasing the Ctrl key.

Transposing Data

If you have data you originally entered across a row and then decide it would be better placed in a column, you can tell Excel to transpose the data. The same is true if you have data in a column that you want moved to a row. Use these steps:

1. Select the cells you want to transpose.

2. Choose Home>Clipboard>Copy (or press Ctrl+C).

The Transpose feature will not work if you choose Cut instead of Copy.

3. Click the cell where you want the transposed cells to begin.

4. Choose Home>Clipboard and click the down arrow below Paste.

5. Choose Transpose. As you see in Figure 8-20, Excel copies the selected cells into the new area, transposing rows into columns or columns into rows.

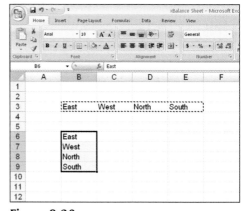

Figure 8-20

Change the flow of data by transposing cells.

Working with Range Names

I F YOUR WORKSHEET DOESN'T CONTAIN massive amounts of data, then working with individual cells is generally quick and easy. However, as your worksheet data expands, performing operations cell by cell can become tedious and can allow for more human error. Instead, you can work with a group of cells in a single operation. You have already experienced working with ranges if you selected more than once cell at a time to move, copy, or delete. Let's take that to the next level. If you repeatedly go to or use in a formula a specific cell or group of cells, it will help you to assign those cells a range name.

A *range name* is basically a descriptive name for a specified worksheet area, making them much easier to remember than actual cell addresses. Formulas can use range names, and the Go To box can recognize range names.

Naming a Range of Cells

Giving cells intuitive names makes locating data easier. It also can help make formulas more logical and easier to understand. (You'll work with formulas in Chapter 9.) Use the following steps to assign a range name:

1. Select the cells you want to name.

   Ranges can be a single cell, a contiguous group of cells, entire rows, or entire columns.

2. Choose Formulas>Defined Names>Define Name. The New Name dialog box appears.

3. In the Name text box, type a name for the range (see Figure 8-21). Name the range something that clearly identifies the area, such as Income or Grades. Range names are not case sensitive; however, range names must follow these conventions:

Selected cells

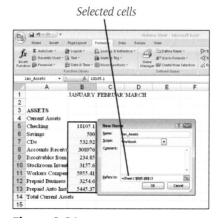

Figure 8-21
Creating a range name.

▶ **Range names must begin with a letter, an underscore, or a backslash.**

▶ **Range names cannot include spaces.**

▶ **Range names cannot include operator symbols. (+, -, *, /, <, >, or &).**

▶ **Range names can be up to 255 characters; however, shorter is better.**

▶ **Range names cannot be the same as a cell address. For example, you can't name a range AB32.**

4. Click OK.

Optionally, enter a range name into the Name box located at the left end of the Formula bar.

Using Named Ranges

Jumping to a remote area in the worksheet is only a mouse click away when you use range names, because Excel provides a convenient drop-down menu that you can use to move around quickly.

Click the down arrow in the Name box which displays a list of named ranges such as you see in Figure 8-21. Select the range name you want to access and Excel immediately highlights the named cells.

Figure 8-22
Quickly locate an area by choosing a range name.

Optionally, display the Go To dialog box and double-click on the range name you want to access.

Managing Range Names

Excel worksheets can accommodate an almost unlimited number of range names. However, if your workbook has quite a few, it can be difficult to manage or remember what each range represents. To assist you with range names, Excel includes the range Name Manager feature.

Choose Formulas>Defined Names>Name Manager which displays the Name Manager dialog box shown in Figure 8-23. You can select from the following options:

Figure 8-23
Use the Name Manger to add, edit, or delete range names.

▶ Click the New button, which displays the New Name dialog box in which you can enter a range name and enter the cell location it refers to. Instead of typing the range cell locations, click the Collapse button, which moves aside the New Name dialog box. You can then use your mouse to select the desired cells. Press Enter or click the Collapse button again to return to the New Name dialog box. Click OK when you are finished.

▶ Click an existing range name and then click the Edit button, which displays the Edit Name dialog box shown in Figure 8-24. Use this dialog box to change the range name or the range cell location reference, and click OK to apply your changes.

▶ Click an existing range name and then click the Delete button. A confirmation message appears making sure you want to delete the range name; click OK to do so.

Collapse button

If you have a lot of range names, you can click the Filter button and elect to display only the items meeting selected criteria.

Click the Close button to close the Name Manager dialog box.

Figure 8-24
Editing a range name or cell location.

Using Data Validation

WHEN YOU CREATE A WORKSHEET, you want the data you or others input to be accurate. Typos can destroy the integrity of your collected data. Fortunately, Excel provides a Data Validation feature that can restrict what is entered into a cell. For example, if you were entering student grades, which usually have values that range from A through F, you would want Excel to stop the input if someone entered H or 6. Another example might be that you want all State designations to comply with the two-character postal code, such as CA or IN. You can tell Excel to stop (or warn) you if someone enters IND or Indiana.

The following steps show you how to create cells with data validation.

1. Select the cell or cells you want Excel to validate.

2. Choose Data>Data Tools>Data Validation. The Data Validation dialog box displays with three tabs.

3. In the Settings tab, open the Allow drop-down list and choose the type of validation, such as:

    ▶ Values such as Whole Number or Decimal where you specify the upper and lower limits of allowable data values.

    ▶ Lists such as a list you define, a range of cells in the existing worksheet, or a named range (see Figure 8-25).

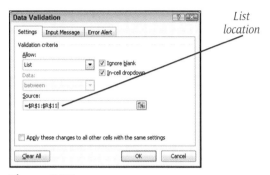

List location

Figure 8-25
Create a list of acceptable options or select one from the worksheet.

When creating a list, if you want the available choices to appear when the cell is selected, make sure to select the In-Cell drop-down check box.

▶ Dates or Times where you specify ranges or limitations such as greater than or less than, or even a specific date.

▶ Text Length where the number of characters in the data must be within the limits that you specify.

4. If necessary, display the Data drop-down list and select criteria such as Between, Greater Than, and so on.

5. Select criteria such as maximum and minimum values, or specify a data location. Enter values or cell addresses. Precede a value with an equal sign (=) to specify a range name.

6. From the Input Message tab, optionally enter a comment to display whenever someone clicks on the validated cell. Think of it as a help message.

7. On the Error Alert tab, choose from the Style drop-down list whether you want Excel to warn you or completely stop you from entering an invalid entry (see Figure 8-26).

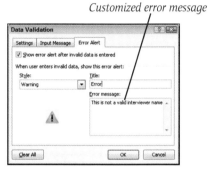

Figure 8-26

Determining the action to take when invalid data entry occurs.

On the Error Alert tab of the Data Validation dialog box, you can customize the error message Excel displays if an invalid entry is entered.

8. Click OK.

When you enter data into a cell that has a validation requirement, one of two things happens:

▶ **If the data meets the validation rules, Excel accepts the entry and moves to the next cell down.**

▶ **If the data does not meet the validation rules, Excel displays an error message similar to the one you see in Figure 8-27.**

Figure 8-27

Entering invalid data into validated cells.

Depending on the setting chosen when the data validation rule was set, choose an option:

▶ **Stop: Choose Retry or Cancel. You cannot leave invalid data in the cell. Retry returns you to the cell where you can change the value. Cancel deletes your entry and returns the cell to its previous value.**

▶ **Warning: Choose Yes or No or Cancel. Choosing Yes retains the value you entered, choosing No goes back to the cell where you can change the value, and choosing Cancel deletes your entry and returns the cell to its previous value.**

▶ **Information: Choose OK or Cancel. Choosing OK retains the value you entered, and choosing Cancel deletes your entry and returns the cell to its previous values.**

Figure 8-28 shows a cell where, due to data validation options, you pick from a list.

Cells that contain invalid data may display a small green triangle in the upper left corner.

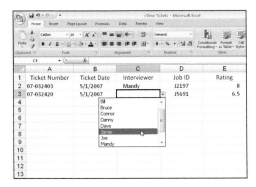

Figure 8-28
Picking from a data validation list.

If you need to locate which cells in the worksheet contain data validation, you can tell Excel to show you which ones. You can also tell Excel to show you only the cells that contain invalid data. Remember that when setting the validation, you can tell Excel to warn you of an invalid entry or to go ahead and accept it.

To have Excel show you all cells that have data validation, choose Home>Editing>Find & Select>Data Validation. Cells with validation restrictions become highlighted, as seen in Figure 8-29.

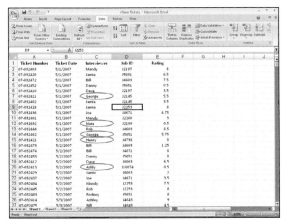

Figure 8-29
Locating cells with data validation restrictions.

To have Excel show you cells that contain invalid data, choose Data>Data Tools and click the arrow next to Data Validation. Choose Circle Invalid Data. Excel places circles around any invalid data (see Figure 8-30).

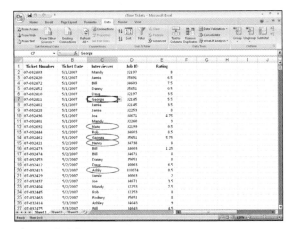

Figure 8-30
Indicating cells with invalid data.

Validation circles do not print. To remove the circles, repeat the previous step but choose Clear Validation Circles.

If you want to remove data validation, select the cells for which you want to remove validation and then choose Data>Data Tools>Data Validation. From the Data Validation dialog box, click the Clear All button and then click the OK button.

9

Working with Formulas and
Functions

PICTURE YOURSELF AT TAX TIME without a computer, a calculator, or a nearby tax firm or accountant. Can you imagine all the figuring that occurs? Calculate your wages less deductions times the tax percentage. Now take that amount and do a hundred other calculations around it. Sound daunting? It is. And you thought that math was never your strong point in school anyway! Fortunately, in today's age, we have accountants, calculators, and computers readily accessible, so we don't have to do all that manual calculating.

One of Excel's strengths is its ability to perform almost any type of calculation. Excel performs everything from simple addition to complex scientific and calculus notations with ease and, most importantly, with accuracy. This chapter introduces you to Excel formula generation. You'll also become acquainted with the more complex formulas called *functions*, all of which are designed to provide you with accurate information so you can make more informed decisions about the task at hand.

Working with Formulas

MANY PEOPLE USE A WORKSHEET to perform mathematical calculations. By using formulas, if a value in a referenced cell changes, any formula based on the cell automatically adjusts to accommodate the new value. Excel can accommodate both simple formulas, such as adding two values together, and complex formulas, such as adding two values together and multiplying the result by another number. In addition, Excel can include the values from many different worksheet cells.

Creating Formulas

All formulas must begin with the equal (=) sign, regardless of whether the formula consists of adding, subtracting, multiplying, or dividing. Formulas can reference either a static value or the value in a referenced cell.

Creating a Simple Formula

An example of a simple formula is to add two cell values together. For example, you could choose to add the values of E2 and F2. Just follow these steps:

1. Click the cell in which you want to place the result.

2. Type an equal (=) sign to begin the formula.

3. Type the cell address of the first cell to be included in the formula. This is called the cell reference. Excel references the cell address in color and places a matching color box around the referenced address (see Figure 9-1).

> Worksheet formulas are not case sensitive. For example, F2 is the same as f2.

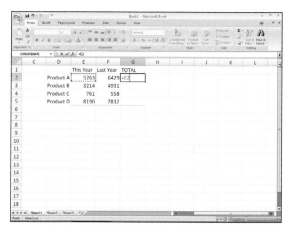

Figure 9-1
Referenced cells are bounded by a colored box.

4. A formula needs an operator to state the next action to be performed. Operators are plus (+), minus (-), multiply (*), or divide (/) symbols. Type the operator.

5. Type the reference to the second cell of the formula. Excel references the second cell address in a different color and places a matching color box around the referenced address.

6. Press the Enter key. The result of the calculation appears in the cell (see Figure 9-2).

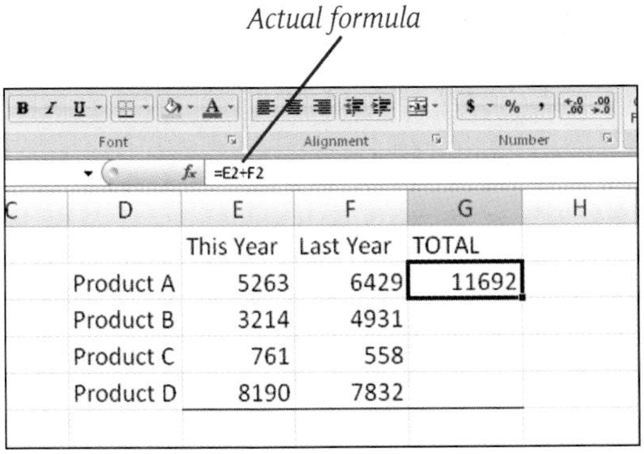

Actual formula

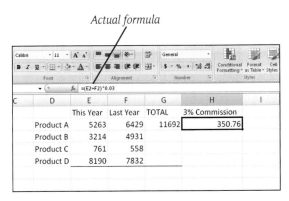

Figure 9-2

The calculation results.

Notice how the result appears in the cell, but the actual formula, =E2+F2, appears in the Contents box of the Edit line.

Creating a Compound Formula

You use compound formulas when you need more than one operator. Examples of a compound formula might be =B7+B8+B9+B10 or =B11-B19*A23.

When you have a compound formula, Excel will do the multiplication and division first, then the addition and subtraction. If you want a certain portion of the formula to be calculated first, put it in parentheses. Excel will do whatever is in the parentheses before the rest of the formula. For example, the formula =B11-B19*A23 will give a different answer than =(B11-B19)*A23. It's the old mathematical "rule of priorities."

In the cell where you want the formula answer, type an equal sign (=) to begin the formula and type the reference to the first cell of the formula. Next, type the operator and then type the reference to the second cell of the formula. Type the next operator and then the reference to the third cell of the formula. Repeat adding operators and references until the formula is complete, adding parentheses wherever necessary. Press Enter to accept the formula. Figure 9-3 illustrates a cell with a compound formula.

Actual formula

Figure 9-3

A compound formula.

If you are following the examples in this book, try changing one of the values you originally typed in the worksheet and watch the answer to the formula change.

You edit formulas in the same way you edit any other Excel data, either by retyping the formula or double-clicking the cell and making corrections. When editing formulas, Excel color codes each cell address to its corresponding cell. When you press the Enter key, Excel recalculates the formula.

Copying Formulas

Now that you've created a formula, there's no reason to type it repeatedly for subsequent cells. Let Excel copy the formula for you! When you copy a formula, the formula changes depending on where you put it. It is said, therefore, to be *relative*— relative to the position of the original formula.

Copying with AutoFill

If you're going to copy a formula to surrounding cells, you can use the AutoFill method. You first learned about the AutoFill command in Chapter 8, "Creating a Basic Excel Worksheet." Follow these steps to copy a formula:

1. Click the cell that has the formula.

2. Position the mouse pointer on the lower right corner of the cell. Make sure the mouse pointer turns into a black cross.

3. Press and hold the mouse button and drag to select the next cells to be filled in.

4. Release the mouse button. Excel copies the formula.

When Excel copies a formula, the references change as the formula is copied. If the original formula was =E2+F2 and you copied it to the next cell down, the formula would read =E3+F3. Then, if you copied it down again it would be =E4+F4, and so on. Take a look at the copied formula in Figure 9-4.

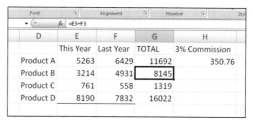

Figure 9-4
Copying a formula changes the formula references.

Copying with Copy and Paste

If the originating cells and the recipient cells are not sequential, you will find it easier to use the Copy and Paste commands. You first learned about copy and paste in Chapter 3, "Editing a Worksheet."

1. Select the cell with the formula that you want to duplicate.

2. Press Ctrl+C or choose Home>Clipboard>Copy. A marquee appears around the copied cells.

3. Highlight the cells in which you want to place the duplicated formula and either press Ctrl+V or choose Home>Clipboard>Paste.

> Press the Escape key to cancel the "marching ants" marquee.

Copying Values Instead of Formulas

As you've seen when you copy a formula, you don't copy the formula results, you copy the formula's underlying mathematical expression. What about those times where you just want the resulting value, but not the formula? Fortunately, Excel includes a tool that provides the value only. Copy the cells containing the values you want and then in the cell where you want the answers, click the arrow below the Paste button shown in Figure 9-5 and choose Paste Values. Excel then pastes in only the results, not the formula.

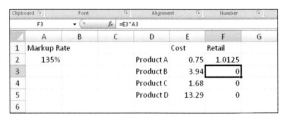

	A	B	C	D	E	F	G
1	Markup Rate				Cost	Retail	
2	135%			Product A	0.75	1.0125	
3				Product B	3.94	0	
4				Product C	1.68	0	
5				Product D	13.29	0	
6							

Figure 9-6
Not using an absolute reference creates an incorrect answer.

Figure 9-5
Pasting in values.

Creating an Absolute Formula Reference

Occasionally when you copy a formula, you do not want one of the cell references to change. That's when you need to create an *absolute reference*. To indicate an absolute reference, you use the dollar sign ($).

It's called an absolute reference because when you copy it, it absolutely and positively stays that cell reference and never changes. An example of a formula with an absolute reference might be =B22*B24. The reference to cell B24 will not change when copied.

Figure 9-6 shows a formula that is supposed to take the cost of an item and multiply it to the mark up rate. The result is the retail cost of the item. The first formula is fine, but, as you can see, when the formula is copied or filled down, the other products display an erroneous retail price of 0.

The original formula was =E2*A2, where A2 is the mark-up percentage rate. When the formula is copied down to the next cell, it becomes =E3*A3, and the cell in A3 is not the mark-up percentage rate cell. Use the following steps to create an absolute reference:

1. Click the cell in which you want to place the formula answer.

2. Type the formula. If any references are to be an absolute (unchanging) reference, add dollar signs ($) in front of both the column reference and the row reference.

> When typing the cell reference, press F4 to automatically create the absolute reference.

3. Press the Enter key. Excel displays the answer in the cell.

> **Compound formulas can also have absolute references.**

4. Copy the formula to adjacent cells using one of the methods you discovered earlier in this chapter.

Using Excel Functions

WHILE CREATING A FORMULA provides mathematical calculations, Excel includes a much more powerful feature called functions. Functions are a fast way to enter a complex formula. Excel has hundreds of different functions you can use, and it groups them together by categories, such as mathematical, statistical, logical, and date and time. Using functions can save considerable room in the Formula bar and cuts down on typographical errors that are so easy to make when typing formulas.

Understanding Function Syntax

Functions consist of several different parts. Like a formula, a function begins with an equal (=) sign. The next part is the function name, which might be abbreviated to indicate what the function does. Examples of function names include SUM, AVERAGE, and COUNT. After the name, you enter a set of parentheses and enter arguments within those parentheses. For every open parenthesis there must be a closing parenthesis.

Arguments are additional pieces of information that clarify how you want the function to behave. Arguments can consist of one or more components, ranging from cell addresses such as D13 or a range of cell addresses like D13:D25 (every cell from D13 to D25), to other variables such as a number of digits you want Excel to do something to. With only a few exceptions, all functions in Excel must follow that pattern. This function structure is called the *syntax*. Following are a few examples of function syntax. You'll learn throughout this section what these functions do.

▶ **=SUM(B3:B21)**

▶ **=AVERAGE(F1:G6)**

▶ **=IF(B3>B4,"yes", "no")**

***

Function names are not case sensitive.

***

Creating a Total with the SUM Function

The most commonly used function in Excel is the SUM function, which adds two or more values together and displays the total in the current cell. If any of the values change, the SUM total will automatically update. There are a number of different methods to enter the SUM function, but the following section describes two of the most common ways. The syntax for the SUM function is =SUM(*range of values to total*).

Entering a SUM Function

One way to enter a SUM function is to type the function in its syntax directly into a cell where you want the answer. Like other formulas, Excel displays the answer in the current cell, but displays the actual function in the Formula bar (see Figure 9-7).

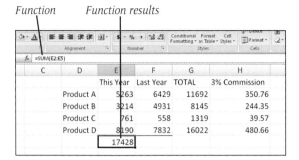

Figure 9-7
Using the SUM function.

The following steps show you how to enter a SUM function:

1. Click in the cell where you want the total of the values to display. Type an equal sign (=). The blinking insertion point appears after the equal sign, but do not press the Enter key until the function is complete. Type the word SUM and then type an opening parenthesis.

The arguments for a SUM function require that you enter the cell addresses you want to add. When you enter function arguments, you type the cell addresses you want to add. If the cell addresses are adjacent to each other, you separate them with a colon (:). For example, typing B2:B5 will add the values in B2 plus B3 plus B4 plus B5. If the cell addresses you want to add are not adjacent, you separate them with a comma. For example, entering B2, B5, B13 will add the values in cells B2 and B5 and B13 but not the value of any cells in between. You can also combine adjacent and non-adjacent cells, such as B2, B5, B13:B15, which would add the values in cells B2 and B5 and B13, B14, and B15.

Instead of typing cell addresses, you can use your mouse to highlight the desired cells. Highlighting the cells instead of typing them makes it easier to see that you have selected the correct cells.

2. Type the cell addresses you want to add together, using a colon or comma to separate the addresses. As you type the cell addresses, Excel puts a border around the cells so you can quickly see if you typed the correct cell address.

3. Type a closing parenthesis and then press the Enter key. The resulting value appears in the cell, but as with formulas, the Formula bar still reflects the function and its arguments.

Using the AutoSum Button

Since the SUM function is the function used most, Microsoft includes a button for it on the Ribbon. In fact, you'll find the AutoSum button on the Ribbon twice—once on the Home tab and again on the Formulas tab. The AutoSum button looks like this: Σ (a Sigma). Using the AutoSum button makes creating a simple addition formula as easy as clicking a mouse! Begin with these steps:

1. Click the cell below or to the right of the values you want to total.

2. Choose Home>Editing>AutoSum or Formulas>Function Library>AutoSum. Click on the AutoSum button. The cells to be totaled are highlighted. Excel first suggests the values in the cells directly above it, but if no values are directly above the current cell, Excel looks for values in the cells to the left (see Figure 9-8).

AutoSum button

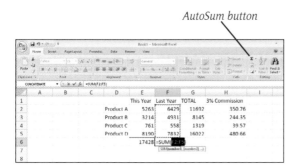

Figure 9-8

The AutoSum feature in action.

In the following examples, I list the function syntax. However, in many cases the description of the arguments are *my* interpretation of them—not necessarily the complex terms sometimes used by Excel.

> If you want to total different cells than Excel has highlighted, select them with your mouse.

3. Click the AutoSum button again or press the Enter key. Excel enters the total value of the selected cells.

Using Other Functions

As mentioned at the beginning of this section, Excel includes hundreds of different built-in functions that are divided into categories according to their purpose. The SUM function, for example, is considered a mathematical function.

This section will show you some of the function categories. Don't get discouraged when viewing the functions and their arguments. Excel provides a great tool to assist you with them. You'll learn about that tool shortly.

Calculating with Mathematical Functions

One category of functions is comprised of mathematical and trigonometric functions. You find the mathematical and trigonometry functions by choosing Formulas>Function Library>Math & Trig and then choosing the function you want. Following are some common mathematical functions.

▶ **INT: The INT function rounds a number down to the nearest integer. The number can be a specific number you type or, more commonly, the reference to a specific cell. The syntax is =INT(cell address or number). For example, to find the integer of cell B3, you would enter =INT(B3).**

> Functions can be nested. For example, to find the integer of the SUM of a range of cells, you might type =INT(=SUM(B3:B10)). Excel will add each cell and round down the total.

▶ **ROUND**: Whereas the INT function displays whole numbers for you, the ROUND function takes a value and rounds it to a specified number of digits. The ROUND function contains two different arguments—one to specify which cell you want to round and the second to tell Excel how many decimal places you want to display. The syntax is =ROUND(*cell address or number,num of digits*). For example, if cell D1 has a value of 27.6358 and you want it rounded to three decimal places, you would enter =ROUND(D1,3); then Excel would display the answer of 27.636. Excel also includes the ROUNDUP and ROUNDDOWN functions, which specifically round the answer up or down the number of digits you specify. See Figure 9-9 for an example.

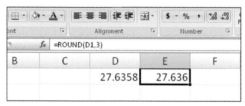

Figure 9-9
Rounding a value.

▶ **SQRT**: Finds the square root of a cell or cell range total. The syntax is =SQRT(*cell range*).

▶ **RAND**: The RAND function simply provides a random decimal value in a cell. The value is always greater than 0 but less than 1, and every time the worksheet recalculates any other value, the random value changes. The RAND function has no arguments, so the syntax is =RAND(). There is also a similar RANDBETWEEN function that lets you specify a low and high value range. =RANDBETWEEN(2,50) extracts a random whole number between 2 and 50.

▶ **POWER**: Raises a number exponentially. There are two arguments in this function. The first argument refers to the number (or cell address) you want to raise and the second argument is to what power. The syntax is =POWER(number or cell, power). Entering =POWER(5,3) results in 125.

▶ **ROMAN**: Displays the Roman numeral value of a cell. The syntax is =ROMAN(*number or cell*). So if in cell B3, you had a value of 17 and in cell B4 you entered =ROMAN(B3), the result is XVII. Using negative values or values greater than 3999 results in an error. Figure 9-10 illustrates an example where the year 1968 is converted to Roman numerals.

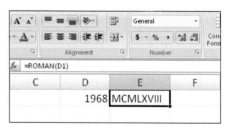

Figure 9-10
Converting a value to Roman numerals.

Analyzing with Statistical Functions

Statistical-based functions provide a means for analysis of data. Statistical analysis helps you explore, understand, and visualize your data. You access statistical functions from Formulas>Function Library>More Functions>Statistical. Here are the more common statistical functions:

▶ **AVERAGE:** The AVERAGE function finds an average of a range of values. The syntax for this function is =AVERAGE(*range of cells or values to average*). An example might be =AVERAGE(B7:D7), which would add the values in the three cells B7, C7, and D7, then divide that total by three to get the average value. Figure 9-11 shows the average value of a range of cells.

C	D	E	F	G	H
		This Year	Last Year	TOTAL	
	Product A	5263	6429	11692	
	Product B	3214	4931	8145	
	Product C	761	558	1319	
	Product D	8190	7832	16022	
	TOTAL	17428	19750	37178	
	AVERAGE	4357			
	MAX	8190			
	MIN	761			
	COUNT	4			

Figure 9-11
Finding the average value of a cell range.

▶ **MAX and MIN:** Two other common statistical functions are the MAX and MIN functions. The MAX function will display the largest value in a range of cells, whereas the MIN function will display the smallest value in a range of cells. The syntax is =MAX(*range of values*) or =MIN(*range of values*).

▶ **COUNT:** The COUNT function is handy for finding out how many numerical entries are in a specified area. The syntax is very simple: =COUNT(*range of cells to count*).

▶ **COUNTA:** The COUNTA function is similar to COUNT except it is not limited to numerical entries; it will count any non-blank cell, no matter what type of information the cell contains. The syntax is =COUNTA(*range of cells*).

▶ **COUNTBLANK:** The COUNTBLANK function determines the number of blank, or empty, cells in a range. The syntax is =COUNTBLANK(*range of cells*).

Choose Formulas>Function Library or Home>Editing and click the arrow next to the AutoSum button to quickly select the commonly used SUM, AVERAGE, COUNT NUMBERS (which is the same as COUNT), MAX, and MIN commands (see Figure 9-12).

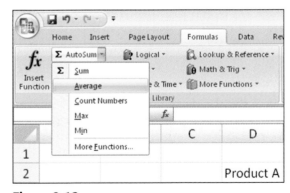

Figure 9-12
Save time by choosing from the AutoSum functions list.

Using Date Functions

Date functions are commonly used to enter the current date into a worksheet, or to calculate the difference between two or more dates. Excel stores dates as sequential serial numbers so they can be used in calculations. By default, January 1, 1900 is serial number 1, and July 20, 2005 is serial number 38553, because it is 38,553 days after January 1, 1900. When you type a date in Excel, it displays the date in a regular date format, such as 20-Jul-05, but behind the scenes Excel still considers that date a serial number. You will discover in Chapter 10 how to put dates into a more understandable format. Access the date or time function by choosing Formulas>Function Library>Date & Time.

> Because dates and times are values =(date serial numbers), they can be added, subtracted, and included in other calculations.

> ▶ **NOW:** If you enter the NOW function in a cell, Excel will display the current date and time. The date and time are dynamic in that the current date and time will change whenever you recalculate anything in the worksheet. By default, Excel recalculates the worksheet whenever any changes, additions, or deletions are made. The NOW function does not contain any arguments, so the syntax is =NOW().

> ▶ **MONTH:** The MONTH function returns the month number of a date serial number or a date in a cell. The syntax is =MONTH(*serial number or cell address*). If you have a date of 19-May-99 in cell C16 and you enter =MONTH(C16), Excel returns the value of 5 since May is the 5th month in the calendar year.

> ▶ **NETWORKDAYS:** The NETWORKDAYS function returns the number of working days between two dates. Working days exclude weekends and identified holidays. The syntax also includes an optional argument where you can enter any additional number of days to exclude. The syntax is =NETWORK-DAYS(*StartDate, EndDate, optional holidays*). For example, if you enter a start date of August 15, 1985 and an end date of March 23, 2007 using the standard number of holidays, Excel returns a result of 5,637. See Figure 9-13 for another example.

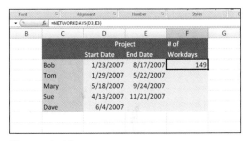

Figure 9-13
Calculating days worked.

> A quick way to calculate the number of days between two dates is to enter =NOW() in one cell and another date in another cell. Then create a formula to subtract the older date from the newer date. Excel displays the difference in a date format, so you'll need to format the value as a number.

Figuring with Financial Functions

Financial functions perform elaborate calculations such as returns on investments or cumulative principal or interest on loans. Functions exist for calculating future values or net present values on investments and for calculating amortization. Take a look at the PMT function and how you can use it.

The PMT function calculates the payment for a loan based on a constant interest rate. You will need to enter the interest rate, the number of payments, and the amount of the loan. The syntax is =PMT(*rate,nper,pv,fv,type*) where *rate* is the interest rate, *nper* is the number of payments and *pv* is the loan amount. There are two other optional arguments: including *fv* (future value),which Excel assumes to be zero unless you enter a *fv*, and *type*, which refers to when the payment is due. The following steps show you how you enter this function.

1. In separate cells, enter a loan amount, an interest rate, and the number of payments you intend to make. See Figure 9-14 for an example.

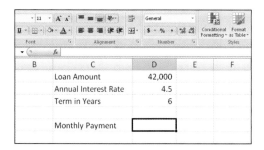

Figure 9-14
Preparing to calculate payments.

2. Type =PMT(in the cell where you want to display the payment amount. Excel will immediately identify the entry as a function and display a function ScreenTip with the function syntax.

Be uniform about the units you use for specifying *rate* and *nper*. If you make monthly payments on a six-year loan at an annual interest rate of 8 percent, use 8%/12 for *rate* and 6*12 for *nper*. If you make annual payments on the same loan, use 8 percent for *rate* and 6 for *nper.*

3. Click on the cell or type the cell address you entered for the interest rate. The referenced cell will have a border around it.

4. Type a comma to separate the arguments.

5. Click or type the cell address you entered for the number of payments and then type another comma.

7. Click or type the cell address you entered for the value of the loan and then type the closing parenthesis.

9. Press the Enter key. Excel calculates and displays the payment amount as you see in Figure 9-15

B	C	D	E	F
	Loan Amount	42,000		
	Annual Interest Rate	4.25%		
	Term in Years	6		
	Monthly Payment	($661.89)		
	The above formula is =PMT(D2/12,D3*12,D1)			

fx =PMT(D2/12,D3*12,D1)

Figure 9-15
The net payment amount.

The payment amount returned by PMT includes principal and interest only.

Understanding Logical Functions

You have seen that most functions work basically the same way. You enter the equal sign, enter the function name, and then tell the function which data to use. Most functions involve some sort of mathematical calculation. Logical functions are different in that they use operators such as equal to (=), greater than (>), less than (<), greater than or equal to (>=), less than or equal to (<=), and not equal to (<>).

One of the most commonly used and most powerful logical functions is the IF function. IF evaluates a condition and returns one of two answers, depending on the result of the evaluation. The IF function has three parts. The first part determines if a situation is true or false; the second part determines the result to display if the first part is true; and the third part determines the result to display if the first part is false. It's really not as confusing as it may sound. The syntax is =IF(*item to test, value if true, value if false*).

For example, suppose in cell C1 you want to find out if the value in cell B5 is greater than the value in cell B6. If B5 is larger than B6 (true), you want to enter "Yes" in cell C1; if B5 is not larger than B6 (false), you want the answer "No" in cell C1. You would enter the function as =IF(B5>B6,"Yes","No"). Look at the steps needed to create an IF function and its arguments:

1. Type =IF(in the cell in which you want to display the answer. Excel will immediately identify the entry as a function and display a tip box with the function syntax.

2. Type the first argument including an operator. This is the condition you want Excel to evaluate.

3. Type a comma to begin the second argument and then type the result you want if the evaluation is true. The true result can be a value, a calculation, or text.

> If you want the result to be text, the result must be enclosed in quotation marks. The quotation marks will not be displayed in the answer. No quotation marks are needed if the result is numeric.

4. Type a comma to begin the third argument and type the result you want if the evaluation is false. The false result can also be a value, a calculation, or text.

5. Type the closing parenthesis and then press the Enter key. Excel calculates and displays the evaluation result.

In the example in Figure 9-16, the IF function checks whether the total project days is less than the goal of 130 days. If it is, Yes! is displayed; if not, No is displayed.

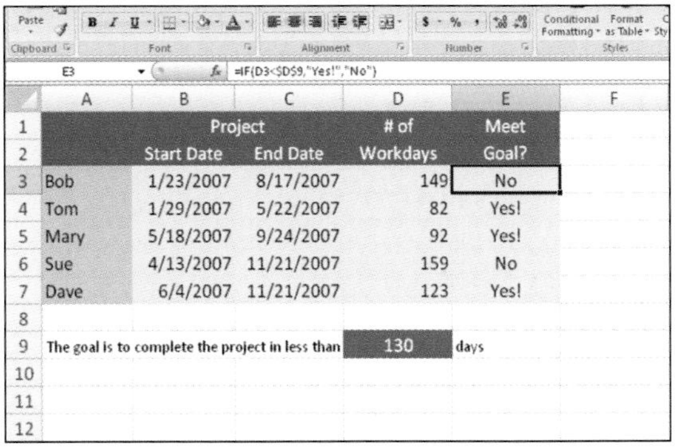

Figure 9-16
Using the IF function.

Looking Up with Lookup Functions

The Lookup category contains functions designed to save you time by finding related data. If you work with large lists in Excel, you can use lookup functions to retrieve individual records from those lists quickly. Two commonly used lookup functions are the VLOOKUP and the HLOOKUP.

The V stands for vertical and the H stands for horizontal. You use VLOOKUP when you need to search through columns of information, and you use HLOOKUP when you need to search through rows of information.

The VLOOKUP actual syntax is VLOOKUP (*lookup_value,table_array,col_index_num*), but let's see if we can translate that into something a little simpler. To understand this formula, take a look at the table in Figure 9-17. We'll use it to illustrate the VLOOKUP function.

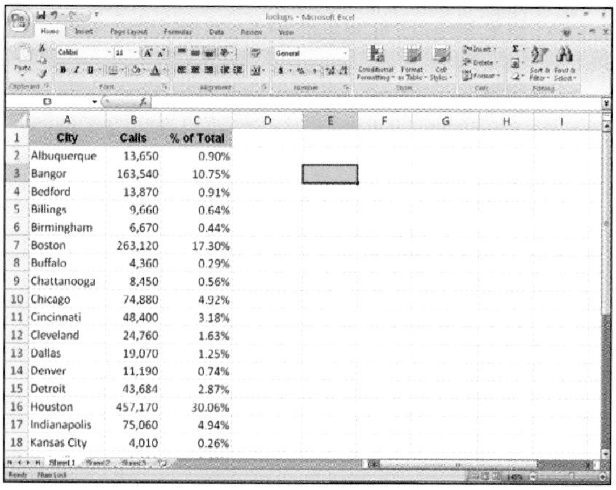

Figure 9-17
A typical lookup table.

The first argument *lookup_value* is really asking for where Excel finds the value you want to match, so we'll rename it *lookup cell*. In our example, we want to know how many calls were made to a specific city, which we will enter in cell E3, so the first argument is in cell E3. (For ease in understanding, I highlighted the *lookup cell* in yellow.)

> One important factor with VLOOKUP (and HLOOKUP) is that the first column (or first row) MUST be in alphabetical order. See Chapter 11, "Managing Large Amounts of Data" for instructions on sorting your data.

The second argument *table_array* is prompting you to specify where you have your list. We'll call it *list area*. You can enter a range name or you can specify the range of cells. Do not include column headings. In our example, our list is in cells A2 through C31, which we specify as A2:C31.

The third argument asks which column of the list we want to extract. Again referring to our example, since we want the number of calls, we need the second column.

So after translating the VLOOKUP to read =VLOOKUP(*lookup cell, list area, column number*) we need to enter =VLOOKUP(E3,A2:C31,2), which gives us a result of 9,490. If you type another city in cell E3—Boston, for example—you get a result of 263,120. You can verify those results by manually looking up Louisville or Boston in the list (see Figure 9-18).

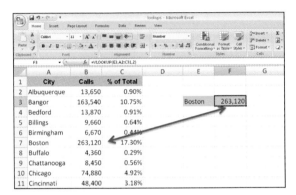

Figure 9-18
VLOOKUP results.

The steps in the previous section used the VLOOKUP function because the data resided in columns. In a VLOOKUP the data resides in rows. HLOOKUP works just like the VLOOKUP except it looks in the top row of the list and returns the value of the indicated cell.

The HLOOKUP syntax is HLOOKUP(*lookup_value,table_array,row_index_num*) or as we translated earlier, =HLOOKUP(*lookup cell, list area, row number*). Figure 9-19 illustrates the HLOOKUP function in action.

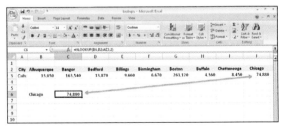

Figure 9-19
HLOOKUP results.

Writing Text Functions

The text category typically works with the text in a cell. The cell could have numbers, but the function in the category doesn't handle them as values in that it doesn't add values such as 2+3 to equal 5. Depending on the text function it might add them together as cells so that a cell with 2 and a cell with 3 becomes 23, or APPLE and PIE become APPLE PIE. Other functions reveal only a specified number of characters such as the 3 characters on the left side of the cell (YORKSHIRE becomes YOR) or the right four characters (YORKSHIRE becomes HIRE). Take a look at a few of the text functions:

▶ **CONCATENATE: This function joins together several text cell strings into a single text string. For example, if in cell A2 you had Mary and in cell B2 you had Jones, if you concatenate them you end up with Mary Jones. The syntax is =CONCATENATE (***cell address or value or text1, cell address or value or text2, cell address or value or text 3***). You can add together up to 255 different text strings, numbers, or cell references. Let's look at the above example. If you simply entered the function as =CONCATENATE(B2,C2) you end up with MaryJones. You need to enter =CONCATENATE(B2," ",C2) like you see in Figure 9-20, which provides Mary Jones. The second argument was a space, and all manually entered text must be enclosed in quotes.**

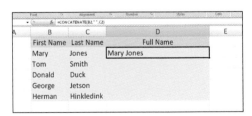

Figure 9-20
Adding several text cells together.

- **RIGHT: Provides a specified number of characters from the right side of a cell. (There's also a LEFT function that provides a specified number of characters from the left side of a cell.) As an example, beginning at cell A2, you have a list of inventory items that begin with a two-digit vendor code and then a three-digit part number such as 63174. For your purpose you need only the part number, which is the three characters on the right. The syntax is =RIGHT(*cell address, number of characters*), so you would enter =RIGHT(B2,3), which returns the value 174 (see Figure 9-21).**

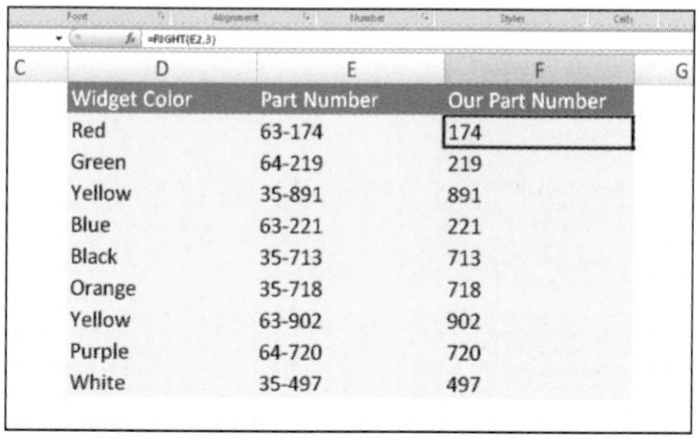

Widget Color	Part Number	Our Part Number
Red	63-174	174
Green	64-219	219
Yellow	35-891	891
Blue	63-221	221
Black	35-713	713
Orange	35-718	718
Yellow	63-902	902
Purple	64-720	720
White	35-497	497

Figure 9-21
Extracting characters.

- **PROPER: The PROPER function capitalizes the first letter in each word of the cell text. If you have The *dog is gone* in cell G5, using the PROPER command results in *The Dog Is Gone.* The syntax is =PROPER(*cell address*).**
- **UPPER: Converts cell text to all uppercase letters. The syntax is =UPPER(*cell address*). If the value of cell C3 is John Smith, entering UPPER(C3) results in JOHN SMITH. There is also a LOWER command that uses the same command to convert cell text to all lowercase letters.**
- **TRIM: The TRIM function removes any extra spaces but leaves one space between each word. The syntax is =TRIM(*cell address*).**
- **REPT: The REPT function allows you to repeat characters a specified number of times. The syntax is =REPT(*what characters, number of times to repeat).* If cell G5 had a value of 12, then if you enter =REPT("*", G5) the answer cell would show 12 asterisks. You can specify more than one character such as */ or <>.**

Getting Help with Excel Functions

With each Excel function having a different syntax, it becomes almost impossible to remember the syntax of each function. You've already seen that when you begin typing the function and the open parenthesis, Excel displays a function Screen Tip to help you, but you can get even more help with functions by using the Insert Function feature. Just follow these steps:

1. Click the cell where you want to enter a function.
2. Choose Formulas>Function Library>Insert Function. Excel automatically inserts the equal (=) sign in your selected cell and the Insert Function dialog box opens.
3. Click the "Or select a category" arrow and choose a function category. If you don't know the category, choose All (see Figure 9-22).

If you don't know the name of the function you want, in the search box, type a description of what you want to do, then click Go. Excel displays a list of possible functions to meet your needs.

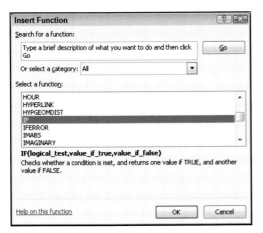

Figure 9-22

Selecting a function from the Insert Function box.

4. Choose the function you want. The function syntax and a description of the function displays under the function list.

5. Click OK, which opens the Function Arguments dialog box. In the selected cell, Excel inserts the Function name and the parentheses.

Since some function arguments are optional, in the Function Arguments dialog box, Excel lists the required arguments in bold.

6. In the first argument box, type the cell address, actual value, or click on the cell that contains the argument.

7. Click in the next argument box and repeat the previous step. As you click in each argument, Excel displays a description. Repeat until all required arguments have a cell reference or a value. Figure 9-23 illustrates the IF function arguments dialog box and Figure 9-24 illustrates the VLOOKUP arguments dialog box.

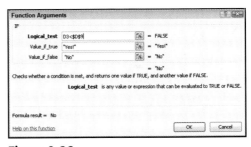

Figure 9-23

The IF function and its arguments.

Figure 9-24

The VLOOKUP function and its arguments.

8. Click on OK. The Function Arguments dialog box will close and Excel displays the function result in the selected cell.

Troubleshooting Errors

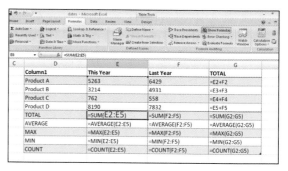

Figure 9-25
Displaying the actual formulas.

G IGO: GARBAGE IN, GARBAGE OUT. That's what happens if you enter incorrect data into your worksheet. The answers become garbage and are useless. To help you locate potential problems, Excel provides a number of tools.

Viewing Formulas

As you've already seen, when you create formulas, the result of the formulas is what Excel displays in the worksheet. Although the Edit bar displays the actual formula, you can view only one formula at a time. Excel provides a method to view the formulas in the cells. Having the formulas display is a wonderful tool for proofing and troubleshooting formula errors in your worksheet.

Choose Formulas>Formula Auditing>Show Formulas. Excel displays the formulas in each cell instead of the formula result. Each cell reference in a formula is assigned a color and a corresponding colored box surrounds the referenced cell whenever you click a cell with a formula (see Figure 9-25). If you print the worksheet while the formulas are displayed, the formulas will print, not the formula results.

> A shortcut key to turn formula display on and off is Ctrl+` (grave accent).

Understanding Common Formula Error Messages

There are a number of error messages that may appear when you type a formula. Some are typing mistakes and some may be a result of a cell value.

> Often when you enter a formula with an error, Excel notifies you of the error and either attempts to correct the error for you or offers suggestions for correcting the error.

Other errors may appear in the formula result cell. Following are a few of the more common error messages.

▶ **#DIV/0!: This means that the formula is trying to divide by either an empty cell or one with a value of zero (see Figure 9-26).**

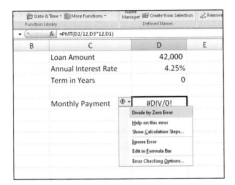

Figure 9-26
Divide by zero error.

▶ **#REF!:** This may mean that the formula includes an invalid cell reference.

▶ **Circular:** This means that a formula in a cell refers to the same cell. Excel displays a circular reference notation in the status bar. Excel may also display an error box and display a Circular Reference help window to assist you in locating the erroneous formula. In Figure 9-27, the formula in B10 is trying to add itself to the total, thereby creating the circular reference.

Figure 9-27
Circular reference error.

Identifying Formula Precedents and Dependents

The Formula Auditing features can assist you in tracing through formulas such as when resolving worksheet errors. The Formula Auditing features display tracer arrows, which are arrows that show the relationship between the active cell and its related cells. It traces *dependents*, which are other cells that are affected *by* the current cell, and *precedents*, which are other cells that affect the current cell.

Select a cell that contains a formula or one that is referenced in one or more formulas and choose Formulas>Formula Auditing>Trace Precedents, or choose Formulas>Formula Auditing>Trace Dependents. As you see in Figure 9-28, Excel displays one or more blue arrows pointing out dependents or precedents. You see where cell E3 is the dependent for cells E6, E7, E8, E9, and G3.

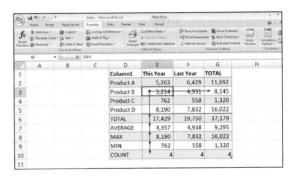

Figure 9-28
Viewing formula precedents.

To remove the dependent or precedent tracings, click Formulas>Formula Auditing>Remove Arrows.

10

Making Your Worksheet Look
Good

PICTURE YOURSELF GROWING A BONSAI tree. It begins as a small root and though careful shaping and care becomes a beautiful work of art. The overall artistic effect is of great significance in growing the trees. Everything must be proportional: the size of the tree, its leaves or needles, its flowers or fruit, and the container in which it grows. The container, especially, must be chosen to harmonize with the tree in size, shape, and color.

In Excel, you begin with a blank worksheet, add in your data, and then you find that columns often aren't wide enough, fonts are too small to read, dates display in an unusual manner, and when you have columns of data stacked next to each other, sometimes the information begins to overlap. It just plain looks boring.

Fortunately, Excel includes a plethora of features with which you can make the worksheet more interesting and easier to read. Change the fonts, or make the numbers easier to read by adding numeric formatting. Liven up your worksheet with effective use of borders, lines, and color. Whoever said "Looks aren't everything" wasn't staring at an unformatted Excel spreadsheet. This chapter is about shaping your worksheet into its own work of art.

Changing Cell Formats

YOU CAN CHANGE THE SIZE or appearance of any cell regardless of content. For example, by default, values are displayed as general numbers; however, you can choose to display values as currency, percentages, fractions, dates, and many other formats. You can make your titles large and bold so they are quickly noticed.

Formatting Values

The Excel Ribbon provides several methods you can use for formatting values. First, there are buttons on the Home tab of the Ribbon that include several popular number styles: accounting, percentages, and commas. You can also choose from the Number Format drop-down list, or you can open the Format Cells dialog box where you'll see all available options.

Select the cells you want formatted. You can select a few cells, entire rows, entire columns, or the entire worksheet. Choose Home>Number>and select from the following options (see Figure 10-1):

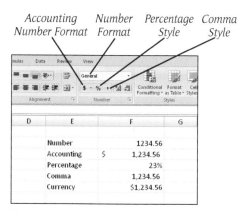

Figure 10-1
Numeric values formatted with different styles.

▶ **Accounting Number Format:** The Accounting option has a drop-down list from which you can select different international currency symbols.

▶ **Percentage Style:** When changing numbers to display as a percentage, Excel automatically multiplies the cell value by 100 and displays the result with a percent symbol and no decimal points. For example, if the cell has a value of 15, Excel displays 1500%; however, if the cell has a value of 0.15, Excel displays 15%.

▶ **Comma Style:** When you apply a comma style to selected values, Excel separates the thousands, making the data easier to read. The Comma option also automatically adds two decimal places but does not include a dollar sign.

▶ **Number Format:** Choose the drop-down arrow to display a list of options such as seen in Figure 10-2. This figure illustrates values formatted in various Excel styles. Notice the different dollar sign placement in the Accounting and Currency types. Accounting and Currency format may appear the same, but they really are different. The difference is in the placement of the dollar sign. In currency style, the dollar sign is right next to the numbers, but in accounting style, the dollar sign is on the left edge of the cell.

Figure 10-2
Choose from several format options.

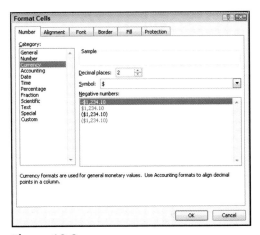

Figure 10-3
The Format Cells dialog box.

Another method for selecting number formatting is using the Number Dialog Box Launcher, which displays the Format Cells dialog box seen in Figure 10-3. Number format selections are on the Number tab.

The Format Cells dialog box allows you to select from several different number formatting styles, including choosing whether to display negative numbers in red, choosing the number of decimal points, and even selecting the desired type of currency symbol. There is also a "Special" category where you can format numbers to match the pattern for telephone numbers or social security numbers.

As mentioned earlier, by default, the comma and currency styles include two decimal places, and percentages don't include decimal points. If you have a number in a formatted cell with more than the two decimal points, Excel rounds up the number. So if you enter 75.257 in a cell, then format that cell to comma or currency, Excel displays $75.26. There are Ribbon buttons, however, that allow you to increase or decrease the number of decimal places. Excel numbers can display up to 30 decimal places.

Select the cells you want formatted and choose Home>Number>Increase Decimal. Each click of the button adds another decimal digit to the right of the decimal point (see Figure 10-4).

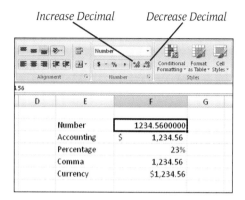

Figure 10-4

Easily add or remove decimal places.

If a formatted value cannot fit within the width of a cell, Excel may display a series of ###. You will discover how to widen a column later in this chapter.

To remove digits to the right of the decimal point, choose Home>Number>Decrease Decimal. Each click removes a number from the far right of the decimal point and rounds the value in the cell.

Designing with Fonts

Excel uses a default font of Calibri, but from the Home tab of the Ribbon you can easily change the font typeface, size, and style. *Fonts* are typefaces in different styles that give your text character and impact. Your selection of fonts varies depending on the software installed on your computer.

The default font size in an Excel worksheet is 11 points. There are approximately 72 points in an inch, so a 10-point font is slightly less than one-seventh of an inch tall.

Additionally, Excel includes three different font styles other than plain text that you can select from the Ribbon. Font styles include **bold**, underline, and *italics*. Here are the steps you take to change fonts and font attributes:

1. Select the cells you want to format.

2. On the Home tab, open the Font drop-down menu and select a font. If you hover your mouse over a font before clicking it, Excel displays the selected cells in the different fonts (see Figure 10-5).

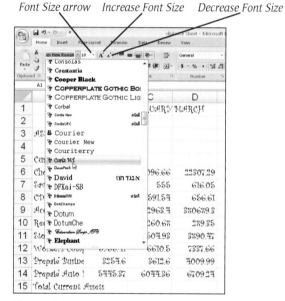

Figure 10-5

Direct attention to cells by changing the font face.

3. From the Home>Font group, click the Font Size arrow and select a font size.

Optionally, click the Increase Font Size or the Decrease Font Size button to increment or decrease the font size one step at a time.

4. From the Home>Font group, click an attribute such as Bold, Italic, or Underline (see Figure 10-6). The Bold, Italic, and Underline buttons are toggle switches, meaning that one click turns them on, but if you click again, Excel turns them off.

Bold   Italic   Underline

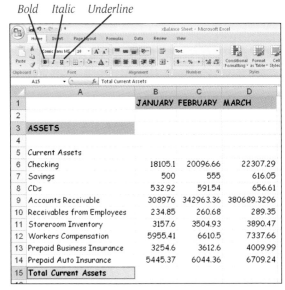

Figure 10-6
Enhance cell data with text attributes.

Shortcut keys for Bold, Italic, and Underline are Ctrl+B, Ctrl+I, and Ctrl+U, respectively.

Underlining is not the same as a cell border. (Cell borders are discussed later in this chapter.) The default underline style is a single underline. Click the Underline button down arrow to select Double Underline. Or, choose additional underline options through the Font Dialog Box Launcher, which displays the Format Cells dialog box. Underline options appear on the Font tab, as in Figure 10-7.

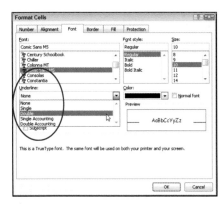

Figure 10-7
Choose from these underline options.

To change the default Excel font, choose Office>Excel Options. From the Popular section, click the "Use this font" drop-down arrow and select the font you want in all new workbooks. Click OK twice.

Changing Data Color

If you want to add color to your worksheet, try changing the font color. Select the cells you want to format and choose Home>Font and click the Font Color drop-down arrow to select a color. Excel's Live Preview feature, as you see in Figure 10-8, shows you the selected cells in the new font colors.

The colors you see depend on which theme you are using. See "Working with Themes," later in this chapter.

Figure 10-8
Choosing a color for your text.

Another method to select Font color is through the Font group Dialog Box Launcher, which displays the Format Cells dialog box. Font color selection is on the Font tab.

Working with Date Formats

As you learned in Chapter 8, "Creating a Basic Excel Worksheet," Excel may not display a date in the same format as you entered the data. A couple of date format options are accessible through the Number Format drop-down list, but more extensive options are offered in the Format Cells dialog box.

Select the cell that has a date you want formatted and then, from the Home tab, click the Number Dialog Box Launcher, which displays the Format Cells dialog box. Click the Date category, as seen in Figure 10-9, which displays a variety of different date formats. Select a format for the selected cells and click the OK button.

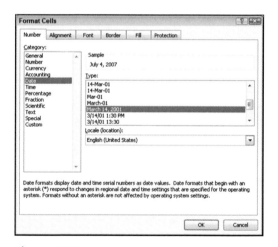

Figure 10-9
A few of the available Excel date formats.

Working with Alignment and Spacing

IN THE PREVIOUS SECTION, you worked with font face, size, color, and so forth of cells. In this section, you discover how to change the worksheet itself so you can see more (or less) of the information in the individual cells, and especially how the cell contents line up with the cell edges.

Adjusting Column Width

By default, Excel columns are 8.43 points wide. When the content of a cell is too long to fit into its cell, depending on the type of data, Excel may automatically widen the column or display the information in a different format. You can manually resize a column so all data displays correctly.

If a label does not fit into the cell, the contents spill into the next cell to the right, if the next cell is empty. If the next cell is not empty, Excel displays only the amount of text that fits into the cell. The extra text is not cut off, it's just not displayed.

If a value is too wide, Excel may do one of several things:

▶ **Display the number in scientific notation so it displays in fewer characters.**

▶ **Automatically widen the cell.**

▶ **Truncate the value's decimal points.**

▶ **Display the data as a series of number signs (#).**

The following steps show you how you can widen a column:

1. To adjust the width of columns headings, select the headings of the columns you want widened. If you want to adjust a single column, click any cell in that column or select the column heading.

2. Choose a method to adjust column width:

▶ **To manually change the width of columns, position the mouse pointer on the right boundary of the column heading until it turns into a double-ended arrow. Drag until the column is the width that you want. As you move the pointer, a ScreenTip displays the new width. In Figure 10-10 you see the expansion of column A.**

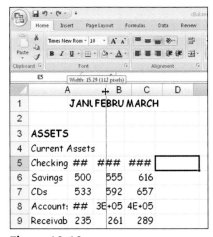

Figure 10-10
Manually changing column width.

Excel displays cell width in characters and pixels instead of in inches. The minimum column width is 0 characters, and the maximum is 255 characters.

▶ **To set column width to a specific setting, choose Home>Cells>Format> Column Width. The Column Width dialog box, shown in Figure 10-11, appears. Type the exact width you want; then click OK.**

Figure 10-11
The Column Width dialog box.

▶ **To automatically change the column width so it fits the widest entry, double-click the boundary on the right side of the column heading or choose Home>Cells>Format>AutoFit Column Width. The column automatically expands to fit the widest entry in the column.**

The default column width is 8.43 based on the default 11-point Calibri font. If you change the default font type or size, Excel may also change the standard column width. You can manually set a default column width by choosing Home>Cells>Format>Default Width.

Changing Row Height

When you change to a larger font, Excel usually enlarges the row height to accommodate the larger font size. You can also manually resize the row height. Highlight the row headings whose height you want to adjust and do one of the following:

Excel displays row height in characters and pixels instead of in inches.

▶ **Manually change the row height. Position the mouse pointer on the bottom boundary of the row heading until it turns into a double-ended arrow. Drag until the row is the height that you want. As you move the pointer, a ScreenTip displays the new height. In Figure 10-12, you see the height of row 1 increasing.**

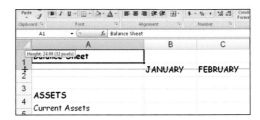

Figure 10-12
Increasing row height manually.

▶ **Set row height to a specific setting by choosing Home>Cells>Format>Row Height. The Row Height dialog box appears. Type the exact height you want, and then click OK.**

▶ To automatically change the height of the row so it fits the tallest entry in the row, double-click the boundary on the bottom of the row heading or choose Home>Cells>Format>AutoFit Row Height. Excel examines the rows contents and sets the height slightly larger than the tallest entry.

The default row height is 15 points based on the default 11-point Calibri font. If you change the default font type or size, Excel may also change the standard row height. You cannot manually set a default row height.

Aligning Data

By default, Excel makes labels left-aligned and values right-aligned to their cells. You can change the alignment of cells individually or in a block so they are aligned left, right, centered, or full justified. You can also wrap text in the cells when the text is too long to fit in one cell and you don't want it to overlap to the next cell. Additionally, Excel aligns text vertically to the bottom of the row, but you can also center it or align it to the top of the cell.

Begin by selecting the cells you want to align and choosing Home>Alignment. Then, select one of these alignment buttons:

▶ **Align Text Left**: Horizontally aligns the data along the left edge of the cell.

▶ **Center**: Centers the data horizontally in the middle of the cell. If you modify the column width, the data remains centered to the new column width. Cells B2 through D2 are center-aligned in Figure 10-13.

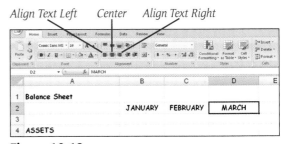

Align Text Left   Center   Align Text Right

Figure 10-13
Aligning cell contents horizontally.

▶ **Align Text Right**: Horizontally aligns the data along the right edge of the cell.

Values formatted as accounting display only as right aligned. You can change alignment on all other formatting styles.

▶ **Top Align**: Aligns the data vertically along the top edge of the cell.

▶ **Middle Align**: Centers the data vertically in the cell.

▶ **Bottom Align**: This is the default option and aligns the data along the bottom edge of the cell. Notice the heading in Figure 10-14. Cell A1 shows a top center alignment whereas cells B2 through C2 show the default bottom alignment.

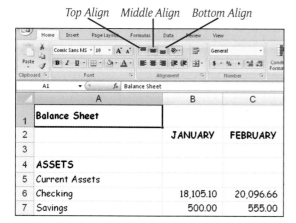

Figure 10-14

Vertical cell alignment.

Optionally, you can view additional alignment options and align both the horizontal and vertical alignment at the same time using the Format Cells dialog box. From the Home tab, click the Alignment group Dialog Box Launcher. If necessary, click the Alignment tab and then set any desired alignment options, and then click OK.

Merging Cells

Sometimes the rectangular grid can get in the way of your design creativity. Perhaps just one cell in the worksheet is too small, or you want to center text across a group of columns to create attractive headings. Fortunately, you can merge multiple cells. Select the cell containing the data you want to merge and the cells you want to include in the merge. The data cell must be in the left cell of the selection and the other cells cannot contain data, as shown in Figure 10-15.

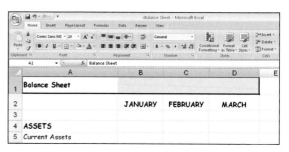

Figure 10-15

Selecting the cells you want to merge.

Choose Home>Alignment>Merge & Center. All the selected cells merge into one larger cell, and the data is centered horizontally. If you select cells vertically and choose the Merge and Center command, Excel merges the cells and vertically bottom-aligns the data. See Figure 10-16, which shows cells A1 through D1 merged horizontally and cells A4 through A5 merged vertically.

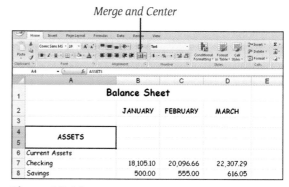

Figure 10-16

Merging cells can create a title for the worksheet.

In this example, it appears that the heading is located in Columns B and C; however, the text is still in Column A. If you need to change the text, be sure to select Column A, not Column B, C, or D.

After clicking Merge & Center, you can change the alignment. Click the Merge & Center button again to unmerge the cells from each other.

Indenting Cell Data

What about those cells that you want left aligned, but not all the way to the edge? You could insert some spaces in front of the text, but because of font styles, the text doesn't always line up evenly. If you insert spaces in front of values, Excel simply ignores them. So what can you do? You can use the Indent buttons. Just follow these steps:

1. Select the cells you want to indent

2. Choose Home>Alignment>Increase Indent. Each Increase Indent click adds a small amount of space between the cell border and the data itself. See Figure 10-17, where cells A7 through A15 are indented. How Excel indents depends on how you format the cell:

► **If the data is left aligned, Excel indents to the left.**

► **If the data is right aligned, Excel indents to the right.**

► **If the data is centered, with the first click Excel indents to the right, but subsequent clicks cause Excel to move the data to the left.**

Click the Decrease Indent button to remove indentation.

Wrapping Text in a Cell

The Wrap Text feature treats each cell like a miniature word processor, with text wrapping around in the cell.

1. Select the cells you want to format.

2. Choose Home>Alignment>Wrap Text. As in Figure 10-18, if the selected text cells contain more text than will fit the width of the cell, Excel displays it on multiple lines. Notice that Excel automatically increases row height to accommodate the additional text lines.

To force a new line of text in a wrapped cell, press Alt+Enter where you want the new line to begin.

Decrease Indent   *Increase Indent*

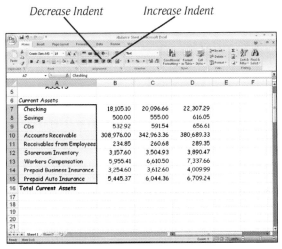

Figure 10-17
Indenting helps set data apart from other cells.

Wrap text button

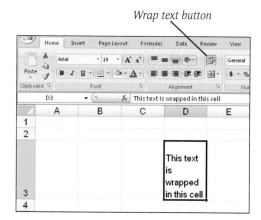

Figure 10-18

A worksheet cell with wrapped text.

If you open the Format Cells dialog box, you see a Shrink to Fit option on the Alignment tab. This option allows Excel to automatically change the font size in the selected cell to force the data to fit within the cell's current width. Use caution with this option; the text may become so small that it's unreadable.

Rotating Cell Text

Another feature you can use to dress up your worksheet is to rotate the text. Rotating text is often helpful for headings, but I wouldn't recommend it for your actual data. It can be a little difficult to read. The following steps show you how to rotate text:

1. Select the cells you want to format.

2. Choose Home>Alignment>Orientation. A list of options appears:

   ▶ **Angle Counterclockwise:** Angles the text in the cell from left bottom to right top.

   ▶ **Angle Clockwise:** Angles the text in the cell from left top to right bottom.

   ▶ **Vertical Text:** Centers the text and places one letter on top of the other.

   ▶ **Rotate Text Up:** Places the text on the lower-right side of the cell and runs it vertically up the cell.

   ▶ **Rotate Text Down:** Places the text on the upper-left side of the cell and runs it vertically down the cell.

Choose Format Cell Alignment to open the Format Cells dialog box where you can select a specific degree of rotation.

3. Choose an option. The selected cells take the rotation you choose. In Figure 10-19, you see heading cells angled counterclockwise.

Orientation button

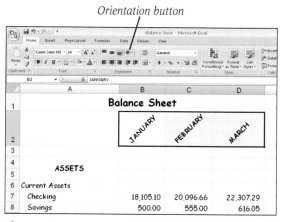

Figure 10-19

Rotating cell data to add a special effect.

Adding Borders and Shading

ON THE SCREEN, each cell has a light gray border around it, but those borders do not print by default. That's called the grid, and it is there for the ease of viewing each cell independently. In fact, you can turn the grid display off and on by clicking View>Show/Hide>Gridlines. If you want borders around your cells, whether around the entire cell, or just on a part of the cell, Excel provides a tool to easily create printable lines. You can also add pizzazz to your worksheet by adding backgrounds and patterns.

Figure 10-20
Creating cell border lines.

Placing Borders Around Cells

You can add border lines to individual cells and groups of cells. A border can appear around all sides of the cell or only on certain sides, such as the top or bottom. Different from an underline, which runs directly under letters and numbers, a border flows across the entire width or height of a cell.

To add a border, select the appropriate cells. Choose Home>Font and then click the arrow next to the Borders button. A variety of border options appears, as you see in Figure 10-20.

> The Borders tooltip button may display Bottom Border, Top Border, or whatever border was last used.

Select the border you want. Excel applies the border to the selected cells. Optionally, click the More Borders option, which opens the Format Cells dialog box. From there you can select even more border styles, colors, and options.

Applying Cell Background Colors

Adding a background color to a cell or group of cells can make your worksheet more interesting and can call attention to specific areas of the worksheet. Excel calls the background color the Fill color.

Select the cells to which you want to add background color. From the Home tab, in the Font group, click the down arrow next to the Fill Color icon. A gallery of colors appears (see Figure 10-21).

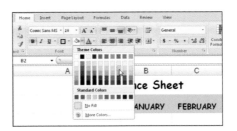

Figure 10-21
Choosing a color for cell background shading.

Select the cell background color you want or choose More Colors to create your own shading color. To remove cell background shading, choose No Fill.

> A good combination to use with a black and white printer is a black background and a light font color.

Adding Cell Patterns

You can use a pattern instead of a single color as a background to your cells. A pattern uses two colors, arranged in some design, such as stripes or dots. Each pattern has both a background and a foreground color. The background color is the base color, whereas the foreground color is the color of the stripes or dots. Be careful using patterns because they can be distracting to the reader.

The following steps show you how to add fill patterns.

1. Select the cells you want formatted.

2. Choose Home>Cells>Format>Format Cells as you see in Figure 10-22, which launches the Format Cells dialog box.

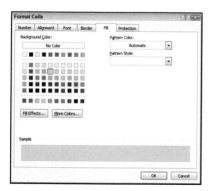

Figure 10-22
Format Cells options.

> Optionally, click the Dialog Box Launcher from either the Font, Alignment, or Number group.

3. From the Fill tab, click the down arrow next to Pattern Style and select a pattern of your choosing (see Figure 10-23).

> Click the Fill Effects button to choose a gradient instead of a pattern.

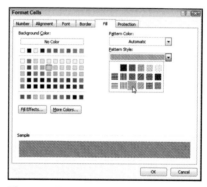

Figure 10-23
Choosing a cell pattern.

4. From the Pattern Color drop-down list, optionally choose a color for your pattern.

5. Click the OK button.

Discovering Formatting Shortcuts

SO FAR YOU'VE LEARNED quite a few ways to dress up your worksheet. There appears to be a button for just about anything. Now, however, you need to speed up the process of formatting worksheets. Fortunately, Excel includes several features to assist you.

Using the Mini Toolbar

In Chapter 3, you discovered that while formatting text in Word, you could use the Mini Toolbar to provide quick access to commonly used formatting features. Excel also provides a Mini Toolbar which contains many of the formatting commands available on the Home tab, making it unnecessary for you to actually switch to the Home tab. The usefulness of the Mini Toolbar comes from the fact you don't have to move your mouse so far to select the commands from the Ribbon.

Along with a context-sensitive shortcut menu, the Mini Toolbar appears whenever you right-click on a cell or group of cells (see Figure 10-24). Choose the formatting attribute you want to apply. The cells take the selected attributes and the Mini Toolbar remains open for you to make additional selections. Click any cell to close the Mini Toolbar.

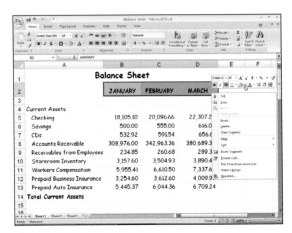

Figure 10-24
Save mouse movement by using the Mini Toolbar.

Copy Formatting

Sometimes it takes a lot of time and effort to get the formatting of a cell just the way you want it. Rather than duplicate all those steps for another cell, Excel includes a Format Painter feature that copies formatting from one cell to another. Copied formatting includes font size, color, style attributes, shading, and alignment. When you copy the formatting, the values in the cells are not affected.

1. Click a cell containing formatting you want to copy.

2. Choose Home>Clipboard>Format Painter. The mouse pointer is a white plus sign along with a paint brush like the one you see in Figure 10-25.

Double-click the Format Painter tool to lock it in so you can paint additional cells without having to reselect the tool. Click the Format Painter tool again to unlock it.

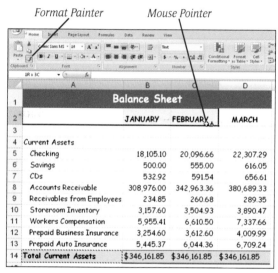

Figure 10-25
Use the format painter tool to duplicate formatting selections.

3. Click or drag across the cells you want to format. Excel immediately applies formats such as font, size, colors, borders, and alignment.

To quickly copy the width of one column to another column, select the heading of the first column, click the Format Painter tool, and then click the heading of the column where you want to apply the column width.

Working with Themes

In Chapter 3, you discovered that you could use Office themes, which are professionally designed predefined sets of colors, fonts, and other effects that you can apply to your Office documents. Themes are consistent throughout all Office documents, so using them brings continuity to your work. The default theme used by Excel is called the Office theme, but there are quite a few others. Take a brief look at how changing a theme changes the options Excel provides.

Themes are available in Word, Excel, PowerPoint, and Outlook. They are not available in Publisher.

In Figure 10-26, which has the standard Office theme, you see that the default font is Calibri 11 point and you see some of the coordinating colors available from the Fill Color drop-down list.

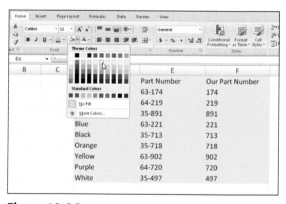

Figure 10-26
Office theme options.

Now look at Figure 10-27, which is the Verve theme. The default font is Century Gothic and the theme colors available under the Fill Color drop-down list are much more vibrant, than the ones available with the standard Office theme.

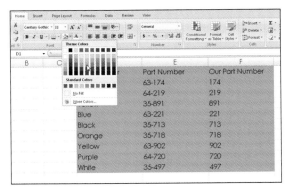

Figure 10-27

Verve theme options.

To choose a different theme for your Excel Worksheet, choose Page Layout>Themes>Themes. A variety of theme choices from which you can select appears, as you see in Figure 10-28.

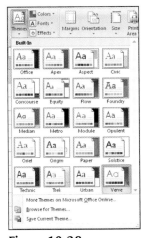

Figure 10-28

Choose your favorite theme.

Using Cell Styles

Based on themes, Cell Styles let you quickly apply a group of formatting options to a selected group of cells. The choices you have available depend on the theme you choose for your document. The following steps show you how to apply Cell Styles.

1. Select the cells you want to format.

2. Choose Home>Styles>Cell Styles. In Figure 10-29, you see that Excel displays a gallery of predefined styles. This worksheet is using the Flow theme.

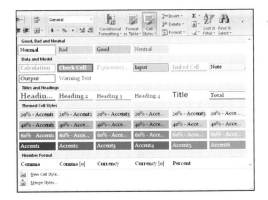

Figure 10-29

Select from many different cell styles.

Excel styles include Normal (the default style for regular cell text), Heading 1 through Heading 4 (suitable for worksheet headings), Accent1 through Accent6 (font and fill effects to make text stand out), and several data model styles (Calculation, Input, Output, and so on).

3. Excel's Live Preview shows your choice before you actually apply it. Select the style you want to use.

Conditional Formatting

WHEN YOU USE CONDITIONAL formatting, you can instruct Excel to change the formatting for a cell if the cell's value meets a certain criteria. You use conditional formatting to visually annotate your data for both analytical and presentation purposes or to easily find exceptions and to spot important trends. For example, if sales for any salesperson falls beneath their quota, you could have Excel automatically format it in red or with shading or borders. Follow these simple steps:

1. Select the cells to which you want to apply conditional formatting.

> Reasons for using conditional formatting might include locating dates that meet a certain condition (such as falling on a Saturday or Sunday), specifying highest or lowest values in a range, or indicating values that fall under or over a specified amount.

2. Choose Home>Styles>Conditional Formatting>Highlight Cell Rules.

3. Select the criteria you want to use. Criteria options include Greater Than, Less Than, Between, Equal To, Text That Contains, A Date Occurring, and Duplicate Values. A dialog box opens where you can specify the value. In Figure 10-30, in order to see which items went over budget, you use the Greater Than criteria.

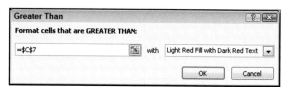

Figure 10-30
Specifying conditions for formatting.

4. Enter the values you want to reference in the text box. The number of boxes depends on the criteria you selected in Step 3. You can type a value here, such as 500, or you can reference a cell address such as F13.

5. Click the drop-down arrow next to the format options so you can specify the format options to employ if the condition you specified is true. Live Preview shows you what your data will look like.

> Click the Custom Format option where you can create your own format, selecting from font styles and color, numeric and other formats, borders, patterns, or background color.

6. Click OK. (In Figure 10-31, you see formatting options applied to three cells that meet the specified criteria of being greater than the budget amount).

7. Repeat Steps 2 through 6 to apply any additional conditions.

	A	B	C
1		Current Month	Current Month
2		Actual	Budget
3			
4	**Expenses**		
5	Auto	0.00	1,500.00
6	Depreciation	2,361.88	2,500.00
7	Insurance	422.10	250.00
8	Cleaning	300.00	350.00
9	Legal	657.38	0.00
10	Office	0.00	75.00
11	Payroll Tax	1,437.87	2,850.00
12	Rent	2,500.00	2,100.00
13	Salaries	8,059.09	16,350.00
14	Utilities	97.64	400.00
15			
16	**Total Expenses**	15,835.96	26,375.00

Figure 10-31

Cells with conditional formatting applied.

> To clear conditional formats, go to the Home tab and choose Styles>Conditional Formatting>Clear Rules>Clear Rules from Selected Cells.

Another form of conditional formatting, new to Excel 2007, are Data Visualizations. With Data Visualizations, you see your data conditions even better in the form of gradient colors, data bars, and icon sets.

Select the cells to which you want to apply formatting and choose Home>Styles>Conditional Formatting. Select from the following options. (Figure 10-32 shows an example of all three data visualizations.)

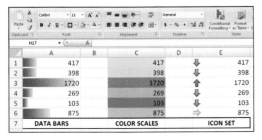

Figure 10-32

Using data visualizations.

▶ **Data Bars**: A gradient-style bar helps you see the value of a cell relative to other cells. The length of the data bar represents the value in the cell, so a longer bar represents a higher value and a shorter bar represents a lower value. The data bars have six different color options designed to match Excel themes.

▶ **Color Scales**: Designed to visually help you understand your data, color scales compare a range of cells by using two colors representing higher or lower values or three colors representing higher, middle, or lower values. The color scale bars come in eight different color themes, including red, yellow, and green. You can also create your own scheme by choosing More Rules under the Color Scales options.

▶ **Icon Sets**: Icon sets help you classify data into three, four, or five categories with each icon representing a range of values such as higher, middle, and lower. As shown in Figure 6-33, icon sets include arrows, traffic lights, clocks, and even flags.

Figure 10-33

Select the icon symbol you want to use to represent your data.

> The icon size you see depends on the cell font size. You may need to adjust the column width to accommodate the icon.

11

Managing Large Amounts of
Data

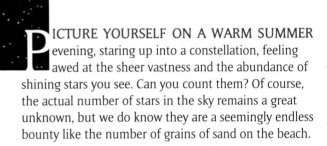

PICTURE YOURSELF ON A WARM SUMMER evening, staring up into a constellation, feeling awed at the sheer vastness and the abundance of shining stars you see. Can you count them? Of course, the actual number of stars in the sky remains a great unknown, but we do know they are a seemingly endless bounty like the number of grains of sand on the beach.

Sometimes working with large amounts of data can make you feel like you'll never find your way through it. Fortunately, Excel contains quite a few tools specifically designed to manage volumes of information.

This chapter is about that volume and how you can easily manage all the data whether on a single sheet, on multiple worksheets, or even in multiple workbooks.

Working with Multiple Worksheets

FIRST LET ME CLARIFY A COUPLE of terms. A *worksheet*, sometimes called a spreadsheet, is a collection of cells that can have more than one million rows down and over sixteen thousand rows across. Each cell of each sheet can contain over 32,000 characters.

By default, each time you create a new Excel file, it contains three worksheets. Technically, Excel calls files with multiple sheets *workbooks*. Think of a workbook as a three-dimensional worksheet. Each workbook, however, can have an almost unlimited number of worksheets, limited only by your computer's memory. The resulting possible number of cells in a single workbook is too huge to even dream about, but the fact remains that you could create a single huge workbook. Realistically, however, you'll probably have a number of different workbooks, each with a number of worksheets.

Excel makes it easy to work with multiple worksheets. You can easily maneuver between the worksheets; insert, delete, move, and copy worksheets; rename the tabs that reference them; and create formulas that reference other worksheets or workbooks.

Moving Between Worksheets

By default, a new blank workbook includes three worksheets named Sheet1, Sheet2, and Sheet3. You can move from worksheet to worksheet using the mouse or the keyboard. With the mouse, click on any desired tab.

If your workbook has more worksheets than you can see at the bottom, click the First, Previous, Next, or Last navigation buttons in the bottom-left corner of the workbook.

You also can use the keyboard to move from worksheet to worksheet. Press Ctrl+Page Up to move to the previous sheet or press Ctrl+ Page Down to move to the next sheet.

Inserting Additional Worksheets

If you need extra worksheets in your workbook, you can easily add them. Whenever you save the Excel file, all worksheets in the workbook are saved. Excel provides several methods to insert additional worksheets:

▶ **Choose Home>Cells>Insert (arrow)> Insert Sheet. Excel automatically inserts a new blank worksheet on top of the currently selected sheet. Excel automatically assigns the next number, such as Sheet4**

▶ **Click the Insert Worksheet tab. It's located after the last named worksheet tab.**

▶ **Right-click a worksheet tab and select Insert from the resulting shortcut menu. The Insert dialog box opens (see Figure 11-1). Choose Worksheet and then click OK.**

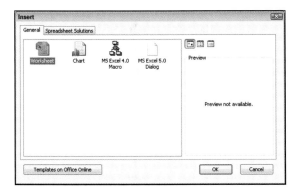

Figure 11-1
Inserting a new worksheet.

Deleting Worksheets

If you have created a worksheet in an Excel file that you no longer need, you can delete it. Deleting unnecessary worksheets can save on file size and make the file quicker to open and close.

Choose Home>Cells>Delete (arrow)>Delete Sheet. If any cells in the selected sheet have data in them, a warning message appears, as shown in Figure 11-2. A worksheet with no data in it will not display the warning message. Click the Delete button. Use caution when deleting worksheets. The Undo feature does not work with the Delete Sheet function.

Figure 11-2
Deleting a worksheet.

Another way to delete a worksheet is to right-click the worksheet tab and choose Delete from the resulting shortcut menu.

Renaming Worksheets

Since Excel uses the rather generic naming scheme of Sheet1 or Sheet2, you can more easily identify the type of data each worksheet contains if you give your worksheets more descriptive names. Names for sheets can be up to 31 characters long and are not case sensitive; however, a worksheet name cannot be left blank and cannot include a few special characters: [−] * / \ ? : [ ]. Just follow these steps to rename a worksheet:

1. Click anywhere on the sheet you want to rename.

2. Choose Home>Cells>Format>Rename Sheet. The worksheet tab becomes highlighted. Leave it highlighted so that you can replace it with a new name.

   Optionally, right-click the worksheet tab and select Rename.

3. Type a unique name for the worksheet, as shown in Figure 11-3. Remember that two worksheets in a single workbook cannot have the same exact name.

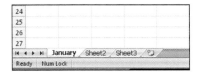

Figure 11-3
Renaming a worksheet.

4. Press Enter to accept the change.

   Be descriptive, but keep the name short. When you have lots of worksheets with long names, it can be more difficult to maneuver from one to the next.

Copying Worksheets

In that if you need a worksheet similar to one you already have, you can copy the worksheet. Then all you have to do in the new worksheet is modify the parts you need changed. You don't need to start at the beginning. The following steps show you how to copy a worksheet:

1. Click anywhere on the worksheet you want to duplicate.

2. Choose Home>Cells>Format>Move or Copy Sheet. The Move or Copy dialog box appears.

> Optionally, right-click the worksheet tab and select Move or Copy.

3. Check the Create a copy check box (see Figure 11-4).

Figure 11-4
Duplicating a worksheet.

4. Select where in the order of the worksheets you want the duplicate sheet placed.

5. Click OK. Excel duplicates the sheet, gives it the same name as the copied sheet, and numbers it sequentially.

> To move a worksheet, drag the worksheet tabs left or right.

Moving Worksheets to a Different Workbook

Although it certainly may be what you need, use caution when you move worksheets to other workbooks. Calculations or charts based on worksheet data might become incorrect when you move a worksheet to another workbook.

> You cannot copy or move a worksheet created in an Excel 2007 workbook to one created in an earlier version of Excel.

1. Open both the workbook containing the sheets you want to move and the workbook to which you will move the sheets.

2. Click anywhere on the worksheet you want to move. If you don't see the sheet you want, click the tab scrolling buttons until you see it.

> If you want to move or copy multiple worksheets, hold down the Ctrl key and click additional tabs. If you want to move or copy all the existing worksheets to another workbook, right-click a sheet tab and choose Select All Sheets.

3. Choose Home>Format>Move or Copy Sheet. The Move or Copy dialog box opens.

Optionally, right-click a selected tab and choose Move or Copy.

4. From the To book drop-down list, shown in Figure 11-5, select the workbook to which you want to move or copy the sheets.

Figure 11-5
Select the workbook you want to move to.

5. If you want to duplicate the sheets to the other workbook, click the Create a copy check box.

6. Select where in the order of the existing worksheets you want the moved sheet placed.

7. Click OK. Excel moves or copies the worksheets to the other workbook. In Figure 11-6, the sheet named Hours by Job was moved from the Time Tickets workbook to the Balance Sheet workbook.

If you opted to copy a sheet to another workbook in which a sheet has the same name, Excel keeps the same name but adds a sequential number to the end.

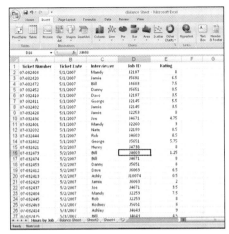

Figure 11-6
Moving a worksheet to a different workbook.

Hiding Worksheets

A worksheet can be hidden from view but still contain active working formulas and data. Click anywhere on the worksheet that you want to hide and choose Home>Cells>Format>Hide & Unhide>Hide Sheet. Excel hides the worksheet from view. All formula references to a hidden worksheet are still valid even when a worksheet is hidden.

To unhide the worksheet, select Choose Home>Cells>Format>Hide & Unhide>Unhide Sheet. A dialog box like the one in Figure 11-7 appears listing all currently hidden worksheets in the active workbook. Select the worksheet you want to unhide and click OK.

Optionally, right-click a worksheet tab and select Hide (or Unhide).

Figure 11-7

Choosing a worksheet to unhide.

Changing Worksheet Tab Colors

Each worksheet tab has its own unique name. Earlier in this chapter, you discovered how you can easily rename sheets. It may be helpful to assign a color to the sheet tabs. This can make them easier to locate, especially for a frequently used sheet or in a workbook with lots of worksheets.

To recolor the worksheet tab, click anywhere in that worksheet and choose Home>Cells>Format >Tab Color. The Tab Color gallery that you see in Figure 11-8 appears. Select a color or select No Color to remove a tab color. The color choices you see depend on your current worksheet theme.

Figure 11-8

Assigning colors to worksheet tabs.

Optionally, right-click a worksheet tab and choose Tab Color to display a Tab Color gallery.

When a worksheet with a colored tab is the current worksheet, Excel does not display the tab color in full. It displays only a colored line under the tab name. The tab becomes full color when the worksheet is not the active one.

Generating References to Other Worksheets

Sometimes you need to refer to information stored in another worksheet—for example, when you have a workbook with sheets for each company division, along with a worksheet that totals the individual worksheets. You can create a reference in the Totals worksheet that instructs Excel to reference the data in the various monthly worksheets. When you create a reference to different sheet, Excel will use the name of the sheet first, then the cell location. Use the following steps to guide you:

1. Select the cell into which you want to enter a reference.

2. Perform one of the following actions:

   ▶ **If you want to display a value located in another cell on the same worksheet, type the equal sign and then the cell address. For example, type =A2. If the value in A2 changes, the cell with the reference to A2 also changes (see Figure 11-9).**

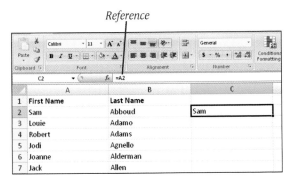

Figure 11-9
Creating a reference to another cell.

▶ **If you want to display a value located in a cell on a different worksheet but in the same workbook, type the equal sign. Next, click the worksheet tab containing the cell you want to reference and then click the actual cell you want to reference. Press the Enter key. Excel displays the equal sign, the worksheet name, an exclamation point, and the cell reference (see Figure 11-10).**

Formulas referencing other worksheets or other workbooks can also be compound formulas or used in a function.

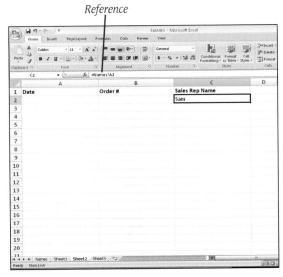

Figure 11-10
Referencing a cell on another worksheet.

Optionally, you can manually type the referenced sheet and cell address, but you must be sure to include the exclamation point.

Notice in all of the previous examples, the answer is displayed in the worksheet, but on the Edit line the originating cell location is displayed. The linked reference is the sheet name followed by an exclamation point and the cell location. If the value in the originating cell changes, the value in the cross reference cell will also change.

Cross-Referencing Other Workbooks

Similar to creating a link to a different worksheet in the current workbook, you can also create links to specific locations in other workbooks. The easiest method to create a workbook link is to have both the origination and the destination workbooks open.

If, when updating links, the originating workbook was renamed, deleted, or moved, an information dialog box will appear notifying you it could not update the link. You have the option of continuing, leaving the data as it was last saved, or clicking an Edit Link button to change the link references.

1. Open the workbook to which you want to refer. For illustration purposes, we'll call the file *Original*.

2. Click the desired cell in the workbook where you want to create a reference. Again, as an example, we'll call this file *Reference*.

3. In *Reference*, begin the formula or reference with an equal sign.

4. If using a function or formula, enter any portion that you want to precede the cross reference.

5. Click the cell that you want to reference from *Original*.

6. Finish the remainder of the formula or press the Enter key. Excel displays the equal sign, an apostrophe, and then the *Reference* file name in brackets followed by the worksheet name, a closing apostrophe, an exclamation point, and then the absolute cell reference. For example, [NAMES.xlsx]Sheet1!A2 refers to the value in cell A2 of Sheet1 in the Excel file named NAMES. See Figure 11-11 for an example of a cross reference.

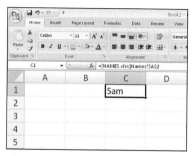

Figure 11-11
Creating a cross reference to different workbook.

> Excel uses absolute references (with dollar signs) when referring to other workbooks.

When you open a workbook containing a cross reference, Excel displays a message such as the one shown in Figure 11-12, prompting you with a security warning so it can determine whether to update the cross referenced cell. Click the Options button and then choose "Enable this content" (also seen in Figure 11-12) if you want Excel to check the originating workbook for changes to the referenced cell.

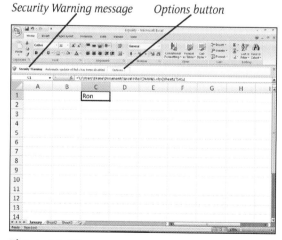

Figure 11-12
Giving permission to update a cross reference.

Inserting a Hyperlink

In Chapter 7, you saw how you could insert a hyperlink into a Word document which would, when clicked, take you to another document area, another document, an Internet site, or even launch an e-mail. You can accomplish the same task in Excel. Select a cell or graphic object and then choose Insert >Links>Hyperlink. The Insert Hyperlink dialog box appears. If you clicked a blank cell before beginning, in the "Text to display" box you can type the text you want the cell to display. If you started with a cell already containing data or an object, you can change the displayed text.

> Click the ScreenTip button to enter text you want displayed, such as a prompt or hint that appears whenever the user pauses the mouse over the link.

Select the option you want to use and enter any relevant information. Click OK when you are finished. Figure 11-13 illustrates an Excel worksheet with a hyperlink.

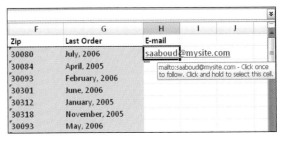

Figure 11-13
An Excel hyperlink.

> To remove a Hyperlink, right-click the link and select Remove Hyperlink.

Managing Worksheet Views

S OMEONE ONCE WROTE ABOUT the importance of seeing and being seen. Although I'm sure that quote referred to people, it also can apply to your Excel worksheets. You need to see them in many different contexts. This section teaches you how to show your worksheets from different perspectives.

Zooming In or Out

The Zoom feature enlarges or shrinks the display of your worksheet to allow you to see more or less of it. Excel can zoom your worksheet in percentages, with the normal display of your worksheet being 100%. Zooming in or out does not affect printing. Chapter 4 shows you zooming in on a Microsoft Word document.

Choose View>Zoom>Zoom or click the Zoom level button next to the status bar Zoom controls. The Zoom level button displays the current zoom percentage. Select a magnification percentage from the Zoom dialog box. A higher zoom setting makes the text appear larger so you see less on the screen; a lower setting shows more on the screen, but the data appears smaller. Click OK.

Select the Custom option and enter your own setting from 10% to 400%.

You can also use the Zoom control slider to manually set the magnification. Drag the Zoom slider bar to the right to increase magnification or drag it to the left to decrease magnification. Click the Zoom In or Zoom Out buttons on the Zoom control slider, which changes the magnification percentage by 10% for each click of the Zoom In button (see Figure 11-14).

Figure 11-14
Zooming in on your data using the Zoom controls.

The Zoom percentage displays on the Status bar.

Changing Worksheet Views

When working with a larger worksheet, it can become difficult to see the entire worksheet on the screen. As you scroll down or across the worksheet, you may lose track of which column or row of data you are entering. Excel contains several tools to help you view your worksheet from different perspectives.

▶ **Page Layout**: Choose View>Workbook Views>Page Layout. As in Figure 11-15, the Page Layout view displays your worksheets on individual pages that correspond to printed pages. A ruler appears on the top and in the header and footer area. See Chapter 12 for more on headers and footers.

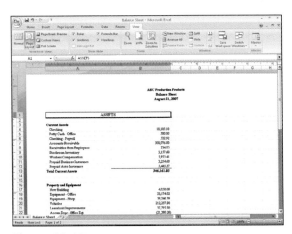

Figure 11-15
Page Layout view with headers and footers.

Use the Zoom controls to increase or decrease magnification.

▶ **Normal**: Choose View>Workbook Views>Normal. Excel returns to the default Normal view, which shows one continuous page of columns and rows.

While in Normal, Page Layout, or Page Break Preview modes, you find three icons on the Status bar next to the Zoom Controls. You can use these to quickly switch among the Normal view, Page Layout view and Page Break Preview modes (see Figure 11-16).

▶ **Page Break Preview**: Choose View>Workbook Views>Page Break Preview. A Welcome to Page Break Preview dialog box appears. Click OK. The Excel mode changes to Page Break Preview, where Excel indicates page breaks with horizontal lines. You can drag these lines to modify where pages break. (See Chapter 12 for more on using page breaks.) To return to the Normal view, choose View>Workbook Views>Normal.

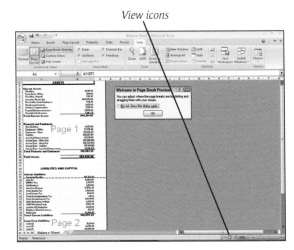

Figure 11-16
Page Break Preview.

If you do not want to see this dialog box when you enter Page Break Preview, click Do Not Show This Dialog Again.

▶ **Full Screen:** Choose View>Workbook Views>Full Screen. As shown in Figure 11-17, you see only the worksheet itself with its row and column headings, worksheet tabs, and the title bar. The Ribbon, Quick Access Toolbar, and the Status bar are hidden. Press the Escape key. Excel returns to Normal view.

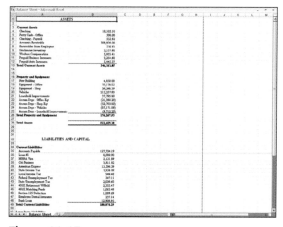

Figure 11-17
Full Screen view.

Freezing Worksheet Titles

When working with a long or wide list, as you add more data you might lose track of which column or row you are entering data into. It would be helpful if you could see which column or row label you are working with. You can freeze the column headings and row labels so they remain visible no matter where you are working in your worksheet.

Typically, when you press Ctrl+Home, Excel takes you to cell A1, but when you have the Freeze Panes feature active, Excel takes you to the cell just below and to the left of the frozen headings.

Choose what you want to freeze:

▶ **Columns:** Select the column to the right of the columns you want to freeze. For example, click cell B1 to freeze only column A.

▶ **Rows:** Select the row below the rows you want to freeze. For example, click cell A4 to freeze rows 1, 2, and 3.

▶ **Columns and rows:** Click the cell below the rows and to the right of the columns you want to freeze. For example, click cell B2 to freeze both column A and row 1.

Freezing panes affects only the current worksheet. If you want to freeze other worksheets, you must select them individually and freeze them.

Choose View>Window>Freeze Panes>Freeze Panes. A thin black line appears to separate the sections. As you see in Figure 11-18, as you scroll down and to the left, row 1 and columns A and B remain visible even though you see rows 40 through 59 in the bottom section and columns D through I on the right. Choose View>Window>Freeze Panes>Unfreeze Panes to remove the freeze from row and column headings.

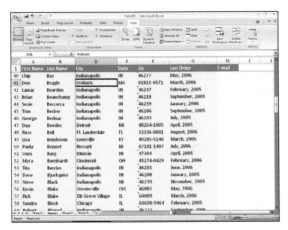

Figure 11-18
Freezing column titles.

Splitting the Excel Screen

Sometimes you need to see two or more different sections of your worksheet at the same time, but your worksheet is too large to view both sections. Excel includes a feature which allows you to split a window into two or four sections which you can move independently of each other.

Click anywhere in a row and column where you want to split your screen. This is usually somewhere around the middle of the screen. Choose View>Window>Split. Excel splits the window horizontally into two or four panes, each separated from other panes by bars. Each pane has its own set of scroll bars (see Figure 11-19).

Drag the horizontal split bar up or down, or drag the vertical split bar left or right to resize the window sections, or double-click any part of the bars that divide the panes to remove that particular split.

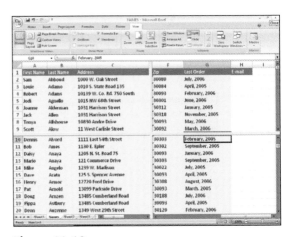

Figure 11-19
Splitting a window into multiple panes.

Choose View>Window>Split again to remove the split.

Hiding Rows and Columns

If you have rows or columns you don't really need to see, or that you don't want to print, you can hide them from view. Hiding them doesn't delete them or make their data inaccessible; it only keeps them out of view. When you hide rows or columns, Excel is actually changing the row height or column width to zero.

> **You can hide multiple columns at one time or multiple rows at one time, but you can't hide both columns and rows in a single step.**

Select the rows or columns you want to hide and choose Home>Cells>Format>Hide & Unhide>Hide Rows or Hide Columns (see Figure 11-20). Optionally, right-click over a selected column or row and choose Hide.

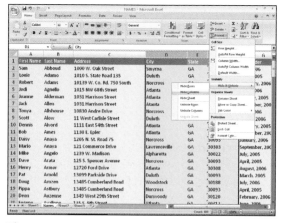

Figure 11-20
Select the columns or rows you want to hide.

The selected rows or columns remain hidden. In Figure 11-21, columns D, E & F are hidden from view.

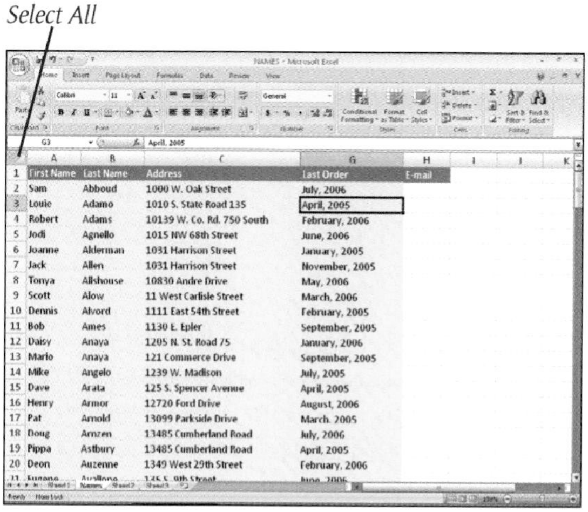

Select All

Figure 11-21
Hidden columns or rows.

When you are ready to unhide rows or columns, select the rows or columns on both sides of the hidden rows or columns. If you have hidden column A or row 1, you cannot select columns or rows on both sides. In this situation, click the Select All button to the left of column A and above row 1 (as shown in Figure 11-21). Choose Home> Cells>Format>Hide & Unhide>Unhide Rows or Unhide Columns. Again, you can optionally right-click the selected rows or columns and choose Unhide.

Sorting Data

SOMETIMES WORKSHEETS BECOME quite large, making locating particular pieces of information time-consuming and difficult. If your data is in an array, you may find the data easier to view if it is sorted in a particular manner.

Perhaps you have multiple worksheets, and you want to locate every occurrence of a specific value. Or, maybe you're just a neat freak and want everything to be in a particular order. Excel contains features to help your arrange your worksheets in an easy-to-manage sequence.

Sorting from the Ribbon

As with most Excel tasks, there are two ways to sort your data: the easy way and the powerful way. Sorting from the Ribbon is the easy way, and, while it doesn't provide as many options as the alternative sorting method, you'll find it works for most of your sorting tasks. Just follow these steps:

1. For the easiest sorting, create a list in contiguous order and with headings specifying the contents of each column. Figure 11-22 illustrates an ideal data array.

2. In the column you want to sort by, click any cell containing data. If the data is not in a contiguous list, you must first select the entire list.

> If Excel finds unselected data in columns next to the selected data, it may prompt you for more information.

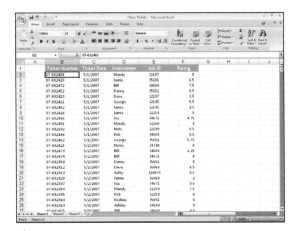

Figure 11-22
Data for sorting.

3. Choose Data>Sort & Filter>Sort A to Z. (If the current cell contains a value, the button says Sort Smallest to Largest.) Excel sorts the entire list in ascending order. Sorting text data in ascending order sorts text A–Z; sorting numeric information in ascending order sorts low to high (1–10); and sorting dates in ascending order places the earliest date first.

Excel sorts in the following pattern: numbers, spaces, special characters, including ! " # $ % & ( ) * , . / : ; ? @ [\ ] ^ _ ` { | } ~ + < = > and, finally, letters. Blanks are always placed last.

Optionally, choose Data>Sort & Filter>Sort Z to A (or Largest to Smallest). Excel sorts the entire list by descending order. Figure 11-23 shows the Ticket Date column sorted in descending order.

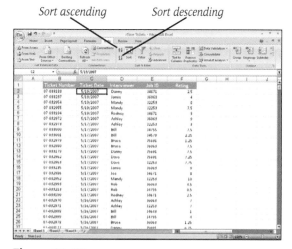

Figure 11-23
Sorting your data.

If Excel incorrectly sorts a cell that contains a value, make sure the cell is formatted as a number and not as text.

Working with the Sort Command

Okay, now for the more powerful way of sorting Excel data. The Excel Sort command not only supplies several ways you can sort your data, it provides options for sorting your data horizontally and even whether or not to sort by capitalization. The following steps show you how to use the Sort command:

1. Select or click in the list of data you want to sort.

Select only a single column of data if you want to sort that column independently of the rest of the data.

2. Choose Data>Sort & Filter>Sort. The Sort dialog box opens (see Figure 11-24).

Figure 11-24
The Sort dialog box.

3. If your data includes column headings, make sure the "My data has headers" option is checked. Excel does not include header rows in the sort process. If the data doesn't include column headings, deselect the option.

4. From the Sort By drop-down list, select the column by which you want to sort (see Figure 11-24).

If you do not have header rows, Excel displays Column A, Column B, and so forth.

5. From the Sort On drop-down list, choose Values.

6. From the Order drop-down list, select how you want to sort the data:

▶ **To sort text values, choose A to Z or Z to A .**

▶ **To sort numeric data, choose Smallest to Largest or Largest to Smallest.**

▶ **To sort by dates, choose Oldest to Newest or Newest to Oldest.**

Click the Options button if you want to make the sorting case-sensitive so that non-capitalized words appear before capitalized words.

7. Click OK.

You can also sort your data horizontally. Choose Data>Sort & Filter>Sort. Click the Options button and choose Sort Left to Right, and then click OK. Define your sort choices in the Sort dialog box and click OK. Figure 11-25 shows data sorted by their color in row 2.

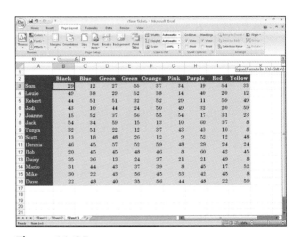

Figure 11-25
Data sorted horizontally.

Sorting by Multiple Criteria

What about those times when, after sorting your data, you have multiples of the same item? For example, if you sort an employee list by last name and you have three employees with the last name Wilson, you can apply a secondary sort on first name. Doing so would then list Barbara Wilson, John Wilson and then Stephen Wilson. Just follow these steps:

1. Select or click in the list of data you want to sort.

2. Choose Data>Sort & Filter>Sort. The Sort dialog box opens.

3. Select whether or not to include column headings in the sort.

4. Set up the primary sort criteria as in the previous section.

Excel sorts dates formatted with slashes such as 11/22/68, as numeric data. Dates with the day or month spelled out must be sorted differently. See the section, "Sort by Day, Month, or Custom List" later in this chapter.

5. Click the Add Level button.

6. In the "Then by" section, select the secondary column you want to sort by if two or more items are identical in the first "Sort by" option (see Figure 11-26).

Figure 11-26

Selecting a second sorting level.

7. Select how you want to sort the second data criteria. Repeat as needed. You can have up to 256 sorting levels.

> To delete an entry, select the sort entry and choose Delete Level. You must keep at least one sort entry in the list.

8. Click OK. Excel performs the sort process. Figure 11-27 illustrates data rows sorted first by Ticket Date and then by Interviewer.

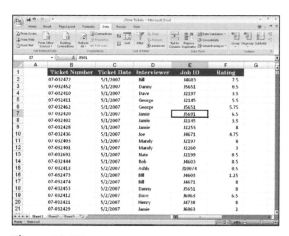

Figure 11-27

Data sorted by multiple criteria.

> During an Excel sort, apostrophes (') and hyphens (-) are ignored, unless two text strings are the same except for a hyphen. In that situation, the text with the hyphen is sorted as the latter.

Removing Duplicate Records

After sorting your data, you may discover you have some records in the list more than once. You could manually scan the data and delete the extras one by one or, better yet, let Excel remove any duplicate records. Follow these steps:

1. Select or click in the list of data you want to work with.

2. Choose Data>Data Tools>Remove Duplicates. The Remove Duplicates dialog box appears (see Figure 11-28).

Figure 11-28

Easily remove duplicate records.

3. Check or uncheck the columns you want Excel to examine.

4. Click OK. Excel looks for and removes duplicates. A message tells you how many duplicates were removed (if any) and how many unique values remain.

5. Click OK.

Filtering Data

AFTER YOU CREATE AN EXCEL database and assemble a large amount of data, you probably want to analyze it. You may want to ask yourself questions about your data. "Who are my best customers?" "Which inventory items are provided by a specific supplier and cost less than a certain amount?" "Which employees work the least amount of hours?" Excel includes several tools you can use to answer these questions and study your data so you can make better decisions.

Filtering means that Excel can pull out specific records for review. This provides you with an easy way to break down your data into smaller, more manageable chunks. Filtering does not rearrange your data; it simply temporarily hides records you don't want to review so you can clearly examine those you do.

Creating an AutoFilter

AutoFilter provides a quick and easy way to find and work with a subset of data in a range. A filtered range displays only the rows that meet the criteria you specify for a column. You use the AutoFilter, which includes filtering by selecting from available choices.

Unlike sorting, filtering does not rearrange a range. Filtering temporarily hides rows you do not want displayed. When Excel filters rows, you can edit, format, chart, and print your range subset without rearranging or moving it.

1. After clicking anywhere in your database, choose Data>Sort & Filter>Filter. Excel displays a filter arrow in each database column.

> The AutoFilter feature is unavailable for protected worksheets.

2. Click the arrow in the column heading from which you want to find a common value. Excel displays a drop-down list, which includes one of each unique entry (up to 10,000 entries) in the selected column (as you see in Figure 11-29).

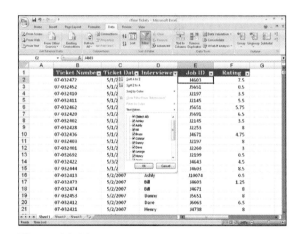

Figure 11-29
Select the item you want to filter.

3. Remove the check mark from Select All. All items become unselected.

4. Click the entry or entries you want to filter and then click OK. Excel displays only the records that match your choice. In Figure 11-30, for example, you see only the interviewers named Danny or Dave. Also notice that the filter arrows on filtered columns take on a different appearance to indicate that a filter is in use.

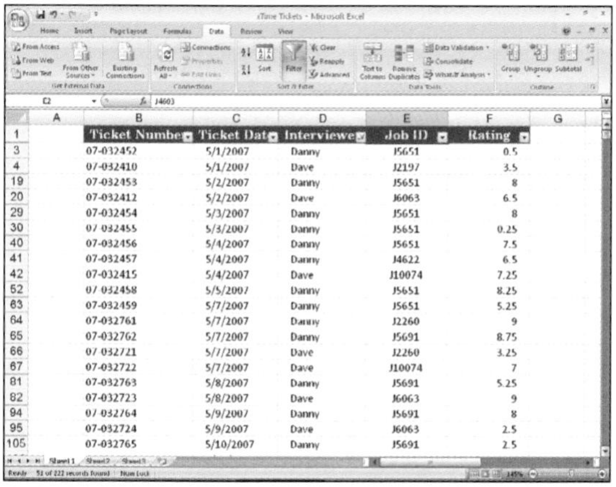

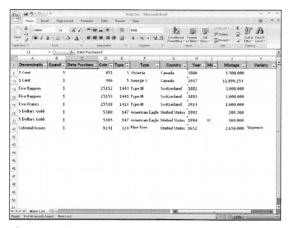

Figure 11-30
Filtered data.

To sort any column after filtering, click the column filter arrow and choose a sort option.

From the column containing the filtering you want removed, click the column filter arrow and choose Clear Filter from "field name." If you want to turn off the AutoFilter, choose Data>Sort & Filter>Filter. You can turn the AutoFilter on and off as often as you need to.

Searching for Blank Cells

Suppose you are a coin collector and you have your existing coins and the coins you'd like to obtain all in an Excel database list. One of your columns is for the date you obtained the coins, so for the coins you don't yet have, the date obtained field would be blank. By using the AutoFilter, you can advise Excel to locate only the records where a particular field (date obtained, in this example) is blank.

Make sure the AutoFilter option is on and your database columns contain filter arrows. Click the arrow in the column heading where you want to find a blank cell. Remove the check mark from Select All and then scroll to the bottom of the list and check the Blanks entry. It should be the only one selected. Click OK, and Excel displays only the records with blank cells in the column you selected, which in Figure 11-31 is the Date Purchased column.

Figure 11-31
Locating records with blank data.

To filter for only non-blank values, make sure Select All is chosen in the AutoFilter menu at the top of the list of values. Then, at the bottom of the list, remove the check mark from Blanks.

Performing a Secondary Filter Selection

Secondary filters are used when you want to be even more specific than with a single filter. With a single filter, you pick, for example, a country like the United States. The secondary filter comes into play when you want to see only the coins of a specific type from the United States. Here's how you perform a secondary filter selection:

1. Make sure the AutoFilter option is on and your database columns contain filter arrows.

2. Click the column arrow by which you want to filter data first.

3. Choose the data you want to filter. In Figure 11-32, you see only selections that display United States in the Country column. Note, however, that there are three different coin denominations of 1 Cent, 5 Dollars Gold, and Colonial Issues.

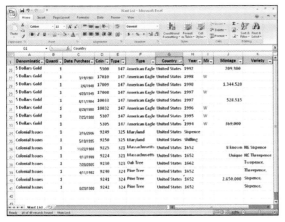

Figure 11-32
Data filtered using the AutoFilter.

4. To further isolate specific items, click the filter arrow at the top of another column.

Each additional filter is based on the current filter and further reduces the subset of data.

5. Select the field by which you want to perform the second filter. In Figure 11-32, the primary option was to filter by the country of the United States. In Figure 11-33, the data is additionally filtered to show only 5 Dollar Gold coins.

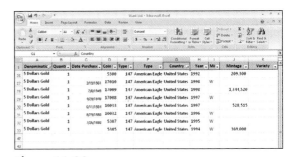

Figure 11-33
Data filtered twice.

6. Repeat Steps 4 and 5 to further filter by as many fields as necessary.

7. When you're finished working with your filtered data, choose one of these options:

   ▶ **To return to the first filter only: Click the second filter column arrow and choose the Clear Filter From option.**

   ▶ **To return to the first filter only: Click the second filter column arrow and choose Clear Filter from "field name."**

   ▶ **To return to viewing all records: Choose Data>Sort & Filter>Clear.**

When working with filters, it's best not to mix text, number, and date formats in the same column because only one type of filter command is available for each column. If a mix of formats occurs, the command displayed has the format that is used most frequently.

Choosing Text Comparison Filters

Text comparison is when you specify a range such as "begins with" or "does not equal." Other options might be "exactly" or "contains." Following are the different options:

► **Equals or Does Not Equal: Equals locates all records in which the selected field cells exactly match or don't match the text you specify. For example, if you look for records matching "Chicago," only the records with Chicago appear. Records containing East Chicago, Chicago Hill, Las Vegas, Chicagoan, Seattle, or Boston do not appear. If you chose Does Not Equal you might see East Chicago, Chicago Hill, Las Vegas, Chicagoan, Seattle, or Boston, but not Chicago.**

► **Begins With or Ends With: Locates all records in which the selected field cells begin or end with the text you specify. If you chose Begins With, you'll see Chicago, Chicago Hill, and Chicagoan, but not East Chicago, Las Vegas , Seattle, or Boston. If you chose Ends with, you would see the records for Chicago and East Chicago, but not Chicago Hill, Las Vegas, Chicagoan, Seattle, or Boston.**

► **Contains or Does Not Contain: Locates all records in which the selected field text contains or doesn't contain the text you specify. The text could be at the beginning, middle, or end of the field cell value. If you choose Contains, you will see Chicago, East Chicago, Chicago Hill, and Chicagoan, but not Las Vegas, Seattle, or Boston.**

Click the filter arrow for the text column by which you want to filter data and choose Text Filters. From the following submenu of comparison filters, make a selection. The Custom AutoFilter dialog box you see in Figure 11-34 appears. The comparison filter you selected appears in the Line description box, but you can click the drop-down list and select a different comparison function. In the first list box on the right, type the data you want to filter and then click the OK button.

Selected field name

Figure 11-34
The Custom AutoFilter dialog box.

Choosing Additional Comparison Criteria

When you want your data to meet more than one criteria on, Excel can support that as well. For example, you want to locate your clients in Cleveland OR Cincinnati. The OR means that *either* criteria on fits what you want. Another example would be if you want to view only the customers in California whose sales are more than a specified amount.

In that situation you would use the AND criteria. The AND criteria specifies that *both* criteria must be met. Take a look at the steps for multiple comparison criteria:

1. Follow the instructions from the previous section "Choosing Text Comparison Filters."

2. Select the And or the Or option.

3. From the drop-down list, select a second comparison filter.

4. Enter the second comparison filter value. Figure 11-35 shows an example.

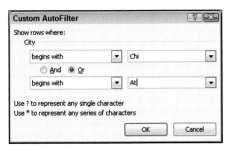

Figure 11-35
Choosing a comparison filter.

If you need to locate cells that share some of the characters you entered but not others, you can use a wildcard character. Entering one or more question marks finds single characters and entering an asterisk finds any number of characters. For example, if you enter Bos???, you would find Boston, Bosnia, Bosart, Boshel—any word that begins with Bos but has only six characters.

5. Click OK to display the filtered records.

Reviewing Other Filter Options

Still need more filter options? Excel has plenty of others. You can filter comparison by numbers. For example, you can show the customers who have purchased more than 1000 units but less than 2000 units. Filtering by the top ten allows you to show the 10 best (or the 10 worst) territories. Or, you can use filters to display only the employees with the above average work ratings.

Click the filter arrow by which you want to filter and then choose one of the following:

▶ **Filter for Numbers: Click the filter arrow for the numeric column by which you want to filter data, and then choose Number Filters. A submenu of comparison filters appears. Some of the choices include Equals, Does not Equal, Greater Than, Greater Than or Equal To, Less Than, Less Than or Equal To, and Between (see Figure 11-36). Select the comparison filter you want to use and Excel displays the Custom AutoFilter dialog box. Enter your filter criteria and then click OK.**

Figure 11-36
Filtering for number types.

► **Filter for Top or Bottom Numbers:**
Click Number Filters and choose Top 10. In Figure 11-37, you see the Top 10 AutoFilter dialog box. Select whether you want the Top (highest) or Bottom (lowest) values and, in the second option, select the number of items you want to see (from 1 to 500). In the third option, select whether you want to filter the items by their names or by their percentiles. For example, choose to list the top 10 customers per their sales dollars, or list the top 10% of your customer base. Click OK. Excel displays the records that match your criteria.

Figure 11-37
Filtering for top or bottom values.

► **Filter for Above or Below Average Values:**
Click Number Filters and choose Above Average or Below Average to filter by numbers that meet either condition. In Figure 11-38, only the records with Ratings above the total average appear.

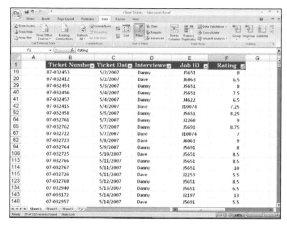

Figure 11-38
Filtering for average values.

Filtering by Date or Time

Another filter option is to filter by date or time. By default, dates in the database are grouped by years, months, and days, in that order. Excel includes two types of date filters: Common and Dynamic. Common filters are those based on comparison operators such as Equal To, Greater Than, Less Than, or Between. Dynamic filters are those for which the criteria can change when you reapply the filter. They include Today, Tomorrow, Next Month, Last Year, and Year-to-Date. Look at the steps needed to filter by a date or a time:

1. Click the filter arrow for the date column by which you want to filter data and choose Date Filters (see Figure 11-39).

Figure 11-39
Available date filters.

2. Select a date filter. If you select a Common filter, you see the Custom AutoFilter dialog box. If you selected a dynamic filter, Excel immediately applies the filter.

> To filter by a date range, select Between.

3. In the box on the right, enter a date or time or, optionally, click the Calendar button to select a date.

4. Click OK. Figure 11-40 shows only those records with dates after May 13th.

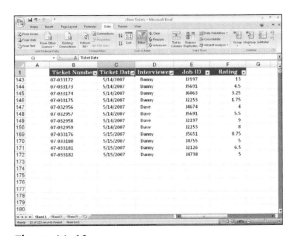

Figure 11-40
Data filtered by date.

> Years and quarters always start in January of the calendar year.

Splitting Data into Multiple Columns

In Chapter 9, you discovered how you can combine columns using the Excel CONCATENATE function. So if you had a first name (Mary) in column A and a last name (Jones) in column B, you created a formula that resulted in firstname lastname (Mary Jones). Sometimes, you want to break the data down instead of combining it. If you have a column with Mary Jones in it but you really need a column with the first name and another column with the last name, you can have Excel do this task for you.

Look at Figure 11-41. You see data with a combined first and last name. The following steps show you how to break that into two separate columns:

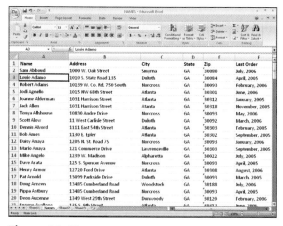

Figure 11-41
Combined data.

1. If necessary, insert blank cells to the left of the cells you want to split. If you will have data in three columns, you must have two blank columns.

2. Select the cells containing the data you want to split into columns.

3. Choose Data>Data Tools>Text to Columns. You see the Convert Text to Columns Wizard.

4. Select Delimited and then click Next.

5. Choose the characters you use to separate your text. In this example, the data is split up by a space, which separates the first and last names , so we'll choose space. The Data preview space shows you how your split data will appear (see Figure 11-42).

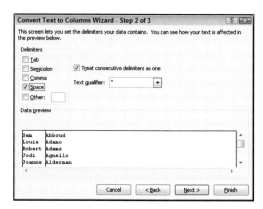

Figure 11-42
The Convert Text to Columns Wizard.

6. Click Next.

7. If you want any specific format for your columns—for example, if you had a zip code and you wanted it treated as text instead of numeric or a date as a specific date format—select the column you want formatted and choose a Column Data Format.

8. Click Finish. Excel converts the data into separate columns (see Figure 11-43).

This feature isn't perfect. For example, it cannot recognize whether a city (such as New York), includes two words. It puts each word into its own column. You may have to work on the data after you split it up.

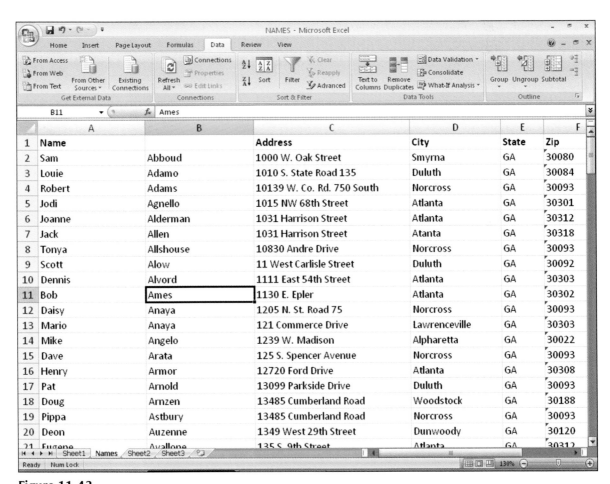

Figure 11-43
Separated data.

12

Setting Security and Printing

Options

PICTURE YOURSELF AND YOUR FAMILY all snuggled together sharing the beauty of a blazing fire. You feel safe and warm. As you share a big bowl of popcorn, you reflect how comforting it is knowing you are sheltered in your home.

To share or not to share. That's what this chapter is about. If you want to share your workbook with others, you can print it or e-mail a copy of it. If you don't want to share it, you need to protect your work and keep it safe.

Keeping Workbooks Secure

WORKSHEETS OFTEN CONTAIN numerical information that is confidential in nature, such as financial or payroll data. In today's world of electronic snooping, it's up to you to protect your work against prying eyes. Fortunately, Excel provides a large number of security tools such as password protection, hiding sensitive worksheet areas, or locking data against unwanted changes.

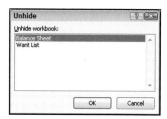

Figure 12-1
Redisplaying a hidden workbook.

Hiding a Workbook

Suppose you are working on a payroll benefits report and nosy Ned approaches to ask you a question. You don't want him to see your work, so you need to hide it from his view. There are a couple of steps you can take to shelter your work from curious onlookers:

▶ **Choose View>Window>Hide. Excel hides the current workbook, leaving the Excel program open and visible. If you have another workbook open, you see that workbook but not the hidden workbook. To redisplay the workbook, choose View>Windows>Unhide. (If no workbooks are hidden, the Unhide button is unavailable.) Excel displays the Unhide dialog box listing all hidden workbooks, as you see in Figure 12-1. Select the workbook to unhide and click OK.**

▶ **Press the Windows key plus the M key to quickly minimize all open items and display the Windows desktop.**

Inspecting for Private Information

In Chapter 7, you discovered the Document Inspector, which searched through Word documents for metadata. Excel also provides the Document Inspector which can help remove hidden information that you might not want others to see. Just follow these steps:

1. Save the workbook and then choose Office Button>Prepare>Inspect Document. The Document Inspector dialog box appears.

2. Deselect any option you do not want to check and then click Inspect. Excel inspects the document for the selected information.

3. When the inspection is complete, the Document Inspector reappears with information as in Figure 12-2.

4. Click the Remove All button next to any option you want removed. Excel removes the selected data. After removing the data, the Remove All button next to the option disappears.

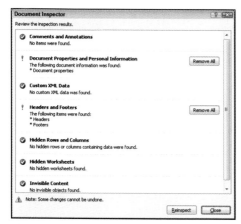

Figure 12-2
Remove the items you don't want in the file.

You cannot undo some changes done with the Document Inspector.

5. Repeat Step 4 for any additional items you want to remove.

6. Click Close and resave your file.

Protecting Worksheets

You will probably want to ensure that no one can either accidentally or intentionally make unauthorized changes to your data. Excel provides protection at several different levels including protecting the worksheet, specific cells of the worksheet, or the entire workbook.

1. Click anywhere on the sheet that you want to protect and then choose Review>Changes> Protect Sheet. The Protect Sheet dialog box appears, as shown in Figure 12-3.

Figure 12-3
Locking your sheet against unwanted changes.

A good reason to protect a worksheet is to prevent accidental changes to formulas.

2. Make sure the option Protect Worksheet and Contents of Locked Cells is checked.

3. Optionally, in the Password to Unprotect Sheet text box, type a password. For privacy reasons, only a series of dots appears. Passwords are case-sensitive.

4. From the Allow All Users of the Worksheet To box, select any options a user is allowed to change without unprotecting the worksheet.

Deselecting the Select Locked Cells option doesn't allow an unauthorized user to even click a locked cell. All cells are considered locked unless you unlock them, as you see in the next section.

5. Click OK.

6. If you generated a password, a Confirm Password dialog box appears. Retype the password and then click OK again.

To unprotect the worksheet, choose Review>Changes>Unprotect Sheet. Enter the password if prompted.

When anyone attempts to change a locked cell, they see an error message such as the one shown in Figure 12-4.

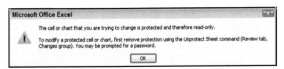

Figure 12-4
No access is allowed to locked cells on a protected worksheet.

Unlocking Cells

You may have a worksheet in which you want only yourself or others to enter data in specific cells and to not have access to formulas or other definite data. You can designate the cells you want editable and leave the remainder of the worksheet protected.

Select the cells you want users to be able to modify and choose Home>Cells>Format>Lock Cell (see Figure 12-5). Because, by default, Excel locks all cells, choosing this option turns the Lock Cells option off. Click the option again to relock the cells again. Protect the worksheet to protect all but the unprotected cells.

Optionally, select Home>Cells>Format> Format Cells, which displays the Format Cells dialog box. Click the Protection tab and deselect the Locked option. Click OK.

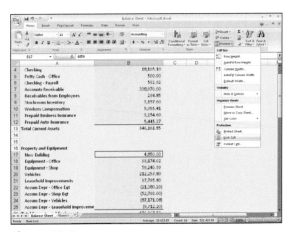

Figure 12-5
Selecting cells you want to unprotect.

Hiding Cell Formulas

You've seen how you can keep others from changing cells by protecting the worksheet, but they can still view the cell contents and formulas. Excel provides a feature with which you can hide the formula so that only the result in the cell is visible. Select the cells containing formulas or information you want to hide. Choose Home>Cells>Format>Format Cells. This displays the Format Cells dialog box. Click the Protection tab and select the Hidden option. Click OK and then protect the worksheet.

In Figure 12-6, although you see the results of the formula in cell B49, the formula bar does not display the actual formula.

No formula seen

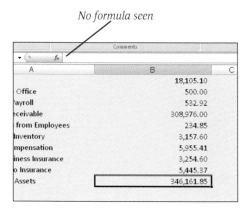

Figure 12-6
Displaying only the formula result, not the actual formula.

Marking a Workbook as Final

To protect your workbook against accidental changes, Excel, like Word, includes a feature called Mark as Final. Marking the workbook as final is the similar to placing the workbook into a read-only state in that the workbook cannot be changed.

Choose Office Button>Prepare>Mark as Final. Click OK at the acknowledgement message that appears. If you have not yet saved the file, the Save As dialog box appears. Enter the file name and save the file. Otherwise, Excel saves the file, displays a confirmation message, and the words Read-Only appear next to the file name on the Title bar (see Figure 12-7). Also notice that all items on the Ribbon are grayed out and unavailable.

Figure 12-7
Changes cannot be made to a file marked as final.

Marking the workbook as final disables every option in the Ribbon that could change the workbook in any way. An icon appears in the status bar indicating the document is marked as final, and if you attempt to make any changes, the icon changes to a message stating the modification is not allowed.

The Mark as Final feature is designed to prevent accidental changes and is not permanent. If you find you need to make changes to the workbook, choose Office Button>Prepare>Mark as Final again to turn off the Read-Only function.

Assigning a File Password

Another method to protect your workbook is applying a password to keep others from even opening it. You can also apply a password to allow them to view it but not make any changes, anywhere in the entire workbook. This type of password protection, called *file level* protection, is accomplished through the Save As dialog box. Follow these steps to assign file level passwords:

1. Choose Office Button>Save As, which displays the Save As dialog box.

2. Click the Tools button and then select General Options. Excel provides two levels of password protection. You can use either or both password options.

3. Type a password in the Password to Open text box (see Figure 12-8). The Password to Open box prevents unauthorized users from even opening the workbook.

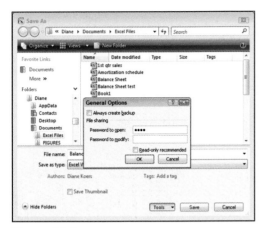

Figure 12-8
Assigning passwords to protect the file.

4. Optionally, type a password in the Password to Modify text box. The Password to Modify box prevents users, once the workbook is open, from making any changes.

Optionally, check the "Read-only recommended" option to recommend (not require) that the user open the file as read-only. This means before they can save the file, they must assign it a different file name or folder.

5. Click OK.

6. Retype the password to open, and then click OK. Retype the password to modify, and then click OK.

7. Click Save.

Click Yes if you're prompted to overwrite the file.

When someone attempts to open the password protected file, they see the Password dialog box shown in Figure 12-9. Type the Open password, and then click OK. If prompted, type the password to allow modifications and click OK. The protected file opens.

Figure 12-9
Enter the password to access the file.

Checking for Errors

BEFORE YOU PRINT OR GIVE YOUR Excel file to someone else, you should check it for spelling errors. You want to eliminate typos that can scream out to the world, "I can't spell." Excel includes a built-in dictionary you can use to check your workbooks for misspellings; however, it can't read your mind, so if you type *too* instead of *two*, Excel probably won't indicate that as an error. But, combine the spell check with careful proofreading on your part, and you'll find it becomes a very helpful tool.

Spell Check reviews all cell values, comments, embedded charts, text boxes, buttons, and headers and footers, but it does not check protected worksheets, formulas, or text that results from a formula.

Choose Review>Proofing>Spelling. If there are no errors in the worksheet, a message box appears advising you the spell check is complete; otherwise it displays the Spelling dialog box seen in Figure 12-10, referencing the first error. Choose one of the following:

Optionally, press F7 to launch the Spell Check.

▶ **Change or Change All:** Choose one of the suggestions; then, click Change to change just this incident of the spelling mistake or select Change All if you think you could have made the mistake more than once.

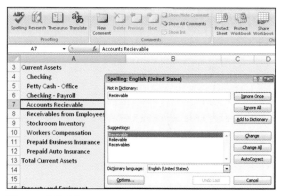

Figure 12-10
Using spell check to improve your worksheet.

▶ **AutoCorrect:** Have Excel, in future workbooks, automatically correct the mistake with the selected replacement.

▶ **Ignore Once:** Click this button if you don't want to change the spelling of the highlighted instance of the spelling.

▶ **Ignore All:** Click this button if you don't want to change the spelling of any identical instances of the spelling.

▶ **Add to Dictionary:** Add a word, such as a proper name or medical or legal term, to Excel's built-in dictionary so that Excel won't flag it as a potential error in the future.

If, when you began the spell check, the current cell was not at the beginning of the workbook, Excel asks you whether to check the beginning of the worksheet. When the spell check is complete, a dialog box notifies you. Click OK.

Using Find and Replace

THE EXCEL FIND AND REPLACE feature lets you locate specific worksheet text or formulas and optionally replace the found data with something different. The Find feature can search through formulas, values, or comments. If you select formulas, the Find feature will look through both the underlying formulas and the values for the selected data. If you select values, Excel will look only in the results, not in the formulas. If you select comments, Excel will look only in comments.

Searching for Data

Especially with large workbooks, sometimes it's difficult to locate specific entries. You can let Excel locate the data for you. Choose Home>Editing> Find & Select>Find or just press Ctrl+F. The Find and Replace dialog box appears. In the Find what box, enter the value or word you want to locate.

Click the Options button and specify any desired options (see Figure 12-11):

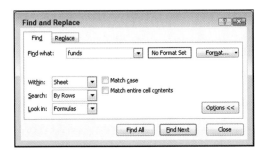

Figure 12-11
Specify where and what to search.

▶ **Within:** Search just the current worksheet or the entire workbook. By default, Excel searches only the current worksheet

▶ **Search:** Select whether to search first across the rows first, or down the columns first.

▶ **Look in:** Select whether you want to search through the values or formula results, through the actual formulas, or if you want to look in the comments.

> Select Formulas when you are looking for a formula that references a specific cell address.

▶ **Match case:** Check this box if you want your search to be case case-specific (for example, Daniel instead of DANIEL or daniel).

▶ **Match entire cell contents:** Check this box if you want your search results to only list only the items that exactly match your search criteria.

Click the Find Next button. Excel jumps to the first occurrence of the match. If this is not the entry you are looking for, click the Find Next button again. Excel advises you if it does not locate the data you are searching for. Click the Close button when you have located the entry you want.

Optionally, you can locate all occurrences of the data you want to locate. In the Find and Replace dialog box, click the Find All button. The Find and Replace dialog box expands as you see in Figure 12-12, showing a list of each cell entry that contains your data. You can click any entry to select that cell.

> To resize the Find and Replace dialog box, drag the resize handle in the lower right box corner.

Resize handle

Figure 12-12
See all occurrences of found data at once.

> In Chapter 7 you discovered how you could use the Find or Find and Replace features to locate text with specific formatting in Word. The same feature is also available in Excel. Click the Format buttons to specify a cell format.

Replacing Cell Data

Excel can locate specific data for you and automatically replace it with different data. Choose Home>Editing>Find & Select>Replace, which displays the Find and Replace dialog box, with the Replace tab on top (see Figure 12-13).

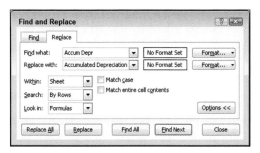

Figure 12-13
The Replace tab.

Type the data you want to replace in the Find what text box. Next, type the replacement data in the Replace with text box. If desired, click the Options button for more Find options. The Replace Options box has the same options available in the Find dialog box. Click Find Next to begin the search. Excel locates the first occurrence of the selected text.

Click Replace if you want to replace the found data with the replacement data. Excel will make the replacement and proceed to the next occurrence; or, click Replace All to have Excel replace all occurrences of the original data with the replacement data. Excel notifies you of the total number of occurrences.

When finished, click the Close button.

Adjusting Page Layout

WITH JUST A SINGLE CLICK, you can print your worksheet. But before you print it, you might want to specify what paper size you want to use, how large you want the margins, and whether or not to print the gridlines. You might also want to only print a portion of the worksheet instead of printing it in its entirety.

Managing Manual Page Breaks

As you have probably already noticed, when you have more data on your worksheet than will fit on a printed page, Excel automatically starts a new page for you. Excel indicates page breaks as dotted lines vertically and horizontally on the screen. You can, however, tell Excel how to manage these page breaks. The easiest way to manage page breaks is through Page Break Preview.

Choose View>Workbook Views>Page Break Preview. Click OK at the Welcome to Page Break Preview message box. Your worksheet appears in Page Break Preview mode and shows blue dotted lines at the natural page breaks (see Figure 12-14).

> To hide future occurrences of the Welcome to Page Break Preview box, check Do not show this dialog again.

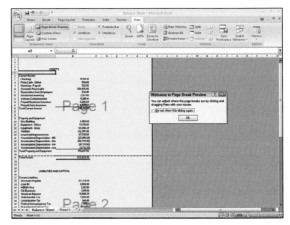

Figure 12-14
Viewing page breaks.

To set page breaks manually, position your mouse over any blue dotted line. The mouse pointer turns into a double-headed arrow, and you can drag the line until it is in the position where you want the page to break. If you drag the page break so the page is longer, Excel scales the page to fit when printing. Manual page breaks appear as solid blue lines.

When you are finished creating manual page breaks, choose View>Workbook Views>Normal.

> To remove the manual page breaks, choose Page Layout>Page Setup>Breaks> Reset All Page Breaks.

Specifying a Print Area

When printing, Excel assumes you want to print the entire worksheet area, or just specified pages. If you only want to print a portion of the sheet, you need to specify a specific print range, called the *print area*. This is especially useful if you have several different tables in your worksheet and you only want to print one of them. Setting the print range is a matter of selecting the range and then issuing the command to make that range the print area. Just follow these steps:

1. Highlight the area you want to print.

2. Choose Page Layout>Page Setup>Print Area>Set Print Area. Dotted lines appear around the print area. When you print the worksheet, only the area contained within the dotted lines prints (see Figure 12-15).

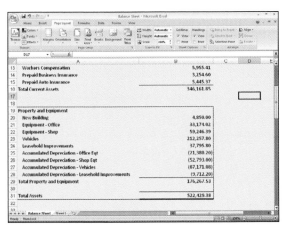

Figure 12-15
Setting the area you want to print.

Optionally, highlight the area you want to print and, from the Print dialog box, choose Selection in the Print What section.

To reset Excel to print the entire worksheet, choose Page Layout>Page Setup>Print Area>Clear Print Area.

Setting the Paper Orientation and Size

If your worksheet uses quite a few columns, you might want to change the orientation or paper size. The default size is $8^1/_2 \times 11$-inch paper in portrait orientation (the short side at the top and bottom). Changing to landscape orientation will print with the long edge of the paper at the top and bottom.

To select the paper orientation, choose Page Layout>Page Setup>Orientation and then select whether you want Portrait or Landscape orientation.

To change the paper size, choose Page Layout> Page Setup>Size. From the drop-down list of paper sizes that appears, select a paper size. The paper-size choices you see depend on the currently selected printer. The two most common US choices are Letter, which is 8.5×11 inches, and Legal, which is 8.5×14 inches (see Figure 12-16).

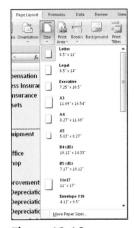

Figure 12-16
Choosing a paper size.

From the Size list, click the More Paper Sizes option to open the Page Setup dialog box. From there you can select additional paper sizes.

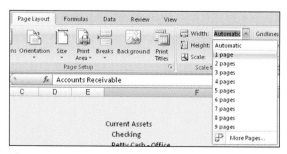

Figure 12-17
Tell Excel how to shrink your document.

Shrinking Worksheets to Fit

Instead of struggling with resizing columns and fonts to make your worksheet fit on a certain number of pages, Excel allows you to scale your document. Scaling makes Excel resize the print area as needed to fit in the specified number of pages. You could also manually tell Excel to shrink the worksheet by a percentage amount. For example, your worksheet prints on two pages, but there are only three rows on the second page. You can tell Excel to squeeze it just enough so it fits on a single page. Just follow these steps:

Don't try to shrink your document too much. Because Excel shrinks the font, trying to fit too much on a page can make the document typeface too small to read.

1. Choose Page Layout>Scale to Fit.

2. From the Width drop-down list, select the number of pages wide you want to print (see Figure 12-17).

3. From the Height drop-down list, select the number of pages wide you want to print.

Optionally, in the Scale text box, enter a percentage to reduce or enlarge the document. Values range from 10 to 400.

Setting Page Margins

By default, Excel uses a top and bottom margin of .75 inch and left and right margins of .70 inch. You can change these margins to meet your needs. You can select from several predefined settings or you can create your own custom margins. Follow these steps:

1. Choose Page Layout>Page Setup>Margins. Figure 12-18 shows a list of margin options.

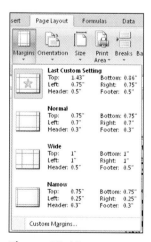

Figure 12-18
Select from the margin options.

2. Select from the margin options shown or choose Custom Margins to open the Page Setup dialog box (see Figure 12-19) that enables you to set your own margin options.

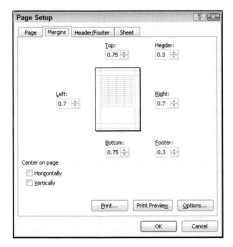

Figure 12-19
Selecting margin options.

From the Page Setup dialog box, click the option Horizontally and/or the option Vertically in the Center on Page section to center the worksheet on the page, regardless of the margins.

Indicating Repeating Rows and Columns

In Chapter 11, you learned how to freeze worksheet titles so they remained on the screen even when you scrolled to other areas of the worksheet. If your worksheet will be more than one printed page in height or width, you may want to print one or more rows or columns on each page—in effect, "freezing" titles for each page. To specify which rows and columns should be repeated on each page, follow these steps:

1. Choose Page Layout>Page Setup>Print Titles. The Page Setup dialog box opens.

2. On the Sheet tab, type a dollar sign ($) followed by the row numbers or column letters you want to print as titles in the Print Titles section. Entering $1:$2, as you see in Figure 12-20, repeats rows 1 and 2 at the beginning of each page. If you want a specific column on each page, enter $A:$A (or whatever columns you want) in the Columns to repeat at left box.

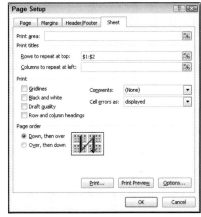

Figure 12-20
Specifying which columns and rows to print on every page.

Click the Collapse Dialog button on the right to collapse the Page Setup dialog box so you can select the rows or columns you want to include. Click the button again to return to the Page Setup dialog box.

3. Click OK.

Printing Gridlines and Headings

Although you see them on your screen, Excel does not print the gridlines that divide the rows and columns. The same is true for the row and column headings. It would be extremely difficult to tell where Column D is if it wasn't referenced at the top. Sometimes you want to print the gridlines or the row and column headings so while viewing the printout, you don't have to rely on any borders you've added.

Choose Page Layout>Sheet Options and select from the following options:

▶ **Gridlines:** Check the Print option to print the gridlines surrounding each cell in the worksheet. By default, the Gridlines View option is checked. If you don't want to see the gridlines while you're working on the worksheet, uncheck this item.

▶ **Headings:** Check the Print option to print the row numbers or column letters around the worksheet. Figure 12-21 illustrates a worksheet as it would look printed with gridlines and row and column headings.

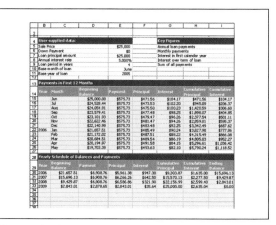

Figure 12-21
A worksheet with gridlines and headings.

By default, gridlines are a lighter shade of blue. You can change the gridline color by choosing Office Button>Excel Options. Click the Advanced section and scroll down to the Display options for this worksheet section. Click the Gridline color arrow and select a different gridline color.

Working with Headers and Footers

HEADERS AND FOOTERS ARE SIMPLY text that appears either at the top (header) or bottom (footer) of every page. The type of information you might include in a header or footer might be a report title, the current date, page number, or file name. You typically manage headers and footers through the Page Layout View.

Adding a Standard Header and Footer

You can select from one of the predefined headers and footers or you can create you own. The easiest method is to pick from one of the predefined headers and footers.

1. Choose View>Worksheet Views>Page Layout. You see the header area of your worksheet.

2. You may have to scroll to the top of the page where you see the Header area. Headers and Footers are divided into three sections: Left, Center, and Right. Excel also now displays a Header & Footer Tools Design tab (see Figure 12-22).

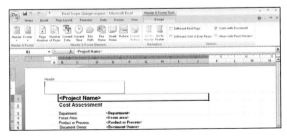

Figure 12-22
The Header & Footer Tools Design tab.

If you want to work on the Footer, click Header & Footer Tools Design>Navigation> Go to Footer.

3. Click in the header section where you want to work.

4. Choose Header & Footer Tools Design> Header & Footer>Header (or Footer). A list of predefined headers (or footers) appears, as you see in Figure 12-23.

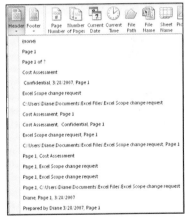

Figure 12-23
Selecting a predefined header.

5. Select the predefined option you want to use.

The Options group of the Header & Footer Tools Design tab supplies other choices you might want applied to your header or footer. Take a look at each of them (Figure 12-24):

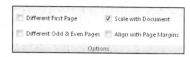

Figure 12-24

Setting options for a header or footer.

▶ **Different First Page:** If you choose this option, Excel won't print the header or footer on the first page.

▶ **Different Odd & Even Pages:** Choose this option if you want a header or footer for the odd-numbered pages of the document different from the one that prints on the even-numbered pages.

▶ **Scale with Document:** This option is selected by default and tells Excel to use the same font size and scaling as the worksheet. If you want the header and footer font size and scaling independent of the worksheet scaling, clear this check box.

▶ **Align with Page Margins:** Choose this option to align the header and footer with the left and right margins of the worksheet. If this is unchecked, the header and footer margins print independently of the worksheet margins.

Creating Custom Headers and Footers

If none of the predefined headers or footers meets your needs, you can easily create your own. While in Page Layout View, choose the desired header or footer section in which you want to work. Type the text you want for the header (or footer), which, as you see in Figure 12-25, you can format just as you would any cell data. You can also choose from any options in the Header & Footer Elements group:

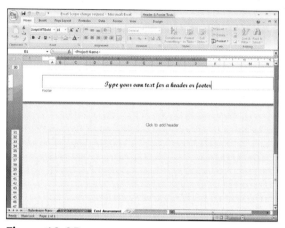

Figure 12-25

Creating your own header or footer.

▶ **Page Number:** Insert a code that indicates the page number.

▶ **Number of Pages:** Insert a code that indicates the total number of pages.

You can add text to the Page text. For example, "Page &[Page] of &[Pages]" will print "Page 3 of 5" or "Page 1 of 2".

▶ **Current Date or Current Time:** Insert the print date or time of day.

▶ **File Path, File Name, or Sheet Name:** Include file information.

▶ **Picture:** Insert a graphic image such as a company logo.

▶ **Format Picture:** Resize, rotate, or crop a header or footer graphic image.

To continue editing the worksheet, when you are finished working in your header or footer, click a cell outside the header or footer area.

Printing Your Worksheet

WHEN YOU FINISH COMPILING your worksheet, you may want to print a hard copy or e-mail a copy to someone. Once you have specified any print specifications and options, you can print the worksheet with only a couple of mouse clicks.

Previewing Your Work

You may want to preview the worksheet on the screen before you print, just to make sure you have all the options set correctly. Using the Print Preview feature can save lots of paper by allowing you to see the worksheet on your screen before actually printing it to paper.

1. Click the Office button and pause your mouse over the Print option.

2. Choose Print Preview. The document appears in Print Preview mode (see Figure 12-26). Don't strain your eyes trying to read the text in the Preview window. You are looking at the overall perspective here, not necessarily the individual cell contents. You cannot edit the worksheet cell contents while in Print Preview mode.

> Optionally, press Ctrl+F2 to open the Print Preview mode.

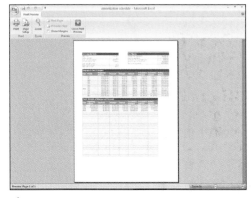

Figure 12-26
Taking a sneak peak with Print Preview.

3. Select from the following options:

   ▶ **If you have multiple pages, click the Next Page or Previous Page buttons to view additional pages.**

   ▶ **Use the scroll bars to view different areas of the worksheet.**

   ▶ **Click the Zoom button to enlarge the view. Click a second time to reduce the view.**

   ▶ **Click the Print button to display the Print dialog box.**

   ▶ **Click the Page Setup button to display the Page Setup dialog box.**

   ▶ **Click the Show Margins check box to display the page margins; then drag any margin line to manually set margin sizes. Click the Margins button again to turn off the margin lines.**

4. Click the Close Print Preview button to return to Normal view.

Printing a Worksheet

Typically, the end result of creating a worksheet is to get the information onto paper. Now that you've checked all your printing options, you are ready to print. You can print with the "no questions asked" method, or you can specify additional printing options through the Print dialog box. Just follow these steps:

1. Choose Office Button>Print. The Print dialog box appears, as shown in Figure 12-27.

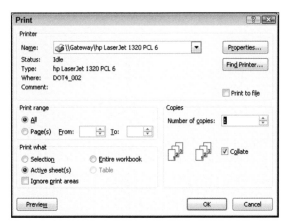

Figure 12-27
The Print dialog box contains many options.

Optionally, choose Office Button>Print> QuickPrint, which immediately prints the worksheet using the default printer.

2. Choose from the following options:

▶ **Name:** Select a printer different than the default printer.

▶ **Print range:** Specify whether to print the entire worksheet as determined by the print area or whether to print only specific pages.

▶ **Copies:** Select the number of copies you want to print.

▶ **Print what:** Choose whether to print the current worksheet, a preselected area, or the entire workbook.

3. Click OK.

E-Mailing Workbooks

As with a Word document, you can e-mail your Excel file. Recipients must have Excel installed on their systems to open the workbook file.

Choose Office Button>Send>E-mail. As you see in Figure 12-28, your e-mail program launches with the worksheet as an attachment. Enter the recipient e-mail information and any additional text in the body of the message and then click the Send button.

Figure 12-28
E-mailing an Excel workbook.

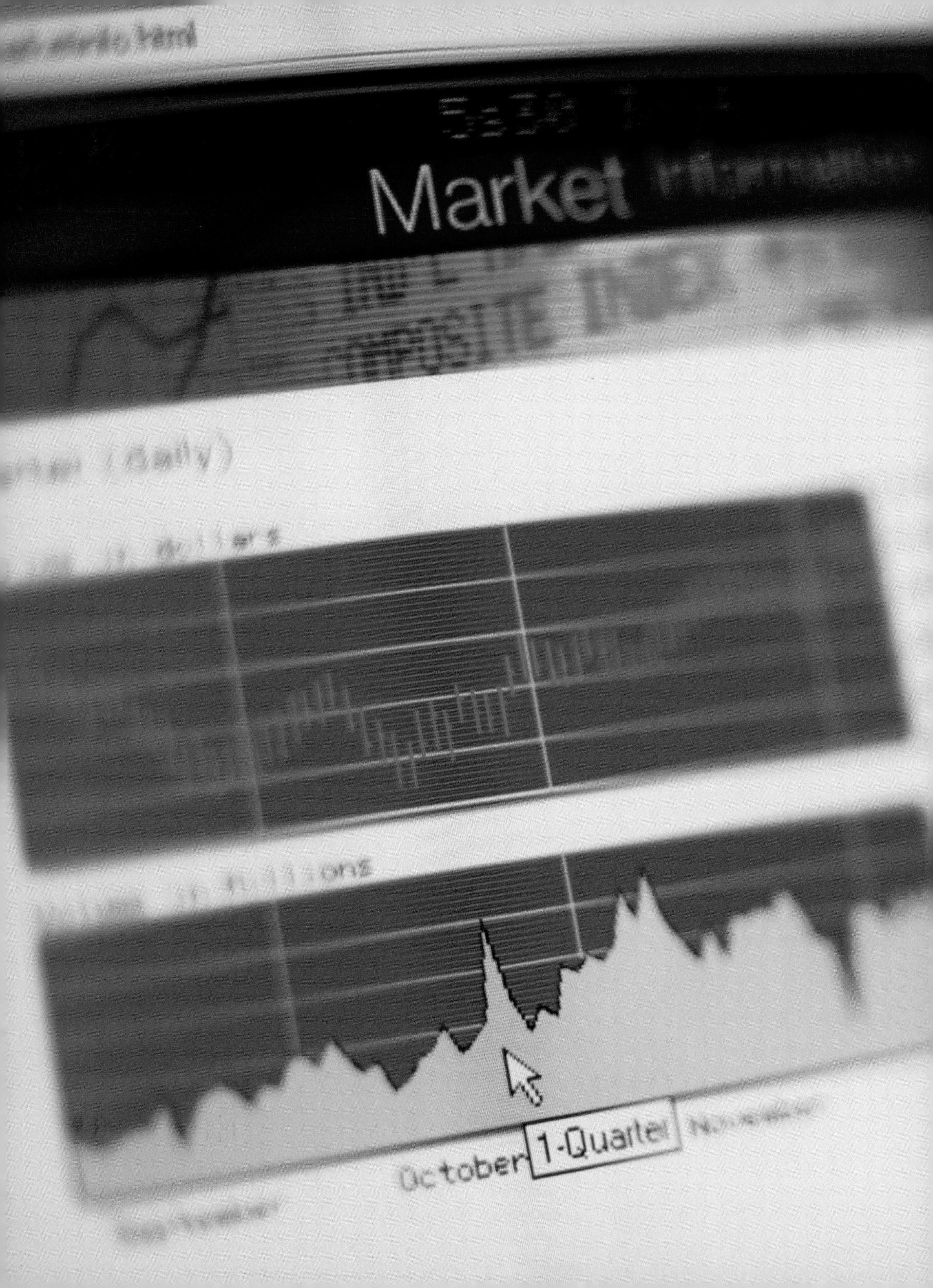
Market
1-Quarter
October

Generating Excel
Charts

PICTURE YOURSELF TRYING TO WORK on a jigsaw puzzle without the box to show you the overall picture. Without seeing the complete picture, the pieces may not come together as you think. It's the same with a chart. Whoever said a picture is worth a thousand words certainly could have been referring to a chart.

Let's face it...we like looking at pictures more than we like looking at sheets of data. Charts, sometimes referred to as graphs, provide an effective way to illustrate your worksheet data by making the relationships between numbers easier to see. The chart turns numbers into shapes and enables you to compare the shapes to each other. Charts let you get your thoughts across with simplicity and strength, and, because different charts may cause you to draw varied conclusions, they also prod you to ask questions about what you are seeing. Whatever the idea you are trying to convey, charts make it easier.

If you've ever spent hours drawing a chart on graph paper, you'll really appreciate the ease with which you can create dozens of different chart styles using your Excel data. And you don't really have to draw a thing! With just a few decisions on your part and a few clicks of the mouse, you have a two- or three-dimensional illustration of your data.

Creating a Basic Chart

EXCEL PROVIDES TWO METHODS FOR putting your data into a chart. The first method, which is the really quick way, involves telling Excel where your data is located and pressing a single key on the keyboard. Excel creates a chart that you can then edit or move. Take a look at the first method and the components of a chart.

> Throughout this chapter you learn how to edit the look and style of a chart.

The steps are very simple. First, select the data (sequential or nonsequential) you want to plot in the chart. See Figure 13-1, in which cells A2 through D11 are selected as an example of sequential data for a chart.

> Typically, if you are selecting values such as monthly figures, you don't want to include totals in your chart.

Second, press the F11 key. Excel immediately adds a new sheet called Chart1 to your workbook with the data plotted into a column chart. Each subsequent chart page is numbered sequentially such as Chart2, Chart3, and so forth.

> Some newer keyboards use a different function for the F11 key. If your F11 key does not produce a chart, use the Insert tab as explained in the next section.

	A	B	C	D	F	G
1	\multicolumn{4}{c}{**1st Quarter Widget Sales**}		
2	COLOR	JANUARY	FEBRUARY	MARCH	TOTALS	
3	Green	11,062	9,441	10,004	30,507	
4	Yellow	3,500	8,500	11,664	23,664	
5	Blue	15,000	15,100	15,200	45,300	
6	Pink	18,976	22,962	21,069	63,007	
7	Red	14,995	13,157	13,164	41,316	
8	Purple	3,158	3,505	10,890	17,553	
9	Gray	5,955	6,620	7,337	19,912	
10	Black	13,254	13,612	14,009	40,875	
11	Orange	5,445	6,044	6,709	18,198	
12	TOTALS	91,345	98,941	110,046	300,332	
13						
14						

Figure 13-1
Selecting your chart data.

To modify the chart, you first need to know the various components involved in a chart. Figure 13-2 shows you the various components that can make up a chart, and Table 13-1 identifies each of those components.

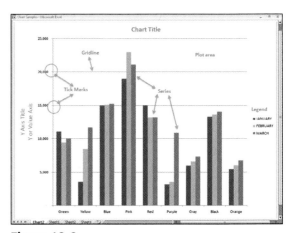

Figure 13-2
Excel chart elements.

Table 13-1 Chart Components

Component	Description
Title	A descriptive name for the overall chart. By default, titles are not added in a basic chart, but you can add them later manually or by using the Chart Wizard.
X or Category Axis	Column or row headings from your selected data, which Excel uses for Category axis names. In a column chart, the categories display along the bottom. In other charts (such as a bar chart), the category axis displays along the left side.
X Axis Title	A descriptive name for the Category axis. By default, a category label is not added in a basic chart, but you can add one later manually or with the Chart Wizard.
Category	A single grouping of data on the Category axis. The Category is identified in the legend.
Y or Value Axis	A scale representing the zero or the lowest and highest numbers in the plotted data. The Value axis is usually located on the left side on a column chart or on the bottom on a bar chart.
Y Axis Title	A descriptive name for the values. By default, a value label is not added in a basic chart, but you can add one later manually or by using the Chart Wizard.
Legend	The box, usually located on the right, identifies the patterns or colors that are assigned to the chart data series. Notice in Figure 13-3 how the legend explains that one shade of color represents January, another shade is for February, and the third color is for March.
Tick marks	The small extensions of lines that appear outside of the gray area that represent divisions of the value or category axis.
Gridlines	These lines extend from the tick marks across the chart area to allow you to easily view and evaluate data.
Series	Excel uses the worksheet cell values to generate the series. Each element, called a data marker, represents a single worksheet cell value. Related data markers make up a data series and have the same pattern or color. In Figure 13-4, you can see the comparison of the data values to the y-axis and the series values.
Plot area	The background that represents the entire plotted chart area.

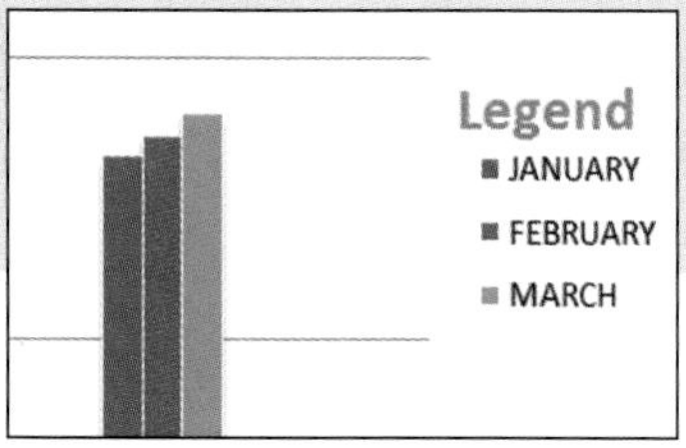

Figure 13-3
A chart legend.

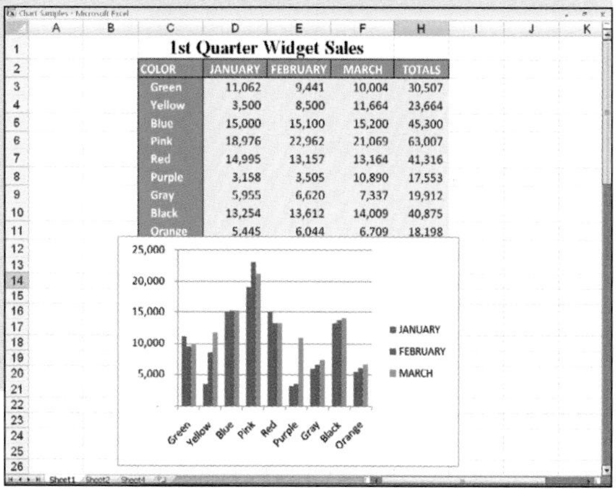

Figure 13-4
Data as displayed in a data series.

Inserting a Chart

THE SECOND TECHNIQUE YOU CAN use for creating a chart allows you to set a couple of options as you create the chart. You get to determine where you want the chart and which chart type you want.

When you insert a chart, you can create the chart on its own sheet such as you discovered in the previous section, or you can tell Excel to place the chart on top of the sheet with the data. Excel calls this an embedded chart. No matter where you place your chart, the data is tied to the chart, so if the data changes, so does the chart. Here are the necessary steps:

1. Select the data you want to plot in the chart.

2. Choose Insert>Charts, and click the chart style you want which displays the chart type gallery: Excel can create many different chart types; each compares data in a different manner (see Figure 13-5). Some of the most commonly used chart types include the following:

Figure 13-5
Select the chart type appropriate for your data.

▶ **Column:** Column charts compare values to categories using a series of vertical columns to illustrate the series.

▶ **Bar:** Bar charts, like column charts, compare values to categories but use a series of horizontal bars to illustrate the series.

▶ **Line:** Line charts are similar to bar charts but use dots to represent the data points with lines to connect them.

▶ **Pie:** This chart compares parts to a whole. Usually a pie chart has only one data series. Figure 13-6 illustrates data appropriate for a pie chart.

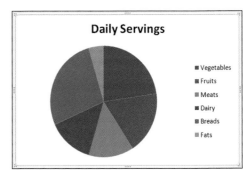

Figure 13-6
A pie chart compares parts to the whole unit.

▶ **Area:** Area charts display the trend of each value, usually over a specified period of time.

▶ **X-Y Scatter:** These charts include two value axes, one showing a set of numerical data along the x-axis and the other showing data along the y-axis.

▶ **Surface:** Shows trends in values in a continuous curve.

▶ **Doughnut**: Displays data similarly to a pie chart; it compares parts to a whole but contains multiple series.

▶ **Stock**: Stock charts are usually (but not exclusively) used to illustrate the fluctuation of stock prices. In a stock chart, the data order is very important and usually the row headings are High, Low, and Close (or Open, High, Low, and Close). See Figure 13-7 for an example of a stock chart.

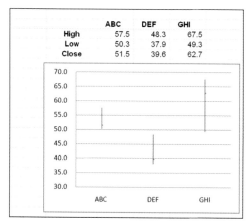

Figure 13-7
Easily track stock progress with a stock chart.

▶ **Radar**: Displays changes in values relative to a center point by comparing the cumulative values of multiple data series.

▶ **Bubble**: These charts are similar to scatter charts but compare three sets of values by displaying a series of circles.

▶ **Cylinder, Cone, and Pyramid**: Excel uses these three chart types to create a column or bar chart using three-dimensional cylindrical, conical, or pyramid shapes.

4. Choose a chart subtype. Depending on the chart type, some chart subtypes show the data series next to each other; others show the data elements stacked on top of each other. Some charts are two-dimensional, and others are three-dimensional. As you see in Figure 13-8, Excel creates the chart on the worksheet where your data resides. The chart is an object on the sheet and floats on top of the sheet. You will discover later in this chapter how to resize, modify, or move the chart. Also, notice in Figure 13-8 that three new Chart Tools tabs appear on the Ribbon.

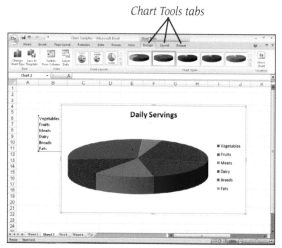

Figure 13-8
Creating an Excel chart.

Workbooks can contain multiple charts. Excel saves all charts as part of the workbook.

Changing the Chart Options

YOU JUST DISCOVERED HOW SIMPLE it is to create a chart. But you probably will want to enhance your chart to improve its appearance. Some of the items you can change include the size, style, color and placement.

However, like many other Excel features, you must select the area you want to change before you can change it. When a chart is on the same page as the data, and the chart is selected, you see eight dotted handles around the outer edge of the cart as well as a thick colored line. Each chart, no matter where it resides, has two windows. The outer window is a frame in which the chart appears. When a chart is on a sheet by itself, that frame is entire sheet. When the chart is an object on a worksheet, the frame appears as the box that surrounds the chart.

Click anywhere on the chart to select it, or click outside of the chart to deselect it. If a chart is on its own sheet, you don't need to select it. Just having the chart displayed makes it eligible for modifications.

If you create a chart and then decide you don't want it, you can easily delete it. No data is deleted, only the chart compiled from the data. If the chart is an object on the data page, select the chart and press the Delete key. If the chart is on its own sheet, right-click the chart sheet tab and choose Delete. Click Delete at the confirmation message that appears.

Resizing a Chart

When a chart appears on the same page as the worksheet, it may be too small to read the data correctly, or it may be so large that it covers the worksheet data. Either way, it's easy to resize a chart.

Select the chart which displays the eight selection handles. Position your mouse pointer over one of the handles. The mouse pointer changes to a double-headed arrow as you see in Figure 13-9. Drag the handle and you see a dotted line that indicates the new chart size. When you release the mouse button, the chart is resized.

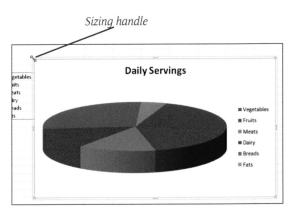

Figure 13-9
Changing the chart size.

Hold down the Shift key while you drag the chart to maintain the height-to-width chart ratio.

Changing the Chart Type

If you want to change the chart type, you can select a bar, area, line, pie, or any of the other types, many of which can also be thee-dimensional. Be careful when changing the chart type that you don't change the intended chart message. For example, if you change your chart from a bar chart to a pie chart, the emphasis shifts from what each value represents to the values in relationship of the percentage of the whole.

Select the chart and choose Chart Tools Design>Type>Change Chart Type. The Change Chart type dialog box appears. Select the chart type and subtype you want and then click OK (see Figure 13-10).

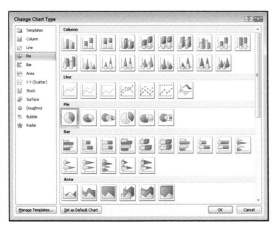

Figure 13-10
Choosing a different chart type or subtype.

Moving the Chart

When a chart is on the worksheet page, you can easily move it to any location on the page or you can move it from the data page to its own sheet. You cannot move a chart that's on its own sheet except to move it from its own sheet to the data page.

To move the chart located on the data sheet, to a different location on the data sheet, select the chart and position the mouse over the edge of the chart, but not over one of the handles. Your mouse pointer should be a four-headed arrow. Drag the chart border to a new location. As you move the chart, you see an outline such as you see in Figure 13-11, which represents the new chart position.

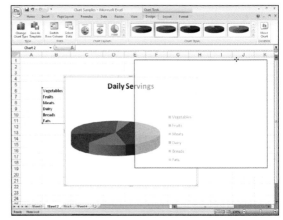

Figure 13-11
Moving a chart object around on the worksheet.

If you want to move the chart from its own sheet to the data sheet or from a data sheet to its own sheet, just follow these simple steps:

1. Select the chart that you want to move.

2. Choose Chart Tools Design>Location>Move Chart. The Move Chart dialog box seen in Figure 13-12 appears.

Figure 13-12
Changing the chart location.

3. Select a location:

▶ **New sheet**: Creates a new worksheet and places the chart on the sheet.

▶ **Object in**: Moves the chart to an existing sheet in the workbook. Click the drop-down arrow to select the worksheet to which you want to move the chart.

4. Click OK. Excel moves your chart to the location you specified.

Adding Descriptive Chart Text

A good way to make your chart more readable is to add some descriptive text that helps put the chart into a proper context. The Chart Title appears above or in the chart itself, and provides a brief description of the overall chart. You can also add axis titles to more clearly define your X or Y axis information.

Adding a Chart Title

To add a chart title, you first select the chart you want to modify and then choose Chart Tools Layout>Labels>Chart Title. A list of options appears. If you choose None, which is the default choice, no title will be displayed. You'll also use this option if you want to remove a chart title. Choose Centered Overlay Title to center the title

within the chart plot area. This option retains the existing chart size. Choose Above Chart if you want to center the title above the chart.

> **Depending on the data you select when creating a chart, some chart types automatically create a chart title.**

Make a selection. A box with the words Chart Title (as you see in Figure 13-13) appears on the chart. Double-click the Chart Title and drag across the words Chart Title to highlight them and type your own text.

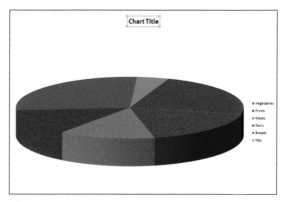

Figure 13-13
Adding a title to the chart.

Optionally, choose Chart Tools Layout>Labels> Chart Title, More Title Options. From the Format Chart Title dialog box seen in Figure 13-14, you can select Fill and then choose any desired background options for the chart title. Excel's Live Preview feature lets you view various options without first selecting them. You can also select from Border Styles, Border Color, Shadows, 3-D Format, and Alignment.

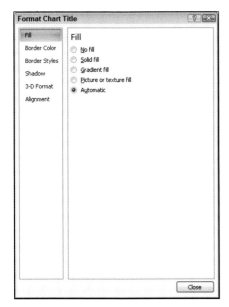

Figure 13-14
Enhancing a chart title.

You can't apply 3-D formatting or select a shadow if your title doesn't have a border line around it.

Adding Axis Text

You can add additional text to either the X or Y axis that can assist you or someone viewing your chart in better understanding the chart information. For example, adding the text *in millions* to the value axis helps the reader understand that a value of 12 really means 12 million. Or adding a category axis of *2007* might help the reader understand that the January, February, and March they are seeing are from the year 2007.

If you want to add a Category axis title, choose Chart Tools Layout>Labels>Axis Titles>Primary Horizontal Axis>Title Below Axis. Again replace the default text with your own description.

If you want to add a Value axis title, choose Chart Tools Layout>Labels>Axis Titles>Primary Vertical Axis and select a value axis title type. You have several choices for the vertical axis title:

> ▶ **None:** Removes an existing value axis title.

> ▶ **Rotated Title:** The title runs parallel with the Y axis from bottom to top.

> ▶ **Vertical Title:** The title runs from top to bottom with each letter stacked on top of each other.

> ▶ **Horizontal Title:** The title runs horizontally, which makes it easy to read but decreases the chart plot area. Use this title type for very short text.

Figure 13-15 illustrates three positions for vertical axis text and a category axis text.

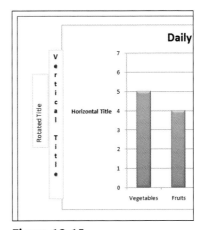

Figure 13-15
Adding axis text.

Right-click any title, which displays the Mini Toolbar. From there you can change the formatting of the selected title.

Selecting Additional Axis Options

Besides adding a title to the axis, you can also choose a few other options pertaining to the axis. For example, you can choose whether or not to display gridlines to help your reader relate to the values. Besides the default display of horizontal gridlines along the major values, you can also display vertical gridlines, or you can choose not to display gridlines at all. Choose Chart Tools Layout>Axes>Gridlines. You can add, change, or remove horizontal or vertical gridlines. You can also select More Options to modify the gridline color. Figure 13-16 illustrates a chart with both major and minor gridlines displayed.

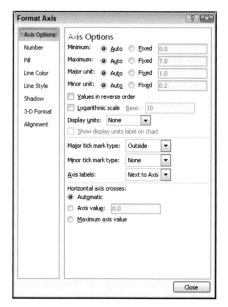

Figure 13-17
Setting value axis options.

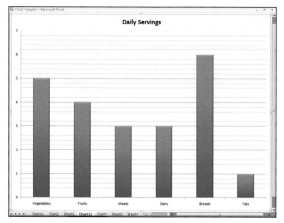

Figure 13-16
Adding minor horizontal gridlines.

Choose Chart Tools Layout>Axes>Axes to change the way Excel displays either the horizontal or vertical axis. You can choose not to display an axis or you can change the value representation along the vertical axis. Click the More button to change choices such as axis-number high or low limits or axis number formatting (see Figure 13-17).

Working with the Legend

For most charts, Excel automatically adds a legend that helps explain each series. For example, if you have only red, blue, and yellow bars without a legend, you or your reader wouldn't know what the red bars mean versus the blue or yellow bars. You can turn the legend off, move it around to a different chart area or change the options associated with a legend.

Choose Chart Tools Layout>Labels>Legend. From there you can select from the seven options seen in Figure 13-18. Remember, if you turn off the legend, you may have difficulty understanding the chart data. Optionally choose More Legend Options, which displays the Format Legend dialog box where you can select a border, fill color, shadow, or a number of other legend options. Also, like chart titles, you can right-click the legend and select formatting options.

Figure 13-18
Modifying the chart legend.

Optionally, click anywhere on the legend box to select it and manually drag the legend box wherever you want it.

Adding a Data Table

When you place a chart of the same worksheet as its data, you have one advantage over placing it on its own sheet: you can put the chart right next to the data it represents so you can see firsthand where the chart data comes from. But if you have your chart on its own page, you can add a data table.

Data tables appear in the form of a grid beneath the chart and display the numeric data that makes up the chart. They are very helpful if a reader needs to see exact values along with a graphical display, such as when using a 3-D chart. The following steps show you how to add a data table:

Data tables are not available for pie, scatter, bubble, radar, or surface charts.

1. Click anywhere on the chart you want to modify.

2. Click Chart Tools Layout>Labels>Data Table. Options include a choice not to show a data table, show a data table but not show a chart legend, or to show a data table and include the chart legend identifiers.

3. Make a Data Table selection. A data table, as seen in Figure 13-19, displays at the bottom of the chart showing the actual values.

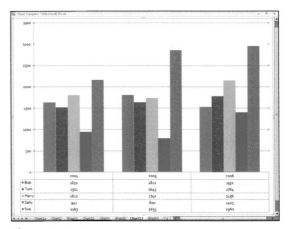

Figure 13-19
Adding a data table.

Double-click the data table to set data table formatting options.

Displaying Data Labels

Another form of text you can add comes in the form of text to the individual data markers. By default, adding data labels shows only the value of the data point, but you can also include the series name and, depending on the chart style, either the category name or the X and Y values.

1. Select the chart you want to modify and choose Chart Tools Layout>Labels>Data Labels. A menu of data label placement options appears. The options you see depend on your chart style.

> You can use Data Labels to help identify the data series values, which are sometimes difficult to read on the y-axis scale.

2. Depending on your chart type, either select Show, which turns on the data labels without any options, or choose a placement option. Figure 13-20 shows the data labels with a placement of Outside End.

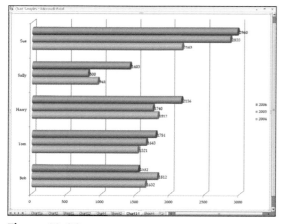

Figure 13-20
Adding data labels.

3. Choose Chart Tools Layout>Labels>Data Labels>More Data Label Options. The Format Data Labels dialog box appears.

4. If you don't want the data label to be the series value, choose a different option from the Label Options area (such as the series or category names).

5. In the Number area, select a number style for the data labels.

6. Select any additional options and then click OK.

Editing the Chart Data

Suppose that you make a wonderful chart but then decide that you want to include more data, or exclude some of the data you've chosen. Excel provides two different ways to change the data area—both of which are very easy.

The first method you can use when you want to quickly add or delete a series to a chart located on the same worksheet as the data. Click anywhere on the chart that you want to edit. Notice that Excel surrounds the chart with selection handles and marks the source data in the worksheet with a colored border. Drag the corner handle of the worksheet source range to add or subtract cells. Be sure your mouse pointer is a double-headed arrow before you drag a corner handle (see Figure 13-21).

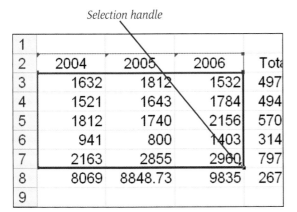

Selection handle

1				
2	2004	2005	2006	Tot
3	1632	1812	1532	497
4	1521	1643	1784	494
5	1812	1740	2156	570
6	941	800	1403	314
7	2163	2855	2960	797
8	8069	8848.73	9835	267
9				

Figure 13-21
Changing the data you want plotted.

You can also change the chart data by following these steps:

1. Click anywhere on the chart that you want to modify.

2. Choose Chart Tools Design>Data>Select Data. The Select Data Source dialog box opens with the current chart data selected in the worksheet (see Figure 13-22).

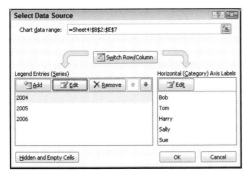

Figure 13-22
The Edit Data Source dialog box.

3. Drag in the worksheet to select the new data range. The Select Data Source dialog box collapses so you can easily see your data.

Optionally, type the cell location in the Chart data range.

4. Release the mouse button. The Edit Data Source box reappears, and the new data range appears in the Chart data range box.

5. Click OK. The Edit Data Source dialog box closes and the chart reflects the new data area.

Altering the Chart Color Style

You've already discovered how you can quickly change many options on your chart. You can also change the look by applying any of the many different predefined chart styles. Chart styles are based on the current Excel workbook's theme, and include options such as colors and fonts.

Even if you don't like some of the predefined options, you can still change any chart options individually. Right-click on any element you want to change and select Format (chart item). Most changes can be made directly from the Format dialog box. Just follow these steps to apply a chart style:

1. Click anywhere on the chart you want to modify.

2. Choose Chart Tools Design>Chart Styles and click the More button, which displays the Chart Styles gallery seen in Figure 13-23. This figure illustrates the chart styles based on the Metro theme.

See Chapter 10, "Making the Worksheet Look Good," for a refresher on themes.

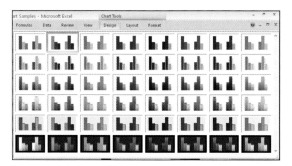

Figure 13-23
Selecting a chart style.

3. Select a chart style. You may need to scroll down. The available styles vary depending on the chart type.

Enhancing a 3-D Chart

Because 3-D charts have depth and dimension, you can alter how Excel displays the chart perspective. For example, you can rotate the chart, deepen the floor, or even change the series bevels, lighting, and materials. Let's review the steps required to enhance a three-dimensional chart.

1. Select the 3-D chart you want to modify.

2. Choose Chart Tools Layout>Background>3-D Rotation. The Format Chart Area dialog box, shown in Figure 13-24, appears. The options you see depend on the chart type. Figure 13-24 shows you the options for the column chart you also see in the figure.

To change the 3-D options for a specific chart component, click the chart component. The options in the Format Chart area box apply to the selected component.

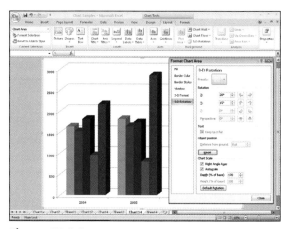

Figure 13-24
Changing three-dimensional options.

3. Click the 3-D Rotation option and choose from options such as the following:

The options you have available depend on the chart style you selected.

▶ Click the x-axis left or right rotation arrows or enter the degree of left/right rotation (between 0 and 360) you want for the chart in the Rotation box. This rotates the series left or right.

▶ Click the y-axis up or down rotation arrows or enter the degree of up/down rotation.

▶ Click the Perspective up or down arrows to change the "camera" view or the view from the top. On pie charts, you can optionally type the elevation angle (between 10 and 80) in the Elevation text box. Figure 13-25 illustrates changing the depth of the column chart base, which made the bars wider as well as

changed the axis rotation and perspective. Compare this chart to the one in Figure 13-24.

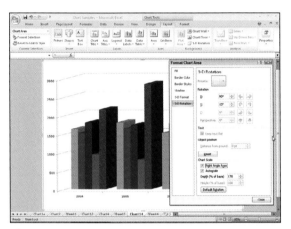

Figure 13-25
After changing three-dimensional options.

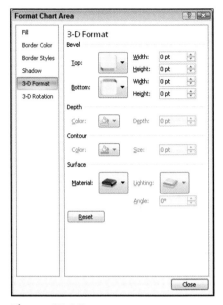

Figure 13-26
3-D Format choices.

4. Select options from the available 3-D Format choices such as those you see in Figure 13-26:

> **Again, the options you have available depend on the currently selected chart style**

▶ Choose an option to select a bevel style for the top or bottom of the chart border.

▶ Change the thickness of the bars or height of pie slices by entering a value (between 5 and 500) in the Height box.

▶ Change the Depth option to deepen series bars and the chart floor. This option does not apply to pie charts. Values range from 0 to 2000.

▶ Change the Surface material option.

5. Click Close. The chart appears on-screen, rotated to the angles you selected. Figure 13-27 shows a 3-D pie chart before and after changing the elevation and rotation.

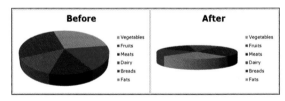

Figure 13-27
Enhancing a pie chart.

Placing a Picture in a Data Series

When Excel creates a chart, the slices, bars, or lines are typically a solid color. Earlier in this chapter you discovered how to change the entire chart style. You could also change the worksheet theme, which would change the chart colors.

One other option is to change the individual data series so that it reflects a specific color other than the default choices. Or you can add a texture or gradient to the colors you select. In some situations, however, you can get your message across even better by using a graphic instead of the solid color bar or pie slice.

1. Right-click the data point you want to modify. A shortcut menu appears.

2. Choose Format Data Series. The Format Data Series dialog box appears.

> If you are working with a pie chart or a bar or column chart with only one series, the option will say Format Data Point.

3. Click the Fill choice in the list at the left. Fill options appear on the right side.

4. Select Picture or texture fill (see Figure 13-28).

> If you just want to change the series color, select Solid fill and pick a color.

Figure 13-28
Format Data Point fill options.

5. Click File. The Insert Picture dialog box appears.

> Optionally, click the ClipArt button to select a ClipArt object instead of an image.

6. Locate and select the picture you want to use.

7. Click Insert. The Format Data Series dialog box reappears.

8. Choose whether you want Excel to stretch the picture to fill the series or to multiply them and stack them on top each other. Typically you would use the stretch option if you are modifying a pie chart. Using the stretch option with bar or column charts distorts the image.

9. Click OK. Figure 13-29 illustrates a pie chart where one series was replaced with a photograph, one with clip art, and one with a gradient fill. Data labels were also added for clarity.

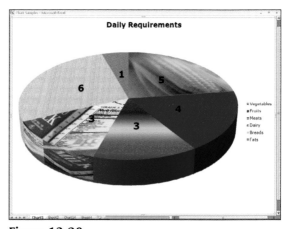

Figure 13-29
Liven up your charts with graphic images.

Part IV
PowerPoint

Very seldom anymore do you attend a conference, seminar, meeting or trade show without seeing a PowerPoint presentation, since PowerPoint is ideal for presenting concepts and lecture material. PowerPoint is the feature-laden Microsoft Office program that allows you to create presentations and optional audience handouts. Through the creation of PowerPoint slides, you can add color, images, sounds, animation, and movies to an otherwise text-based presentation.

This section takes you through creating a PowerPoint presentation that will help you get your message across efficiently.

14

Creating a PowerPoint
Presentation

PICTURE YOURSELF ATTENDING A MEETING. It's a long meeting, and the presenter has been droning on and on about something, but you are not sure about what. His monotone voice is putting you to sleep, and he just stands there reciting fact after fact about his topic. It all becomes a blur, and you know you aren't getting anything out of this meeting.

Now picture yourself at a meeting with a vibrant presenter who not only gives you the topic facts, but backs them up with colorful charts and illustrations all presented in a logical and interesting manner. This speaker is using a PowerPoint presentation to help get the point across, and, by golly, it's working!

Now it is time for you to give a presentation. If you are not sure where to begin, don't worry. PowerPoint includes quite a few tools to help you take that first step. Actually, you already know a lot more than you think. By working in Word and Excel you have learned about many of the tools you will use in PowerPoint when you create your first dynamic presentation.

Starting with the Basics

EVERY PROJECT NEEDS A STARTING
point, and if you are using PowerPoint for the
first time, you will want to begin with a quick
exploration of the PowerPoint program window.
When you open the PowerPoint application, a blank
slide appears and the program is in Normal view.

Perusing the PowerPoint Window

First, I will review a few of the common Office features. Take a look at Figure 14-1. Just like Word and
Excel, PowerPoint includes the Office button where
you can access your file management commands
such as Save, Open, and Print. You also see the
Quick Access Toolbar with its Save, Undo and
Repeat buttons. You also see the PowerPoint
Ribbon with seven different tabs displayed when
working with a new PowerPoint presentation. You
will see other Ribbon tabs appear as certain
processes occur such as adding graphics or tables
to your slides.

Down in the lower right corner you see the familiar
Zoom control where you can zoom in for a closer
look, and you also see three other View buttons
next to the Zoom control. PowerPoint has three
working views: Normal, which is the default view;
Slide Sorter view, which you will see in Chapter 15;
and Slide Show view, which you will work with in
Chapter 17. The three View buttons next to the
Zoom control take you quickly into any of the
three PowerPoint views.

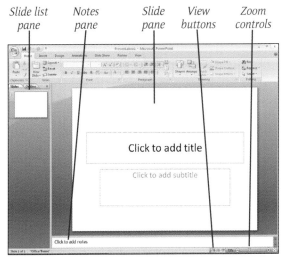

Figure 14-1
The PowerPoint window.

The left pane on the PowerPoint screen is called
the Slide list, where you can see the slides in
your presentation. As you add multiple slides to
the presentation, you will see a scroll bar appear.
It is also where you will view and work with your
outline. I will cover the outline later in this chapter.
The right side pane is the Current Slide window
where you perform the actual work on the slides
such as adding text or graphics.

The bottom pane is the Notes pane. That is were
you can jot down notes to yourself (or to the presenter) as reminders when giving the presentation.
I will cover creating Notes in Chapter 17, "Showing
Your Presentation."

Adding a Little Advice

Okay, so this section does not have you actually *do* anything, but it gives you something to think about. A lot of research has gone into creating the perfect presentation, and here are several tips to help you when planning your presentation:

▶ **Consider your audience. The way you present information to a group of school children is very different than the way you might present it to your co-workers. (Most of the time, anyway.)**

▶ **Keep it simple. Do not try to shove every thought on to a slide. The slides become jumbled and you lose your audience. Keep the text simple and direct. You can do more explaining as you present.**

▶ **Remain focused. Keep the slides and your speaking focused on the current topic.**

▶ **State your intentions. State what your presentation is about and what you intend to prove with the presentation.**

▶ **Make it personal. Tell the story that illustrates the problem and through the presentation, show how to solve the problem. Provide solutions...not just problems.**

▶ **Use graphics such as charts and tables to illustrate your key points. People like pictures and they understand and retain pictures better than words.**

▶ **Don't under or over design. Follow the KISS ("Keep It Simple, Stupid") theory. While you certainly want some design elements, keep the design elements consistent through the entire presentation and don't add too many so you don't distract your audience. Figure 14-2 illustrates two slides: one so boring it makes you yawn and one with too much design.**

Figure 14-2
Not too much, not too little.

▶ **Know your material. If you are the one who will present the material, make sure you know it inside and out. Rehearse, rehearse, rehearse.**

Keeping those few items in mind will help you get your point across to your audience in just the way you intend.

Understanding the Presentation Process

Although it is certainly not written in stone, the following tasks are the typical actions taken when creating a presentation. Other than the first and last items, the tasks are pretty much interchangeable. Take a look at Figure 14-3, which illustrates the following list:

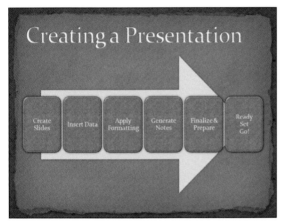

Figure 14-3
The process of creating a presentation.

▶ **Create the slides**: Although a presentation could consist of a single slide, they rarely do. You can select from the preformatted slide layouts designed to present your information.

▶ **Insert the data**: Once you have some slides, you need to make them project the information you are trying to relay. You do that in the form of text, tables, charts, and shapes.

▶ **Apply a design**: You can create a background for your slides and apply a theme, all of which helps maintain the continuity of your presentation.

▶ **Generate speaker notes**: You can jot down reminders of what you want to say to your audience when you are giving the presentation.

▶ **Prepare for presentation**: To liven up your presentation, you can add multimedia such as video, sounds, or narration, or you can animate the items on a slide.

▶ **Present the presentation**: The culmination of all your work, you present the slides to an audience, during which you can draw on the slides or make them run automatically.

Creating a New Presentation

When you started PowerPoint, you saw a new, blank presentation ready for you to work with. If you do not want to start with the blank presentation provided when you open PowerPoint, you can select from the many pre-designed, pre-formatted PowerPoint templates. These templates illustrate that you need not be an artist to create a good-looking presentation, complete with a background and other images.

Press Ctrl+N to create a new blank presentation with a title slide.

Choose Office Button>New. The New Presentation window seen in Figure 14-4 launches.

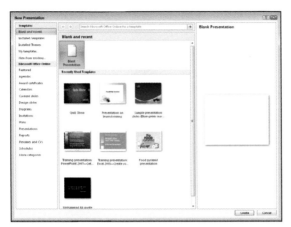

Figure 14-4
Select the template you want to use.

Figure 14-5
Save time by beginning with a predesigned template available online.

From the left side, chose a category. If you don't have an Internet connection, choose Installed Templates or My Templates. If you have an Internet connection, PowerPoint can also display choices from the hundreds of templates available from Microsoft Office Online.

If you just want a plain blank template, from the Blank and recent category choose Blank Presentation and then click Create. If you want one of the already installed templates, from the Installed Templates category, choose a template and click Create. If you select one of the templates from Office Online, click the template you want, such as seen in Figure 14-5, and then click Download. PowerPoint downloads the template and displays it on your screen.

You only have to download a template once. The next time you want the template, you see it listed under the Blank and recent category or under My Templates.

Adding New Slides

A FTER YOU CREATE THE presentation, you can begin working on the first blank slide for the presentation title, or you can start inserting the slides. Slides use slide layouts, which are preformatted slide designs that help you enter text, graphics, and other things. Some layouts have text placeholders for entering titles and other text, while some contain content placeholders for inserting tables, charts, diagrams, pictures, clipart, images, or video.

Inserting Blank Slides

When you insert a slide, you must select the layout that best resembles the slide you want to create. Don't worry—you can change to a different layout or change any component of the slide later.

Choose Home>Slides and click the arrow at the bottom of the New Slide button. A list of slide layouts appears as seen in Figure 14-6. Choose the layout you want. With one exception, all the slide layouts contain some combination of text placeholders or text and content placeholders. It is up to you to decide which of the nine slide layouts you want to use. The following list explains each slide layout and what placeholders it contains:

Deleting an unwanted slide is as easy as selecting the slide and choosing Home> Slides>Delete.

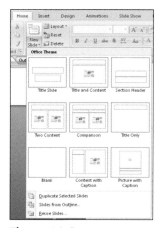

Figure 14-6
Select the layout you want for your new slide.

► **Title Slide:** Contains two text placeholders. Typically you use the larger text box for the presentation title and the smaller one for a presentation description.

► **Title and Content:** Contains one text placeholder, usually used for the slide title, and one content placeholder.

► **Section Header:** Very similar to a Title slide, the section header contains two text placeholders. Section header slides are usually used to break a presentation into separate areas.

► **Two Content:** Contains one text placeholder for the slide title and two side by side content placeholders

▶ **Comparison**: Contains three text place-holders and two side-by-side content placeholders. One text placeholder is used for the slide title, and the other two are positioned above the content placeholders.

▶ **Title Only**: Contains one text placeholder positioned for the slide title.

▶ **Blank**: Contains no placeholders at all.

▶ **Content with Caption**: Contains two text placeholders and one content placeholder. One text placeholder is for the slide title and the other for content explanatory text. Figure 14-7 illustrates a slide from a Content with Caption layout.

▶ **Picture with Caption**: Contains two text placeholders and a modified content placeholder. One text place-holder is for the slide title and the other to explain the content placeholder. The content placeholder is modified to insert pictures only.

Figure 14-7
A slide made in the Content with Caption layout.

As you add slides to your presentation, they appear in the Slide list; however, the Slide list pane does not show placeholders. Only the Slide pane on the right shows the placeholders. To switch to a different slide, simply click the slide in the Slide list.

Copying Slides

To save time and effort, if you have already slides that are similar to a new slide you want, you can duplicate them. You can copy a slide from the current presentation or from another saved presentation.

Copying From the Current Presentation

If you need a new slide similar to one in the current presentation you can save yourself time by dupli-cating the slide and then editing the duplicate as needed. Just follow these steps:

1. From the Slide list pane, click the slide you want to duplicate.

   If you want to duplicate multiple slides, hold down the Ctrl key as you click on each slide you want to duplicate.

2. Choose Home>Slides and click the New Slide arrow.

   If you don't click the arrow and just click the New Slide button, PowerPoint auto-matically adds a Title and Content slide.

3. Choose Duplicate Selected Slides. PowerPoint creates a copy of the slide and inserts the copy directly below the selected slide (see Figure 14-8).

Figure 14-8
Duplicating slides can save you lots of time.

Figure 14-9
Select the presentation you want to copy from.

Keep source formatting

Figure 14-10
Reusing slides from other presentations.

Using Slides from Another File

If you have a saved presentation with slides that can help you in the current presentation, you can copy them, thereby saving lots of time. You have the option of not only copying the slide content, but also copying the formatting. Just follow these easy steps:

1. Choose Home>Slides and click the New Slide arrow.

2. Click Reuse Slides. The Reuse Slides pane, seen in Figure 14-9, opens on the right side of the screen.

3. Click the Browse button and choose Browse File.

4. Locate and click the PowerPoint presentation from which you want to select slides.

5. Click Open. All the slides in the selected presentation appear in the Reuse Slides pane (see Figure 14-10).

6. By default, the reused slides use the design elements in the currently open presentation. If you also want the design formats in the saved presentation, click the Keep source formatting option.

7. Select the slides you want to reuse. PowerPoint inserts the slide into the presentation.

8. When you are finished selecting slides to reuse, click the Close (x) button to close the Reuse Slides pane.

Adding Slide Objects

NOW THAT YOU HAVE SELECTED a slide layout, it is time to begin adding data to the slide. That data can be in the form of text, whether titles or bullets, photographs or clipart, charts or diagrams, tables, or just drawn shapes. In this section you will see how to add each of these elements to your slide. In Chapter 15, "Editing the Presentation," you will see how to edit the objects after you add them.

The sections below first assume you want to add the object into the slide placeholder, but you can add any of these objects anywhere on the slide. I will also give you instructions on how to optionally place the object on the page without using the content placeholder.

Including Text on Slides

Think of each text placeholder as a miniature Word program in that you can type text into it. The text stays constrained to the placeholder, but, if needed, PowerPoint wraps the text around in the placeholder box. The default font is determined by the slide layout and the current theme, but you can change it as needed to suit your purpose.

Begin by clicking any text placeholder. The placeholder text (which, by the way, does not print) disappears and a blinking insertion point appears. Type the desired text and use the same editing techniques as you discovered in Chapter 2, "Getting Started with Word." Typically, if you are working on a title text placeholder, you only want one or two lines of text since the font size is already very large.

If you want to freely place text on a slide without using a placeholder, you use a text box. Choose Insert>Text>Text Box. Bring your mouse to the slide and draw an imaginary box about the size you want the entire block of text. When you release the mouse button, the text box appears with a blinking insertion point where you type your text. If the text box is too small, you can continue typing, although all the text may not display. In Chapter 15 "Editing Your Presentation," you will see how to move or resize the text box.

Content placeholders display a "Click to add text" guideline. If you want to create a list of bullet points for the slide, click the "Click to add text" line and begin typing. Each time you press the Enter key, the slide displays another bullet as you see in Figure 14-11. Click anywhere outside of the content placeholder to deselect the placeholder boundaries.

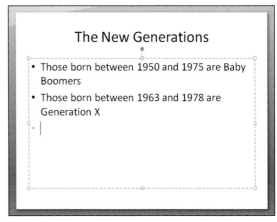

Figure 14-11
Press the Enter key to display a new bullet point.

Attaching Graphic Images

When working with a content slide, you can, as you just discovered, add bullet point text. Another type of element you can add to a content slide is graphic images that come in the form of pictures, which are usually photographs but can be any saved graphic image or clip art that is a graphic and is small in size, usually an illustration or line drawing.

A slide content placeholder has six icons in the middle as you see in Figure 14-12. As you pause your mouse over each icon, the icon brightens and a ScreenTip appears to describe the type of content. The six content icons are Insert Table, Insert Chart, Insert SmartArt Graphic, Insert Picture from File, Clip Art and Insert Media Clip.

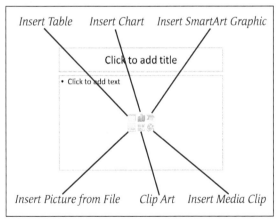

Insert Table   Insert Chart   Insert SmartArt Graphic

Insert Picture from File   Clip Art   Insert Media Clip

Figure 14-12
Click to insert content into a content placeholder.

Adding Clip Art

While most Office applications have the ability to insert clip art into a file, adding clip art to a slide, especially one with quite a few bullet points, brings interest to an otherwise dull slide. Office ships with hundreds of clip art images and thousands more are available online, free from Microsoft. Office stores clip art in collections with keywords so you can easily locate the image you want. Whatever the topic, you are sure to find a clip art image that compliments it. Here is how you can add clip art to a slide content placeholder:

1. Choose the slide you want to place clip art and in the content placeholder, click the Clip Art icon. If you do not want the Clip Art in the content placeholder, but just as a separate screen object, choose Insert> Illustrations>Clip Art. Either way, the Clip Art pane appears on the right side of the screen.

   In Word or Excel, you can insert clip art by choosing Insert>Illustrations>Clip Art. In Publisher, you choose Insert>Picture> Clip Art.

2. In the "Search for" box, type a word or short phrase that best describes the image you want. For example, typing *dairy* brings up a collection of artwork ranging from cows to cheese to milk cartons.

3. Click the Go button. Office displays the available clip art that matches your request (see Figure 14-13).

Figure 14-13
Click the clip art graphic you want to use.

4. Click the image you want. The image appears in the slide as you see in Figure 14-14.

5. Click the Close button to close the Clip Art pane.

Close button

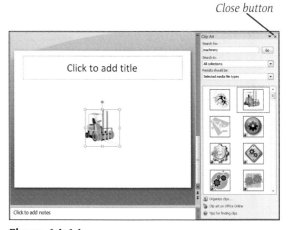

Figure 14-14
The clip art image appears in your slide.

Chapter 15 "Editing the Presentation," shows you how to move, resize, and otherwise manage graphic images.

Adding Saved Pictures

If you have a digital photograph or other graphic image such as a company logo, you can place it on the slide as well. To insert an existing graphics file into your slide, follow these steps:

1. In the content placeholder for the slide you want a picture, click the Insert Picture from File icon. If you do not want the image in the content placeholder, but just as a separate screen object, choose Insert>Illustrations> Picture. The Insert Picture dialog box opens.

2. Locate and select the image you to insert.

3. Click Insert. PowerPoint inserts the image you selected into the content placeholder or elsewhere on the slide (see Figure 14-15.)

Figure 14-15
Adding a picture to the slide.

Inserting Tables

If you want to present your data in a row and column, use a table on the slide. Tables are a great way to display the numerical facts that backup your topic. In Chapter 5 "Working with Columns and Tables," you discovered a great deal of information about inserting and managing a table in Word. A great deal of the Words table features are mirrored in PowerPoint.

Begin by selecting the slide on which you want and table and then clicking the Insert Tables icon on the content placeholder. The Insert Table dialog box appears prompting you for the number of columns and rows you want in your table. Enter the numbers you want and click OK. If you need more columns or rows, or fewer, you can change that after you create the table. PowerPoint inserts the table into your document. If you already have applied a design to your presentation, the table picks up the styles and colors associated with that design.

> If you do not want to use the content placeholder, you can optionally choose Insert>Tables>Table, which provides a grid where you can select the table size.

Just like a Word table, you add any text into the individual cells by typing the text and then either clicking in the next cell or using the Tab or Shift+Tab keys to move around the table (see Figure 14-16).

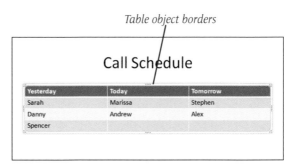

Table object borders

Figure 14-16
Illustrate data in a table.

Because the table is an object in the slide, when a table is active you see a border surrounding it. The border has a series of dots in each corner and at the middle of the top, bottom, left, and right sides. In Chapter 15 "Editing the Presentation," you will see where you can use the border and the border dots to move or resize the table. You can inactivate the table by clicking anywhere outside of the border and reactivate it by clicking anywhere in the table.

When you insert a table, and while the table is active, PowerPoint adds two contextual tabs to the Ribbon: Table Tools Design and Table Tools Layout, both of which you see in Figure 14-17. The Table Tools Design tab helps you manage the overall table appearance, and the Table Tools Layout tab primarily helps you manage the table plan.

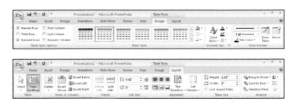

Figure 14-17
The Table Tools tab.

You will find the Table Tools Layout tab is very similar to the Word Table Tools Layout tab. It includes tools with which you can insert and delete rows, merge and split cells, change row height and column width, and manage text directions.

The PowerPoint Table Tools Design tab also is almost identical to the Word Table Tools Design tab. From there you can select styles, borders, and fill options for your table.

Building Charts

In Chapter 13, "Generating Excel Charts," you learned about creating charts. The charts you create in a PowerPoint slide have one major difference. In PowerPoint, you decide on the chart first, *then* you enter the data. The following shows the steps involved:

1. From the slide you want to place a chart, click the Insert Chart icon on the content placeholder, or, if you are not using a content placeholder, choose Insert> Illustrations>Chart.

> If you want to place a chart in you Word document, you also can choose Insert> Illustrations>Chart. The remaining steps are identical in both Word and PowerPoint. You can also create a chart in Publisher, but I will cover that in Chapter 20, "Adding Artwork to a Publication."

2. From the Insert Chart dialog box seen in Figure 14-18, select the chart style you want and then click OK. Your PowerPoint window resizes itself to half the screen and an Excel worksheet window with sample data in it appears on the right.

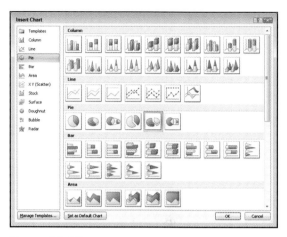

Figure 14-18
Choosing a chart style.

3. Edit the worksheet data so the labels and values portray the data you want shown. As you make the changes, the chart in the PowerPoint window immediately reflects the changes (see Figure 14-19).

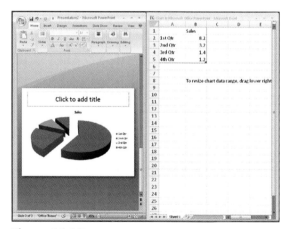

Figure 14-19
Enter the chart data into the Excel worksheet.

4. When you finish editing the data, close the Excel window. You do not need to save changes as they are already saved in PowerPoint.

5. Since the PowerPoint window displays three Chart Tools tabs (Design, Layout and Format) while the chart is selected, you can edit the chart design as you learned for editing an Excel chart.

> To edit the chart data, choose Chart Tools Design>Data>Edit Data, which reopens the data in the Excel window.

Creating SmartArt

Another element you can place on a content slide is called SmartArt. SmartArt objects are diagrams that show relationships, product cycles, workflow processes, and such. Using a diagram allows your viewers to better visualize a concept or idea.

> **Diagrams are also available in Word and Excel.**

First you must select the diagram type and then you can customize it to meet your specific needs. There are seven basic diagram types, although each type contains quite a few variations. Here are the different diagram types:

▶ **List:** Use this type for describing related items, usually sequential or showing a progression.

▶ **Process:** Use this type for describing how a concept or physical process changes over time.

▶ **Cycle:** Use this type to show progress from one stage to another when the process repeats itself.

▶ **Hierarchy:** Use this type to describe relationships between items or people. A company organization chart is an example of a Hierarchy diagram.

▶ **Relationship:** Use this type to describe how two or more items are connected to each other.

▶ **Matrix:** Use this type for showing the relationship between the whole and its components.

▶ **Pyramid:** Use this for showing proportional or interconnected relationships. The famous Food Pyramid seen in Figure 14-20 is a classic example of a pyramid diagram.

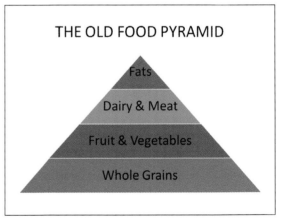

Figure 14-20
The Food Pyramid created from SmartArt.

Begin by clicking the Insert SmartArt Graphic icon in the content placeholder or by choosing Insert>Illustrations>SmartArt. The Choose a SmartArt Graphic dialog box seen in Figure 14-21 appears. Select the diagram type you want, and then from the List section, choose the diagram subtype and click OK. For the illustrations in this section, I am using an organization chart.

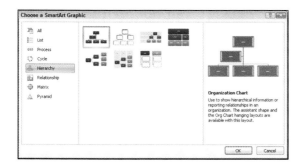

Figure 14-21
Choose the type of SmartArt you want to create.

Removing Shapes

Later in this chapter you will see how you can add additional shapes to your diagram. If, however, your diagram has shapes you do not want or need, you can easily delete them. In Figure 14-22, you see an organization diagram that automatically begins with a high level, an assistant level, and three sublevels. If you don't want the Assistant box, for example, you can remove it. Simply click the border edge of the shape you want to remove. When the shape is selected, you see eight selection handles around the box. Press the Delete key to delete the unwanted shape.

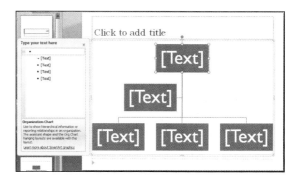

Figure 14-22
Deleting unwanted shapes.

Adding Text to a Diagram

Notice that each box in the diagram has a text placeholder. To add text to your diagram you *could* click each individual placeholder and type the desired text. A faster way, however, is to use the Text pane that appears on the left side of the diagram (see Figure 14-23). Selection handles surrounding the graphic shape are tied to your insertion point location on the Text pane. As you enter text, it automatically resizes to fit in the selected diagram shape.

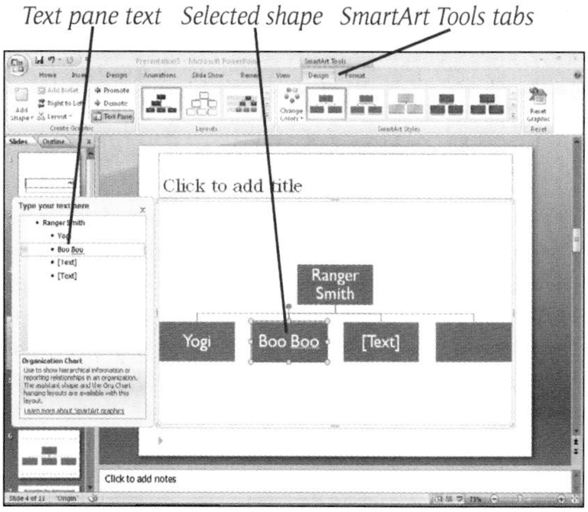

Text pane text   Selected shape   SmartArt Tools tabs

Figure 14-23
Entering text into the Text pane.

To close the Text pane, choose SmartArt Tools Design>Create Graphic>Text pane. Click it again to redisplay the Text pane.

Working with Hierarchy Levels

In the Text pane, when you press Enter, another blank line and a corresponding shape appear on the slide. Since a hierarchy diagram (such as our organization chart), usually includes different levels, called branches, PowerPoint by default provides several higher headings and a few lower headings. You can promote or demote these headings as needed. In the Text pane, click anywhere in the line you want to promote or demote and do one of the following:

▶ **Press the Tab key to demote to a lower level. Optionally, choose SmartArt Tools Design>Create Graphic>Demote.**

▶ **Press the Shift+Tab key to promote to a higher level. Optionally, choose SmartArt Tools Design>Create Graphic>Promote.**

As you promote or demote the text, the slide graphic immediately reflects the changes (see Figure 14-24).

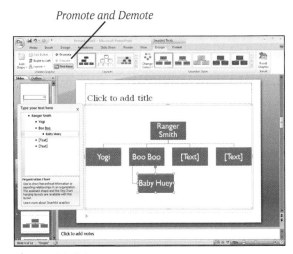

Promote and Demote

Figure 14-24
Promoting and Demoting in an organization chart.

Adding Diagram Shapes

The SmartArt Tools Design tab contains a button to add shapes; however, in most situations it is generally easiest to add shapes using the Text pane. Simply click at the end of the text in the shape located before where you want the new shape. Press Enter and the Text pane provides another line for typing and a shape to go with it. You can then add as many shapes as you want.

Unlike the hierarchy type diagrams, the list, process, cycle, relationship, and matrix diagrams do not have branches, which makes them travel in a single direction. Look at the Text pane and diagram in Figure 14-25 where you see three shapes forming a circle. When working with these types of diagrams, all the Outline text lines are on the same level.

Figure 14-25
A single-level outline.

When adding shapes to a hierarchy diagram, you have additional decisions to make such as at what level you want the new shape placed. If you are adding a peer-level shape, you use the Text pane. Click at the beginning of the line where you want the new shape and press the Enter key. On the resulting blank line, type the text for the new shape.

If, however, you want to add an assistant-level shape, follow these steps:

The Add Assistant feature is available only if you are working with an Organization Chart.

---

1. In the Text pane, click the line for the shape to which you want to add an assistant..

2. Choose SmartArt Tools Design>Create Graphic and click the Add Shape arrow. A list of choices appears.

3. Choose Add Assistant. The Assistant box appears. In the Text pane, instead of a bullet point like the other shapes, the Assistant appears at the bottom of the list with a right-angled arrow (see Figure 14-26).

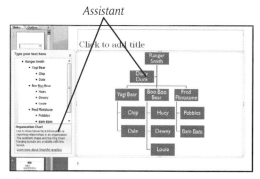

Figure 14-26
Adding an assistant.

Changing the SmartArt Layout

If after working on your diagram you decide you should have chosen a different style, you do not have to start all over. Choose SmartArt Tools Design> Layouts and select from the layouts. As you pause your mouse over any layout, Live Preview shows you your chart as it would appear in the new layout. In Figure 14-27, you see the original organization chart changed to a Horizontal Hierarchy.

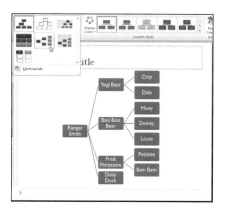

Figure 14-27
Select a different layout.

Remember that only an organization chart can have an assistant, so in this example, choosing a different layout forces the assistant to a peer level.

Changing Shapes

If you want to call special attention to a certain area of your diagram, you can change the shape of an object. Optionally, you can change the shapes for all the diagram shape objects. For example, you want the assistant to be in the form of a circle instead of the square cornered box. Or perhaps you want a box to have rounded corner boxes instead of the square corners.

Select the shape you want to change and choose SmartArt Tools Format>Shapes>Change Shape. A gallery of shapes like the one you see in Figure 14-28 appears. Choose a new shape and the diagram reflects the change.

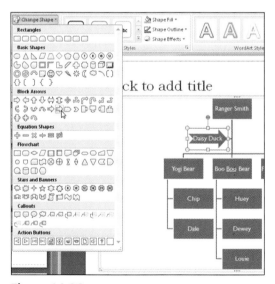

Figure 14-28
Selecting a new shape.

Changing shapes may force the text size on all the shapes to change. If your shape size needs modified, choose SmartArt Tools Format>Shapes and choose Larger or Smaller.

Changing a Diagram Style

If you want to add a little style to your diagram, you can select from a variety of predefined styles that are coordinated and would look good with your current diagram layout. You can also change the colors assigned to the diagram. The color choices available depend on the PowerPoint presentation theme. You will see how to apply designs and themes in Chapter 16, "Formatting Your Presentation."

If you want to change the diagram colors, choose SmartArt Tools Design>SmartArt Styles>Change Colors. A drop-down gallery similar to what you see in Figure 14-29 appears. Again, as you pause your mouse over any choice, Live Preview shows you how it looks on your diagram.

Figure 14-29
Adding a little color to your diagram.

If you want to change the box styles, such as adding an shadows, embossing, or three-dimensional angles, choose SmartArt Tools Design>SmartArt Styles and click the More button. Select from the choices you see. In Figure 14-30, you see the diagram with an intense color depth and shadows.

You can also change an individual shape color or effects by selecting the shape and choosing SmartArt Tools Format>Shape Styles and choosing from the number of different options provided which include the shape fill color, outline attributes, and shape effects. See the Assistant shape in Figure 14-31.

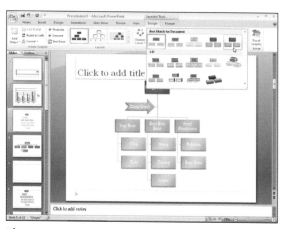

Figure 14-30
Adding diagram special effects.

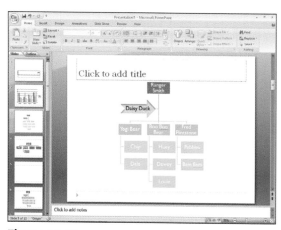

Figure 14-31
Changing the individual shape attributes.

Adding Photo Albums

A UNIQUE PRESENTATION YOU CAN create with PowerPoint is a Photo Album. In a Photo Album, each slide displays one or more photos. While you could do this manually by creating lots of slides and inserting an image on each slide, you can also let PowerPoint do this automatically. You simply tell PowerPoint which pictures you want. The following steps show you how to create a Photo Album presentation.

1. Choose Insert>Illustrations>Photo Album. The Photo Album dialog box seen in Figure 14-32 opens.

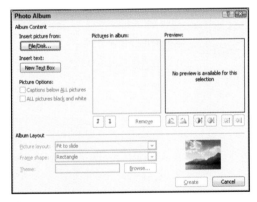

Figure 14-32
Creating a Photo Album presentation.

2. Now you need to designate which photos you want included in the album. Click the File/Disk button. The Insert New Picture dialog box opens.

3. Navigate to the folder containing the pictures you want to use.

4. Select the pictures you want. You can select multiple pictures by holding down the Ctrl key while clicking the individual pictures (see Figure 14-33).

Figure 14-33
Select the images you want to include.

5. Click the Insert button. The Insert New Picture box closes and you return to the Photo Album dialog box. The dialog box lists all the pictures you selected. From this box you can select an image from the list and do any of the following (see Figure 14-34):

   ▶ **Remove an image**

   ▶ **Move an image up or down in the list**

   ▶ **Rotate an image**

   ▶ **Add an image caption**

   ▶ **Change the image contrast**

   ▶ **Change the image brightness**

Rotate buttons   Change contrast   Change brightness
                         buttons   buttons

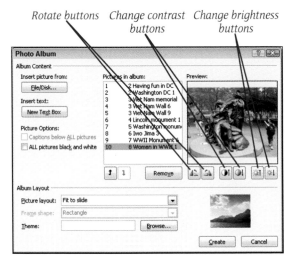

Figure 14-34
Choosing options for the Photo Album presentation.

6. Click the Picture layout drop-down arrow. You can choose how many images you want on a single slide: 1, 2, or 4.

7. Click the Frame shape drop-down arrow. You can choose from a variety of frames to place around your image. If, in step 6, you choose Fit to Slide, the Frame option is unavailable.

8. Optionally, click the Browse button next to Theme and choose an Office theme for your Photo Album.

If you want to insert a blank text slide so you can perhaps journal information about the images, click the New Text Box button.

9. Optionally, click Captions below ALL pictures. Each image will display its file name as the caption.

10. Optionally, if you want your Photo Album to display the images in black and white instead of color, click ALL pictures black and white.

11. Click the Create button. A new PowerPoint presentation like the one shown in Figure 14-25 appears with the options you selected. PowerPoint creates the first slide as a title slide.

Figure 14-35
A Photo Album presentation with a title slide.

To return to the Photo Album dialog box, choose Insert>Illustrations and click the Photo Album down arrow. Choose Edit Photo Album. After making any desired changes, click the Update button.

Working with Outlines

THROUGHOUT THIS CHAPTER, YOU discovered how to create a presentation by adding slides one at a time. Another, and typically much faster method for creating a presentation is to use an outline. You first worked with outlines in Word in Chapter 7 "Discovering Word Tools." Working with a PowerPoint outline is very similar. In fact, you can create your presentation based on an outline that you saved in Word.

The pane on the left side of a presentation has two tabs. The first tab is for the Slide list pane, but behind that tab is the Outline tab. Click the Outline tab to begin working with the presentation outline in the Outline pane.

Creating the Outline in PowerPoint

The best way to begin the outline is to create the slides and their titles. PowerPoint treats the first line of outline text as the first slide title. Usually the first slide in a new presentation is a title slide layout, so on the first line you should type a title for your presentation. When you press the Enter key the insertion point moves to the next line and PowerPoint creates another slide, which by default is in a Title and Content layout. Again, the text you type in the outline becomes the slide title. You keep typing the slide titles until you have the slides you want. Figure 14-36 illustrates the Outline pane with the slide titles.

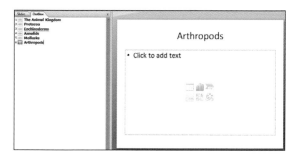

Figure 14-36
Typing in the Outline pane.

The second level in a PowerPoint outline is for items such as subtitles and bullet points. Click at the end of the slide you want to add a subtitle or bullet point. Press Enter to create a new line and press the Tab key. Pressing the Tab key indents the text and makes it into a second level heading. If the current slide is in a Title layout, the second level text becomes a subtitle like the one you see in Figure 14-37. If the current slide is a Title and Content layout, the second level text becomes bullet points as you see in Figure 14-38.

Figure 14-37
Adding subtitles in the outline.

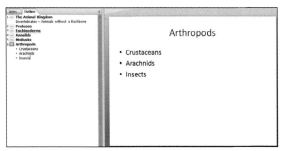

Figure 14-38
Adding bullet points in the outline.

To shift second level text back to first level text, press Shift+Tab

File type drop-down arrow

Figure 14-39
Choose the Word file containing the outline you want.

Importing an Outline from a Word File

Since slide titles are similar to the headings you created when you typed a Word outline, you can import the outline from a Word document that uses Heading styles. When you import the text from Word, you get one slide for each Level 1 heading which creates the slide title. Level 2 headings form the first bullet level, Level 3 headings for the second bullet level, and so forth. Any body text in the outline is ignored during the import.

The following steps show you how to create an outline from an existing Word file.

1. Choose Office Button>Open. The Open dialog box appears.

2. Click the file type drop-down arrow and choose All Outlines.

3. Navigate to the folder containing the outline and select the outline you want to use (see Figure 14-39).

4. Click the Open button. PowerPoint imports the outline and creates the necessary slides. The text appears in the Outline pane as you see in Figure 14-40.

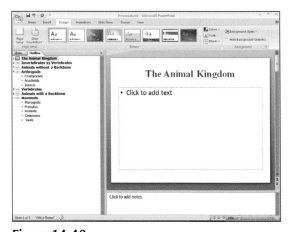

Figure 14-40
An outline imported from Word.

To print the outline, see Chapter 17, "Showing Your Presentation."

Editing Your
Presentation

PICTURE YOURSELF ASSEMBLING A BICYCLE. You have all the parts laid out in front of you and you slowly begin putting all the pieces together. Carefully and meticulously, you adjust the seat and handle bars so everything is right where you need it, and then you add the decals and emblems for a few final flourishes.

Whether you create your presentation from a blank beginning or from one of the PowerPoint templates that provide some rather impressive slides, you will want to make modifications to any presentation you create. This chapter is about editing. You have created the slides you need, and now you need to adjust the slide content until everything is in just the right place.

Changing Views

HAVE YOU EVER HEARD THE OLD expression that sometimes you can't see the forest for the trees? When your presentation has a number of slides, sometimes you become so concentrated on the individual slides that you need to sit back and look at your presentation from another perspective. Fortunately, PowerPoint includes a couple of different ways to do just that.

Working in Slide Sorter View

Depending on your task, you will probably switch frequently between the three main PowerPoint views. Up to this point you have been working in the Normal view. When you are editing the individual slide elements, you can work best in the default Normal view.

However, for a good overall look at the presentation and an easy way to manipulate entire slides, it is easiest in the Slide Sorter view. The Slide Sorter view provides a thumbnail size view of each slide in the presentation. You cannot edit slide content in Slide Sorter view, but you can change the order in which the slides appear as well as easily delete slides.

Change to Slide Sorter view by clicking the Slide Sorter icon from the View icons or by choosing View>Presentation Views>Slide Sorter. Figure 15-1 shows a presentation in Slide Sorter view.

The third main view, Slide Show view, lets you present the show in its entirety. You will work in Slide Show view in Chapter 17, "Presenting Your Presentation."

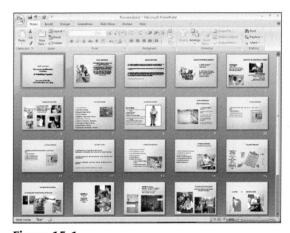

Figure 15-1
Viewing slides in the Slide Sorter.

Viewing Slides in the Slide Sorter

From the Slide Sorter view you can view the overall effects of your presentation, including the ability to view a slide close up or in other color modes. Here are a couple of your options:

▶ Use the zoom controls at the bottom to zoom the slide collection to a larger or smaller size. Optionally, if your mouse has a scroll wheel, hold down the Ctrl key and roll the scroll wheel forward to enlarge the view or roll it backward to shrink the view (see Figure 15-2).

▶ Double-click a slide to display the slide in Normal view.

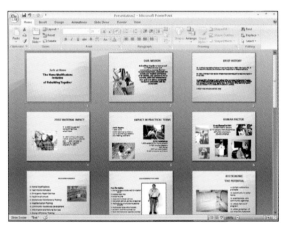

Figure 15-2
Zoom the slides in or out.

Selecting Slides

Before you can manipulate the slides, you need to select the them. Simply click once on an individual slide. Selected slides have a heavy border around them. If you want to select multiple slides, do one of the following:

▶ To select a sequential group of slides, click once on the first slide, hold down the Shift key, and click the last slide in the group. All the selected slides display a heavy border around them. In Figure 15-3 slides 3 through 10 are selected.

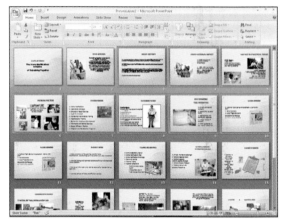

Figure 15-3
Selecting slides.

▶ To select a non-sequential group of slides, click once on the first slide, hold down the Ctrl key, and click on each additional slide you want.

Deleting Slides

Using the Slide Sorter view makes deleting slides only a keystroke away. Simply select the slides you do not want and press the Delete key. Optionally, after selecting the unwanted slides, choose Home>Slides>Delete.

If you accidentally delete the wrong slides, immediately click the Undo button on the Quick Access Toolbar or press Ctrl+Z.

Rearranging Slides

You might decide that you would rather display slides in a different order than you originally created. First select the slide you want to move and then drag the slide into a new position. As you drag the mouse, a solid line indicating the new slide position appears between two slides, as seen in Figure 15-4. When you release the mouse button, the selected slide moves into the new position.

New slide position

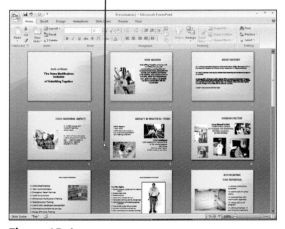

Figure 15-4
Moving a slide in the Slide Sorter view.

Exploring Other View Options

If you are planning on printing your slide show and you only have a black and white printer, you might want to see how it would look before your print it. PowerPoint provides a couple of other views to see how your presentation looks in grayscale or black and white.

From either Slide Sorter view or Normal view, choose View>Color/Grayscale>Grayscale to see how your presentation would look in shades of gray. A new tab as seen in Figure 15-5 appears while in Grayscale mode. Using the Grayscale tab in Normal view you can select any individual slide object and adjust its tone. Choose Grayscale>Close>Back to Color View to return to color mode.

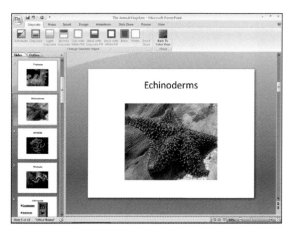

Figure 15-5
The Grayscale tab.

▶ Choose View>Color/Grayscale>Pure Black and White to see how your presentation would look in black and white. Figure 15-6 shows a slide in its full color mode, in grayscale mode, and in black and white mode. Similar to grayscale mode, a new tab appears while in black and white mode. Use the Black and White tab to adjust any image. Choose Black And White>Close>Back to Color View to return to color mode.

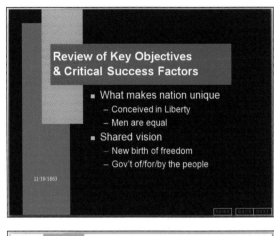

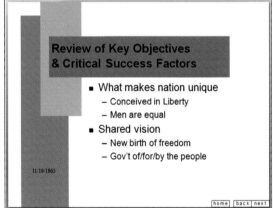

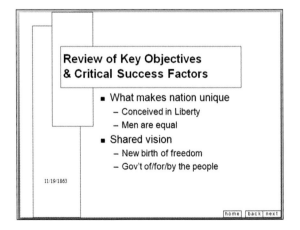

Figure 15-6
A slide in Color mode, Grayscale mode, and Black and White mode.

Modifying Slide Layouts

WHEN YOU FIRST CREATE A NEW slide, you must choose a slide layout; however, as you work on the slide, you might find that you need to change the layout. For example, you might need to change a Title and Content layout slide to a Two Content slide.

You can change layouts from either Normal view or Slide Sorter view. Select the slide or slides you want to change and choose Home>Slides>Layout. A gallery of slide layout options appears as you see in Figure 15-7. If you have a design applied to your presentation, the available layouts reflect the design.

Choose the layout you want. The slide layout changes and all objects are rearranged. Depending on the layout and the current view, you may see new placeholders.

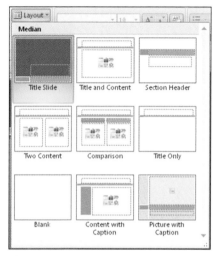

Figure 15-7
Choosing a different layout.

Adding Additional Objects

IN THE PREVIOUS CHAPTER you discovered how to place objects into the slide, primarily by using the content placeholder icons. One content placeholder icon not discussed in the last chapter was multimedia, which includes audio and video files. In this section, you discover how to add multimedia to your slide as well as a creative art object called WordArt. You will also learn how to add and format your own lines and shapes to any slide.

Inserting Multimedia

Multimedia is described as the use of computers to present text, graphics, video, animation, and sound files in an integrated way. PowerPoint by itself is a multimedia application because it can use those file types in a presentation. For the purpose of this book, the term multimedia file will refer to an animation, video, or sound file.

You can insert a multimedia file either in a content placeholder or anywhere on the slide. Because multimedia files typically have an action or sound associated with them, sometimes you will only see an icon that represents the file. The media action or sound in the file becomes apparent whenever you run the presentation in a slide show.

Inserting Sounds

If you have a sound file that you want to play when viewing a particular slide, you can add it to the slide. Because sound files typically have no picture associated with them, you see only an icon on the slide in the shape of a speaker. To insert a

sound file, first select the slide on which you want the sound file. Next, choose Insert>Media Clips and either click the Sound button or click the arrow on the Sound button. Clicking just the Sound button displays the Insert Sound dialog box, and clicking the arrow displays additional options as you see in Figure 15-8.

Figure 15-8
Choosing a sound clip.

Choose one of the following:

> ▶ **Just like clicking directly on the Sound button, the Sound from File option displays the Insert Sound dialog box seen in Figure 15-9. From there you locate the sound file you want to use and click Open. A message box appears asking you if, when displaying the slide in a slide show, you want the sound to automatically begin when the slide comes up, or if you want to play the sound manually. Click the button of your choice.**

Figure 15-9
Locate the sound you want on your slide.

Figure 15-10
Select a sound from the Clip Art pane.

▶ Choose Sound from Clip Organizer, which opens the Clip Art pane and displays a list of sound files included with Microsoft Office and available from Microsoft online. Optionally, enter a category, such as insects, in the Search For box, and then click Go to filter the sound files that appear. Click the sound file icon to insert it into your slide, or, if you want to hear the sound before you insert it, pause your mouse over a sound file and from the arrow that appears, choose Preview Properties. The Preview Properties dialog box appears and your sound plays. Close the Preview Properties box and if you want the sound file on your slide, click its icon. Figure 15-10 shows the Clip Art pane. After you make your selection, a message box appears asking you if, when displaying the slide in a slide show, you want the sound to automatically begin when the slide comes up, or if you want to play the sound manually when you click the icon. Click the button of your choice.

▶ Choose Play CD Audio Track, which prompts you to insert an audio CD into your CD drive. The Insert CD Audio dialog box also displays options for which track you want and for how long you want it.

▶ Choose Record Sound if you have a microphone hooked up to your system and want to record your own sound file.

When you have a sound clip on your slide, you can select it by clicking on its icon. The icon is very small, and by default PowerPoint places it in the middle of your screen. You will see very soon how you can move it. When the sound clip is selected, a new tab appears on the Ribbon. The Sound Tool Options tab, as seen in Figure 15-11, provides tools for you to preview the sound, adjust the sound volume, and choose other sound options.

Sound clip icon

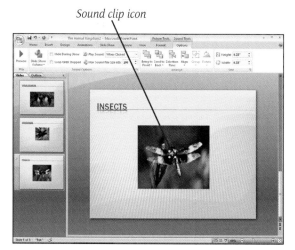

Figure 15-11
Change sound preferences from the Sound Tool Options tab.

Inserting a Video Clip

Placing a video clip onto a slide is very similar to adding a sound clip. However, you do get more than just an icon when you insert a video clip. You get the first image on the video. You can select your video from a saved file on your computer or from the Clip Art gallery, which also checks for videos from Microsoft Office Online. Choose Insert>Media Clip>Movie or click the Movie drop-down arrow. Clicking the arrow gives you the option of adding a Movie from File or selecting a Movie from Clip Art organizer. Clicking just click the Movie icon is the same as choosing Movie from File. It displays the Insert Movie dialog box. You locate and select the movie you want and choose Open.

No matter whether you choose a movie from a file or from Clip Art, PowerPoint asks you how you want your movie to start in the slide show. Choose Automatically or When Clicked.

PowerPoint places the movie in the middle of the slide and displays the movie image in the middle of the current slide. Like a sound file, if you select the movie image it becomes selected and the Movie Tools Options tab appears where you can manage the movie file (see Figure 15-12).

Figure 15-12
The Movie Tool Options tab.

Designing with WordArt

Adding text and art to a slide is one way to add visual excitement, but if you're the creative type or if you want your text to have more impact, WordArt might be your solution. With WordArt, you can take headings or key words and add decorative color schemes, shapes, and special effects. The following steps show you how to create a WordArt object.

1. Select the slide on which you want the WordArt and choose Insert>Text>WordArt. A gallery of options appears as you see in Figure 15-13.

You can add WordArt to any Word, Excel, PowerPoint, or Publisher document. In Publisher, choose Insert>Picture>WordArt. The choices in Publisher are slightly different than Word, Excel, or PowerPoint.

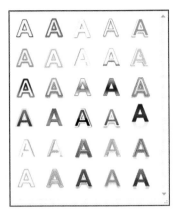

Figure 15-13
The WordArt gallery.

2. Select a style. A WordArt text box appears on the slide and a Drawing Tools Format tab appears.

3. Type the text you want, and when you are finished click outside of the WordArt text box to see your WordArt object (see Figure 15-14). Limiting WordArt to a single line of text is a good idea; the elaborate formatting can make lengthier text difficult to read.

To edit the text, simply double-click anywhere in the WordArt text and make a correction.

Welcome Home

Figure 15-14
Creating WordArt.

4. Click the Drawing Tools Format tab. If you do not see the Drawing Tools Format tab, click once on the WordArt box.

To change only a portion of the WordArt, highlight the portion you want to change before you make the change.

5. Use the tools in the WordArt Styles group to modify the WordArt text characteristics. All options include Live Preview, so as you pause your mouse pointer over any option, you see its effect on your WordArt object:

▶ **Styles changes the text style from the one you selected in step 2.**

▶ **Text Fill changes the text color, gradient, or pattern.**

▶ **Text Outline modifies the outer edges of the text.**

▶ **Text Effects applies special effects such as shadow, reflection, rotation, bevel, and transformation (see the next section).**

6. Optionally apply a background to the WordArt object, by choosing Drawing Tools Format>Shape Styles and then click the More button. A gallery of themed styles appears as you see in Figure 15-16. Select a background option or click the Other Theme Fills arrow to select from several gradient options.

If you want to change the font or font size, double-click the WordArt object to select it and choose Home>Font and make any desired font changes.

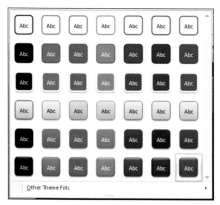

Figure 15-15
Select a style for the object.

In addition to changing the size and style of the WordArt text, you can also change the shape of the WordArt object. The WordArt shape options include placing the WordArt object in a circular or semi-circular pattern, or even a wave, triangle, or octagonal shape.

Click the WordArt object to select it and choose Drawing Tools Format>WordArt Styles>Text Effects>Transform. A gallery of shapes will appear (see Figure 15-16). Choose the shape you want.

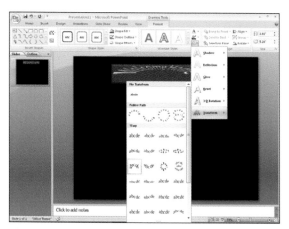

Figure 15-16
Transforming the WordArt Shape.

Some shapes will make your text hard to read, while others will add an exciting or fun tone to your words. You may have to experiment with the different choices to find the shape that best fits your text.

Figure 15-17 shows you the example's final result.

Figure 15-17
WordArt after adding a gradient background and transforming.

Drawing Shapes

Even if you do not have an artistic bone in your body, you can still draw with the Microsoft Office drawing features. You can draw arrows, boxes, stars, circles, callouts, and dozens of other objects. The Shapes feature is available in Word, Excel, and PowerPoint. In Publisher, it's called AutoShapes. You'll discover AutoShapes in the section "Drawing with the Drawing Tools" in Chapter 19.

Follow these steps to draw a shape:

1. Select the slide on which you want to draw.

2. Choose Insert>Illustrations>Shapes. A gallery of shapes appears as seen in Figure 15-18.

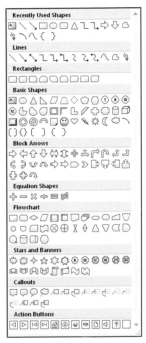

Figure 15-18
Selecting a predefined shape.

3. Choose the shape you want. The gallery closes and your mouse pointer turns into a small black plus sign.

4. Drag in the slide until the shape that appears is about the size you want (see Figure 15-19). When you release the mouse button, the shape object becomes selected.

To constrain the shape so it is equally sized, such as a perfect circle or a completely straight line, hold down the Shift key when drawing.

Figure 15-19
Drawing shapes.

After you draw the shape you can apply many different style changes to it. After you select the object, choose Drawing Tools Format>Shape Styles. From there, you can:

▶ **Click the Shape Styles More button and select from the available styles. The choices you have depend on any theme you have assigned to your presentation (see Figure 15-20).**

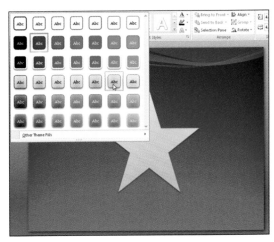

Figure 15-20
Changing a shape style.

▶ Click the Shape Fill option to change the object fill. Choices include solid fills, gradients, pictures, or textures.

▶ Click the Shape Outline option to change the border around the object. You can select a border color, size, and style.

▶ Click the Shape Effects option to add special effects such as shadows, borders, or rotation (see Figure 15-21).

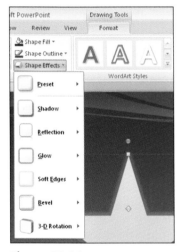

Figure 15-21
Adding shape effects.

Figure 15-22 illustrates a three-dimensional star with a glow and an arrow with a reflection along with a few other shapes. Notice that you can right-click any shape except lines and arrows and choose Edit Text to type text into the shape.

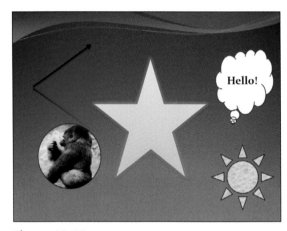

Figure 15-22
Adding cool shapes!

Managing Objects

N OW THAT YOU HAVE ALL OF these objects on your slides, you probably need to manipulate them a little. You can move them to a different location, adjust their size, change brightness or contrast, or just delete an object you don't want. If you have multiple objects, you can align them, group them, or even place one object on top of or beneath another. In this section you will discover how to take any of those actions.

> If you want to edit the text on a slide, simply click in the text you want to edit. If the text is in a text placeholder, you can also edit it in the Outline pane.

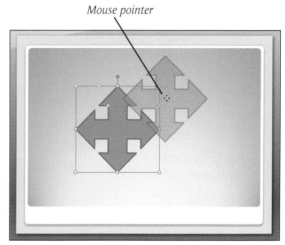

Mouse pointer

Figure 15-23
Dragging the object to a new position.

Moving Objects

If an object is not where you want it, you can easily move it to another place on the slide. Click the image to select it and then position the mouse pointer over any part of the selected image *except* the selection handles or the green rotation handle. The mouse pointer has four arrow heads. Drag the image to the desired position. As you see in Figure 15-23, a lightly transparent version of the object indicates the new position. When you release the mouse button, the object moves to the new location.

If you want to move the object just a little bit, you may find it easier to use the keyboard. After selecting the object, use the up, down, left, or right arrow keys to nudge the object into a different position.

> If you want to place the object on a different slide, use the cut and paste features.

Deleting Objects

Okay, this process is so simple it really doesn't deserve its own section, but putting it in one makes it easier for you to find. To delete an unwanted object, click the object border and press the Delete key.

Resizing Objects

The object may not fit on the page exactly as you envisioned it. You can easily make the object smaller or larger. Just follow these steps:

1. Select the object you want to resize. The selection handles appear around the object.

2. Position the mouse pointer over one of the eight handles. Do not select the green rotation handle. Your mouse pointer turns into a white double-headed arrow as you see in Figure 15-24.

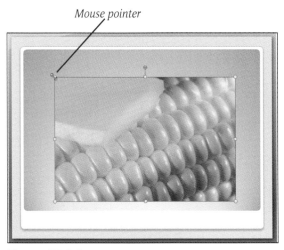

Mouse pointer

Figure 15-24
Resizing an object.

3. Drag a selection handle in one of the following manners:

> **When you begin dragging a handle, the mouse pointer turns into a plus sign.**

- ▶ **Drag a top or bottom handle to change the object height.**
- ▶ **Drag a left or right side handle to change the object width.**
- ▶ **Drag a corner handle to resize both the height and width at the same time.**

4. When the object is the desired size, release the mouse button.

Rotating Objects

Most graphic objects appear onto the slide in a horizontal or vertical pattern. And most of the time, that's exactly what you want. But in some cases, tilting the object at an angle provides just the right touch to a slide. PowerPoint objects come with a rotation handle with which you can rotate an object clockwise or counterclockwise.

Select the object you want to rotate and position the mouse pointer over the green rotation handle. Drag the rotation handle clockwise or counterclockwise until the graphic object is at the angle you want. Notice in Figure 15-25 that the mouse pointer turns into a circular arrow.

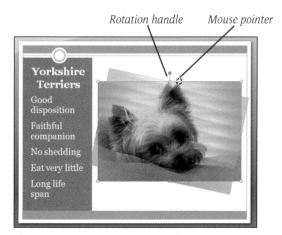

Rotation handle   *Mouse pointer*

Figure 15-25
Rotating an object.

Flipping an Object

If you want to reverse the direction of a picture or other object, you can flip it either vertically or horizontally. Take a look at the dog in Figure 15-26. In the picture on the top the dog is facing right, but on the bottom image, which is the same photograph, the dog is facing left. To flip an object, select the object and choose Home>Drawing> Arrange>Rotate and choose Flip Horizontal or Flip Vertical.

Figure 15-26
Flipping an image.

Aligning Multiple Objects

If your slide contains multiple graphic objects, like the ones you see in Figure 15-27, you may want some of them to line up with each other. PowerPoint includes a tool to make aligning objects quick and easy. Just follow these steps:

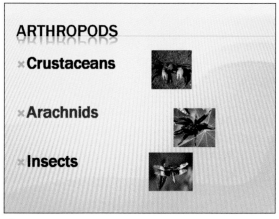

Figure 15-27
Multiple objects that need aligning.

1. Select the first object you want to align and then hold down the Ctrl key and select each additional object.

2. Choose Home>Drawing>Arrange>Align. A menu of alignment options appears (see Figure 15-28).

3. Choose one of the following alignment options:

   ▶ **Align Left:** Aligns the objects along their left edges

   ▶ **Align Center:** Centers the objects horizontally along their middles

   ▶ **Align Right:** Aligns the objects along their right edges

Figure 15-28
Selecting an alignment option.

▶ **Align Top:** Aligns the objects along their top edges

▶ **Align Middle:** Centers the objects vertically along their middles

▶ **Align Bottom:** Aligns the objects along their bottom edges

Two additional options on the alignment choices apply when you have three or more objects selected. Distribute Horizontally calculates the total space from the left edge of the left most object to the right edge of the right most object and evenly divides the space between the selected objects. Distribute Vertically calculates the total space from the top edge of the top object to the bottom edge of the bottom object and evenly divides the space between the selected objects.

> Optionally, from the Align options, choose View Gridlines to display a grid that you can use to manually align the objects.

Stacking Objects

When you have multiple objects, sometimes you want them to overlap. Depending on the order in which the images were created, you may have on object covering up another object you don't want covered. In Figure 15-29, you see a chart, an arrow, and a circle, with the circle being the topmost object. In this sample, the circle should be on the bottom and the arrow on the top, making the chart in the middle of the three objects.

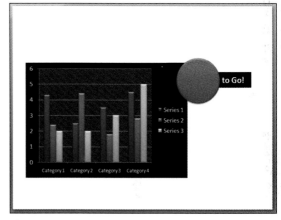

Figure 15-29
Incorrectly stacked objects.

When you restack objects, you can send an object back one object at a time or push it to the lowest object. Or, you can bring an object forward one object at a time or bring it to the top of the stack. Follow these steps:

1. Select the object you want to reorder.

2. Choose Home>Drawing>Arrange.

3. Choose one of the Order Objects options: Bring to Front, Send to Back, Bring Forward, or Send Backward.

Now take a look at the objects in Figure 15-30.

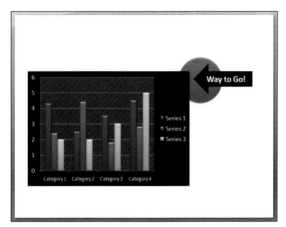

Figure 15-30
After changing the stacking order.

Grouping Objects Together

You can group multiple objects together to form a single object, which makes moving, resizing, and reshaping objects much easier. For example, instead of resizing each of four objects individually, you can group them and resize only one. A really nice feature about the group function is that if you need to, you can easily ungroup the object, make any desired individual changes, and then quickly regroup them.

Select the objects you want grouped together and choose Home>Drawing>Arrange>Group. In Figure 15-31, you see three independent objects on the left and one grouped object on the right. If you want to ungroup the object, select it and choose Home>Drawing>Arrange>Ungroup. To regroup, select any one of the original objects and choose Home>Drawing>Arrange>Regroup.

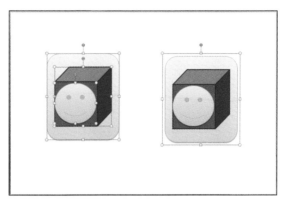

Figure 15-31
Grouping objects.

Reshaping an Object Shape

You may have noticed one or more small yellow diamond on some of the graphic shapes. While you won't see them on some shapes such as arrows, lines, circles, or squares, you will see them on WordArt, stars, smiley faces, callouts, and so forth. The yellow diamond is called a reshaping handle, and you can use it to remodel the graphic shape.

What it actually remodels depends on the shape. For example, it can change the depth of a three-dimensional object, change the smile on a smiley face to a frown, change the head or shaft on an arrow. The following steps show you how to reshape an object:

1. Select the graphic object you want to reshape. If you do not see the yellow diamond shape on the object, it does not support reshaping.

2. As you position your mouse over the diamond, the mouse pointer takes on a wedge shape. Take a look at the callout in Figure 15-32. The reshaping handle, although it's a little hard to see, is on the stem of the callout. Drag the yellow handle to modify the image shape.

Reshaping handle

Figure 15-32
Reshaping a graphic.

3. Release the mouse button to complete the reshape action.

As you see in Figure 15-33, the callout handle is now longer. And, I also changed the smiley face to a frowning face.

Figure 15-33
After reshaping graphics.

Using Picture Tools

When you place a picture on a slide (or a Word file or Excel worksheet), you get quite a few options to perform some fairly sophisticated tasks. You can adjust the image brightness and contrast, apply a color accent, give it a frame, or rotate it three-dimensionally. You can even crop it to get rid of unwanted areas. You accomplish all of these picture tasks by using the Picture Tools Format tab that appears on the Ribbon when you select a picture. Figure 15-24 shows you the Picture Tools Format tab.

Figure 15-34
The Picture Tools Format tab.

Making Picture Adjustments

The Adjust group contains six different buttons:

▶ **The Brightness button displays a gallery where you can adjust the image brightness. The original image begins at 0% and you can make the image up to 40% brighter or darken it by 40%. See Figure 15-35.**

Figure 15-35
Adjusting the picture brightness.

▶ The **Contrast** button displays a gallery where you can adjust the image contrast by a range of +40% to -40%.

▶ The **Recolor** button applies a coloring effect such sepia, black and white, or other color variations.

▶ The **Compress Pictures** button applies a compression algorithm to the all the presentation pictures in order to reduce the document size.

▶ The **Change Picture** button displays the Insert Picture dialog box where you can replace the current picture.

▶ The **Reset Picture** button undoes any editing and formatting you performed on the selected picture. Trust me...this button will become your friend!

Working with Picture Styles

The Picture Styles group on the Picture Tools Format tab offers a gallery of styles with preformatted shapes and three-dimensional effects. Click the More button to see the complete gallery, as shown in Figure 15-36.

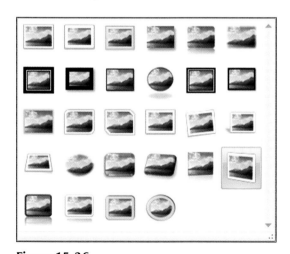

Figure 15-36
Applying a picture style.

In the same group you also have options to change the picture shape and border or to add effects. Through the Picture Shape option you can make your picture take the shape of an arrow, circle, callout, or any of the many different shapes. The Picture Border allows you to assign a color to the frame around your picture. The Picture Effects option provides options for adding shadows, glows, soft edges, and other options. You discovered the effects options when working with objects earlier in this chapter.

Figure 15-37 shows a slide with two images displaying applied picture styles.

Figure 15-37
After applying picture styles.

Cropping the Picture

The process of cropping removes unwanted portions of an image.

1. Select the picture you want to crop and then choose Picture Tools Format>Size>Crop. Your mouse pointer turns into a cropping tool, and instead of selection handles the picture has cropping handles as you see in Figure 15-38.

Cropping handles   Mouse pointer

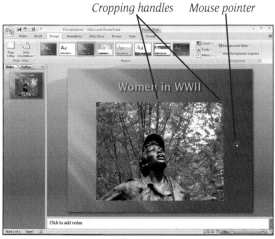

Figure 15-38
Cropping handles surround the picture.

2. Drag a cropping handle to begin the cropping process. You may need to crop from several sides of your image. As you drag a cropping handle, a line appears representing the new picture edge.

If you crop too much off the image, drag the cropping handle the opposite way. What you cropped reappears.

3. Click the Crop button or press the Esc key to turn off the cropping feature.

Figure 15-39 shows the image after cropping and applying a frame.

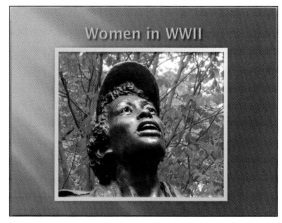

Figure 15-39
Cropped and framed.

16

Formatting Your

Presentation

PICTURE YOURSELF WALKING DOWN THE grocery aisle. You immediately recognize many products because of their appearance. The soup brand you use totes a half red and half white label. Your favorite peanut butter has red, blue, and green stripes with white lettering, and your usual laundry detergent is in a big orange bottle. What you count on is the consistency of the brand label. Think about it. When certain delivery people walk into your presence, you know who they represent because of their uniform appearance.

Uniformity is also important when creating a presentation. It not only shows professionalism, but maintaining consistency helps your audience know that you are still working on a particular topic. What you don't want, however, is a completely boring presentation where all slides look the same. A certain amount of variety is important, but the basic design on a presentation topic should be consistent. This chapter is about the look and consistency of a PowerPoint presentation. You will discover how to quickly apply a professionally designed look to your presentation as well as modify that look or even create your own.

Applying Themes

POWERPOINT COMES SUPPLIED WITH a gallery of themed designs, and more are available from Microsoft Office Online. Themes come with a preset font, coordinated color palette, background, and placeholder arrangement, and with a single click you can apply all these attributes to every slide in your presentation. You can change to a different theme at any time.

The theme you select sets the tone for your entire presentation. If you are giving a presentation on an arctic oil exploration you probably want a presentation with cooler color tones, but if you are giving a presentation on global warming, you want one with warmer colors. For vibrant presentations, use one with bright distinctive colors shades. Choosing a theme is a very personal choice. Only you can decide which one is right for your presentation.

To apply one of the predefined themes, choose Design>Themes and click the More button. A gallery of themes appears as seen in Figure 16-1.

Figure 16-1
Choosing a theme.

As you pause your mouse over any theme, Live Preview shows you in the Slide pane what your slides would look like with the new theme. Select the theme you want, and all slides in your presentation take on the new look. Figure 16-2 illustrates the same slide with three different themes beginning with the original Office theme that appears when you launch PowerPoint.

The templates you discovered in Chapter 14 are all based on different themes. One time saver is to choose one of the templates and then fit your presentation to the template. Better yet, modify the theme so it fits your presentation.

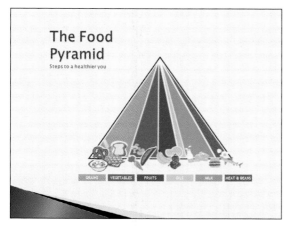

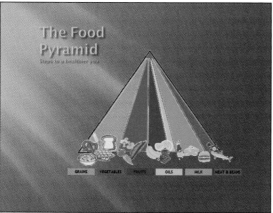

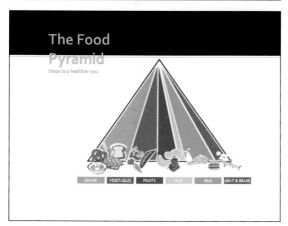

Figure 16-2
A sample slide with different themes.

Changing Theme Options

Suppose you apply the theme, but you want to modify the theme colors or font. You can easily change options using the Design tab, and the changes affect the entire presentation. Begin by applying the theme of your choice. For an example, in Figure 16-3, you see the Concourse theme as it is applied to the entire presentation. Notice on the status bar that PowerPoint displays the current theme name.

Current theme

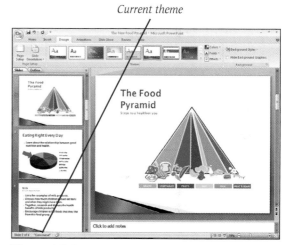

Figure 16-3
After applying a theme.

Choosing a Background

While a predefined theme already has a background, you can select something different. For a background you can have a solid color, a transparent color, a gradient blend of two colors, a texture, or a picture.

By default, background changes apply to the current slide or all slides. If you want to change the background for a group of slides, for example to indicate the presentation is changing focus, from the Slide Sorter view, select the slides you want to change before changing the background. The following steps walk you through changing the slide background.

1. Choose Design> Background>Background Styles. A gallery of styles appears as seen in Figure 16-4. As you pause your mouse over an option, Live Preview shows you the result on the current slide.

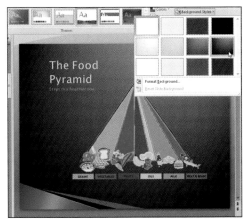

Figure 16-4
Choosing a background style.

2. If you want one of the background styles, select it. The background applies to all your slides. If you want to create your own background, choose Format Background, which displays the Format Background dialog box, and continue with these steps.

3. If not already highlighted, click the Fill option on the dialog box left side.

4. Choose one of the following options:

   ▶ **Solid fill: This option provides a single uniform color. Click the Color button and select a color. As you choose a color, you immediately see it on the current slide. Optionally, drag the transparency slider to the right to lighten the color hue.**

   ▶ **Gradient fill: This option gives the background a mixture of two colors gradually blending into each other. When you choose this option, the dialog box changes to provide the options you see in Figure 16-5. Select the two colors you want to blend. You can also control the Type, which is the direction the colors blend together, and the Stops, which control how smoothly they blend.**

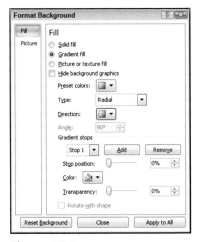

Figure 16-5
Creating a background gradient fill.

▶ **Picture or texture fill**: This option provides a means to select either a texture for the background or an image. If you want a texture, click the Texture button and select an option from the gallery seen in Figure 16-6. If you want a picture for your background, either click the File button and choose your picture or click the Clip Art button and choose the clip art you want for your background. You can also adjust the transparency and other options for the texture or image.

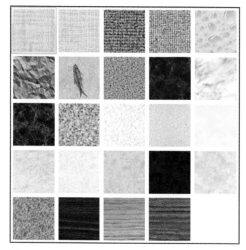

Figure 16-6
Choosing a texture or a picture for a background.

Using pictures for a slide background can be extremely distracting from the slide content, especially if the image has lots of colors. Use this feature sparingly, and if you do use it, adjust the transparency so the image is light in the background.

5. If you want the new background for all the slides, choose Apply to All. If you just want the choice for the current slide, click the Close button.

Click the Reset Background button to start all over.

Applying Theme Effects

PowerPoint also has Theme Effects you can apply to your presentation. Theme effects are the attributes applied to lines and filled objects. If you draw an arrow, for example, while you can certainly change the individual arrow effects, if you have multiple arrows or other shapes, you probably want them to have a consistent appearance throughout the presentation.

Choose Design>Themes> Effects and click the theme effect you want to use from the gallery seen in Figure 16-7.

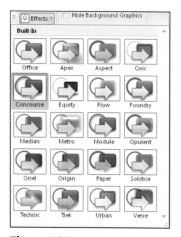

Figure 16-7
Choosing a theme effect.

Working with Slide Masters

YOU ALREADY KNOW THAT consistency in a presentation is important. For example, in each slide layout, the fonts and font sizes are consistent, the placeholder frames are in the same position, and all the bullet point items have the same style bullet.

Often, one of the themed templates is almost, but not quite, right for your presentation. Perhaps a color is slightly different than you really want, or you want your company logo on each slide, or maybe you want a different font than supplied with the template. If your presentation already has a lot of slides, it would be tedious to place the logo or change the font or color on each and every slide.

Instead, you can work with the Slide Master. Think of the Slide Master as the control center for the presentation. The Slide Master view controls the fonts, sizes, bullet styles, colors, alignments, spacing, and more for each slide type of your presentation. It is also where you place any art, such as a logo, that you want on every slide in exactly the same position and in the same size.

Choose View>Presentation Views>Slide Master. As seen in Figure 16-7, on the Slide List pane, you have the various masters for each slide layouts and a master slide and in the slide pane, you have the current slide layout master. Switching to Slide Master view presents a Slide Master tab with tools for working with the Slide Master.

If you already have slides in your presentation, the Slide List pane can show you which slides are used by each layout. Pause your mouse over a layout to reveal the information. As you also see in Figure 16-8, as the mouse pauses over the Title and Content slide, a tool tip appears indicating that the layout is used by slides 3 through 8.

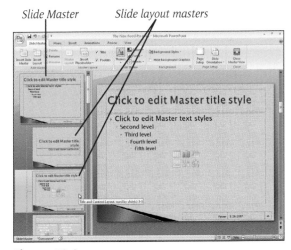

Figure 16-8

Working with Slide Masters.

In the Slide List, the top slide is called the Slide Master and the ones below it are the individual slide layout masters. Changes you make to the master slide affect all layouts, but you can still individualize a specific layout by choosing the slide layout master you want modified and making changes to it.

To make any changes to the master, select the master you want to modify and if the item you want to modify is in a placeholder, select the placeholder. Using the instructions you learned in previous chapters, do any of the following:

▶ **Insert an image such as a logo.**

▶ **Move, delete, insert, or resize a placeholder.**

▶ **Change font, font size, color, or other font attributes.**

▶ **Add borders to any placeholder.**

▶ **Modify the bullet style. See the next section for instructions on changing bullet styles.**

Figure 16-9 shows the Slide Master after the following edits, and because the edits were done on the Slide Master instead of a layout master, the changes apply to all slides.

Figure 16-9
After editing the Slide Master.

▶ **The title font type is changed to Cooper Black.**

▶ **The title font color is changed from gray/black to blue.**

▶ **A shadow is added to the title text.**

▶ **A logo is added in the lower left corner.**

▶ **The content section bullet style is changed from a round bullet to an arrow.**

If you want to make changes to an individual slide layout master, select the slide layout master and make the desired change. In Figure 16-10, a blue and black angled box is added to the Title Slide layout master, giving the bottom of the slide layout a different appearance than the rest of the slide layouts.

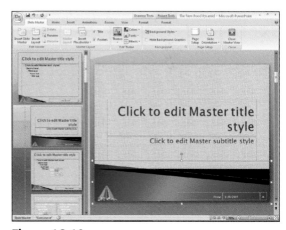

Figure 16-10
Changing options on a specific layout.

When you are finished modifying the Slide Masters, choose Slide Master>Close>Close Master View.

Modifying the Bullet Style

If you want to select different bullet style other than the solid circle, you can choose from a bullet style gallery or even use a picture. You can also change the bullet color.

From the Slide Master, select the bullet placeholder and choose Home>Paragraph and click the arrow next to Bullets. A gallery of bullet styles appears as shown in Figure 16-11.

> If you want to change the bullets for a single slide instead of the Slide Master or a specific slide layout, choose the slide from the Normal view instead of the Slide Master view.

Figure 16-11
Selecting a different bullet style.

Either select one of the bullet styles shown or click the Bullets and Numbering option to display the Bullets and Numbering dialog box (see Figure 16-12). From the Bullets and Numbering dialog box you can change the bullet size or color, select from hundreds of different bullet styles, or choose a picture to use as a bullet.

Bullet size   Bullet color

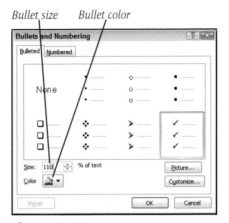

Figure 16-12
The Bullets and Numbering dialog box.

To choose different bullet styles, click the Customize button, which displays the Symbol dialog box. Select the symbol you want to use. Optionally, from the Font drop-down list, choose a different font. Many fonts display different symbols such as the Wingdings symbols you see in Figure 16-13. Click the OK button after you select a symbol. Click OK again if you are finished and want to close the Bullets and Numbering dialog box.

> If you are using numbering on your slides, you can change the number style from the Bullets and Numbering dialog box. Click the Numbered tab to make your selection.

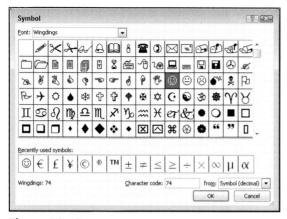

Figure 16-13
The Wingding font provides lots of bullet choices.

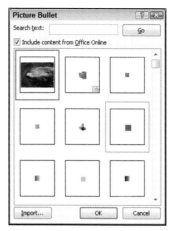

Figure 16-14
Choosing a picture for a bullet.

Another bullet option available from the Bullets and Numbering dialog box is to select a picture to use as a bullet symbol. Click the Picture button to display the Picture Bullet dialog box. By default, the pictures provided are small drawings that work well as bullet points, but if you don't see any you want, you can use your own picture. In Figure 16-14, an image of a dolphin was added as a bullet option. To add your own picture, click the Import button, locate and select your picture, and click Add. Your image is added to the Picture Bullet list. Choose the picture you want and then click OK. Click OK again if you are finished and want to close the Bullets and Numbering dialog box.

> **Keep in mind that bullets are generally very small. If you use a picture, you probably will not see much image detail in the bullet.**

Figure 16-15 shows the Slide Master as it looks using a picture for bullets.

Figure 16-15
Using bullet pictures.

> When you are finished modifying the Slide Masters choose Slide Master> Close>Close Master View.

Generating Footers

In earlier chapters, you discovered how, in a Word or Excel document, you could place a header at the top of every page and place footers at the bottom of every page. PowerPoint also lets you create headers and footers for all your slides. In fact, by default, all new blank presentations come with footer placeholders that place the date on the left, text that you specify in the middle, and the slide number on the right. Take a look at the Slide Master in Figure 16-16 where you see the place-holders at the bottom of the Slide Master. In the Slide Master, optionally drag the placeholders to other positions or delete them if you do not want them.

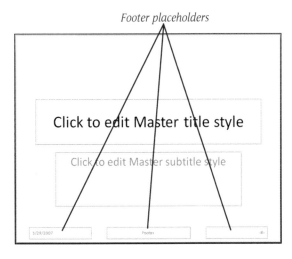

Footer placeholders

Figure 16-16
Positioning the footer placeholders.

However, even though the slides have footer place-holders, the option to display the footer is turned off. You must activate the footer and make a few decisions about its format. From either the Normal view, the Slide Sorter view or the Slide Master view, choose Insert>Text>Header & Footer. The Header and Footer dialog box appears with the following items on the Slide tab:

▶ **Date and time**: Check this option if you want the date and optional time printed on your slides. When you select this option, you see other choices become available. The Update Automatically option creates a dynamic date so when-ever you print the slides or view them in a slide show, you see the current date. Click the date format drop-down arrow to display a variety of date formats and choose the format you want. The Fixed option allows you to manually type a specific date that is static and does not change.

▶ **Slide number**: Check this option if you want the slide number printed on your slides.

▶ **Footer**: Check this option if you want additional text printed on each slide. In the text box, type the text you want. Figure 16-17, shows a company name for the footer text.

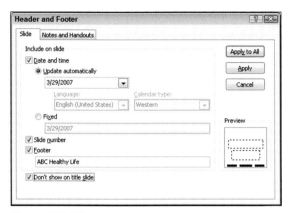

Figure 16-17
The Header and Footer dialog box.

▶ **Don't show on title slide: Click this
option if you do not want to see the
header or footer on the title slide. Most
presentations do not show headers or
footers on the title slide.**

Click the Notes and Handouts tab to set
the options for the speaker notes or
audience handouts. See the next section
for creating the speaker notes and see
"Printing Audience Handouts" later in
this section.

Select the options you want and click Apply to All.
If you have a particular slide (other than a title
slide) on which you don't want the header or footer,
select that slide, redisplay the Header and Footer
dialog box, turn off the options you don't want,
then choose Apply, which applies the options to
only the current slide.

Creating Notes

WHEN YOU CREATE YOUR presentation, you typically keep the actual amount of readable information on the slide to a minimum by using bullet points to present your ideas. Then you, as the presenter, elaborate more on those points, or optionally then break each point down to its own slide.

To assist you in keeping track of what you want to say when a particular slide comes up, you can enter notes, which are sometimes called speaker notes. Entering information in the PowerPoint notes area helps you remember the information you want to relay to your audience. You can then print a hard copy of those notes along with a copy of the slide for your reference.

Separator bar

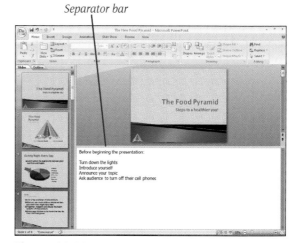

Figure 16-18
Type your notes in the Notes Pane.

Entering Notes

Located below the current slide is an area called the Notes Pane. In Normal view, you could just click anywhere in the Notes Pane and begin typing your text, but since the area is pretty small, it is to your advantage to resize the Notes Pane. Drag up the separator bar that you see between the slide and the Notes Pane. This gives you more room for the notes, although it makes the slide appear smaller. You can move this separator bar up or down as needed (see Figure 16-18).

Another and probably easier way to work on your speaker notes is to view the Notes Page. Choose View>Presentation Views>Notes Page. You see a full screen view with half the page taken by the slide and the other half with a placeholder you can click into and easily type your text (see Figure 16-19).

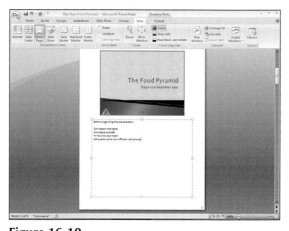

Figure 16-19
Entering notes in the Notes Page.

Editing the Notes Master

Like the Slide Master that controls the slide design and layout, PowerPoint provides a Notes Master. Choose View>Presentation Views>Notes Master. From the Notes Master seen in Figure 16-20, you can change the default font, perhaps making it larger and easier to read when in a dimly lit room. You can move the placeholders, for example, if you prefer the note text on top and the slide on the bottom. Any formatting option you can apply in the presentation, you can also apply in the Notes Master. When you finish setting up your parameters for the Notes Master, choose Notes Master>Close>Close Master View.

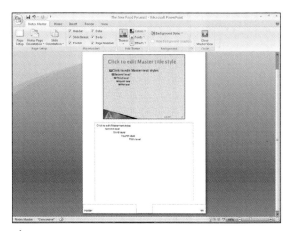

Figure 16-20
Changing the Notes Master.

Finishing Your Presentation

Y OU'VE PUT A LOT OF WORK INTO creating your presentation and you are almost ready to present it. Before you do, however, you want to check it for errors and apply choices to keep it safe. You may also want to print some or all of the presentation.

Checking Your Spelling

Ouch! Nothing can detract more from your presentation than misspelled words. Word and Excel have a tool for checking your spelling, and so does PowerPoint. Like Word and Excel, PowerPoint underlines any potential misspellings with a wavy red underline. You can correct the spelling errors as you type by right-clicking the misspelling and choosing from the shortcut menu options. You can also check the entire presentation at once. Choose Review>Proofing>Spelling, which immediately launches the Spelling dialog box that stops at the first misspelled word (see Figure 16-21).

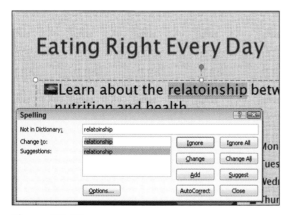

Figure 16-21
Checking for misspellings.

Select a correct spelling and choose Change or Change All, add the word to your dictionary, or ignore the misspelling once or throughout the entire presentation. The spell check runs through the presentation and the Masters and then notifies you when it is complete. Click OK to acknowledge the message.

> The Review tab also has a button labeled Thesaurus. Click anywhere in the word you want replaced and choose Review> Proofing>Thesaurus. A Research pane appears on the right side of the screen and displays various meanings of the current word and possible replacements. When you locate the word that better best fits your document, click the arrow next to it and choose Insert.

Replacing Text

The PowerPoint Replace features lets you locate specific presentation text and replace the found data with something different. For example, suppose you gave the presentation to client ABC and now you want to give the presentation to client XYZ. Let PowerPoint do all the work for you. Choose Home>Editing>Replace. The Replace dialog box seen in Figure 16-22 appears. In the Find What box, enter the word or phrase you want to locate. In the Replace With box, enter the replacement word or phrase.

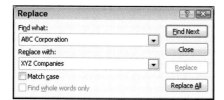

Figure 16-22
Letting PowerPoint quickly replace text for you.

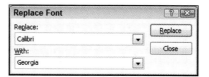

Figure 16-23
Easily replace fonts in your presentation.

Click the Options button and specify any desired options:

> ▶ **Match case:** Check this box if you want your search to be case case-specific (for example, "Some" instead of "SOME" or "some").

> ▶ **Match whole words only:** Check this box if you want your search results to list only words that exactly match your search criteria. With this option checked, when looking for the word "some," PowerPoint ignores "wholesome" or "someone."

Click the Find Next button. PowerPoint jumps to the first occurrence of the match. If this is not the entry you are looking for, click the Find Next button again. Click Replace if you want to replace the found data with the replacement data. PowerPoint will make the replacement and proceed to the next occurrence. Or, click Replace All to have PowerPoint replace all occurrences of the original data with the replacement data. PowerPoint notifies you of the total number of occurrences. Click OK. When finished, click the Close button.

Choose Home>Editing>Replace(arrow)> Replace Fonts to locate a font and replace all occurrences with a different font (see Figure 16-23).

Marking a Presentation as Final

To protect your presentation against accidental changes, just like Word and Excel, PowerPoint includes a feature called Mark as Final. After choosing the option, the presentation cannot be changed unless you choose the Mark as Final option again, which then allows presentation changes. Choose Office Button>Prepare>Mark as Final. A confirmation message appears. Click OK twice.

Marking a presentation as final disables every option in the Ribbon that could change the presentation in any way. An icon appears in the status bar indicating the presentation is marked as final, and if you attempt to make any changes, the icon changes to a message stating the modification is not allowed.

This feature is easily bypassed. Suppose you need to change a date in the presentation or you forgot to list a particular item. You can "unmark" the presentation from being final by simply going back into Office Button>Prepare>Mark as Final.

Inspecting for Private Information

In Chapters 7 and 12, you discovered the Document Inspector, which searched through Word and Excel files for hidden metadata. PowerPoint also provides the Document Inspector, which can help remove hidden information that you might not want others to see. Just follow these steps:

1. Save the workbook and then choose Office Button>Prepare>Inspect Document. The Document Inspector dialog box appears (see Figure 16-24).

Figure 16-24

Inspecting the presentation.

2. Deselect any option you do not want to check and then click Inspect. PowerPoint inspects the presentation for the selected information.

3. When the inspection is complete, the Document Inspector reappears with information with its finding.

4. Click the Remove All button next to any option you want removed. PowerPoint removes the selected data. After removing the data, the Remove All button next to the option disappears.

5. Click Close and resave your file.

Printing Your Presentation

The big day has finally arrived and it is time to give your presentation. Most of the time, presentations are given on a computer screen, in the form of a slide show, which you will discover in the next chapter, "Presenting Your Presentation." Sometimes, however, you just want to print your presentation, including when you want to print your slides on transparencies for display on a projector.

Preparing to Print

When printing, you have quite a few different options from which you can choose. You can print the slides, the outline, the notes, and handouts. Choose Office Button>Print. The Print dialog box seen in Figure 16-25 appears. Here are some of the choices available in the Print dialog box:

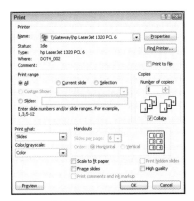

Figure 16-25

The Print dialog box.

▶ **Name:** Choose the printer you plan on printing to.

▶ **Print range:** Choose whether you want to print all slides in the presentation, only the current slide, currently selected slides, or a range of slides. If you want a range of slides, enter the slide numbers separated by a comma for individual slides, or a dash for a range of slides.

▶ **Number of copies:** Specify the number of copies you want printed and whether you want them collated.

▶ **Print what:** This is probably the most important selection in the dialog box. You can choose to print the slides, handouts, notes pages. or outline. You will see shortly about the handouts.

▶ **Color/grayscale:** Click the drop-down list to choose Color, Grayscale, or Pure Black and White. If you choose Color and you print to a black-and-white printer, PowerPoint prints in Grayscale.

▶ **Print hidden slides:** In Chapter 17, "Presenting Your Presentation," you will discover how you can hide slides during your presentation.

▶ **High quality:** Choose this option to print the highest quality your printer can print.

Click the Preview button to preview how the printout looks with your selected options before printing.

Click the OK button when you are ready to print your selections.

Creating Audience Handouts

One of the printing options was for audience handouts. Handouts are thumbnail size versions of your slides that you distribute to your audience. You have the choice of printing one, two, three, four, six, or nine slides to a page.

If you select three slides to a page, PowerPoint automatically prints lines on the right side of the page for your audience to write their own notes.

PowerPoint also includes a Handout Master, as seen in Figure 16-26. Choose View>Presentation Views>Handout Master where you can customize the handout layout including fonts, headers, footers, page numbers, and orientation. After you make any desired changes to the Handout Master, close the Handout Master by choosing Handout Master>Close>Close Master View.

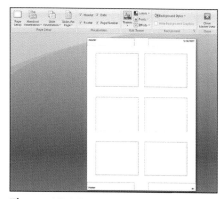

Figure 16-26
The Handout Master.

When you are in the Print dialog box and you choose to print Handouts, you choose the number of slides you want to print per page and whether you want them in a horizontal or vertical format. Figure 16-27 shows the sample presentation's audience handouts printed three per page.

Figure 16-27
Give your audience handouts to follow the presentation.

17

Presenting Your
Presentation

PICTURE YOURSELF STANDING PERFECTLY STILL. Now talk but don't move. It's difficult isn't it? If you are like most people, you naturally move your hands when you speak. You can also make your slides move as they speak by applying transitions and animations. PowerPoint calls the movement from one slide to the next *transitions*. Transitions add mild excitement to the presentation by creating special movements as one slide turns into the next slide.

You are finally ready to give your presentation to your group, so you need to apply a few finishing touches to it. This chapter shows you how to prepare, start, and lead a slide show presentation, as well as give it your own comments in the form of annotations. You also see how you can package the slide show so it can run repeatedly by itself or from a CD that you give to a user.

Transitions and Animations

IT'S TIME TO SHAKE THE BUSH (or rather the presentation) and wake up your audience by rolling a few objects across the screen during the slide show. You can make each slide fade into the background as the next one appears, or you can make bullet points appear one at a time. Transitions can be simple such as just replacing one slide with another or you can select from a number of really fancy transitions.

Setting Slide Transitions

Transitions are wonderful in a presentation if used in moderation. However, some presentations have so many different transitions that they tend to distract the audience with the *Wow*! factor instead of the content. Some transitions are simple in that one slide simply replaces another or dissolves into the next slide, or you can use a transition called News Flash where the slide spins onto the screen. In fact, there are 57 different transitions you can use.

Although you can use Normal view, transitions are easiest to setup while in the Slide Sorter view. When assigning transitions, you not only can assign a transition visual effect, you can set a speed for the transition to occur and you can assign a transition sound. Follow these steps to assign slide transitions:

1. Select the slides to which you want to apply a transition effect.

2. Choose Animations>Transition to This Slide, and click the More button. A gallery of slide transitions appears (see Figure 17-1).

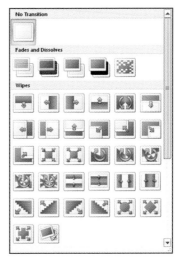

Figure 17-1
Assigning a slide transition.

3. Select the transition you want. A selected slide previews the transition effect.

In the Slide Sorter view, slides with transitions have a small star-shaped transition icon under the slide. In Normal view, the transition icon appears beside the slide in the Slide list pane.

4. Choose Animations>Transition to This Slide, and from the Transition Speed drop-down list, choose a transition speed: Slow, Medium, or Fast. The slide again previews the transition effect.

5. Optionally, choose Animations>Transition to This Slide and click the Transition Sound drop-down list. A list of available sounds appears (see Figure 17-2). Select the sound you want associated with the transition or choose Other Sound if you want to select a sound stored on your computer.

Figure 17-2
Choosing a sound for a transition.

If you want the sound repeated until the next slide, also click Loop Until Next Sound. Please, for the sake of your audience, use this feature sparingly!

6. Choose Animations>Transition to This Slide and specify how the slide should advance to the next slide:

▶ **Choose On Mouse Click if you want the transition to occur when you click the mouse button.**

▶ **Choose Automatically After if you want the transition to occur automatically after a specified time.**

▶ **In the box after Automatically After, enter a number of seconds the slide should display before advancing to the next slide. As shown in Figure 17-3, if you select a timed advance, the number of seconds displays under the slide.**

Transition icon   Slide timing

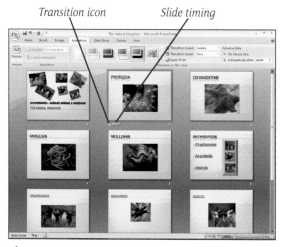

Figure 17-3
Enter the slide timing.

You can also check both options so you can still manually advance the slide if you want to.

7. If you want the selected options to apply only for the currently selected slides, you don't have to do anything else, but if you want the same transitions applied to all slides in the presentation, choose Animations> Transitions to This Slide>Apply To All.

To remove a transition, select the slide, choose Animation>Transitions to This Slide and click the No Transition option.

Assigning Predefined Animations

An animation is similar to a transition, but a transition moves from one slide to another, while an animation moves an individual object on or off the screen within a slide. PowerPoint comes with quite a few preset animation schemes.

1. If necessary, switch to Normal view by choosing View>Presentation Views>Normal. You cannot assign animations in Slide Sorter view because you cannot select the component you want to assign an animation.

2. Display the slide you want to assign an animation and then select the component you want to animate. It could be a slide title or any graphic element. You will see in the next section how to animate a bullet list, and later in this chapter I show you how to apply an animation effect to an individual chart element such as a series or category.

3. Choose Animations>Animations and select from the Animate drop-down list seen in Figure 17-4. While only three animations may appear in this list, you will soon see where you can select from dozens of different animations.

Figure 17-4
Pick an object animation type.

5. Pause your mouse over any of the three animation choices to see your selected object with the animation. Click the animation you want.

> Since an animation is a transition for an element, when you view the presentation in Slide Sorter view, slides with animations have a small star-shaped icon under the slide

Animating Bulleted Lists

Often when giving a presentation using a bulleted list, one point leads into another. By applying animations to certain bullets, you can talk about the main slide items, and then with a click of the mouse illustrate the secondary slide list items.

1. If necessary, switch to Normal view by choosing View>Presentation Views>Normal and display a slide with bulleted text.

2. Select the bullet list component and choose Animations>Animations.

3. Select from the Animate drop-down list seen in Figure 17-5. Notice the choices are slightly different for bullet lists than for other objects. You can have the bullets all arrive at once, or by the first level paragraphs. With the latter option, the next level arrives when you click the mouse or a specific timing interval occurs.

> To remove an animation, select the object and choose Animations>Animations> Animate>No Animation.

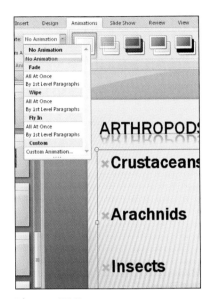

Figure 17-5
Animating bulleted lists.

Animating a Chart by Components

If you use charts in your presentation, you can animate the chart series or the chart categories. For example, if you have a bar chart that shows the number of clients you have in each of your four stores, you could choose to display one store at a time. The following steps show you how to apply an animation effect to a chart:

1. Select the chart you want to animate.

2. Choose Animations>Animations>Animate. For each animation type, the Animate drop-down list seen in Figure 17-6 offers these choices for your chart:

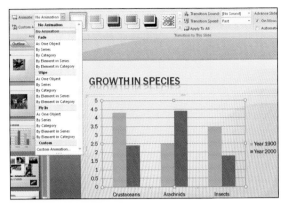

Figure 17-6
Choosing a chart animation.

▶ **As One Object:** This option applies the animation choice to the entire chart.

▶ **By Series:** This option applies the animation to each data series, displaying one data series at a time.

▶ **By Category:** This option applies the animation to each category, displaying one category at a time.

▶ **By Element in Series:** This option applies the animation individually to each data marker in each series.

▶ **By Element in Category:** This option applies the animation individually to each data marker by category.

4. Pause your mouse over any option to see its effect on your chart, and then make a selection.

Creating Customized Animations

Just three different animations? That's all? That hardly seems fair, does it? Actually, there are quite a few different animations; you just have to customize the animation settings. Creating a customized animation allows you to specify exactly what you want to animate and how it should be done.

Choose the component you want to animate then choose Animations>Animations>Custom Animation. The Custom Animation pane appears on the right side of your screen (see Figure 17-7).

Figure 17-7
The Custom Animation pane.

3. Click the Add Effect button. A list of options appears, and each option has its own submenu:

    ▶ **Entrance effects control how the object enters the slide.**

    ▶ **Emphasis effects make the object perform some action after its entrance.**

    ▶ **Exit effects control how the object leaves the slide.**

    ▶ **Motion path enables you to specify exactly where the object travels.**

4. Make a selection. The selected object previews the effect, and the effect is listed on the Custom Animation pane. Optionally from the Add Effect submenu, click More Effects. You see the Add *nnn* Effect menu seen in Figure 17-8, from which you can select additional effects. The choice of effects you see depends on whether you are choosing Entrance, Emphasis, Exit, or Motion Path effects.

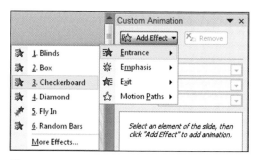

Figure 17-8
The Add Effects dialog box.

5. Click the Speed drop-down list and choose a speed for the effect. Depending on the effect you chose, there may be another option displayed above the Speed box.

Each object can have all four effect types. For example, an image can have an Entrance effect and an Exit effect. This is another feature you should use sparingly so as not to annoy your audience.

Take a look at the Custom Animation pane and the slide in Figure 17-9. The Custom Animation pane lists all the effects you have assigned to the current slide, and the slide lists the order number of the animation effects. To edit or delete an effect, click the effect in the Custom Animation pane, and then click the Change or Remove buttons.

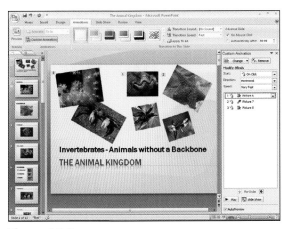

Figure 17-9
Adding customized effects.

Click the Play button to see the entire slide with its effects.

Inserting Action Links

When you run your slide show, you will see controls that enable you to jump to specific slides, but you can perform the action quicker and with more grace by using the hyperlink feature.

In Word and Excel, you discovered how to insert hyperlinks to jump to a Web site or even generate an e-mail. In PowerPoint, you can create hyperlinks to do those things by choosing Insert>Links>Hyperlink. But more commonly, you want to create a type of link called an Action link where your presentation jumps to a specific presentation slide. You can use text or buttons called action buttons for your Action links.

> **You add Action links one at a time on individual slides. Links created in a Slide Master do not work during a slide show.**

You create a text hyperlink by choosing a word or phrase in the slide that acts as the link. Select the slide on which you want to insert the link and highlight the text you want as the link reference. Next, choose Insert>Links>Action. The Action Settings dialog box seen in Figure 17-10 appears.

Figure 17-10
The Action Settings dialog box.

Select one of the two link types to create. One is a Mouse Click where you must click your mouse on the link to make the jump. The other is a Mouse Over, where, during the presentation, you simply pause your mouse over the linked item and it automatically jumps to the link. The choices you select are the same for either link type. Just a word of caution about the Mouse Over option: While it is nice to just point to something and have it jump elsewhere, if you have multiple links on your screen, it may become hard to control the mouse position because it may be jumping to another slide when you did not intend it to.

When you generate the link you can create a hyperlink to a particular slide or run another program. You can also run a macro, which is basically a miniature program that you custom write yourself, or take another action. The last two choices are not commonly used. To activate these two options you must first save your presentation in a special format that enables macros. To do that, you would first choose Office Button>Save As, and from the Save as type drop-down list, choose PowerPoint Macro-Enabled Presentation (see Figure 17-11). Creating macros, however, is beyond the scope of this book.

File type

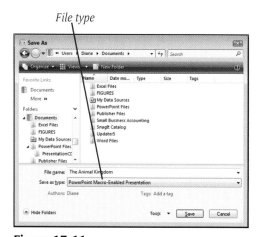

Figure 17-11
Saving the presentation as a macro-enabled presentation.

While in the Action Settings dialog box, choose the Hyperlink To option and then click the display the drop-down list. Choices include: Next Slide, Previous Slide, First Slide, Last Slide, Last Slide Viewed, End Show, Slide, URL, Other PowerPoint Presentation, and Other File. Depending on your choice, you may be prompted for more information. For example, choosing Slide brings up the Hyperlink to Slide box seen in Figure 17-12 where you choose which slide you want to display if the link is activated. When you have made your choices, click the OK button to close the dialog box.

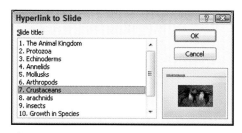

Figure 17-12
Choose the slide you want to jump to.

Inserting Action Buttons

The PowerPoint Action buttons are predefined shape icons. When you select the shape, you also get a predefined action. There are 12 different action buttons, and they are stored with the other shapes. Table 17-1 shows you each button icon, its name, and its predefined action. All choices open the Action Settings dialog box with predefined choices selected or leaving an option for you to select additional information.

Table 17-1 Action Buttons

Icon	Button Name	Button Action
◁	Previous	Jumps to the previous slide
▷	Forward	Jumps to the next slide
◁|	First	Jumps to the first slide
|▷	Last	Jumps to the last slide
🏠	Home	Jumps to the first slide
ⓘ	Information	Nothing
↩	Return	Jumps to the last viewed slide
🎞	Movie	Nothing
🗋	Document	Nothing
🔊	Sound	Plays Applause sound
?	Help	Nothing
☐	Blank	Nothing

The following steps show you how to insert and assign an Action button:

1. In Normal view, display the slide to which you want to add an Action button.

2. Choose Insert>Illustrations>Shapes, which displays the Shapes gallery. Action buttons are the last category on the gallery; you may have to scroll down to see them (see Figure 17-13).

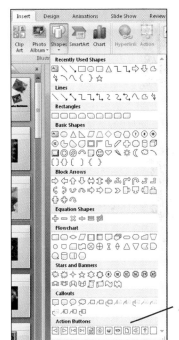

Action Buttons

Figure 17-13
Select an action button.

3. Click the action button you want to use.

4. Drag a rectangle on your slide to draw the shape. When you release the mouse button, you see the Action Settings dialog box.

5. If not already chosen, set the action you want associated with the Action button and then click OK.

Figure 17-14 shows you a slide with the Sound action button.

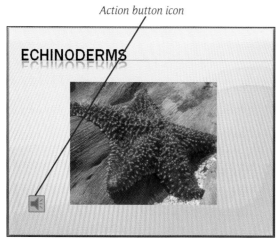

Action button icon

Figure 17-14
An action button assigned to a slide.

Action buttons are objects, and as such you can resize, move, or delete them as you would any other object.

Rehearsing Timings

Why should you rehearse your slide show? Just as actors must repeatedly rehearse their roles, you should rehearse your presentation. The more you rehearse, the more comfortable you become with the task. Besides making you more comfortable, rehearsing can help you examine the amount of time you spend on each slide. If you have only a specified amount of time, you can figure out if your presentation is too short or too long. It also lets you look at each individual slide timing and helps you determine if a particular slide is necessary or whether it would be better served if combined with another slide.

Finally, if you are not sure how much time to allocate for each slide, you can play the slide show and let PowerPoint record your timing as you rehearse your speech.

Before you begin your practice, you will want your speaker notes or any other tool you plan on using during the presentation.

The following steps show you how to rehearse your presentation and record the timings.

1. Choose Slide Show>Rehearse Timings. The slide show will begin, as you see in Figure 17-15, and a Rehearsal bar appears in the top left corner of the screen.

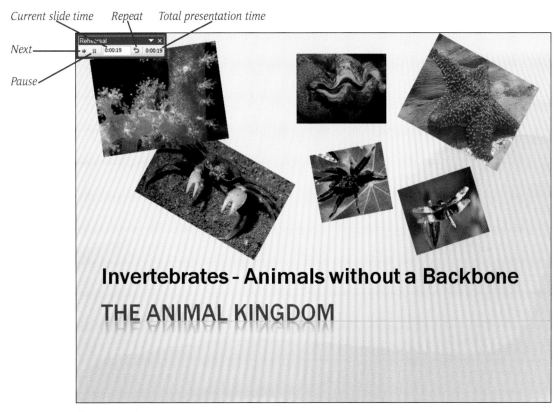

Current slide time   Repeat   Total presentation time

Next

Pause

Invertebrates – Animals without a Backbone

THE ANIMAL KINGDOM

Figure 17-15
Rehearsing Slide Timings.

2. Practice your speech about the current slide and then do one of the following:

   ▶ **Next:** Advance and begin timing the next slide.

   ▶ **Pause:** Temporarily stop recording the timing.

   ▶ **Repeat:** Restart the timing and rehearsal for the current slide.

3. When you complete the rehearsal and have gone through all the slides, the dialog box appears advising you of the total presentation length and asking you if you want to save the slide timings. Click Yes if you are happy with the timing or click No to discard the timings. You can start the rehearsal process again.

Running Your Presentation

THE BIG DAY HAS ARRIVED. You have completed the hard work, so now all you have to do is sit back and enjoy the show.

Setting Up the Slide Show

Before you actually give the presentation, you should set up a few parameters. The Set Up Show dialog box provides you with most of the choices you'll need. Choose Slide Show>Set Up>Set Up Slide Show. The Set Up Show dialog box seen in Figure 17-16 appears with a large variety of slide show options.

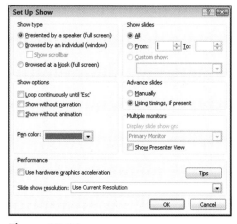

Figure 17-16
The Set Up Show dialog box.

▶ **Show type:** Determines whether to show the presentation in a window or full screen.

▶ **Show options:** Determines whether to repeat the show until you manually stop it and whether to show any animations or narrations. Also allows you to choose a pen color for annotations you make with the electronic felt tip pen. Red is generally the best choice because it is easily seen by most people.

▶ **Show slides:** Determines which slides you want to include in the presentation slide show.

▶ **Advance slides:** Determines whether to advance the slides manually or using the timings you set up for the individual slides or during rehearsal.

▶ **Multiple monitors:** If you are showing the slide show on multiple monitors, controls which monitor to use for the slide show.

▶ **Performance:** Optimizes the show hardware for the best presentation performance.

Select any desired options and then click OK.

Starting the Slide Show

Finally! You are ready to view your presentation in a slide show. You can actually launch the slide show from several places:

▶ **Click the Slide Show view button at the bottom of the presentation window.**

▶ **Choose Slide Show>Start Slide Show>From Beginning.**

▶ **Choose View>Presentation Views>Slide Show.**

To launch the slide show with the keyboard, press the F5 key.

Figure 17-17 illustrates the slide in full screen view during the slide show.

Figure 17-17
A PowerPoint slide show.

When your slide show completes, a black screen appears advising you to click the mouse button.

Navigating Slides

If you assigned timings to your slide show and during the Slide Show setup you elected to use the timings, you don't have to do anything but sit back and watch the show. That is…unless you want to take control over the timings. You can use either the mouse or the keyboard to control the actions in your slide show.

Navigating with the Mouse

When you are in the midst of a slide show presentation, your mouse pointer hides itself until you move the mouse. Then, if you position the mouse over the lower left corner of the slide, you see the slide show controls. They are fairly transparent until you point directly to one of the four buttons: Previous, Pen, Slides, and Next. Table 17-2 shows you the four buttons and their functions.

Table 17-2 Slide Controls Function

Icon	Button Name	Button Function
⬅	Previous	Jumps to the previous slide
✏	Pen	Displays the pop-up menu seen in Figure 17-18 where you can choose annotating pen options
▤	Slides	Displays a pop-up menu for making slide selections
➡	Next	Jumps to the next slide

Figure 17-18
Pen options from the slide show controls.

Other mouse options include simply clicking the left mouse button, which advances you to the next slide. If you click the right mouse button, a short-cut menu appears such as you see in Figure 17-19, from which you can make additional choices. Many audience members, however, find seeing the shortcut menu in the middle of a presentation extremely distracting.

Figure 17-19
Right-click shortcut menu.

Navigating from the Keyboard

Sometimes navigating with the mouse while giving the presentation can be difficult and is often annoying to the audience. A PowerPoint slide show includes quite a few intuitive keystrokes you can use to maneuver in the presentation. Table 17-3 shows you some of these keystrokes.

Table 17-3 Slide Show Keystrokes

Press This	Get This
N	Next animation or next slide
Spacebar	Next animation or next slide
P	Previous animation or previous slide
Ctrl+P	Change pointer to pen
Ctrl+A	Change pointer to arrow
E	Erase annotations
S	Stop (pause) (Press S again to resume.)
B	Pause and show black screen (Press B again to resume.)
W	Pause and show white screen (Press W again to resume.)
Esc	End the presentation

To go to a certain slide, enter the slide number and press Enter.

Pausing the Presentation

Perhaps during the presentation an audience member asks a question that you need to address. You can temporarily pause the presentation and optionally blank out the screen so the audience focuses on you and what you have to say.

If you have an occasion where you want the audience to not look at the presentation screen—for example, if you want them to concentrate on something you are saying—you can temporarily blank the screen. The slides timings do not advance. If you just want to pause the presentation, press S on the keyboard or click the Slide control button and choose Pause. To resume the presentation, press S again or click the Slide control button and choose Resume. When you pause the presentation, the presentation remains visible on the screen.

If, however, you don't want the audience to see the presentation screen during the pause, you can turn the screen to black or white. Figure 17-20 illustrates a slide show with the screen paused and turned black. If you look carefully, you can see the control buttons in the lower left screen corner. To pause the presentation and turn your screen black, press the letter B (or W for white) or, optionally, click the Slide control button and choose Screen>Black Screen (or White Screen). To resume the presentation, press the letter B (or W) again or, optionally, click the Slide control button and choose Screen>Unblack Screen (or Unwhite Screen).

Figure 17-20
Pausing the presentation and blacking the screen.

Annotating Slides

During the presentation you can draw on your screen with an electronic pen or highlighter. You might draw to underline words or check off key points as you discuss them. You actually have two types of pens: a Ballpoint pen that provides a thin line, or a Felt Tip pen that draws thicker, heavier lines. Additionally, the Highlighter draws wide, fairly transparent lines.

To annotate your slides, choose the pen you want to use from the Pen control button. You can also choose the pen ink color and even switch colors in the middle of the annotating. The keystroke to switch to the pen is Ctrl+P.

Draw on your screen. The drawn image appears on the slide. Take a look at Figure 17-21 where you see some annotations made with a red felt-tip pen.

Figure 17-21
Annotating your slides.

To cancel the pen and return to the normal arrow pointer, simply press the Esc key once. Be sure to only press Esc once. Pressing it a second time cancels the slide show.

To erase the screen annotations, press the letter E or click the Pen control button and choose Eraser or Erase All Ink on Slide.

When the slide show ends, a prompt appears (see Figure 17-22) asking you if you want to keep your annotations. Choose Keep or Discard. If you choose to keep them, PowerPoint adds the drawing as objects on the slide.

Figure 17-22
Choosing whether to keep or discard annotations.

Using Hidden Slides

At some point during a presentation, you will probably receive questions from your audience. Before you deliver your presentation, try to anticipate some of the questions you might be asked. Make slides that will answer the questions or provide additional background. Your audience will certainly think you are brilliant! To mark slides as hidden, from either Normal or Slide Sorter view, select the slides and choose Slide Show>Set Up>Hide Slide.

When you are giving the slide show and want to display a hidden slide, click the Slide navigation button and choose Go to Slide, which displays a list of all slides. Hidden slides display with their number in parentheses, like slide 4 in Figure 17-23. Choose the slide you want to display.

Figure 17-23
Showing hidden slides.

Packaging Your Presentation

I F YOU PLAN ON HANDING OFF THE presentation for others to view at their convenience, you want to make sure you have all the necessary files. If you have sound clips, video, or other data linked to your computer, you need to make sure the audience has access to those files as well. Additionally, if your recipients do not have PowerPoint on their computers, they need the PowerPoint viewer that allows them to view the presentation.

The PowerPoint Package for CD feature takes the PowerPoint Viewer, the presentation, *and* all the media links necessary to make the presentation run and puts them all together either ready to burn to a CD or into a folder that you can then e-mail or burn to a CD at a later time. Just follow these steps to create the presentation package.

1. Choose Office Button>Publish>Package for CD.

2. An informational message may appear. Click OK.

3. The Package for CD dialog box appears as seen in Figure 17-24. Perform one of the following steps:

    ▶ **If you want to burn the CD now, give the CD a different name and then click Copy to CD. A warning message will appear. Click Yes, insert a blank CD into the drive, and the CD burn process begins. When finished, PowerPoint asks you if you want to burn another CD.**

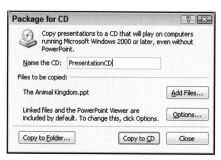

Figure 17-24
The Package for CD dialog box.

▶ **If you want to copy all the files to a folder for distribution at a later time, click Copy to Folder. The Copy to Folder dialog box appears, prompting you for a folder name and folder location. If desired, change the folder name or location and then click OK. PowerPoint creates the folder and saves all the files.**

4. Click the Close button to close the Package for CD dialog box.

Figure 17-25 shows the contents of the saved folder or CD. You can see that it includes not only the PowerPoint presentation file, but other files that make up the PowerPoint Viewer program. All the recipient need do is insert the CD and, if prompted, choose Run Viewer. The slide show presentation immediately begins.

Happy Presenting!

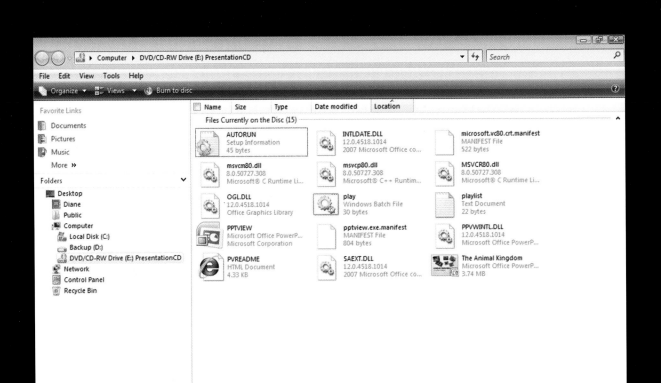

Figure 17-25
A packaged PowerPoint presentation.

Part V
Publisher

Publisher is the often overlooked application in
Microsoft Office. In fact, it doesn't come with all
Office versions. In the past, when you wanted to create
a publication, you needed a professional printer to help
you with layout and graphic design. Not any more.
With Publisher, you can create brochures, business
cards, calendars, and lots of other printed items.
And you do not need to be a professional printer.
You only need an idea.

18

Creating a
Predesigned Publisher
Publication

PICTURE YOURSELF PLANNING A BIG PARTY. You have so much to do and so little time. One task on your to-do list is creating the invitations. You could go to your local party store and buy ready-made invitations, or you can design your own quickly and easily using Microsoft Publisher.

To create publications without going through a lot of trouble, you use one of the supplied publication designs. A publication design gives you the structure for creating the type of publication you want. The designs provide placeholders for graphics and text, similar to the place-holders you worked with when creating PowerPoint slides.

Selecting a Publication Template

WHEN YOU FIRST LAUNCH Publisher (Start>All Programs>Microsoft Office> Microsoft Office Publisher 2007), you don't get a blank document ready for you to begin working. Instead, you get the Getting Started with Microsoft Office Publisher window that includes hundreds of different predesigned templates on which you can base the document you want to create (see Figure 18-1.) By far, this is the easiest way to create your publication, although in Chapter 19, "Designing Your Own Publication," you will see how to create your own.

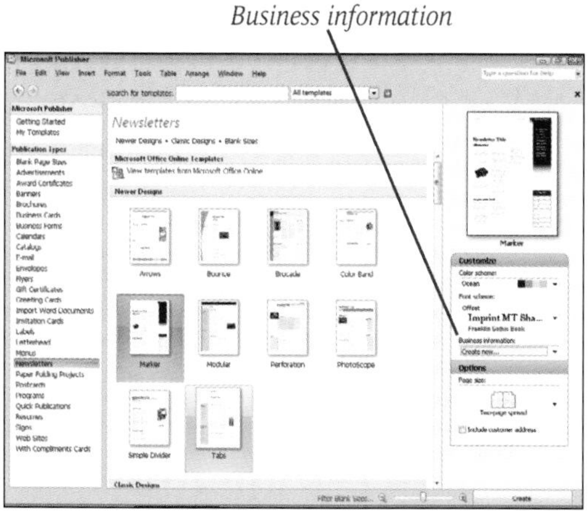

Business information

Figure 18-1

Selecting a publication template.

From the left side of the screen, select a publication type. The center of the screen displays some samples. Be sure to scroll down the screen; there are usually dozens of different samples for each publication type. Click once on the sample you want. A preview appears in the upper right corner. Select any customize options (see the next section) and then click Create.

Customizing Your Publication

On the right side of the screen, you see a section where you can customize the publication to better fit your needs and save you time. When they created the publication template, the designers at Microsoft supplied a group of coordinated colors and fonts; however, you can choose different colors and fonts in the Customize section.

Also, since many publications use common information such as a company name or phone numbers, rather than retyping this information each time you create a publication, you can store this information in the Business Information section. Then, when needed, Publisher automatically populates the publication fields.

Entering Business Information

You can have several different business information sets. Perhaps you have one for your company that includes your boss's name, and maybe you have one that you use for the school PTA. You enter the information and Publisher stores the business information sets for future use as well as in the current publication.

If you have already created a business information set, click the Business information down arrow and choose the set you want. If you have not yet created a business information set, or want to create a new one, click the Business information down arrow and choose Create New. You see the Create New Business Information Set dialog box seen in Figure 18-2.

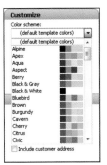

Figure 18-2
Enter your information.

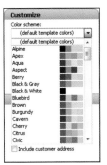

Figure 18-3
Choosing a color scheme.

Enter any relevant information in the Create New Business Information Set dialog box, replacing the existing text with your information. If you have a company logo, you can add it by clicking the Add Logo button, locating and selecting your logo, and choosing Insert. In the Business Information set name, enter a descriptive name for this group of information and click the Save button. The business information set now appears in the drop-down list for this publication and future publications.

> If you need to edit the business information set, from the Publisher menu, choose Edit>Business Information.

Changing the Color Scheme

When you create a publication based on a temple, it contains a scheme of colors that harmonize with each other. By default, Publisher assumes you want to use the original color designs; however, if you want to change the colors to a different theme, click the Color scheme down arrow, which displays color groups as they are associated with the different Office themes as you see in Figure 18-3. Choose the colors you want for your publication.

> **You are not limited to only the colors in your selected scheme; however, they appear as the starting point when selecting color for text or shapes.**

Choosing a Font Scheme

Each publication, when it was originally designed, included a set of fonts that complement each other. By default, Publisher assumes you want to use the original fonts. You can, however, customize the font scheme more to your liking or more appropriate for your actual publication. If you want to change the font scheme, click the Font scheme down arrow, which displays fonts as they are associated with the different Office themes (see Figure 18-4). Choose the font scheme you prefer.

Figure 18-4
Select the font group you want to use.

Viewing the Publisher Window

F OR WHATEVER THEIR REASONING, the wonderful folks at Microsoft did not make the major overhaul to Publisher 2007 that they did with Word, Excel, and PowerPoint 2007. If you have used other computer programs, you will recognize the old faithful menu and toolbar structure. In fact, by default, there are six different toolbars displayed (see Figure 18-5).

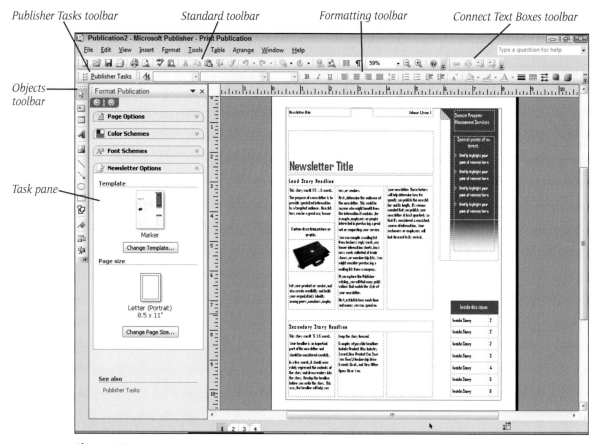

Figure 18-5

The standard Publisher toolbars.

▶ **Standard.** The Standard toolbar contains buttons for features such as those for opening, saving, printing, and zooming. It's the top toolbar, located right under the menus.

▶ **Connect Text Boxes.** Just to the right of the Standard toolbar is a small toolbar with only four buttons. It's called the Connect Text Boxes toolbar, and you use it when your text overflows onto a different area such as another page.

▶ **Publisher Tasks.** The Publisher Tasks toolbar is a very small toolbar with only one button, and it's located on the left side of the second row. This toolbar controls the Task Pane, which I will discuss in the next section.

▶ **Formatting.** Just to the right of the Publisher Tasks toolbar, still on the second row, you find the Formatting toolbar. You use this toolbar when working with changing the appearance of text, shapes, and other objects.

▶ **Objects.** Running vertically, along the left edge of your screen is the Objects toolbar, where you create the various objects you want on your publication. From here you can add tables, WordArt, shapes, and lots of other choices.

▶ **Task Pane.** Just to the right of the Objects toolbar is the Task Pane, which, as mentioned, I will review in the next section.

Some toolbars, such as the Picture toolbar, appear automatically if you are using a function that requires it. But if you don't want to see all the different default toolbars, you can turn any of them off and then back on when you need them. To hide or display toolbars, choose View>Toolbars and click the choice you want to hide or display. A checkmark next to an item means that toolbar is already displayed (see Figure 18-6).

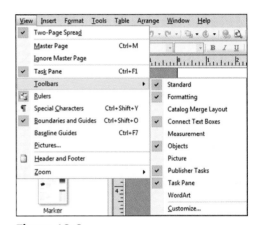

Figure 18-6
Choose a toolbar to display or hide.

Other items you see on the Publisher window include horizontal and vertical rulers, frames, and a few icons on the status bar that you will discern as needed while creating the publication.

Using the Task Pane

The rather large pane on the left side of the screen is the Task Pane. When you first create a new publication, options for formatting the publication appear here. As you work with your publication and select different functions, the Task Pane options may change. Or, you can change the options yourself. Click the down arrow next to Format Publication, which displays a list of the different task panes available with Publisher (see Figure 18-7).

Figure 18-7

Choose a task pane to assist you with your publication.

Manually change to any desired task pane by selecting it from the drop-down list, or you can click the Publisher Tasks button on the toolbar to switch to a common task pane called the Publisher Tasks task pane, which provides links to help you prepare your publication.

If you find the Task Pane annoying (I do), you can hide the Task Pane by clicking the Task Pane Close button. Closing the Task Pane also provides more screen space for you to work on your publication. For the remainder of the Publisher chapters, the Task Pane will be closed unless needed.

Understanding Frames

When you created a PowerPoint presentation, after selecting a slide layout, you saw the placeholders where you entered text or added objects. A Publisher publication also uses placeholders, some for text and some for objects, except that in Publisher they are referred to as *frames.* In Figure 18-8, you see a frame at the top with the words *Newsletter Title,* and there are several more in the middle of the page, prompting for more text information. The picture of the briefcase is a frame for a graphic. A little later in this chapter, we will place a different picture in the graphic frame.

Figure 18-8

Placeholder frames.

Presenting View Options

A S YOU WORK ON YOUR PUBLICATION, you will find yourself needing to look at it from several different perspectives. Perhaps you want to view the detail, or look closer at the ruler, or stand back and look at the overall appearance. Publisher has several options to help you take a better look.

Setting Down Ruler Guides

The Publisher window provides rulers across the top and left side. When working on your publication, you often will want to place a frame in a very precise position on the page. The rulers, with markings in eighths of an inch, guide you in placing your objects.

However, with the rulers being at the far left or at the top it is sometime difficult to line up to a specific position unless you have your publication greatly zoomed in. (You will learn about zooming the screen in the next section.) A better way to work with the rulers is to use ruler guides, which can go anywhere on the page.

Ruler guides are non printing light green lines that you use for visual alignment. You turn them on or off as needed. Choose Arrange>Ruler Guides> and choose Add Horizontal Ruler Guide or Add Vertical Ruler Guide. In Figure 18-9 you see a horizontal ruler guide. You can easily move the guide by positioning your mouse over the guide until the mouse pointer turns into a double-headed arrow. Drag the guide until it is where you want it.

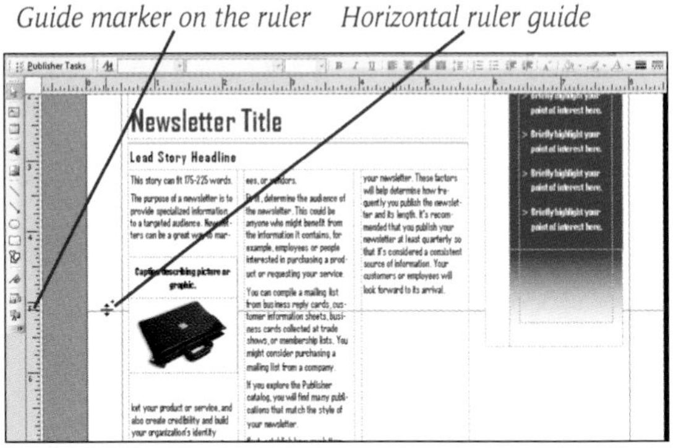

Guide marker on the ruler   Horizontal ruler guide

Figure 18-9
Use ruler guides to align objects.

Notice the guide line displays very lightly on the ruler, and as you move the guide, you see it move on the ruler as well. This helps you tie the guide to the ruler for exact object positioning.

When would you use the guides? Well, one example might be when you need to place the bottom of a picture at precisely 2.375 inches from the top. Place a horizontal guide at 2.375 inches and then drag the picture so its base sits on the guide. Another example when you might use a guide is that at the 2-inch vertical mark, you want to draw a box exactly 1.75 inches tall by 3.25 inches wide. Place two vertical and two horizontal guides so they are the exact dimensions apart and then draw your box in between the guides (see Figure 18-10).

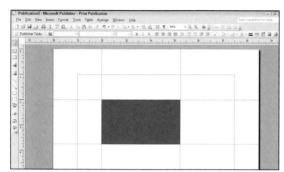

Figure 18-10
Use ruler guides to help you specifically size an object.

Add as many horizontal and vertical guides as needed. When you no longer need them, choose Arrange>Ruler Guides>Clear All Ruler Guides, which clears all the guides. If you just want to remove individual guides, drag the unwanted guide to the ruler on the top or the left.

If you want to hide the rulers, choose View>Rulers. Choose View>Rulers again to redisplay the rulers. Hiding the rulers does not hide the ruler guides.

> Instead of inches, you can set your rulers to measure in centimeters, picas, points, or pixels. Choose Tools>Options. On the General tab is a Measurement Units drop-down list where you can choose your unit of measurement.

Zooming for a Better View

As you create your publication, you will probably need to see the details a little more clearly. When you are viewing the entire page, it can be difficult to read the print. Fortunately, it is very easy to zoom in and zoom out on any section of your publication. In fact, there are several ways you can zoom into or out of your document:

▶ **Click the Zoom In button to zoom in closer on your publication. Each click zooms in a little more (see Figure 18-11).**

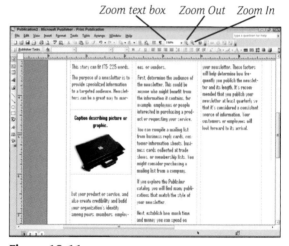

Zoom text box   Zoom Out   Zoom In

Figure 18-11
Zooming in for a closer look.

▶ Click the Zoom Out button to decrease the zoom on your publication. Each click zooms out a little more.

▶ Click the Zoom down arrow, which display a list of common zoom percentages ranging from 10% (really, really tiny) to 800% (enormous—stand back!). You can also choose Whole Page, which generally zooms to the 50% level, or Page Width, which zooms in enough to see the entire width of the document.

▶ Enter a zoom percentage in the Zoom text box and then press the Enter key.

▶ Choose View>Zoom and select an option from the available menu choices.

▶ If your publication has more than one page, choose View>Two Page Spread, which allows you to see facing pages as shown in Figure 18-12 where you see pages 2 and 3.

Navigation buttons

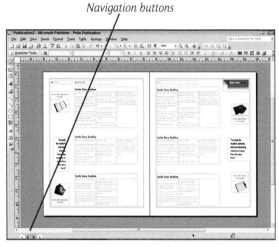

Figure 18-12
Viewing pages side by side.

The individual page numbers are listed on the status bar with a highlight around the currently displayed pages. The page numbers are called Navigation buttons.

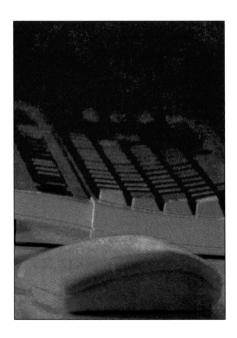

Working with Text

I F YOU ARE READY TO BEGIN EDITING the publication so it contains the content you want, you probably want to begin by entering the text content. One of the first tasks is changing the sample text provided in the template with your own text.

Entering Text in a Text Box

Highlight the text in the text box by either dragging across it completely or by clicking the text box to select it and either pressing Ctrl+A or choosing Edit>Select All. While the text is still highlighted, begin typing your own text. Your text replaces the highlighted sample text. Some publications, such as newsletters, include linked text frames, meaning that as you type the text, if needed, it will automatically flow into the next linked text frame. You can tell where the next frame is located when you click on a frame and look at the icon below it. If there is an arrow pointing to the right, then more text flows into a linked text box elsewhere in the publication. The last linked text box has an icon above it with an arrow to the left to indicate linkage to a previous text box. If the frame does not have an icon with an arrow below it, the box is not linked to other boxes, or is the last box in the group.

Making the Text Fit into the Frames

A huge challenge is making your text fit in the text frame. If the text you entered is too long for the text box, what happens? You actually have a quite a few choices. You can do any of the following:

► Edit the text and remove any unnecessary wording. Editing text in a Publisher frame is just like editing text in a Word document.

► Make the text frame larger. See "Working with Frames" in Chapter 19.

► Shrink the text size so it fits into the box. Choose Format>AutoFit Text>Shrink Text on Overflow. Be cautious with this option, because if you have a lot of text to shrink, it may make it too small to read easily (see Figure 18-13).

AutoFit Text

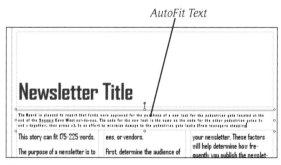

Figure 18-13
Don't make your text too small to read!

► Adjust the character spacing in the text. See "Adjusting Character Spacing" later in this chapter.

► Let the extra text fall into another frame. (See the next section.)

Making Text Flow Across Frames

Notice that most placeholder text shows you approximately how many words will fit in the story frames. When you enter more text than will fit within a frame, you see an icon at the bottom of the text frame. The icon is called Text in Overflow, and it is there to remind you that the entire story is not displayed and that you must make a decision about where you want to place the rest of the text. When you have too much text to fit in a particular frame, you can direct it into another text frame. The target frame could be on the same page or more likely another page. The following steps show you how to make the text flow into another frame:

> A story refers to text that fits across multiple frames.

1. Select the text frame containing the overflow text.

2. From the Connect Text Boxes toolbar, click the Create Text Box Link button. The mouse pointer appears as a small pitcher (see Figure 18-14).

3. Click anywhere in the text box you want the overflow text and Publisher "pours" the overflow text into the second text box. If your story is exceptionally long, you may have an overflow on the second box and need to link it to a third or fourth text box.

Adding Continuation Slugs

When you have a story that flows across different pages, at the end of one page you may want to tell your reader what page to turn to for the rest of the story. You can have Publisher automatically create a *continuation slug* at the bottom of your text frame. Conversely, at the top of the rest of the story, you can add a slug that says "Continued from page….".

Text in Overflow icon   Overflow text box

Figure 18-14
Linking text boxes.

Right-click the text box to which you want to add a slug and from the resulting shortcut menu, choose Format Text Box. Choose the Text Box tab on the Format Text box (see Figure 18-15). Choose either the Include "Continued on page…" or the Include "Continued from page…" option. Click OK to apply the option.

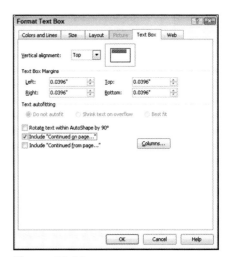

Figure 18-15
Creating continuation slugs.

Formatting Text

When using a predefined publication, most of the formatting is already set up for you, but sometimes you want to make changes. Formatting text in a Publisher text box is very similar to formatting text in a Word document. The difference is primarily in that Word now uses a Ribbon to display the formatting choices where Publisher displays common formatting options on the Formatting toolbar.

Changing Font Formatting

Select the text you want to change and do any of the following (see Figure 18-16).

- ▶ **Click the Font drop-down list and choose a different font.**

- ▶ **Click the Font Size drop-down list and select a font size.**

- ▶ **Click the toolbar buttons to choose Bold, Italic, or Underline.**

- ▶ **Click the Font Color arrow drop-down list and select a font color.**

Adding Bullets and Numbering

If you have text that needs bullets or numbering, you can also add those from the Formatting toolbar. Select the text to which you want to add bullets or numbering. From the Formatting toolbar, click the Bullets button or the Numbering button. The default bullet or numbering style is applied to your text. If you want a special style bullet or numbering, choose Format>Bullets and Numbering, which displays the dialog box shown in Figure 18-17. Select the bullet or number style you want, and then click the OK button.

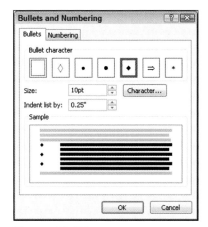

Figure 18-17
Selecting a bullet or numbering style.

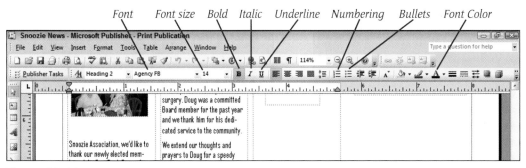

Figure 18-16
Changing character formatting.

Adjusting Character Spacing

When working with headlines you may find you have a lot of unused space, or perhaps your headline is just a little too long. You can tinker with the character spacing to add or remove space between characters. If you want to adjust the space between all selected characters, it is called *tracking*; if you want to adjust the space between two specific characters, it is called *kerning*. Begin by selecting the text you want to adjust and then choose Format>Character Spacing. You see the Character Spacing dialog box in Figure 18-18.

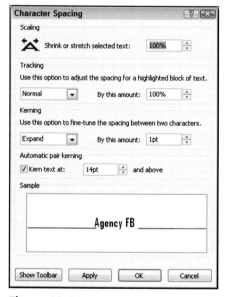

Figure 18-18
Adjusting character spacing.

From the Character Spacing dialog box, choose a Tracking preset option and then click OK. Choices include:

▶ **Normal:** Keeps the text at 100% of its original tracking.

▶ **Very Tight:** Reduces the tracking space by 25% of Normal.

▶ **Tight:** Reduces the tracking space by 12.5% of Normal.

▶ **Loose:** Expands the tracking space by 12.5% of Normal.

▶ **Very Loose:** Expands the tracking space by 25% of Normal.

▶ **Custom:** Reduces or expands the tracking space by a percentage you specify using the spinner boxes.

If you have a block of text that doesn't quite fit into a frame but is not enough to go into another frame, try reducing the character spacing.

Changing Alignments

Just like in Word, you can change the alignment of your text. Horizontal alignment manages the text between the left and right margins of a text box. Vertical alignment manages the text between the top and bottom margins of a text box.

In Chapter 3, "Making a Word Document Look Good," you discovered you can change the horizontal alignment by selecting the text you want to change and clicking one of the four alignment buttons from the Home>Paragraph area. In Publisher, you have the same four choices—Align Text Left, Center, Align Text Right, and Justify—all available on the Formatting toolbar. You can change a headline, all of the text, or a selected story paragraph. You cannot change the alignment for only part of a paragraph.

Horizontal alignments all have shortcut keys. For Align Text Left, use Ctrl+L; for Center, use Ctrl+E; for Align Text Right, use Ctrl+R; and for Justify, use Ctrl+J.

By default, text starts at the top of a text frame, but if you want to change the vertical text alignment, select the text box you want to modify and choose Format>Text Box. The Format Text Box dialog box seen in Figure 18-19 appears. From the Text Box tab, you can select a Vertical alignment of Top, Bottom, or Middle.

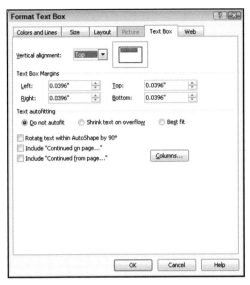

Figure 18-19
Changing vertical alignment.

Adjusting Paragraph Spacing

Another text adjustment commonly used is the spacing before and after paragraphs. Between the paragraphs, instead of placing a full blank line that is determined by the font size, many publications use a fixed amount of space based on point size. The setting is controlled through the Paragraph dialog box and, like horizontal alignment options, applies to the entire paragraph. Just follow these easy steps:

1. Select the paragraphs you want to format.

2. Choose Format>Paragraph.

3. From the Paragraph dialog box, on the Indents and Spacing Tab, set an amount of space you require either before the first line of a paragraph or after the last line of a paragraph, or both (see Figure 18-20).

4. Click OK to apply the settings.

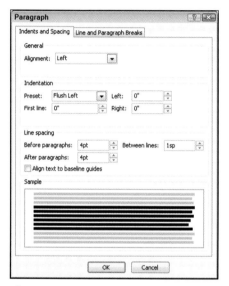

Figure 18-20
Setting paragraph spacing.

From the Paragraph dialog box, you can also set the line spacing, which is the space between individual paragraph lines.

Inserting Drop Caps

A drop cap is a large capital letter typically at the beginning of a story, although you could have a drop cap in any paragraph. Adding drop caps adds a flair of elegance to your story and often captures a reader's eye.

Click the paragraph for which you want a drop cap. You don't have to actually select any part of the text. Publisher will automatically make the first letter in the paragraph the drop cap. Choose Format>Drop Cap, which displays the Drop Cap dialog box as shown in Figure 18-21. Scroll through the various drop cap styles. Click on one to see a preview of your paragraph with the drop cap. Click OK when you find the one you like.

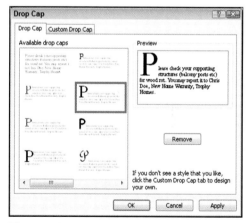

Figure 18-21
Choosing a drop cap style.

Although the drop cap styles in Word are much more limited than those in Publisher, you can easily add one to a Word document too! Click in the paragraph you want to have a drop cap and choose Insert>Text>Drop Cap>Dropped.

Working with Graphics

IN CHAPTER 15, "EDITING YOUR Presentation," you learned how you can manipulate graphics in PowerPoint. Among the options you discovered were how to move, resize, and rotate graphics. Graphics work the same way in Publisher. You select the graphic image, and, using the selection handles, you manipulate the graphic to the size or position you want.

Publisher templates come with placeholders for graphics and text. However, like the text in the text placeholders, the graphics in the graphic place-holders are only samples. You will most certainly want to replace the graphic with one more appro-priate to your publication.

A graphic placeholder may contain only a place for the picture, or it may be two placeholders grouped together—one to contain a place for the picture and another text placeholder for a caption. If your placeholder is just for a picture, you only need to click the placeholder and the Picture toolbar appears. If your placeholder contains both, you need to click the sample image twice, but *not* as a double-click. The first click selects the entire placeholder, and clicking a second time displays the Picture toolbar as you see in Figure 18-22.

> **If you click off of the graphic place-holder, the Picture toolbar disappears.**

Selected graphic   Insert Picture   Picture toolbar

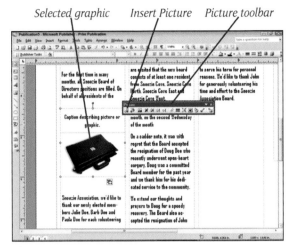

Figure 18-22
Displaying the Picture toolbar.

On the Picture toolbar, click the first button, Insert Picture. Locate and select the picture you want and choose Insert. Publisher replaces the existing picture with your newly selected picture.

> The Picture toolbar also has buttons to adjust the image brightness or contrast, or to crop the picture. Pause your mouse over any button to see a ScreenTip explaining the button's purpose.

19

Designing Your Own
Publication

PICTURE YOURSELF ON THE BEACH, playing in the wet sand. You want to build a sand sculpture, so with an idea in mind, you begin with a handful of sand and slowly transform the wet glob into a work of art.

In the previous chapter you discovered how easy it was to begin with a template that met your needs and just plug in your own text and graphics. The pattern was already laid out and meticulously designed. Most of the time, using a predesigned template is the fastest and easiest way to produce your publication. However, when nothing seems to fit just what you have in mind, you can create your publication from the beginning.

Starting Your Publication

I N THIS CHAPTER, YOU BEGIN WITH A
blank page and transform it into a beautiful
publication. You will discover how to add your
own frames and manipulate them into positions
appropriate for your task. You can add as many
pages as desired to your publication and fill them
with the information you want the world to see.

Planning a Design

The first thing you must do is spend a little time
planning your project. Ask yourself questions such as

▶ **What size paper do I plan on using?**

▶ **In what orientation will I need the
paper?**

▶ **Will I use multiple columns?**

▶ **Will I print this myself or take it somewhere to be commercially printed?**

▶ **What types of things do I want to say?**

▶ **What fonts would look good for the
intended audience?**

The best thing you can do is begin with a pencil
and a blank piece of paper. Sketch out a rough idea
of what you want. It doesn't have to be perfect, but
it will certainly give you a good place to start. Take
a look at Figure 19-1. On the top you see the rough
design of a publication, and on the bottom you see
the final publication. Planning ahead with pencil
and paper will save you time and frustration when
you begin working with your publication in
Publisher.

Figure 19-1
Sketch out your ideas before you begin.

Selecting a Paper Size

The next thing you must do is start Microsoft Publisher and select your blank paper size. Choose File>New if you do not already see the Getting Started with Microsoft Office Publisher 2007 window. From the Publication Types section, click Blank Page Sizes and then choose one of the blank page sizes you see in Figure 19-2. Be sure to scroll down. There are hundreds of different blank page sizes—something for every project. Pause your mouse over any size to see a brief description.

Select the one best suited for your project, and then choose the color and font scheme and the business information set you want to use. If you forgot what the color and font schemes or the business information sets were about, refer back to Chapter 18. After making your selections, click the Create button.

The sample publication created in this chapter is a fold-out brochure so that even though the entire brochure is on a single sheet of paper, the brochure really contains four pages: a front panel, the left inside panel, the right inside panel, and the back panel. On some publication sizes, Publisher may prompt you to insert the additional pages (see Figure 19-3). Choose Yes.

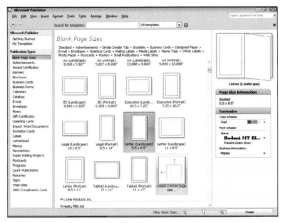

Figure 19-2
Begin by choosing the paper size for your publication.

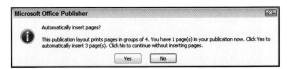

Figure 19-3
Some publication types require multiple pages.

To quickly jump to a project type, click one of the categories at the top.

Setting the Margins

Depending on the layout you selected, the first page of the blank publication appears on your screen with blue lines, which are the page margin guides. Technically, a publication doesn't have margins other than the ones built into some printers, such as a laser printer. The margin guides are just that—guides. You use the guides to ensure that your text and graphics do not stray too far into the margin.

You can change the margin guides at any time: however, it saves time if you change them before you begin placing objects on your screen. Choose File>Page Setup. The Page Setup dialog box shown in Figure 19-4 appears.

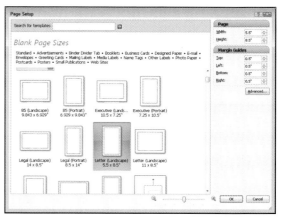

Figure 19-4

Managing the page margins.

You will find the boundary lines very helpful in placing objects on the screen; however, you can turn them on and off by choosing View>Boundaries and Guides or by pressing Ctrl+Shift+O.

From this box you can change your paper size by either selecting a different blank page size, or by changing the width and height measurements under the Page section. Use the spinner boxes to change the Top, Bottom, Left, or Right margin guides. When you are finished, click the OK button.

Working with Frames

EVERYTHING YOU PUT ON YOUR publication appears in a frame. The entire publication is made of combinations of five different frames: text frames, picture frames, table frames, WordArt frames, and Design Gallery frames. (You will discover the Design Gallery later in this chapter.)

You are ready to begin placing frames for the objects you want on the publication. You can place the frames one at a time as you need them, or you can lay out the frames in approximation to your sketched drawing. The choice is up to you, but, personally, I prefer the latter method. It seems to keep me better organized.

Inserting Frames

You insert frames by choosing a button located on the Objects toolbar. Depending on the button you select, the following occurs:

> ▶ **Text Box:** Use the Text Box for headings, paragraphs, or stories. The Text Box tool doesn't ask you for more information. You simply click the tool, drag a rectangular shape in the publication, and then release the mouse button when the frame is approximately the right size. You will see shortly how easy it is adjust the frame size and position. When you release the mouse button, the frame appears with eight selection handles and a rotation handle. Click in the text frame and begin typing your text.

Pause your mouse over a toolbar button to see the button function.

> ▶ **Insert Table:** Use a table to portray facts in a column and row format. After you click the Insert Table button, you draw a rectangular shape in the publication, and when you release the mouse button, the Create Table dialog box appears, like you see in Figure 19-5. Select the number of rows and columns you want and choose a table format. The Sample area displays a preview of the different table formats. Click the OK button when you are finished making your choices and a blank table appears in your publication, ready for your data.

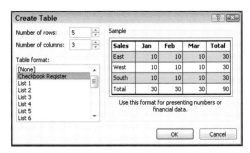

Figure 19-5
Inserting a table frame.

▶ **Insert WordArt:** In Chapter 15, you first discovered WordArt to place on a PowerPoint slide. The Publication WordArt is very similar, although the options are a little different. When you click the Insert WordArt button, the WordArt Gallery seen in Figure 19-6 appears with 30 different options from which you can choose. Select the WordArt style you want and then click the OK button. The Edit WordArt box appears, where you can enter your text and determine more options. For more information, see "Creating WordArt," later in this chapter.

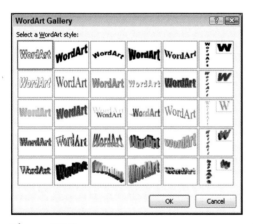

Figure 19-6
Inserting a WordArt frame.

▶ **Picture Frame:** When you click the Picture Frame button, a submenu appears asking you to choose from inserting Clip Art, Picture from File, Empty Picture Frame, or From Scanner or Camera. Choosing Clip Art displays the Clip Art pane where you can select a clip art image (see Chapter 14). If you choose Picture from File, you draw a rectangular shape in the publication and when you release the mouse button, the Insert Picture dialog box appears where you locate and select the picture you want to use. Click the Insert button to fill the frame with the selected picture. Choosing Empty Picture Frame simply allows you to create a blank frame by drawing a rectangle on the publication. You can fill the frame later with the graphic of your choice. Whenever you select the empty picture frame, the Picture toolbar appears. The final menu choice, From Scanner or Camera, displays the Insert Picture from Scanner or Camera dialog box. Follow the onscreen instructions as the instructions vary according to the device connected to your computer.

▶ **Design Gallery Object:** Click the Design Gallery Object button to display the Design Gallery, which is a collection of predesigned objects including decorative buttons, pull quotes, logos, calendars, coupons, and a lot more. See "Using the Design Gallery" later in this chapter.

Modifying Frames

Whether or not you already have text or graphics in the frame, once you have the frame in place, you can easily modify its size or position. You have discovered that with other Office objects you select the object and then you can manipulate it. Since a Publisher frame is also an object, you modify it using the same standard techniques:

▶ **To delete a frame, select the frame and then press the Delete key.**

▶ **To move a frame, select the frame and then move the mouse pointer over the frame edge (but not a handle) and drag the frame to a different position. Make sure the mouse pointer is in the shape of a four-headed arrow before you drag the frame. You can also use the arrow keys to "nudge" a frame up, down, left, or right a small amount.**

▶ **To move a frame to a different page, select the frame and then choose Edit>Cut. Display the page you want the frame placed in and choose Edit>Paste.**

▶ **To change the frame size, select the frame and position the mouse over a selection handle. When the mouse pointer appears as a double-headed arrow, drag the handle until the frame is the size you want (see Figure 19-7). Use the middle handles to drag straight up, down, left, or right, and use the corner handles to change both the height and width. If you have text in a text frame, when you resize the frame the text rewraps to fit the new size. If you have a graphic in a picture frame, be cautious when dragging a side handle as doing so can distort the image proportions.**

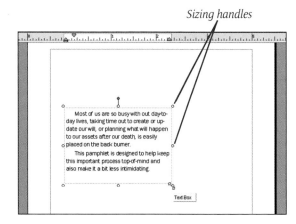

Sizing handles

Figure 19-7
Resizing a frame.

▶ **To rotate a frame and its contents, use the green rotation handle. Position the mouse pointer over the handle until the mouse pointer turns into a small semi-circle. Drag the rotation handle until the frame is at the angle you want.**

Adding Text Frame Borders and Shading

Even though on screen you see dotted lines surrounding a text frame, those lines do not print. They are there to help you visualize the frame location relative to other screen items. Adding a border or background shading to a text frame is a great way to make the frame stand out and attract attention. A border surrounds the frame but does not affect what is inside the frame, and adding background shading fills the entire frame area with a color. The following steps show you how to add borders and background shading to your text frames.

> While you can add borders and shading to any type of frame, typically you use it with text frames.

If you choose a dark background color, you will probably want to change your text color to a light or white color.

1. Select the frame you want to modify.

2. Choose Format>Text Box or right-click the frame and choose Format Text Box.

3. If not already displayed, click the Colors and Lines tab.

4. If you want a background color, click the Fill Color drop-down list and select a color.

5. If you want to lighten the background color, slide the transparency bar to a higher number. The Preview window shows you the current shading (see Figure 19-8).

6. If you want to add borders to the text frame, first click the Line Color down arrow and choose a color for the border lines.

7. Next, choose a line pattern from the Dashed drop-down list. You can select from solid lines to dotted lines to intermittent dashed lines (see Figure 19-9).

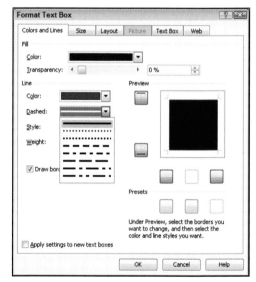

Figure 19-9
Selecting a line pattern.

8. Click the Style drop-down list and choose from a variety of line styles including double or triple lines.

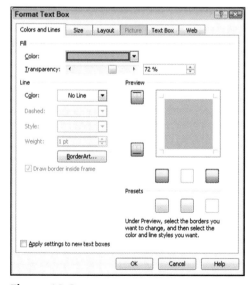

Figure 19-8
Adding shading to a text frame.

9. Finally, once you have the styles you want, you need to tell Publisher where to put the lines. You can have lines on all four sides of the frame or only on the sides you choose. In the Preview box, click the area you want to have the line. Figure 19-10 shows that triple lines will appear at the top and bottom edges of the text frame.

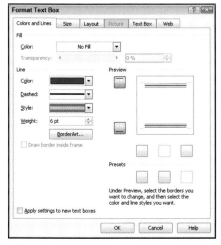

Figure 19-10
Previewing the added borders.

10. Click the OK button when you are finished. Publisher then applies the settings to the selected frame.

Adding Border Art

You often see border art around a scrapbook page, but you can also add it to your publication. Border art is typically a repeating series of small graphics that encompass a frame. Not every publication type should have border art, as it can make the publication look frivolous. However, if you are printing a coupon or some other lively piece of information, border art may be just what you need.

Just follow these steps:

1. Select the frame you want to modify.

2. Choose Format>Text Box or right-click the frame and choose Format Text Box.

3. From the Colors and Lines tab, click the Border Art button. The BorderArt dialog box seen in Figure 19-11 appears.

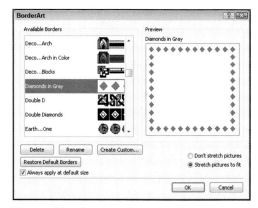

Figure 19-11
Select an artistic border for your text box.

4. Select the border art you want and then click the OK button. Figure 19-12 shows a text box with border art around it.

Figure 19-12
BorderArt can bring attention to special areas.

Adding Other Objects

I F YOU WANT MORE THAN JUST TEXT or pictures in your publication, Publisher includes several other tools to assist you. You can insert decorative text in the form of WordArt, or you can select from a huge group of predesigned objects including decorative buttons, pull quotes, and logos.

Inserting WordArt

With WordArt, you can take headings or key words and add decorative color schemes, shapes, and special effects. The directions for creating WordArt in Microsoft Publisher are slightly different than for the WordArt supplied in Word, Excel, and PowerPoint. Just follow these steps:

1. Click the Insert WordArt button on the Objects toolbar.

2. Make a WordArt style selection from the WordArt Gallery and then click OK. The Edit WordArt Text dialog box shown in Figure 19-13 appears.

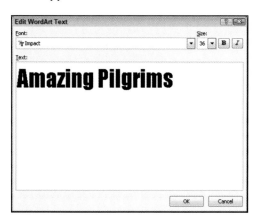

Figure 19-13
Type the text you want molded into WordArt.

2. Type your text. Keep it short; using longer strings of text can be very difficult to read.

3. Click the OK button. The WordArt appears in your publication as you see in Figure 19-14. A WordArt toolbar also appears.

WordArt Gallery   Format WordArt   WordArt Shape

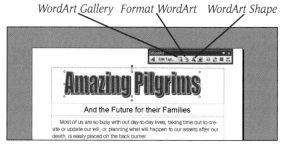

Figure 19-14
A sample WordArt object.

From the WordArt toolbar you can do the following:

▶ **Click Edit Text to modify the text content.**

▶ **Click WordArt Gallery to change the WordArt style.**

▶ **Click Format WordArt to change the fill color or line color surrounding your WordArt.**

▶ **Click WordArt Shape to manipulate the shape of your WordArt (see Figure 19-15).**

Figure 19-15
Mold your WordArt into different shapes.

▶ Click the Text Wrapping button to change the way the WordArt wraps around other text.

▶ Click WordArt Same Letter Heights to make all the characters in the WordArt the same height. (Click the option again to turn off the feature.)

▶ Click WordArt Vertical Text to make the WordArt text run vertically on the page instead of horizontally.

▶ Click WordArt Alignment to stretch or align the text horizontally.

▶ Click WordArt Character spacing to adjust the tracking in the WordArt object. (See "Adjusting Character Spacing" in Chapter 18.) Choices include Very Tight, Tight, Normal, Loose, Very Loose, and Kern Character Pairs.

> If you expand or shrink the WordArt box, the WordArt contents also expand or shrink.

Using the Design Gallery

The Design Gallery is a collection of over 250 theme and color-coordinated objects that you can easily add to your publication. Many Publisher users find them very helpful for filling in blank spaces. You will also find ready-made coupons, reply forms, pull quotes, and even calendars, along with lots of other useful items. And because they are objects, you can manipulate them as you would any other object.

To insert a Design Gallery object, choose Insert>Design Gallery Object or simply click the Design Gallery Object button on the Objects toolbar. From the resulting Design Gallery dialog box seen in Figure 19-16, select a category, then select an object, and then click the Insert Object button.

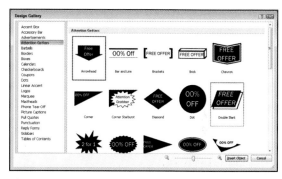

Figure 19-16
Select a ready-made object from the Design Gallery.

Drawing with the Drawing Tools

Well, if none of the Design Tools, WordArt, Clip Art, or other graphic objects quite suit what you have in mind, you can always create your own. In Chapter 15, you discovered that you can add your own shapes to a PowerPoint slide (as well as to a Word document or Excel workbook). Publisher contains some very similar drawing tools.

The Object toolbar contains tools to draw lines, arrows, circles or ovals, squares or rectangles, and several collections of other AutoShapes. You choose the tool you want and then click and drag in the publication until your object is the size you want.

To constrain the shape so it draws only straight lines or perfectly symmetrical shapes, hold down the Shift key when drawing the object.

To alter an AutoShape shape, see "Reshaping the Shape Object" in Chapter 15.

Changing Shape Borders

For arrows, lines, or the border around an object, select the object and choose Format>AutoShape. Depending on the object you select (in this example, an arrow), options appear for the object (see Figure 19-18).

Figure 19-17 illustrates a perfectly shaped cube drawn with the AutoShapes tool and an arrow drawn with the Arrow tool. After you draw the object, you can change the border color, fill in the object with color, reshape the object, or even add text directly on the object.

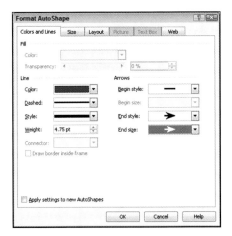

Figure 19-18
Changing an arrow style.

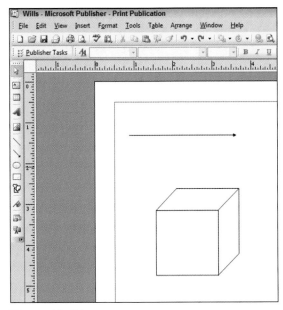

Figure 19-17
Drawing AutoShapes.

From the Line options, select a line color and style. From the Arrow section, choose a style and size for the arrow head and click the OK button when you are finished.

Filling Shapes with Color

Obviously objects such as lines and arrows cannot have a fill, but almost every other shape you draw can be filled with colors, gradients, textures, patterns, or even a picture!

Select the object you want to fill and choose Format>AutoShape. Click the Fill Color down arrow and choose a color related to your color scheme, or click the Fill Effects option. If you select the Fill Effects option you get the Fill Effects dialog box. The different tabs—Gradient, Texture, Pattern, Picture, and Tint—as shown in Figure 19-19, allow you to select the option best for your shape. Choose the fill type, set any desired color shading or other options, and then click the OK button.

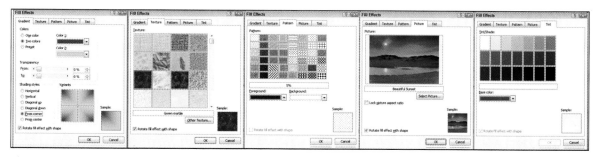

Figure 19-19

Choose a shape fill type and other options.

Figure 19-20 illustrates some various AutoShapes with the different fill effects.

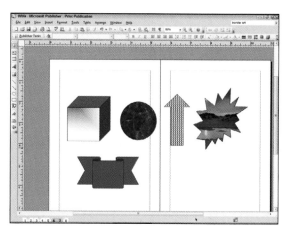

Figure 19-20

Sample fill effects.

Adding Text to a Shape

Any shape object other than arrows and lines can have text applied. You *could* create a text frame and move it inside the object, but that typically makes for a lot of work. A much easier way is to let Publisher enter the text and automatically center it in the shape.

Right-click the shape and choose Add Text from the shortcut menu. A blinking insertion point appears in the object where can type your text. You can then select the text and use any formatting tool to enhance it as you wish. See Figure 19-21 for an example.

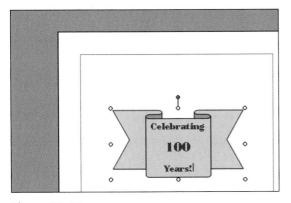

Figure 19-21
Type text in the drawn shape.

Wrapping Text Around a Graphic

By controlling how you wrap text around a frame or graphic, you can make your publication look much more professional. If you look at the graphics in Figure 19-22, you see the same graphic three times inside the text. With the graphic on the top, the Square wrap option wraps text around the graphic in a square pattern. Through wrap is the default choice. The center graphic uses the Tight option, and you see the text wrapped tightly around the graphic, which leaves less white space between the text and graphic.

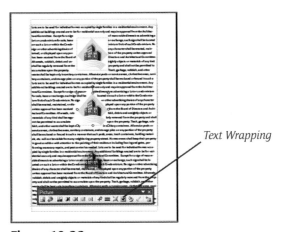

Text Wrapping

Figure 19-22
Making text and graphics play nice together.

The bottom graphic illustrates the Through option, where the text overlays the top of the graphic. If you create the text before you create the graphic, the graphic lays on top of the text. If you right-click the graphic and choose Order>Send Backward, the graphic lays under the text.

To change the way the text wraps around a graphic, select the graphic and, from the Picture toolbar, choose Text Wrapping and select the text wrapping option you want.

Working with Pages

SOME PUBLICATIONS CONTAIN ONLY a single page when you create them. Others may contain 2, 4, or more pages. If you have too many pages, you can delete the extras; and if you need more, you can easily add them.

Inserting New Pages

As you continue working on your projects, you may find you need additional pages. If, for example, your community newsletter has extra articles, you can add pages as needed. Just follow these steps:

1. Choose Insert>Page or press Ctrl+Shift+N. Depending on your publication type, either a blank page appears ready for you to insert objects, or the Insert Page dialog box shown in Figure 19-23 appears.

Figure 19-23
The Insert Page dialog box.

2. Choose how many new pages you want to insert.

3. Select whether you want the new pages placed before or after the current page.

4. Determine whether you want the new pages blank, with a text box, or as a duplicate of a specified page.

5. Click the OK button. The new page numbers appear on the navigation buttons on the status bar.

Deleting Unwanted Pages

To delete extra pages you don't need in the publication, display the page you do not want and choose Edit>Delete Page. Depending on what you are deleting, the following occurs:

▶ **If the page is a single page, not part of a two-page spread, and the page contains no objects, Publisher simply deletes the page with no questions asked.**

▶ **If the page is a single page and the page contains objects, a warning message indicates that the selected page contains objects. Click Yes to delete the page.**

▶ **If the page is part of a two-page spread, you see the Delete Page dialog box prompting you whether you want to delete both pages or just the left or right page. Make a selection and click OK. If the page (or pages) contains objects, you are prompted with a warning message.**

Depending on the publication type, you may also see the warning message displayed in Figure 19-24. Click OK to continue.

Figure 19-24
Publisher warns you if deleting the page may cause complications.

Moving Pages

If you created a page and then decide you want it in a different position in the publication, you can move pages from one place to another.

Display the page you want to move and choose Edit>Move Page. The Move Page dialog box appears, listing all the pages in your publication. You determine the position for the new page and whether it should come before or after the selected page. For example, suppose you have a five-page publication and you want to move what is now page 4. You now want it to be the second page, so you begin by displaying page 4. In the Move Page dialog box shown in Figure 19-25, you would click Page 2 and choose Before. That would move the selected page before the current page 2.

Figure 19-25
Moving pages.

Adding Page Backgrounds

For many publications, a really cool trick is to add a color or gray shaded background to a page. Like filling shapes, you can add backgrounds with colors, gradients, textures, patterns, or even a picture! Follow these steps to apply a background:

1. Display the page you want to format.

2. Choose Format>Background. The Background pane opens on the left side of your screen (see Figure 19-26).

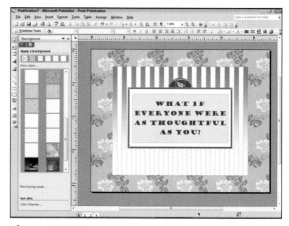

Figure 19-26
Adding a background to a page.

3. Scroll through the choices and click the one you want, or choose the More backgrounds link where you can choose additional gradients, patterns, textures, or a picture.

Managing Master Pages

SIMILAR TO MASTER SLIDES IN PowerPoint, a Publisher publication also uses masters. When you have a publication with many pages, you often want the same background or objects, such as a logo or disclaimer, on all pages. Rather than repeatedly format the background or place the objects on each page, it is easier to format a master page. Objects on the master page appear on every page of the publication.

To open the master page, choose View>Master Page or press Ctrl+M. You switch to the Master view seen in Figure 19-27. An Edit Master Pages toolbar appears along with the Edit Master Pages task pane. Add or change any elements you want on every page, and when you are finished click the Close Master View button on the Edit Master Pages toolbar.

Every page of the publication now has the appearance you assigned in the master page (see Figure 19-28).

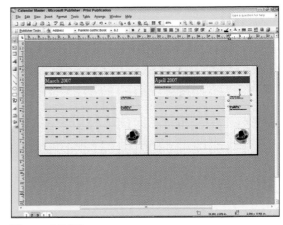

Figure 19-28
Every publication page uses the master elements.

If you don't want a particular page to follow the master page, display the page and choose View>Ignore Master Page.

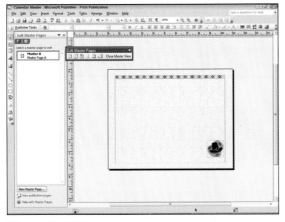

Figure 19-27
Save time by modifying the master page.

Checklist

20

Finalizing Your
Publication

©Olga Rut'ko - FOTOLIA

PICTURE YOURSELF PACKING YOUR CAR for a vacation. You probably have a checklist—either a mental list or a physical list. Did you turn off the stove? Did you pack the sunscreen? And don't forget, even Santa checks his list twice! All types of issues come to mind as you run through the list. When you finish your publication, before you go to the trouble and possible expense of sending it to recipients, you want to make sure it is just right.

Preparing for Printing

BEFORE YOU ACTUALLY PRINT your document, you will want to check it for flaws—both text spelling flaws and potential design flaws. Publisher contains several tools to help keep your document in tip top shape.

Creating Headers and Footers

Just as you've already discovered in other Office applications, you can add headers and footers that print at the top and bottom of every page. The header or footer can contain text that you type, or it can contain fields to represent data such as page numbering or the current date or time. You can create the header or footer on the master page itself, or you can create it on the publication header and footer area, which also places it on the master page for you.

Choose View>Header and Footer. The publication displays the header area and the Header and Footer toolbar.

If you are using a two-page spread and you want different headers and footers on the left page versus the right page, make sure you choose View>Two Page Spread before you choose View>Header and Footer. Publisher then gives you header and footer areas for both the left and right pages.

Type the text you want in the header area and format it as needed. If you want a field code such as page number or date or time, click the appropriate option on the Header and Footer toolbar (see Figure 20-1).

Figure 20-1
Choosing field codes for the header or footer.

When you are finished working with the headers and footers, click the Close button on the Header and Footer toolbar. Your document redisplays with the header and footer as you see in Figure 20-2.

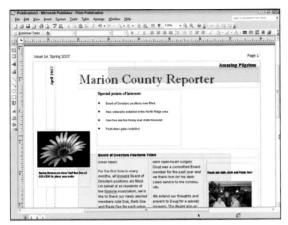

Figure 20-2
A publication with a header.

Running the Design Checker

Just before you produce your publications you should run the Design Checker. The Design Checker examines the publication and looks for potential items such as stories with undesignated overflow, frames out of the print area, text boxes with no text, missing Web links, invisible objects, or even pictures that are out of proportion or missing.

Depending on the publication destination, the Design Checker can run a general design check or look for special problems a commercial printer might run into with the file, or problems you might encounter if you e-mail or create a Web site from the publication. Follow these steps:

1. Choose Tools>Design Checker. The Design Checker task pane seen in Figure 20-3 appears and lists the potential problem areas it located.

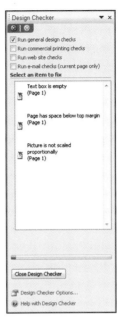

Figure 20-3
Running the Design Checker to look for problem areas.

2. Click directly on an item to jump to and select the questionable area. You can the fix the problem directly, although in some cases the Design Checker offers an automatic fix. Instead of jumping to the problem area, click the down arrow next to a problem. You can choose to Go to this item, which takes you back to the problem, or you may see a Fix such as the Fix: Rescale Picture option shown in Figure 20-4.

3. Click Explain, and a Publisher Help window appears with information about the problem and its possible solutions (see Figure 20-5).

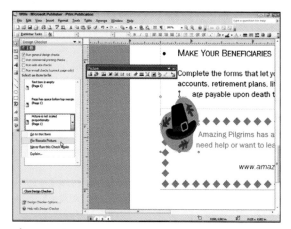

Figure 20-4
Let Design Checker help fix problems.

Figure 20-5
A Help window explaining a suspected design flaw.

To see or control the Design Checker behavior, click the Design Checker Options hyperlink in the task pane. You see the Design Checker Options dialog box seen in Figure 20-6. From the General tab, you can control how the Design Checker displays found errors, and the Checks tab lists all the different potential design errors it should look for.

Figure 20-6
Controlling what the Design Checker looks for.

Checking Your Spelling

Like other Office applications, Microsoft Publisher includes a feature to check for misspelled words. As you type text in your publication, Publisher operates the spell checker tool in the background and identifies problems by displaying a wavy red line under them. Right-click on an unrecognized word and choose from the possible replacement words.

If you want to check the entire publication in a single round, you can choose Tools>Spelling>Spelling or press the F7 key. The Check Spelling dialog box appears with the first error. By default, the Spell Check checks only the currently selected story, but you can either click the Check All Stories option in the Spell Check dialog box, (see Figure 20-7) or choose Yes if Publisher prompts you to check the other stories. When the spelling check process is complete, click Yes to the informational box that appears.

Figure 20-7
Making your publication free of spelling errors.

Printing Your Publication

IT'S BEEN AN INTERESTING PROCESS getting the publication just the way you want it, but now you are finally ready to replicate it.

Running Print Setup

Before you actually print, you need to tell Publisher a few key pieces of information. For example, if you are printing business cards or something similar, you need to determine how many will print on a single sheet of paper. You can plan the printing before you are ready to print by choosing File>Print Setup. You see the Print Setup dialog box shown in Figure 20-8. Depending on the publication type, the choices you see will vary. For example, in Figure 20-8 you see the options for printing some gift certificates, while in Figure 20-9 you see options for printing a fold-out brochure.

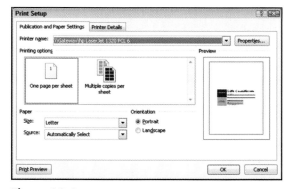

Figure 20-8
Printing options for gift certificates.

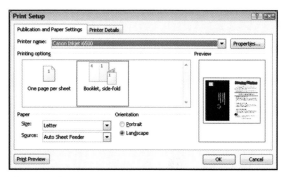

Figure 20-9
Printing options for a fold-out brochure.

If you have access to multiple printers, from the Printer name drop-down list, choose the printer you want to use. You can click the Properties button to modify options specific to your printer such as Paper Type, Paper Source, Print Quality, or Color Intensity.

Click the Print Preview button to preview your publication, or click the OK button to close the Print Setup box.

Printing to Your Printer

Now you are ready to print to your printer. Choose File>Print or press Ctrl+P. The Print dialog box appears (see Figure 20-10). Notice that the Print dialog box has the same options available (plus a few extra) that you just reviewed in the Print Setup dialog box. You can use either option to select your Print settings. Choose the number of copies you want, which pages you want to print, and any other print options relevant to your publication. Click Print when you are ready to print.

> If you click the Print icon on the Standard toolbar, you do not get the Print dialog box where you can specify printing options. The publication goes straight to your default printer, using the default settings and options.

Save yourself time, money, and frustration by consulting with your commercial printer before you begin creating your publication. Determine whether the commercial printer can work with Microsoft Publisher files or whether they prefer your files in another format such as Adobe Acrobat PDF.

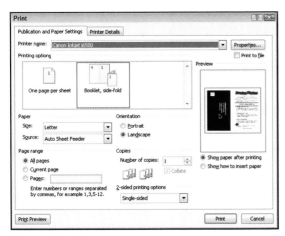

Figure 20-10
Choose your desired print settings.

Preparing for Commercial Printing

Some times you need to send your publication to a commercial printer—for example, when you need to print in large quantities or because you need special trimming or binding options. There are certain conventions a publication must follow, mainly in the color process. Commercial printers use a couple of different color processes, and you need to ask your printer which process they use. Typically, commercial printers use *process colors* or *spot colors*. Some printers can also use a combination of process and spot colors.

Checking Color Systems

You need to prepare your publication so the commercial printer can easily work with the color systems. Follow these steps:

1. Choose Tools>Commercial Printing Tools>Color Printing. The Color Printing dialog box seen in Figure 20-11 appears.

2. Choose the color process recommended by your printer, and you see a confirmation message box.

3. Click OK. If you select Spot colors or Process colors plus spot colors, Publisher prompts you to choose additional spot color inks. These would be specified by your commercial printer.

4. After making your selection, click OK to close the Color Printing dialog box.

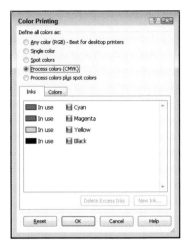

Figure 20-11
Preparing color options for commercial printing.

Checking Fonts

Another convention you must follow is to make sure the commercial printer has access to all the same fonts you do. In most Publisher publications, when you choose to print to your printer, the computer calls the publication fonts from your disk drive as needed. To confirm the font options, follow these steps:

1. Choose Tool>Commercial Printing Tools> Fonts. The Fonts dialog box you see in Figure 20-12 appears.

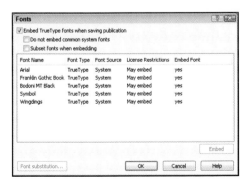

Figure 20-12
Selecting font options for commercial printing.

2. Choose (check) "Embed TrueType fonts when saving publication."

3. Just as a precaution to make sure your printer can access all the necessary fonts, uncheck "Do not embed common system fonts."

4. Click OK.

To make sure the commercial printer has access to the entire publication and all its linked files, you can use the Pack and Go command. The Pack and Go command not only copies the publication but compacts all accessory files such as graphics, fonts, and so forth, into a single compressed file.

To use the Pack and Go command, choose File>Pack and Go>Take to a Commercial Printing Service. The Take to a Commercial Printing Service task pane appears (see Figure 20-13).

Figure 20-13
Identify problems before sending your publication to a commercial printer.

Fix any problems listed and then click the Save button. The Pack and Go Wizard appears. Select a destination to send the publication (usually you will want to Burn to a CD). Click Next, and the entire publication and its supplementary items are burned to a CD or stored to a folder you specify. When the process is finished, the Pack and Go Wizard displays a message and reminds you that if you make any changes to the publication you will need to run the Pack and Go process again.

Using Publisher E-Mail

Microsoft Publisher's e-mail capabilities are tied to the e-mail program you use with other applications, such as Outlook or Outlook Express. You will learn about e-mailing with Outlook Express in Chapter 21.

Sending Your Publication Embedded in a Message

To send your file so the publication appears directly in the body of the e-mail, choose File>Send E-mail> Send as Message. If your publication is a single page, e-mail options appear above the publication (see Figure 20-14) where you can select a recipient, enter a subject, and run the Design Checker to resolve any publication flaws. Click the Send button when you are ready to e-mail your publication.

If your publication has multiple pages, Publisher displays a message box prompting you whether you want to send all pages or just the current page. Select the option you want and then click OK. If you choose to send only the current page, the same options appear as seen in Figure 20-14.

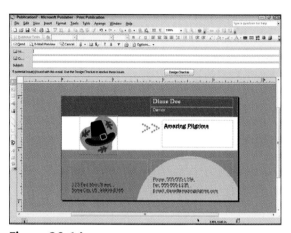

Figure 20-14
Enter a recipient and send your publication via e-mail.

If you chose the Send All Pages option, you see the Send All Pages as Message box shown in Figure 20-15.

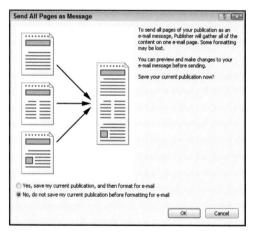

Figure 20-15
Determine which pages you want to e-mail.

The message advises you that to send the publication, some formatting may be unsupported and lost. You can choose to save your publication and then let the program reformat it for e-mail. Either option generates a new publication embedded into the e-mail along with a pane on the left side showing any changes that were made to fit the publication into the e-mail (see Figure 20-16).

At the top of the screen, you also see buttons for selecting recipients and entering a subject, and a button to run the Design Checker if desired. Enter your recipient information and then click the Send button.

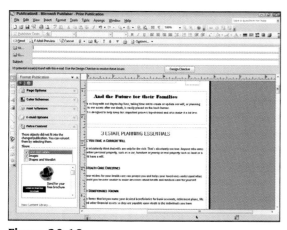

Figure 20-16
You should review the e-mail changes before actually sending the e-mail.

Sending as an Attachment

When you send a publication via e-mail as you just discovered, you can send the publication directly in the body of the e-mail message. To avoid formatting issues, a better option is to send the publication as an attachment. Attachment types can include a PUB (Publisher) file or an XPS or PDF attachment.

If you send the attachment as a PUB file, the recipient must have Microsoft Publisher to open the file. However, if you send the attachment as a PUB file and the recipient has Publisher, they can also modify the file. If you don't want your document modified, send it as a PDF or XPS attachment. (See Chapter 1 for information on PDF and XPS file formats.)

Choose File>Send E-mail and choose the attachment type you want. Publisher opens your e-mail program and displays a blank message with the publication as a .PUB, .PDF, or XPS attachment (see Figure 20-17). Enter the recipient e-mail address, a subject, and an optional message and then click the Send button.

> You must have the Office PDF and XPS add-in utility installed to send your publication as a PDF or XPS file (see Chapter 1).

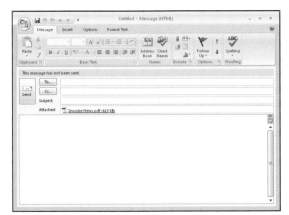

If you have not saved the publication, Publisher prompts you to do so.

Figure 20-17

Sending your publication as an e-mail attachment.

Part VI
Outlook

Microsoft Outlook is a collection of integrated messaging and contact-management programs that allow you to do all the things the other Personal Information Management (PIM) programs do, and it also makes it easier than ever to make your information all work together. For example, you can use the Contacts portion of Outlook when creating e-mails in Outlook or doing a mail merge in Word. You can use the Calendar portion to remind you of upcoming important events, and you can use Outlook's Tasks feature to help keep yourself organized. This section guides you through the ever helpful functions available with Microsoft Outlook.

21

Sending and Receiving Outlook

E-Mail

© sgame – FOTOLIA

PICTURE YOURSELF SITTING at your computer, exchanging e-mail with co-workers, family, and friends, or perhaps even finding romance, as Tom Hanks and Meg Ryan did in the movie *You've Got Mail.*

Using Microsoft Office Outlook, the most widely used e-mail program, you can quickly and easily enter the world of electronic communication. And, besides providing you with e-mail capabilities, Outlook acts as a personal information manager, providing you with a calendar on which you can enter meeting information, helping you keep track of names, addresses (both snail-mail and e-mail), and phone numbers, and letting you create a to-do list for those things you know you're going to forget if you don't write them down.

Looking at the Outlook Window

WHEN YOU FIRST OPEN OUTLOOK, the Outlook Today page appears, showing you what's on your calendar for today, tasks on your to-do list, and a summary of your e-mail situation (see Figure 21-1). Across the top of the window, you see the currently displayed menus and toolbars. In the Outlook Today view, you see the Standard toolbar and the Web toolbar.

The Navigation pane runs down the left side of the screen, and you click the buttons in the Navigation pane to switch to different areas in Outlook. For example, to work with Outlook's to-do list, click Tasks. When you click Mail, Outlook highlights Personal Folders in the Navigation pane and continues displaying the Outlook Today page. You use the items listed below Personal Folders to help you work with e-mail.

If this is the first time you ever opened Outlook, you are prompted to set up and e-mail account. See "Setting Up an Account" later in this chapter.

Figure 21-1

Viewing your agenda in the Outlook Today window.

Customizing Outlook Today

You can customize the Outlook Today page by clicking Customize Outlook Today in the upper right corner of the window. Outlook displays the Customize Outlook Today page (see Figure 21-2).

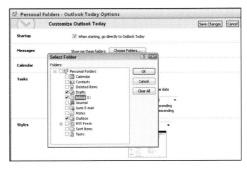

Figure 21-3
Select folders that you want to appear on the Outlook Today page.

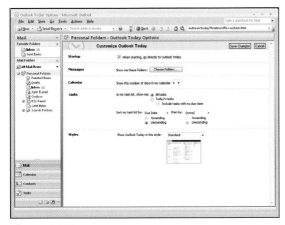

Figure 21-2
Set options for the Outlook Today window.

▶ If you remove the check from the When Starting, Go Directly To Outlook Today box, Outlook doesn't display Outlook Today when you open the program. Instead, Outlook displays your Inbox, which contains e-mail messages you receive.

▶ You can click the Choose Folders button to display the Select Folder dialog box (see Figure 21-3), which you can use to select folders to appear on the Outlook Today page.

▶ In the Calendar section of the Customize Outlook Today page, specify the number of calendar days you want shown on the Outlook Today page.

▶ In the Tasks section, identify the tasks you want to appear on the Outlook Today page and then identify how you want Outlook to sort them.

▶ In the Styles section, you can control the layout and appearance of the Outlook Today page. The default, called Standard, is a three-column layout. You can select to use a two-column layout, a one-column layout, or you can select the Summer or the Winter layout, which both use a two-column layout but present a different appearance of the Outlook Today page.

When you finish setting Outlook Today options, click Save Changes to see the effects of your changes.

Working with E-Mail

THINK OF E-MAIL AS ELECTRONIC letter writing. Using e-mail is a quick and easy way to keep in touch with people both nearby and far away. And, for reasons I can't begin to explain, writing an e-mail seems to take less time than writing a letter. There's no question that e-mail is here to stay.

To use e-mail, you need an Internet connection, an Internet Service Provider (ISP), and an e-mail address. Your computer must contain hardware—a modem or a network card—to support an Internet connection. If you have a *low-speed connection*, your computer contains a modem attached to a telephone line to connect to the Internet. The connection is considered low-speed because standard telephone lines cannot transfer data at rates faster than speeds near 56 kbit/s (kilobits per second). If you have a *high-speed connection* (also called *broadband)*, your computer contains a network card that attaches to a DSL (digital service line) or cable modem to connect to the Internet. The connection is considered high-speed because data is transmitted using unused bandwidth on voice telephone lines or on a cable television network, with upload rates ranging between 384 kbit/s to 6 Mbit/s or more, and download rates almost twice as high as upload rates.

Your Internet Service Provide (ISP) tells you what equipment your computer needs to use the service (and often provides you with some or all of the equipment) and also gives you an e-mail address.

You also can sign up for an e-mail address that isn't connected to a specific ISP. For example, Microsoft offers free Hotmail e-mail accounts and Google offers free Gmail e-mail accounts. Using these accounts, you can collect e-mail using an Internet browser such as Internet Explorer, or you can collect the e-mail in Outlook.

Once you sign up for service with an ISP, set up your Internet connection, and obtain an e-mail address, you're ready to start using the e-mail capabilities in Outlook.

Setting Up an Account

The first time you open Outlook, a wizard appears and prompts you to set up an e-mail account. If you started Outlook and skipped this step, you can set up e-mail accounts at any time. Follow these steps (if you already see the Setup Wizard, you can skip steps 1 and 2):

1. Choose Tools>Account Settings. The Account Settings dialog box appears.

2. From the E-mail tab, click New. The Add New E-mail Account window appears.

3. Click Next and type your name, your e-mail address, and your password on the Auto Account Setup screen of the wizard (see Figure 21-4).

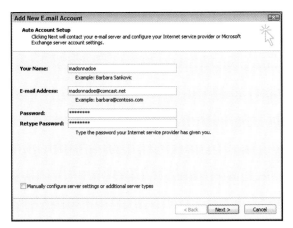

Figure 21-4
Configuring your e-mail.

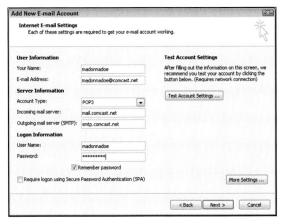

Figure 21-5
Manually configure an e-mail account in Outlook.

4. Click Next. Outlook configures your e-mail account. (The process may take a few minutes.)

If Outlook is unable to automatically configure your e-mail account, check the Manually Configure Server Settings or Additional Server Types check box. Outlook displays the screen you see in Figure 21-5. Your ISP will provide you with the Incoming Mail Server and Outgoing Mail Server (SMTP) information and specify whether you need to check the Require Logon Using Secure Password Authentication (SPA) check box. You can click the Test Account settings to check to see if your information is valid, or simply click Next.

When you finish, Outlook displays the Account Settings window, and you can see your e-mail account as you see in Figure 21-6.

Now you're ready to start working with e-mail.

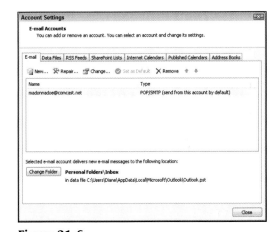

Figure 21-6
Your e-mail account appears in the Account Settings dialog box.

Reading Incoming Mail

To receive incoming e-mail, you don't need to do anything special other than open Outlook. By default, Outlook automatically checks for incoming e-mail for you.

> Expecting a particular message? You can click the Send/Receive button on the toolbar at the top of the window to tell Outlook to check for messages "now."

When you click Mail in the Navigation pane, you see a window divided into three panes (see Figure 21-7). The left pane is the Navigation pane, of course. The center pane contains the folder contents, called the message list, you select in the Navigation pane. The right pane, called the Reading pane, displays the content of any message you select in the center pane. And, to the right of the message content pane, Outlook displays the To-Do bar, which you can display to get a quick overview of what upcoming appointments and tasks you have without leaving the Mail pane in Outlook. See Chapter 24 for details on the To-Do bar.

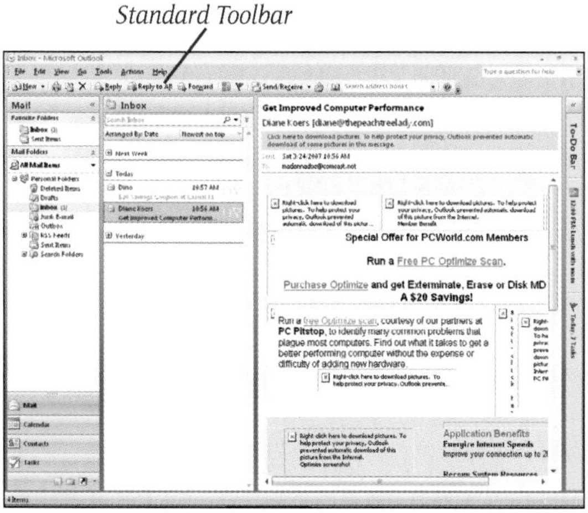

Standard Toolbar

Figure 21-7
Outlook's Inbox, where new mail appears.

> You can click either occurrence of the Inbox folder—the one at the top of the Navigation pane or the one that appears under the Personal Folders.

In Figure 21-7, you see the Inbox in the Navigation pane selected, where new e-mail messages accumulate. The number that appears in parentheses beside the Inbox, and any of the folders in the Personal Folders section, represents the number of unread messages in the folder. The sender's name of an unread message in the middle pane appears in bold when you examine the list of messages. The total number of messages in the Inbox appears in the lower left corner of the screen.

> **Although we're talking specifically about the Inbox in this section, the information here applies to messages in any folder listed in the Personal Folders section of the Navigation pane.**

Outlook organizes messages in the Inbox based on when you received them. In Figure 21-7, only the messages received today are visible. To view messages from other time periods, click the plus sign (+) beside the time period.

To select a message so that you can view its content, click the message in the message list. Outlook displays the message's content in the Reading pane so that you can read it. After you click another message or folder, Outlook automatically marks the message as "read," removing the boldface type from the sender's name in the middle column.

You can double-click a message to open it in a separate window, like the one shown in Figure 21-8, but there aren't many reasons to do so. As you'll see later in this chapter, you can do pretty much whatever you need to do with any message from the Mail pane.

Figure 21-8
An open e-mail message.

In Figure 21-7 and Figure 21-8, you may have noticed a bunch of X's in boxes in the message content in the right pane. The X's represent pictures in the e-mail message that Outlook isn't displaying. By default, Outlook doesn't download pictures in e-mail messages to help you avoid getting e-mail from spammers.

You can view the pictures in any e-mail message if you click the InfoBar at the top of the message and, from the menu that appears, select Download Pictures (see Figure 21-9). Outlook downloads and displays the pictures. If you preview another message and return to the one with downloaded pictures, they will still appear.

Spam **is unwanted e-mail typically sent out in bulk. It usually contains pictures and may try to sell you something. Spammers don't always use legitimate e-mail addresses— often they find a domain name (the part of your e-mail address that appears after the @ sign) and simply use a program to create possible e-mail addresses, in the hopes that some will actually be legitimate. The messages often include links to pictures or sounds on the Internet. If the pictures or sounds are automatically downloaded, you may be verifying your e-mail address for the junk e-mail sender. The junk e-mail sender watches for valid e-mail addresses and then sells them to other spammers, increasing the amount of spam you receive. At best, spam is annoying; at worst, it's offensive and time-consuming to handle.**

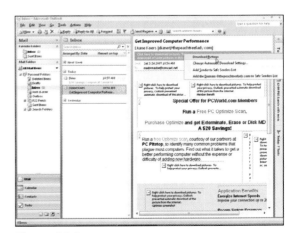

Figure 21-9
Download pictures from an e-mail.

Pictures in E-Mail Messages

You may want Outlook to download pictures from the Internet, either for all e-mail messages or for those from specific senders that you recognize as valid messages that you want to receive. While you can continue to download pictures one message at a time, there are some shortcuts you can use to save time.

For individual messages that you know you want to receive, you can add either the specific e-mail address or all e-mail from a certain domain to Outlook's Safe Senders List. Once you identify these e-mail addresses or domains, Outlook will automatically download pictures in e-mails that come from those senders or domains. In a message containing blocked pictures, right-click any blocked picture or the InfoBar and choose Add Sender to Safe Senders list to add the specific e-mail address. To add any e-mail from the sender's domain, click Add the Domain to Safe Senders list.

You also can simply let Outlook download pictures. When you right-click the InfoBar on a message containing blocked pictures, choose Change Automatic Download Settings. Outlook displays the Automatic Download pane of the Trust Center dialog box (see Figure 21-10).

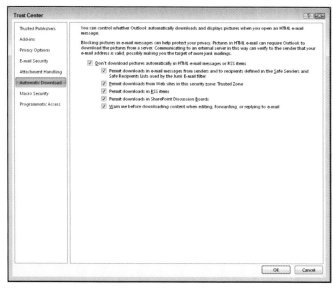

Remove the check from the Don't Download Pictures Automatically in HTML E-Mail Messages or RSS Items check box and click OK. Outlook will download all pictures and sounds in HTML messages.

If you change your mind and want to block pictures and sounds, open the Tools menu and click Trust Center to redisplay the dialog box shown in Figure 21-9. Then, recheck the Don't Download Pictures Automatically in HTML E-Mail Messages or RSS Items check box.

Figure 21-10
Change Outlook's behavior for automatic downloads.

Replying to a Message

Here comes one! And, it's asking you for information. To reply to an e-mail, follow these steps:

1. Click Mail in the Navigation pane.

2. Click the folder containing the message to which you want to reply.

3. In the message list, click the message to which you want to reply.

4. Click the Reply button on the Standard toolbar. Outlook opens a window containing the original message, and the insertion point appears above the original message, waiting for you to type your reply (see Figure 21-11).

Click Reply All if you want to send your reply to everyone who received the original message.

5. Type your reply.

Send button

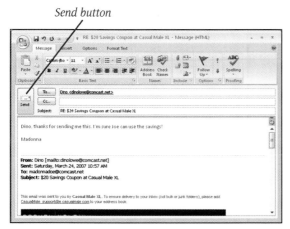

Figure 21-11
Replying to an e-mail message.

6. Click the Send button to the left of the recipient's e-mail address. Outlook places the message in your Outbox. The next time Outlook automatically checks for incoming messages, it will send out your reply and store a copy of it in the Sent Items folder.

You can make Outlook send the message immediately if you click the Send/Receive button on the Standard toolbar.

Forwarding a Message

Suppose Mary just sent you an e-mail message that contains information that you know would be valuable or interesting to John. Without having to retype the e-mail contents, you can forward the message to John by following these steps:

These steps assume that you have stored e-mail addresses in your Contacts list (you can read about creating contacts in Chapter 22). If you have not stored an e-mail address in your Contacts list, type the e-mail address of the person to whom you want to send the message in Step 5. Then, skip to Step 10.

1. Click Mail in the Navigation pane.

2. Click the folder containing the message you want to forward.

3. In the message list, click the message you want to forward.

If you forward a message for which you didn't download its pictures, the pictures are not forwarded to your reply recipient.

4. Click the Forward button on the Standard toolbar. Outlook displays the message in a window, with the Insertion point appearing in the To box (see Figure 21-12).

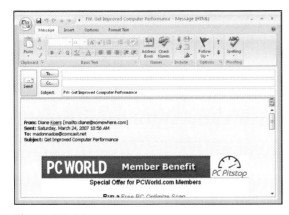

Figure 21-12
Forwarding a message.

5. Click the To button. Outlook displays the Select Names: Contacts dialog box shown in Figure 21-13.

6. Click the name of the person to whom you want to forward the message. Or, you can type some characters of the person's name and Outlook will find the nearest match.

Figure 21-13
Use this dialog box to select contacts when you forward a message.

7. Once you have highlighted the correct contact's name, click the To -> button. Outlook adds the recipient in the To -> text box.

8. Repeat Steps 6 and 7 for each recipient to whom you want to forward the message.

9. Click OK. Outlook redisplays the message window.

10. Optionally, in the body of the e-mail, add any additional message.

11. Click Send. Outlook places the message in your Outbox and sends it the next time it checks for new messages. Outlook stores a copy of the sent message in the Sent Items folder.

Deleting a Message

Once you finish reading a message, replying to it, and forwarding it, you may want to delete it. The concept here is that you don't need the message around for anything anymore. To delete a message, click it in the message pane of the Inbox (or whatever folder contains the message) and then click the Delete button on the Standard toolbar or press the Delete key on your keyboard. Outlook moves the message to the Deleted Items folder.

In the interest of good housekeeping, you should periodically then empty the contents of the Deleted Items folder. To delete the messages in the Deleted Items folder, follow these steps:

1. Click Mail in the Navigation pane.

2. Click the Deleted Items folder in the Navigation pane.

3. Choose Edit>Select All. Outlook highlights all the messages in the middle pane.

4. Click the Delete button on the Standard toolbar or press the Delete key on your keyboard. Outlook displays a message asking if you're sure you want to permanently delete the selected messages.

> Optionally, right-click the Deleted Items folder and choose Empty Deleted Items

5. Click Yes. Outlook deletes the messages.

If you prefer, you can set Outlook options so that Outlook automatically deletes messages in the Deleted Items folder when you close Outlook. Follow these steps:

1. Choose Tools>Options. The Options dialog box appears.

2. Click the Other tab.

3. Place a check in the Empty the Deleted Items Folder upon exiting check box (see Figure 21-14).

Figure 21-14
Setting Delete options.

4. Click OK. When you close Outlook, the program will permanently delete messages in the Deleted Items folder.

Creating a New Message

So you have something that you want to tell somebody and you don't have a message to reply to or forward? No problem. Create your own message by following these steps:

1. Click Mail in the Navigation pane.

2. Click the New button on the Standard toolbar. Outlook displays an empty message window (see Figure 21-15).

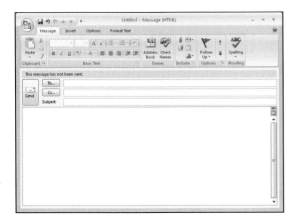

Figure 21-15
A new message, waiting to be created.

3. Type the e-mail address of the person to whom you want to send a message in the To box or, if you've stored the e-mail address in your Contacts list, click the To button. Outlook displays the Select Names: Contacts dialog box.

4. Click the name of the person to whom you want to send the message. Or, you can type some characters of the person's name and Outlook will find the nearest match.

5. Once you have highlighted the correct contact's name, click the To -> button. Outlook adds the recipient in the To -> text box.

6. Repeat Steps 5 and 6 for each recipient to whom you want to send the message.

7. Click OK. Outlook redisplays the message window.

8. In the Subject line, type something that summarizes the purpose of the message. While you don't have to put a subject in the message, many e-mail programs automatically consider them spam and may either delete them or put them into a special junk mail folder.

9. In the large white message box, type your message.

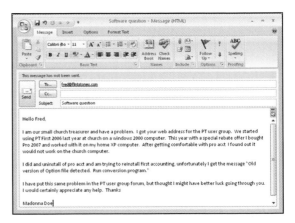

Figure 21-16
Creating a new message.

10. Click Send. Outlook places the message in your Outbox and sends it the next time it checks for new messages. Outlook stores a copy of the sent message in the Sent Items folder.

Working with E-Mail Attachments

YOU'VE HEARD ABOUT ATTACHMENTS: they are files that come along with an e-mail. In fact, you've probably heard never to open an attachment unless you know the person sending it and you're expecting the attachment. That's good advice, by the way. Following that advice will help you avoid getting a computer virus.

You can receive and you can send files attached to an e-mail message.

Receiving an E-Mail Attachment

Assume you receive an attachment from someone you know and you expected the attachment. Now what? Click the e-mail message containing the attachment to select it. You'll notice that a paper-clip appears next to the subject line of the message, below the time the message came in (see Figure 21-17).

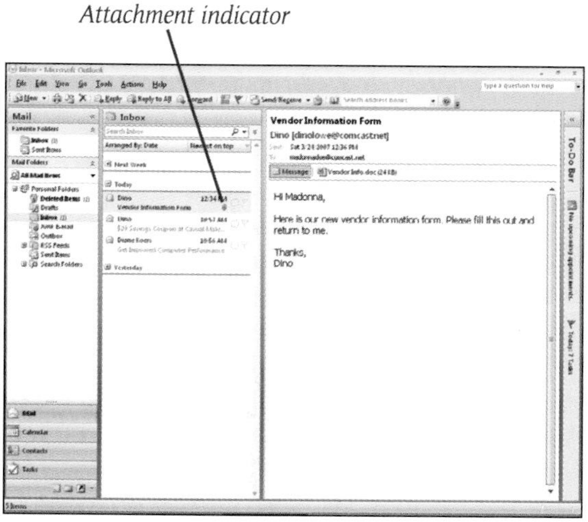

Attachment indicator

Figure 21-17
An e-mail message with an attachment.

In the Reading pane, you'll see two choices below the address information; one for the message and one for the attachment. Click the Message icon to preview the message. Double-click the attachment icon to open it in the program that created it.

> **If you don't have the program that created the attachment installed on your computer, you'll see an error message. You won't be able to open the attachment until you install the program that created it or a viewer for that program.**

If you need to save the attachment you receive for future reference, you can right-click it and choose Save As. In the Save Attachment window, navigate to the folder on your computer where you want to keep the attachment and then click the Save button. Once you've saved the attachment on your computer, you can delete the e-mail if you don't need the information in the message portion.

Sending an E-Mail Attachment

OK, now it's your turn. You need to send a file to someone. Or, you want to send an Outlook item (task, contact, etc.) to someone. No problem. Follow the steps to create, reply to, or forward an e-mail message described earlier in this chapter, but don't click the Send button yet. Choose Message>Include (see Figure 21-18) and then click one of the items shown in Table 21-1.

Attachment indicator

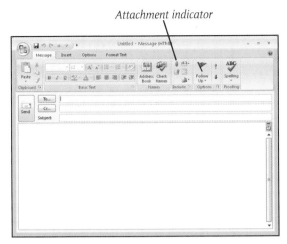

After you select and attach the appropriate item, click the Send button. Outlook places the message in your Outbox and sends it the next time it checks for new messages. Outlook also places a copy of the sent message in the Sent Items folder.

Figure 21-18
The Ribbon.

Table 21-1 Attachment Options

Icon	Purpose	Action
	Attach a file.	Navigate to the location where the file is stored on your computer and select the desired file to attach.
	Attach an Outlook item.	Navigate to the Outlook folder containing the item and select the desired Outlook item.
	Attach an electronic business card.	Select a contact from your Contacts list.
	Attach your Outlook calendar.	Specify the calendar timeframe the recipient doesn't need to use (Outlook to see your calendar).
	Attach an electronic signature.	Clicking this button lets you both create and attach the signature.

Searching for an E-Mail Message

So, you like keeping e-mail messages around. Eventually, you need to find a message you sent or received. You can search any individual folder in the Personal Folders by clicking the folder you want to search in the Navigation pane. If you prefer, you can search all folders by clicking All Mail Items in the Navigation pane, as you see in Figure 21-19. At the top of the middle pane, type your search criteria in the box. Then, click the magnifying glass. Outlook displays all of the messages that meet your search criteria exactly. So, for example, if you want to search for Mary Jones, you cannot type mary jones.

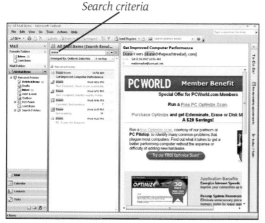

Figure 21-19
Searching for an e-mail message.

Using Personal Folders to Manage E-Mail

Earlier you discovered that you can use the Personal Folders to help you organize e-mail. If you're like me, you may find yourself collecting e-mail from a variety of people on a particular subject. I like to keep my "same subject" e-mail stored in a folder, so, I create my own folders that appear along with the other folders listed under Personal Folders. To create a new folder, follow these steps:

1. Click Mail in the Navigation pane.

2. Choose File>New>Folder. Outlook displays the Create New Folder dialog box (see Figure 21-20).

Figure 21-20
Creating a new folder.

3. Type a name for the new Folder.

4. Open the Folder Contains list to specify the types of Outlook items you'll store in the folder. To store e-mail messages, select Mail and Post Items.

5. In the Select where to place the folder box, choose Personal Folders to create a folder at the same organizational level as the Inbox.

> You can create a subfolder for the Inbox by clicking the plus sign (+) beside Personal Folders and then selecting Inbox.

6. Click OK. Outlook adds the folder in the Personal Folders list.

22

Working with Outlook
Contacts

PICTURE YOURSELF GETTING RID OF YOUR Rolodex, no longer typing or writing contact information on hundreds of little cards that get mashed and smashed as you use them. Imagine knowing exactly where to easily find street addresses, phone numbers, and e-mail addresses without hunting for your address book, wherever you put it. And, best of all, picture yourself no longer typing e-mail addresses because you can have them automatically filled in. These are just some of the advantages of using Outlook's Contacts folder.

Exploring Your Contacts Folder

THINK OF THE CONTACTS FOLDER as an electronic Rolodex without the frayed edges on the cards. Click Contacts in the Navigation pane to display the Contacts folder. In Figure 22-1, you see the Business Cards view of the Contacts folder. This view most closely resembles a Rolodex.

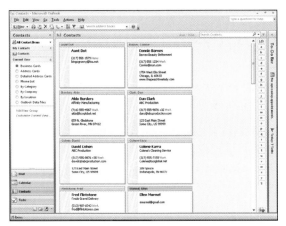

Figure 22-1
The Business Cards view.

You can use your Outlook contacts in a Word Mail Merge. See Chapter 6 for details.

Views of the Contacts Folder

But Outlook's Contacts folder goes beyond the capabilities of the Rolodex, because you can display the information in a variety of ways. Use the options that appear in the Navigation pane to change the appearance of the Contacts folder. Figure 22-2 shows you the Address Cards view, which displays cards that vary in size, depending on the information you've stored for the contact.

When you change to Contacts view, if you do not see the view options, click Current View.

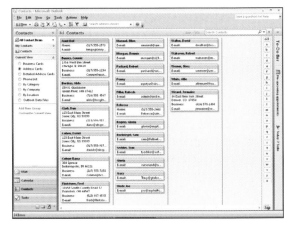

Figure 22-2
The Address Cards view.

The Detailed Address Cards view (see Figure 22-3) includes the names of the fields you're viewing. By default, Outlook displays four columns in this view, and you'll notice that you can't really read the information stored about the contact. But, you can reduce the number of columns, which increases the space allotted to each contact. Place the mouse pointer over one of the lines between the columns, and the mouse pointer changes to a double-headed arrow.

Mouse Pointer

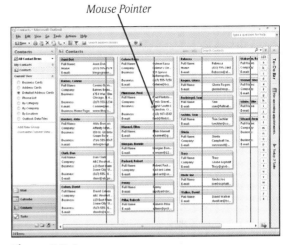

Figure 22-4
Managing the number of columns Outlook displays.

The Phone List view, shown in Figure 22-5, is terrific for helping you focus on finding a phone number.

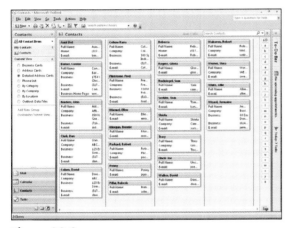

Figure 22-3
The Detailed Address Cards view.

Drag the mouse pointer to the right. You'll see dark lines for each of the column dividers, and when the last one disappears off the screen, release the mouse button. Outlook adjusts the number of columns, widening the space allotted to each contact so that you can see more information per contact (see Figure 22-4).

You can use the same technique to adjust the number of columns Outlook displays in the Address Cards view.

Figure 22-5
The Phone List view.

The By Category, By Company, By Location, and Outlook Data Files views are all variations of the Phone List view.

Outlook provides six color categories that you can assign to contacts so that you can organize and display contact phone information by categories that are meaningful to you. You decide what the various colors mean, and, when you create a contact, you can assign the contact to a color category. Then, you can click the By Category view to name, phone number, and category information for contacts organized by color category.

The By Company view organizes contacts by company name and displays name, company, and phone number information for contacts.

The By Location view organizes contacts by state within the United States and then by country. This view displays name, company, state, country, and phone number information for contacts.

It's possible in Outlook to create multiple data files—for example, you may create a data file that stores messages related to a certain project. The By Outlook Data File view organizes contacts by Outlook data file and displays phone list information.

Customizing a Contact Folder View

You can customize any of the views of the Contacts folder by selecting the view and then clicking the Customize Current View link in the Navigation pane. Outlook displays the Customize View dialog box shown in Figure 22-6. The buttons available depend on the view you selected before opening this dialog box.

Figure 22-6
Customizing a Contacts folder view.

When you click the Fields button, you see the Show Fields dialog box (see Figure 22-7), which gives you the opportunity to select fields that will be visible in the view. To add a field to the view, click the field in the left column (Available fields list) and then click the Add button. To hide a field from the view, click the field in the right column (Show fields list) and click Remove.

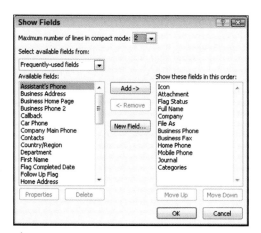

Figure 22-7
Adding or removing fields from a folder view.

The Group By dialog box controls the way Outlook groups contacts in a view (see Figure 22-8). When you choose a field in the Group Items By list, the subsequent Then By list becomes available.

Figure 22-8
Control the way Outlook groups information.

The Sort dialog box seen in Figure 22-9 controls the way Outlook sorts contacts in a view.

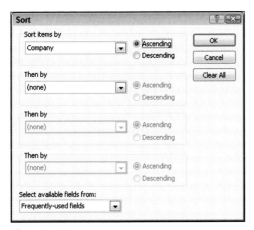

Figure 22-9
Control sorting in a Contacts folder view.

Use the Filter dialog box (see Figure 22-10) to control the contacts that appear in the view. When you don't set any filters, Outlook displays all contacts in the view.

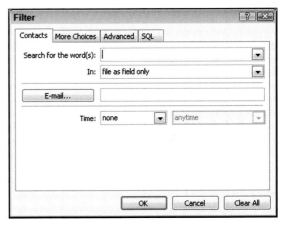

Figure 22-10
Use the Filter dialog box to hide contacts.

From the Other Settings dialog box you see in Figure 22-11, you can control settings like fonts, column sizes, grid line, and group styles.

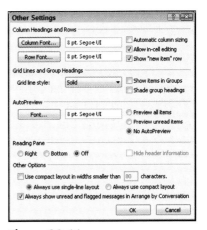

Figure 22-11
Control fonts and column sizes.

Use the Automatic Formatting dialog box shown in Figure 22-12 to control fonts used for various types of contacts. Outlook sets up font rules for some kinds of contacts by default, so that these kinds of contacts are identifiable by the font Outlook uses. You can use this dialog box to add your own rules about the appearance of certain kinds of contacts. When you click Add, the Condition button becomes available. When you click it, Outlook displays the Filter dialog box you saw in Figure 22-10 (without the SQL tab), and you use the Filter dialog box to identify the contacts to whom you want to apply the font rules.

Figure 22-12
Setting up rules.

Finally, use the Format Columns dialog box to format the fields that appear in a view (see Figure 22-13).

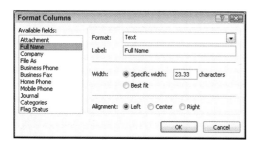

Figure 22-13
Format columns in a Contacts folder view.

Adding a New Contact

So how, you're wondering, do you create a contact? Follow these steps:

1. Click Contacts in the Navigation pane.

2. Click the New button on the Standard toolbar. Outlook displays an empty Contact window.

3. Fill in the window, supplying as much information as you want Outlook to track. As you fill in information, Outlook displays a preview of the contact information (see Figure 22-14).

If you plan to send e-mails to this contact, be sure to supply the contact's e-mail address.

Preview

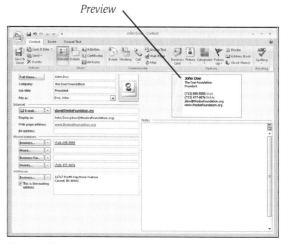

Figure 22-14
Creating a contact.

4. Click the Save & New button on the Ribbon if you want to create another contact. Otherwise, click the Save & Close button. Outlook saves the contact and displays it in any of the Contacts folder views.

Automatically Adding Contacts from E-Mails

You also can add contacts to the Contacts folder from an e-mail you received. Follow these steps:

1. Click Mail in the Navigation pane.

2. Display the e-mail message that contains the contact you want to add to the Contacts folder.

3. In the Reading pane, right-click the e-mail address that appears in the From line and choose Add to Outlook Contacts (see Figure 22-15). In the Contact window that appears, Outlook fills in the contact's name and e-mail address.

Figure 22-15
Add a contact using an e-mail message.

4. Fill in the rest of the window.

5. Click Save & Close on the Ribbon.

Editing Contact Information

You've found a little spare time and you've decided to use it to update your contacts by supplying missing information. The method you use to open a contact's window to add or change information depends on the view of the Contacts folder you use.

▶ **In any view of the Contacts folder, right-click the contact and choose Open.**

▶ **In the Business Cards view, double-click any contact.**

▶ **In the Address Cards view and the Detailed Address Cards view, double-click the contact's name to open the contact information in the Contact window. Or, you can single-click any field and make changes to it. Click outside the field when you finish.**

▶ **In the Phone List view, the By Category view, the By Company view, the By Location view, and the Outlook Data Files view, double-click an entry to display the contact information in a Contact window. Or, click the field you want to edit twice, and you can make changes directly on-screen. When you use this method, click the field twice *slowly*; otherwise, Outlook will assume you're trying to double-click.**

Creating a Distribution List

Suppose that you find yourself sending the same e-mails to a specific group of contacts. For example, you may like to share jokes with a specific group of people, or you may be participating in a project and you need to communicate with the project team regularly. You can set up a distribution list in Outlook.

Using an Outlook distribution list you can simultaneously select several contacts—those included in the distribution list—when you address an e-mail. When you fill in the recipient of the e-mail, you select your distribution list, and Outlook automatically fills in the e-mail addresses of each contact included in the distribution list, saving you lots of time.

To create a distribution list, follow these steps:

1. Click Contacts in the Navigation pane.

2. Choose Actions> New Distribution List. Outlook displays a Distribution List window as shown in Figure 22-16.

Figure 22-16
Use this window to set up a distribution list.

3. In the Name box, type a title for the distribution list.

4. Choose Distribution List>Members>Select Members. Outlook displays the Select members dialog box shown in Figure 22-17.

Figure 22-17
Select contacts to include.

5. Click a name in the list and then click the Members button. Outlook displays each included contact name in the box beside the Members button.

6. Repeat Step 5 for each contact you want to add to the distribution list.

7. Click OK. Outlook redisplays the Distribution List window, and the name and e-mail address of each contact you selected in Steps 5 and 6 appears in the window.

8. Click Save & Close.

To use your distribution list to send an e-mail, create a new e-mail message or forward an existing message. Click the To button and, in the Select Names dialog box that appears, select the name you gave your distribution list and click OK. Then, fill in the rest of the e-mail as described in Chapter 21.

Mapping a Contact's Location

If you store a street address for a contact, Outlook can help you view a map of the address. Follow these steps:

1. Click Contacts in the Navigation pane.

2. Open the contact's window, which you see in Figure 22-18.

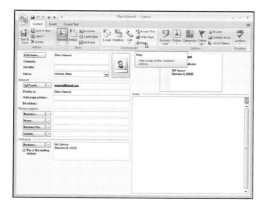

Figure 22-18
Open the contact's window.

3. Choose Contact>Communicate>Map. Outlook opens a Live Search window in Internet Explorer and displays a map, pinpointing the contact's street address (see Figure 22-19).

Figure 22-19
Live Search displays the map.

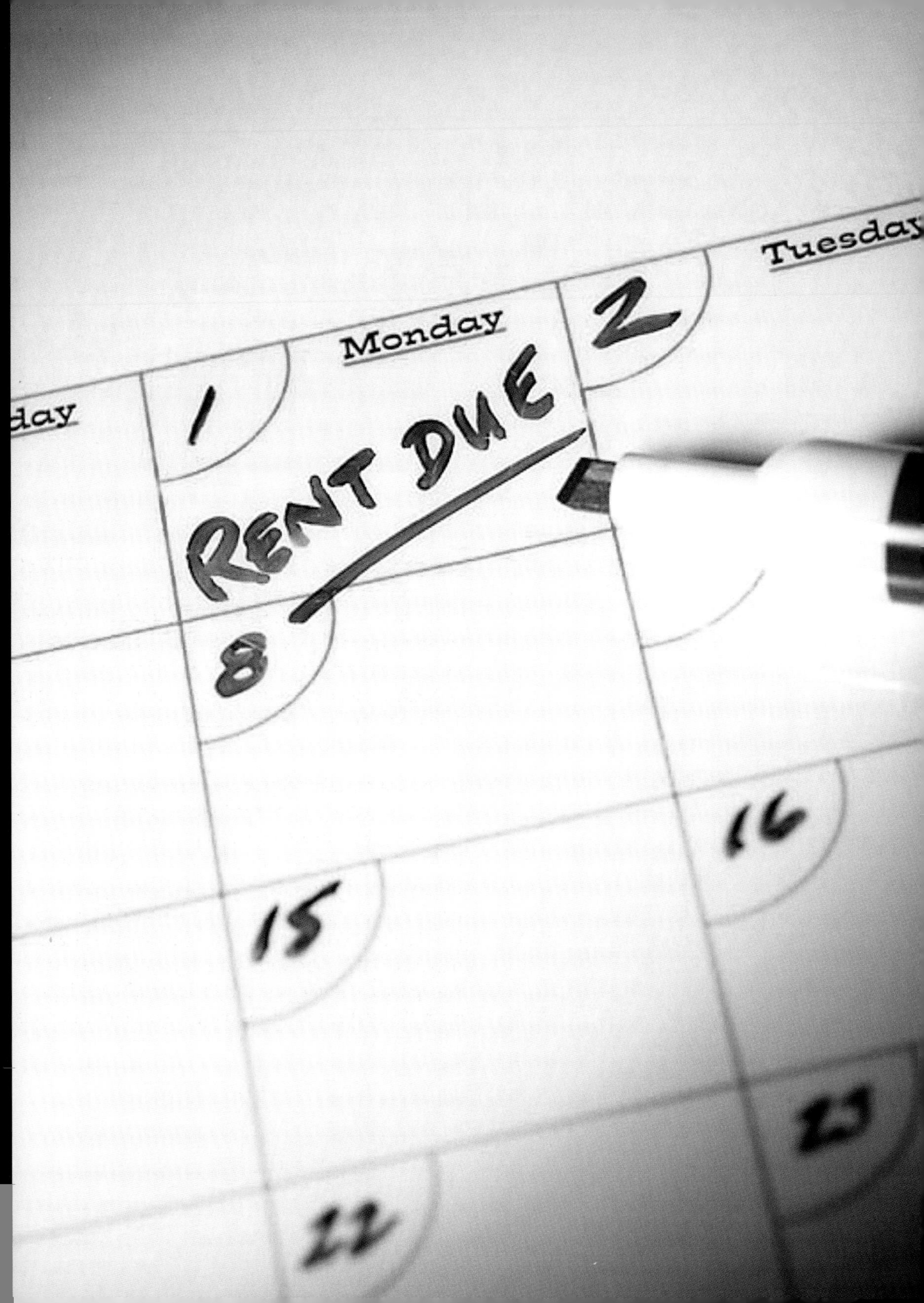
day
Monday
Tuesday
1
2
RENT DUE
8
15
16

23

Using the Outlook
Calendar

PICTURE YOURSELF MANAGING A SCHEDULE
that is meeting-intensive. You have meetings at the
office and away from the office, in the city where
you live, and on the road. Sometimes you initiate a
meeting; other times, you are included by others in
a meeting. And, the original date and time for a meeting
changes, sometimes more frequently than you'd expect.

You need a calendar for your appointments, but the
manual calendar you've been keeping just isn't filling
your needs. You do everything in pencil because of
potential changes, and your book has become so messy
that some days you're having trouble reading it. And
that's not even counting the tasks you need to accomplish in addition to the meetings—you need to be able
to manage both your workload and your schedule so
that you know when you need time *outside* meetings to
accomplish other things on your plate.... Enter Outlook's
Calendar.

Exploring the Calendar

THE CALENDAR VIEW IN OUTLOOK integrates with your e-mail and your tasks so that you can manage more than just your appointments. It lets you view your workload—both appointments and tasks—from a variety of perspectives, and it's neat and clean—no more messy erasures.

Understanding the Calendar Views

Click Calendar in the Navigation pane to view the Day view of the calendar (see Figure 23-1). Outlook displays the Day/Week/Month view of the Calendar folder. In this view, the Navigation pane displays small calendars for the current month and the next month. The right pane shows either a daily, weekly, or monthly view of your calendar. Day, Week, and Month tabs located at the top of the right pane allow you to change views.

The Day view shows you the appointments you have today along with item on your task list that haven't yet been completed.

You can read more about the Tasks view in Outlook in Chapter 24.

In Figure 23-2, you see the Week view of the calendar. Using the option buttons at the top of the Week view, you can view either the work week or the full week. When you view a week that is more than two weeks from "today," you'll see Next Appointment and Previous Appointment tabs at

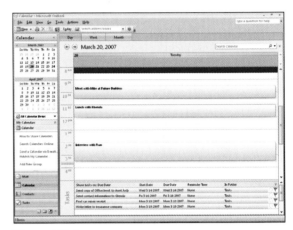

Figure 23-1
A daily view of your calendar.

the right and left sides of the Week view. You can navigate forward or backward one week at a time using those tabs or the arrows that appear at the top of the Week view beside the dates for the week you're viewing.

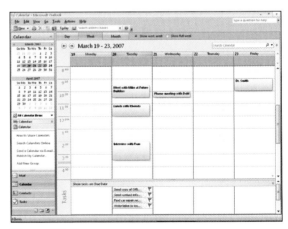

Figure 23-2
The Week view of the Calendar.

The Month view, shown in Figure 23-3, provides a monthly view of your calendar. In the Month view, you don't see tasks that you haven't yet completed. You can use the option buttons at the top of the view to change the level of detail Outlook displays. When you select the Low option, Outlook displays only all day events. If you select the Medium option, Outlook shows all day events and displays solid bars to represent appointments. When you select the High option, Outlook displays events and appointments, including details for appointments. You can view the next month or the previous month using the arrows at the top of the Month view. If you click any date in the Month view, Outlook displays that date in the Day view. And, if you click any of the week markers that appear to the left of each week, Outlook displays the Week view of that week.

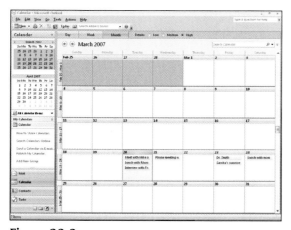

Figure 23-3
The Month view of the calendar.

In addition to the Day/Week/Month view, Outlook provides several other views of the Calendar. You can switch views by choosing View>Current View, and clicking a new view. For example, in the All Appointments view (see Figure 23-4), Outlook lists all appointments stored on your calendar, even those in the past.

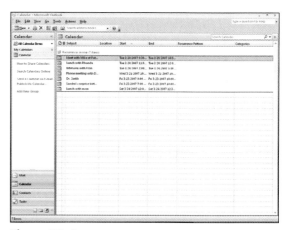

Figure 23-4
View all your appointments in list format.

All of the other available views look just like the All Appointments view, but display different information. Table 23-1 lists the other views and what they show:

Table 23-1 Calendar View Options

View	Shows
Active Appointments	Only appointments that haven't yet occurred
Events	All holidays and other events, such as deadlines, that you set up
Annual Events	Holidays and events that occur annually
Recurring Appointments	Appointments and events that repeat on some regular basis
By Category	Appointments and events organized by category
Outlook Data File	Appointments and events organized by Outlook data file

Adding Holidays

When you first start using Outlook, you won't find any holidays on the calendar, but you can take care of that issue. Follow these steps:

1. Choose Tools>Options. Outlook displays the Preferences tab of the Options dialog box (see Figure 23-5).

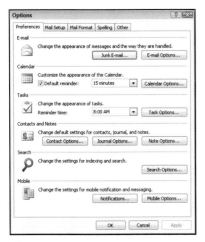

Figure 23-5
The Preferences tab of the Options dialog box.

2. Click Calendar Options. The Calendar Options dialog box appears as seen in Figure 23-6.

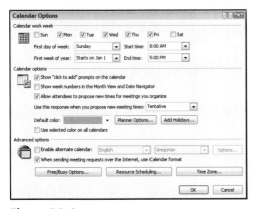

Figure 23-6
The Calendar Options dialog box.

3. Click the Add Holidays button. The Add Holidays to Calendar dialog box appears (see Figure 23-7).

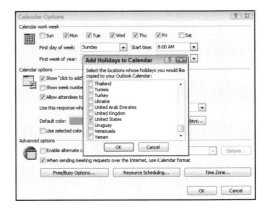

Figure 23-7
The Add Holidays to Calendar dialog box.

4. Place a check in the box beside the country whose holidays you want to appear on your calendar. You can select more than one country.

5. Click OK three times to close each dialog box. Outlook displays the holidays of the country you selected on the calendar.

Working in the Calendar Folder

WHEN YOU WORK IN THE Calendar folder, you can set up both one-time appointments and recurring appointments. You also can create events and schedule (and cancel) meetings.

Setting Up Appointments with Reminders

You can easily add an appointment to your Outlook Calendar by following these steps:

1. Click Calendar in the Navigation pane. Outlook displays your calendar.

2. Click the New button on the Standard toolbar. Outlook displays a new appointment window (see Figure 23-8).

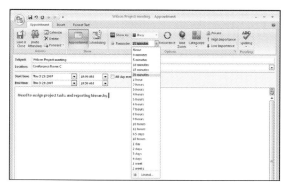

Figure 23-8
Create an appointment and set up a reminder for it.

3. Fill in the subject. This information will appear on your calendar.

4. If you want, fill in a location.

5. Select a start date and time. Outlook fills in the End date and time automatically, but you can change them.

Optionally, display the appointment date on the calendar and double-click the appointment time to open the Appointment window with the time and date already entered.

6. Write any notes about the appointment in the description box.

7. To set a reminder, choose Appointment>Options, click the Reminder down arrow, and select a time.

8. Choose Appointment>Actions>Save & Close. Outlook adds the appointment to your calendar.

If you set a reminder, Outlook will play a sound and display a reminder on-screen like the one shown in Figure 23-9 at the specified time prior to your appointment.

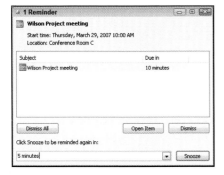

Figure 23-9
A typical reminder.

By default, Outlook assigns a 15-minute reminder to all appointments. If you prefer a different amount of time, you can change this default. Choose Tools>Options. In the Options section, a check appears beside Default Reminder (see Figure 23-10). Open the list box beside the Default Reminder check box and select a different amount of time.

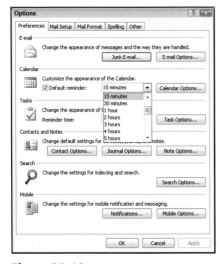

Figure 23-10
Set the default reminder lead time.

Recurring Appointments

So, the manager of the project you're working on has decided on a weekly staff meeting for the next 12 weeks for status updates. Instead of adding the appointment to your calendar 12 times, set up a recurring appointment by following these steps:

1. Click Calendar in the Navigation pane. Outlook displays your calendar.

2. Click the New button on the Standard toolbar. Outlook displays a new appointment window.

3. Fill in the subject. This information will appear on your calendar.

4. If you want, fill in a location and write any notes about the appointment in the description box.

5. Optionally, set a reminder by choosing Appointment>Options>Reminder and selecting a reminder time.

6. Choose Appointment>Options>Recurrence. Outlook displays the Appointment Recurrence dialog box seen in Figure 23-11.

Figure 23-11
Use this dialog box to create a recurring appointment.

7. Set a recurrence pattern. The options in the right portion of the Recurrence Pattern section change, depending on the option you select in the left portion of the section.

8. In the Range of Recurrence section, you can specify an end date.

9. Click OK. Outlook redisplays the appointment window. Just below the Location, you'll see information about how often the appointment recurs (see Figure 23-12).

Figure 23-12
When you create a recurring appointment,
Outlook provides you with recurrence information.

10. Choose Appointment>Actions>Save & Close. Outlook adds the appointment to your calendar.

Scheduling an Event

An event differs from an appointment by Outlook's definition because an event lasts all day. Outlook treats holidays as events. Your birthday is an event. To create an event, follow these steps:

1. Click Calendar in the Navigation pane. Outlook displays your calendar.

2. Choose Actions>New All Day Event. Outlook displays an appointment window, with a check in the All Day Event check box (see Figure 23-13).

Figure 23-13
Creating an event.

3. Fill in the subject and the date and, if appropriate, a location and any notes you need in the Description box.

4. If appropriate, you can choose Appointment>Options> Recurrence and set up information to make the event recurring. For details, see the previous section.

5. Choose Event>Actions>Save & Close. Outlook displays the event at the top of the day on which it occurs, visually representing that no time is associated with the event (see Figure 23-14).

Event

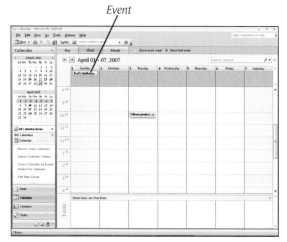

Figure 23-14

Events don't appear near a time slot.

Requesting a Meeting

You can use request a meeting with a contact who also uses Outlook. When you request a meeting, Outlook generates an e-mail that contains meeting information. Typically you and the contact work for the same company. If your company uses Microsoft Exchange Server and shares calendars, you can check schedules for shared calendars to find a meeting time that suits everyone.

When you request a meeting, you initially set up an appointment. To request a meeting with some-one who also uses Outlook, follow these steps:

1. Click Calendar in the Navigation pane.

2. Click New. Outlook displays a new appoint-ment window (see Figure 23-15).

> There is no technological reason why you cannot request a meeting with a user who doesn't use Outlook. But, when you send a meeting request to a user who doesn't use Outlook, the resulting e-mail message looks like gibberish to the recipient.

Invite Attendees

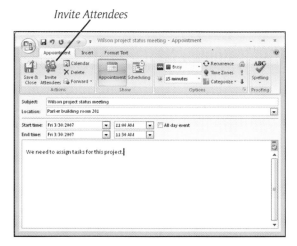

Figure 23-15

Beginning to schedule a meeting by e-mail.

3. Set the proposed meeting start and stop times and, if appropriate, provide additional information in the message area.

4. Fill in the meeting subject information.

5. Choose Appointment>Actions> Invite Attendees. Outlook adds a To line to the Meeting window (see Figure 23-16).

6. Click the To button. Outlook displays the Select Attendees and Resources dialog box (see Figure 23-17).

Figure 23-16
Fill in the meeting request window.

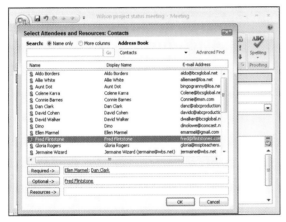

Figure 23-17
Select meeting participants.

7. Click the name of a person you want to attend the meeting. Or, you can type some characters of the person's name and Outlook will find the nearest match.

8. Choose one of the following and Outlook adds the recipient in the appropriate text box.

   ▶ **Choose Required if this person must attend the meeting.**

   ▶ **Choose Optional if the person's attendance is optional.**

   ▶ **Choose Resources if you are selecting a resource.**

9. Repeat Steps 7 and 8 for each meeting participant to whom you want to e-mail the meeting request.

10. Click OK. Outlook redisplays the meeting window, listing Required and Optional attendees in the To box and Resources in the Location box. If you typed a location in the box previously, Outlook asks you if you want to replace the location information.

11. If your company uses Outlook and Microsoft Exchange Server and shares calendars, choose Appointment>Show> Scheduling, and use the tab that appears to help you find the best time for the meeting and to add others to the meeting request.

13. Click the Send button. Outlook saves the meeting on your calendar and places an e-mail in your Outbox for each meeting attendee. The e-mail will be sent the next time Outlook checks for new mail.

Tracking Meeting Request Responses

You can easily identify when someone has responded to a meeting request. Open the meeting on your calendar by double-clicking it. Just above the To line, Outlook displays an overall status on meeting responses. You can choose Meeting>Show>Tracking to see the status of individual responses to the meeting request (see Figure 23-18).

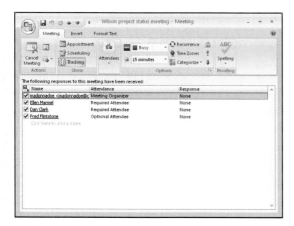

Figure 23-18
Review who has responded to your meeting request.

Cancelling a Meeting

Occasions will arise when you need to cancel a meeting. Open the meeting on your calendar by double-clicking it. Choose Meeting>Actions>Cancel Meeting. Outlook changes the Send Update button to the Send Cancellation button (see Figure 23-19).

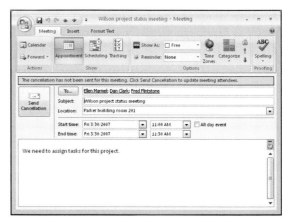

Figure 23-19
Cancelling a meeting.

Click the Send Cancellation button, and Outlook creates an e-mail message addressed to all meeting participants that cancels the meeting—the subject line of the message is the original subject line, preceded by the word "Canceled." Outlook places the message in your Outbox and sends it the next time Outlook checks for new mail.

Tracking Tasks with

Outlook

PICTURE YOURSELF WITH A PILE of work to do that seems to just keep getting bigger and bigger. You need to find a way to keep track of all your tasks, and you'd really like some sense of accomplishment when you get something done so that you'll feel like you're making a dent in the pile.

Using a combination of Outlook's Tasks folder and To-Do list, you can easily create tasks and easily track progress. You can create "one-time" tasks and recurring tasks. You can convert an e-mail into a task, and you can assign tasks to others and still monitor progress. This chapter explores the ways Outlook can help you keep that pile of work under control.

Exploring the Tasks Folder

OUTLOOK OFFERS TWO DIFFERENT ways to look at the Tasks folder, because it distinguishes between tasks and to-do's. A task is an item you create in the Outlook's Tasks folder to track an activity until you complete it. A to-do is any Outlook e-mail message or task flagged for follow-up.By default, Outlook flags all tasks for follow-up, so, all tasks are also to-do items.

Tasks and To-Do's

When you click Tasks in the Navigation pane, Outlook displays the Next Seven Days view of the To-Do List view (see Figure 24-1).

You can manually flag an e-mail message for follow-up (thereby creating a to-do item) by right-clicking that e-mail message, pointing at Follow Up, and selecting a timeframe: Today, Tomorrow, This Week, Next Week, No Date, or Custom.

So, when you initially click the Tasks button in the Navigation pane, you're seeing all to-do items, not just tasks. You can view only tasks if you click Tasks in the My Tasks portion of the Navigation pane (see Figure 24-2). Then, Outlook limits the view to show you only tasks. Compare the In Folder column of Figure 24-1 with Figure 24-2 to see that Figure 24-2 shows only tasks.

Figure 24-1
The Next Seven Days view.

Tasks

Figure 24-2
The Next Seven Days view of the Tasks folder.

> **You can assign a follow-up flag to a contact. When you do, you're really assigning a task to the contact (discussed later in this chapter).**

In the Navigation pane, Outlook provides several views of both the To-Do List and the Tasks folder. The same views are available for both, with one exception. The To-Do List view is available only when you select To-Do List under My Tasks at the top of the Navigation pane. The To-Do List view, shown in Figure 24-3, organizes to-do items by when they are due.

Figure 24-3
The To-Do List view.

Each of the views listed in the Navigation pane for both the To-Do List and the Tasks folder are variations of the view you saw in Figure 24-1 and Figure 24-2, except for the Task Timeline view (see Figure 24-4). This view resembles a Gantt chart like you find in Microsoft Office Project. A Gantt chart provides a visual representation of when a task should be performed and how much time it will take.

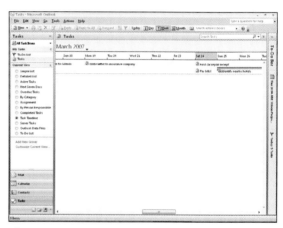

Figure 24-4
The Task Timeline view.

The other views simply provide varying information about the items displayed or organize the items in different ways. For example, the Simple List view shows the task subject and due date, an icon that represents the source of the task (Tasks folder or Mail folder), and a check box you can check to mark an item complete. The Detailed List view shows the source icon, an icon for the priority assigned to the item, an icon indicating if other items are attached to the item, the item's subject, status, due date, percent complete, category, and follow-up flag.

The Active Tasks view shows the same information as the Detailed List view but limits the items displayed to only those that are not yet complete.

Like the Active Tasks view, the Overdue Tasks view shows the same information as the Detailed List view but limits the items displayed to only those that are overdue.

The By Category view organizes task and to-do items by the category to which you have assigned them. The Assignment view organizes tasks by the person to whom they are assigned, the By Person Responsible view organizes tasks by owner, and the Server Tasks view shows tasks listed on the server. These views are useful if your organization uses Microsoft Exchange Server and shares Outlook information.

The Completed Tasks view shows only completed items, and the Outlook Data Files view shows tasks organized by Outlook data files.

Customizing Task and To-Do Views

You can customize any of the views by selecting the view and then clicking the Customize Current View link in the Navigation pane. Outlook displays the Customize View dialog box shown in Figure 24-5. The buttons available depend on the view you selected before opening this dialog box.

Figure 24-5
Use this dialog box to customize a view.

You customize Task and To-Do views the same way that you customize Contact views (see Chapter 22 for details).

Working with Tasks

L ET'S EXPLORE THE KINDS of things you can do with tasks in Outlook:

▶ **Add tasks**

▶ **Create recurring tasks**

▶ **Set task priorities**

▶ **Attach documentation to a task**

▶ **Set task progress**

▶ **Assign tasks to others**

▶ **Delete tasks**

Then, we'll take a look at the To-Do bar.

Adding Tasks

You can easily add a task by following these steps:

1. Click Tasks in the Navigation pane.

2. Click either To-Do List or Tasks under My Tasks.

3. Click the New button on the Standard tool-bar. Outlook displays a new Task window (see Figure 24-6).

4. Type a subject. The subject you type will appear in all views of the Tasks folder or the To-Do List.

5. Select a Start Date. Outlook automatically assigns the same Due Date to the task.

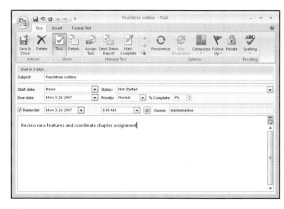

Figure 24-6
Creating a new task.

You don't have to assign a start date to a task, but, from a time management perspective, you are more likely to get the task done if you assign a date to it.

6. If appropriate, select a status other than Not Started.

7. You can set a priority for the task—Low, Normal, or High—and then use any of several views to sort tasks by priority.

8. If you've started the task, you can fill in the % Complete box with an estimate of how far along the task is.

9. You can have Outlook remind you about the task by placing a check in the Reminder box. Then, select a date and time for the reminder.

10. Type any notes about the task in the description block.

11. Choose Task>Actions>Save & Close. Outlook saves the task.

You also can create a task from an e-mail message. Click Mail in the Navigation pane and then find the message in the appropriate folder under Personal Folders. Drag the message onto the Tasks button in the Navigation pane (see Figure 24-7).

Mouse pointer

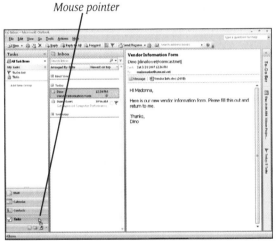

Figure 24-7
Dragging an e-mail message into the Tasks folder.

When you release the mouse button, Outlook opens a Task window with the title of the subject of your e-mail. By default, Outlook doesn't assign a start date, due date, status, priority, or percent complete and Outlook doesn't create a reminder, but you can do all of those things. Outlook *does* display the content of the e-mail message in the description block of the task (see Figure 24-8).

When you choose Task>Actions>Save & Close, Outlook adds the task to the Tasks folder using the subject line of the task (which was the subject line of the e-mail).

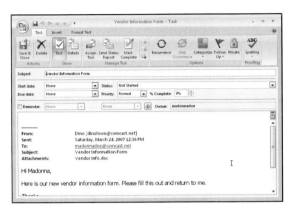

Figure 24-8
Creating a task from an e-mail message.

Editing Tasks

If you find you need to make changes to a task you created, you can easily edit the task. For example, you can edit a task to update its progress by making changes to both the Status and the % Complete fields. Click the Tasks button in the Navigation pane and select a view where you can see the task. Then, double-click any portion of the task's entry. Outlook displays the task in the Task window. Make your changes and choose Task>Actions>Save & Close.

> If you're a Microsoft Office Project user, Project can import task information from Outlook, including status and % Complete.

For example, to record work on a task, you can make changes to the Status and % Complete fields. You also can record Actual Work, mileage and billing information, and the date completed. While viewing the task, choose Task>Show>Details (see Figure 24-9). Then, fill in fields as appropriate and click Save & Close.

Figure 24-9
Recording task progress.

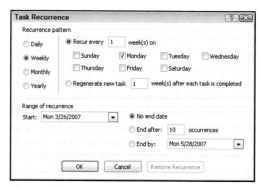

Figure 24-10
Use this box to set up a recurring task.

> **Making changes after you click Details does not change the information you see when you click Task.**

Creating a Recurring Task

Just like the Energizer Bunny, you've got a task that you need to do over and over again. For example, you need to take medication at the same time every day. You can create a recurring task by following these steps:

1. Click Tasks in the Navigation pane.

2. Follow Steps 2 to 10 in the preceding section to set up the task.

3. Choose Task>Options>Recurrence. Outlook opens the Task Recurrence dialog box (see Figure 24-10).

4. Select a recurrence pattern option—Daily, Weekly, Monthly, or Yearly—and the choices to the right of those options change to match your selection.

5. You can set a start and end date for the tasks in the Range of Recurrence section.

6. Click OK. Outlook redisplays the Task window, which now contains a message above the subject line that describes the recurrence.

7. Click Task>Actions>Save & Close.

Attaching Documentation to a Task

Suppose that you've got a task to do and you've got some information in a Word document that pertains to the task. You can attach the Word file to the task and then open it from the task in Outlook. No more hunting. Follow these steps:

1. Click Tasks in the Navigation pane.

2. Follow Steps 2 to 10 in the section "Adding a Task" to set up the task. Or, you can edit the task by double-clicking it.

3. Choose Insert>Include (see Figure 24-11).

Attach File button

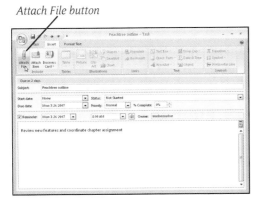

Figure 24-11
Attaching a document to a task.

4. Click the Attach File button, which displays the Insert File window. This window works like any Open or Save dialog box.

5. Navigate to the folder that contains the document you want to attach, select it, and click Insert. Outlook displays an icon representing the file in the description portion of the task (see Figure 24-12).

Figure 24-12
A task containing a Word document.

6. Choose Task>Actions>Save & Close.

To open the file while working in Outlook, open the task and double-click the icon.

Assigning Tasks to Others

If you have your organization's blessing, you can delegate a task to another Outlook user. Outlook refers to this process as making a task request, and you can select options to keep an updated copy on your task list and to receive a status report when the task is complete. Follow these steps to assign a task to someone else:

1. Click Tasks in the Navigation pane.

2. Add or edit a task, making sure that you leave the Task window open (see Figure 24-13).

Assign Task button

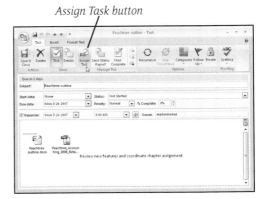

Figure 24-13
Add or edit a task.

3. Choose Task>Manage Task>Assign Task. Outlook changes the appearance of the Task window, giving you the opportunity to supply an e-mail address (see Figure 24-14).

4. Click the To button. Outlook displays the Select Names: Contacts dialog box.

5. Click the name of the person to whom you want to send the task request. Or, you can type some characters of the person's name and Outlook will find the nearest match.

Figure 24-14
Assigning a task to someone else.

6. Once you have highlighted the correct contact's name, click the To -> button. Outlook adds the recipient in the To -> text box.

7. Repeat Steps 5 and 6 for each recipient to whom you want to assign the task.

8. Click OK. Outlook redisplays the Task window with the recipients' e-mail addresses in the To box.

9. Click Send. Outlook places the task request in your Outbox and sends the task request the next time it checks for incoming e-mail. The message box shown in Figure 24-15 appears advising you that the task reminder is turned off since you are no longer the task owner.

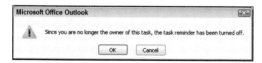

Figure 24-15
Outlook turns off the task reminder.

Outlook and Notes

Outlook contains a Notes feature with which you can create the equivalent of an electronic sticky note. Click the Notes button at the bottom of the Navigation pane. Outlook displays the Notes pane. Double-click any blank spot on the Notes pane and a Note box appears. Just start typing. When you finish, click outside the note.

You can attach an Outlook item, such as a Note, to a task using the steps in this section. Just change Step 4 so that you click the Attach Item button on the Ribbon. Then, select the Outlook folder containing the item you want to attach and, within that folder, select the item.

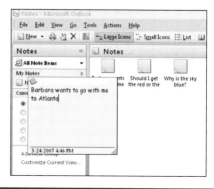

A recipient of a task request can accept or decline the task. The task request arrives as an e-mail message, and when the recipient opens the message, he or she is prompted to accept or decline the task. If the recipient accepts the task, Outlook places it in the recipient's Tasks folder and sends the originator of the task request a message that indicates the task request has been accepted.

If you, the sender of the task request, choose to keep an updated copy of the task on your task list, Outlook notifies you and updates the task in your Tasks folder each time the person to whom you assigned the task updates the task. If you choose to receive a status report when the task is complete, Outlook automatically sends you a status report when the person handling the task marks it complete.

If the recipient of the task request declines the task, the sender of the task request receives e-mail notification that the task request has been declined.

Deleting Tasks

Deleting a task is not the same as completing a task. That said, there are times when you want to delete a task. And, it's easy to do. Click Tasks in the Navigation pane and select the task in any view. Then, click the Delete button on the Standard toolbar. If you select a task to delete, you get no warning; Outlook simply deletes the task. If, however, you created the task from an e-mail message, Outlook warns you that deleting the task will also delete the e-mail.

Using the To-Do Bar

As mentioned in the beginning of this chapter, Outlook distinguishes between tasks and to-do's. A task is an item you create in the Outlook's Tasks folder to track an activity until you complete it. A to-do is any Outlook e-mail message, task, or contact flagged for follow-up. By default, Outlook flags all tasks for follow-up, so, all tasks are also to-do items.

You can manually flag e-mail messages or contacts for follow-up (thereby creating to-do items) by opening that e-mail message or contact and clicking the Follow Up button on the Ribbon or by right-clicking an item and choosing Followup. When you mark an item for follow-up, Outlook offers you timeframes: Today, Tomorrow, This Week, Next Week, No Date, or Custom.

The To-Do Bar (minimized by default) runs down the right side of the screen and is visible in all folders except the Calendar folder (see Figure 24-16).

Expand button

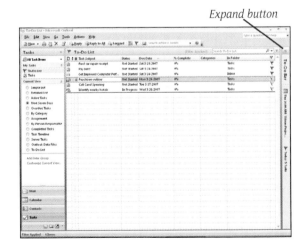

Figure 24-16

The To-Do Bar appears minimized when you view the Mail, Contacts, and Tasks folders.

To open the To-Do Bar, click the Expand button at the top of the bar, and Outlook shows you the complete To-Do Bar, which summarizes your upcoming meetings and tasks (see Figure 24-17).

The To-Do Bar is more than just something you can look at for a quick update. You can click any date on the calendar to switch to the Calendars folder in Outlook for that date. And, you can add to-do's to the To-Do bar. For example, to create a to-do item for an e-mail, drag the e-mail into the appropriate timeframe on the To-Do Bar. The to-do will appear both on the To-Do List (when you click the Tasks button in the Navigation pane and then click To-Do List under My Tasks) and on the To-Do Bar. And, you can right-click the flag of any to-do and choose Mark Complete to clear it from the To-Do List and the To-Do Bar.

Figure 24-17
The To-Do Bar provides a snapshot of your upcoming schedule.

Index